Hiss the Villain

HISS THE VILLAIN

Six English and American Melodramas

Edited, with an Introduction,

by MICHAEL BOOTH

Associate Professor of English, Royal Military College of Canada

ARNO PRESS

A New York Times Company

New York / 1977

Printed in U.S.A. by
NOBLE OFFSET PRINTERS, INC.
NEW YORK 3, N. Y.

Contents

Acknowledgments are due for the following illustrations: to the Victoria & Albert Museum for 'Farley as Grindoff', 'T. P. Cooke as Harry Hallyard', the stock posters for *Ten Nights in a Bar-Room*, *Lost in London* and *Under the Gaslight*, the caricature of Henry Irving, and for the decoration on the title page; to Pollock's Toy Museum for the 'Toy theatre cut-outs' and 'Miss Macarthy as Mary Maybud'; to the Harvard Theater Collection for the stock poster of the sensation scene from *Under the Gaslight*.

Illustrations

——•◦•——

The decoration on the title page is from the Sadler's Wells poster of *My Poll and My Partner Joe.*

Introduction

The melodramas in this book represent a type of drama that has passed away from the stage. They belong to an age which gave birth to the modern theatre, an age of immense theatrical vitality. Melodrama has been treated with general contempt by dramatic historians and critics. The adjective 'melodramatic' is today derisively applied to anything vaguely considered unnatural or exaggerated; sometimes it seems to be used as a synonym for 'old'. Yet melodrama formed a large part of the repertory in the nineteenth century and is the most striking dramatic phenomenon of the period. It deserves at least to be understood.

Essentially, melodrama is a simplification and idealization of human experience dramatically presented. For its audiences melodrama was both an escape from real life and a dramatization of it as it ought to be; uncomplicated, easy to understand, sufficiently exciting to sweep away petty cares. One knows where one is in the world of melodrama; there is no doubt about moral principles, or proper conduct; no confusion about people, no brain-perplexing psychological probing or examination of motives. In its presentation of character, ethics, and social relationships, melodrama presents a world of black and white; there are no greys. Furthermore, it is not a sad or tragic world. Although melodrama is full of violence – stabbing, shooting, hanging, strangling, poisoning, suicide, fire, shipwreck, train wreck, villains of extreme savagery, revenge-seeking ghosts, heroes and heroines who experience a series of fearful physical catastrophes and domestic agonies – these are all signposts along the road to ultimate happiness, the triumph of virtue, and defeat of evil. Everyone knew this and was quite prepared to enjoy the means to an end inevitably and satisfactorily the same. The audiences of melodrama both ate their cake and had it; crime and violence and the utmost exertions of villainy can only produce poetic justice and a re-assertion of a benevolent moral order which, though in temporary upheaval, always rights itself.

In treatment of material, melodrama concentrates on externals; it stays on the surface and never explores the depths. This approach produces two of the form's most notable features: character stereotypes and rigid moral distinctions. The main character types constantly appearing in melodrama are the hero, heroine, villain, comic man, comic woman, old man, old woman, and character actor (usually comic). Other types appear from time to time, and a host of lesser characters are handled in various ways, but the general outlines remain the same for over a century. When they become blurred, and when the sharp divisions of morality are no longer observed, melodrama disappears as a separate form. The building can no longer stand on crumbling foundations.

One of the rules is that the hero and heroine must suffer distress, persecution, and separation, and that their suffering must continue unabated till a few moments before the final curtain, when they emerge united, happy, and triumphant. The heroine comes in for more persecution than the hero, especially as possession of her is frequently the villain's main object. In fact the hero is often of little use to her, either being in prison, or across the sea, or tied up in a cave, or without a weapon at inconvenient times. What intelligence, design, and thought there is in melodrama is resident in the villain and the comic man. The villain may be plural, and sometimes feminine (in later nineteenth-century melodrama villainesses, such as Lady Audley, were popular), or there may be a villain and villainess in the same play. When there are two male villains, one is usually vicious and menacing, the other cowardly, hesitant, and quite willing to desert to the forces of good. The genuine villain is heartless, unprincipled, hateful, and entirely evil. Some attempt may be made to give him a sympathetic motive for his actions, but sympathy never attaches to his present behaviour. The evil of melodramatic villains can make Iago look like a mere dabbler. Continually in pursuit of the property and life of the hero on the one hand and the body of the heroine on the other, absolutely without humane feeling and deaf to the frenzied pleas of the heroine for mercy, justice, honour, etc., the villain meets with a fate such conduct justly deserves. Ruin, imprisonment, or death at the hands of Nature, the hero, or the comic man, is his lot. Occasionally he is allowed reformation or dismissed with contempt, but this is subversive of moral principle and not common. Occasionally, too, the heroine falls victim to vice and pays the penalty: in melodrama as nowhere else the wages of sin is death. The exception to this grim rule includes anybody who, after half-hearted villainy, finally helps out the hero and heroine, and, more surprisingly, the hero himself, who is sometimes allowed a dreadful past of drunkenness, gambling, and desertion of family as long as he finally repents and plays the man. The hero-criminal is another matter, and will be dealt with later.

The three main character types – hero, heroine, and villain – and the relationships between them motivate the action of melodrama, but the others are significant. Small children intensify pathos, and the hero or heroine may have a parent or relative whose sole duty it is to lament evil days, implore Heaven to protect its child, and generally add to the emotional distress. In some melodramas appears a woman unwillingly leagued with villainy (the female counterpart of the lesser villain) who deplores her situation and assists the hero. The character actor may be a drunkard or a jolly sailor or a monster, but whatever he is there is no problem in deciding whether he is on the side of virtue or vice. The comic man is one of the more important characters. His job is to stick loyally by the hero and heroine and frustrate villainy. Very often the comic man – usually of humble station: servant, rustic, or artisan – is much more helpful in foiling the villain than the hero: he overhears his plots, insults him, and intervenes in the nick of time. He is matched with a comic woman, commonly a servant or friend of the heroine, and they have quarrelsome or frolicsome love scenes together.

The presence of the comic man and woman indicates another vital characteristic of melodrama: comic relief. Melodrama would not be complete without the fooling of the comic man, his pursuit of the comic woman or her pursuit of him, and the alternation of scenes of violence and desperate emotion with scenes of ludicrous comedy, as exaggerated in their way as the more serious matter. The writers of melodrama provide not only a rapid sequence of breath-taking incidents and situations, but also a pattern of equally rapid changes from the horrible and the pathetic to the humorous and absurd and back again, without any sense of impropriety.

Indeed, the overall framework of melodrama is one of fast action, where plot and situation are dominant. Character is entirely subordinated to the necessities of plot, and a collection of exciting incidents and situations fraught with emotion comes first. Thus character can only be presented in broad unvarying types; easily identifiable by appearance and action, they were known instantly to the audience for what they are – the melo-dramatist has no time for character development or the study of motivation. Neither has he time for moral searching and questioning; moral positions as well as character must be easily recognizable. In fact the audience of melodrama could identify both at once, for character type and moral viewpoint are insepar-ably linked. Such facility in presentation was a necessary help to the writer, for having set his stage in an instant he could push on without hindrance to the next thrilling situation.

Both exciting incidents and emotional tension can be, and usually are, accompanied by appropriate music, especially in the earlier days. The stage directions of Thomas Holcroft's *The Tale of Mystery* (1802), one of the first important melodramas, contain such instructions as '*Music to express discontent and alarm . . . threatening music . . . violent distracted music . . . music of painful remorse*'. A single striking chord may be employed; for instance, in C. P. Thompson's *The Shade* (1829), the spectre of the murdered Laurent calls on his friend for vengeance:

SHADE (*points to the ruined Cloister*). Blondel – there thy friend was foully murdered! (*Music in a terrific chord*) Blood for blood! (*chord more terrific*) Revenge! (*chord*) Revenge! (*chord*) Revenge! (*chord – thunder*).

That music is an essential part of melodrama is perfectly natural when one considers the immediate background. The word 'melodrama', literally *music-drama* or *song-drama*, comes from Greek by way of French; *le mélodrame* is first recorded in 1772. Rousseau applied it to his *Pygmalion* (1775), a *scène lyrique* in which a character expresses action through speech and dumb show to music.

The word, the dumb show, and the music were borrowed by the Parisian writers of lurid melodramas of blood, revolution, and the violence of situation and pathos of sentiment which characterized early melodrama in English. This type of melodrama, a direct product of the French Revolution, flourished from the late 1790s in the theatres on the Boulevard du Temple (nicknamed, as a consequence, the Boulevard du Crime) such as the Ambigu-Comique, the Folies-Dramatiques, and the Gaîté. Its chief author was Guilbert de Pixérécourt, many of whose plays were instantly anglicized, and whose plots and general approach were borrowed wholesale. *Victor, ou l'Enfant de la Forêt* (1798) and *Coelina, óu l'Enfant du Mystère* (1800) are two of his most influential and famous melodramas, both taken from French novels. Pixérécourt was also inspired by the English Gothic novel, and adapted Mrs Radcliffe in *Les Mystères d'Udolphe* (1798). Bouchardy, Caigniez, and Ducange are only three other names worth remembering in a whole host of French melodramatists of this period. In no sense, however, did French melodrama antedate the English; both reached the stage almost simultaneously, and each influenced the other.

The dumb character, familiar in England from eighteenth-century pantomime, lasted in melodrama for a long time. *The Tale of Mystery, The Dumb Maid of Genoa* (1820), *Frankenstein* (1823), *The Inchcape Bell* (1828), *The Child of the Wreck* (1837), and *The Dumb Man of Manchester* (1837), are only a few of the many popular melodramas containing a dumb person, always a sympathetic figure, who mimed throughout, although musical accompaniment gradually became less emphatic. Early spectacle melodramas relied entirely upon dumb show, and whenever important information or sentiment had to be disclosed, the actors held up crude scrolls with captions like DEATH WHEN I

PROVE FALSE, BIRENO HAS DISCOVERED YOUR LURKING PLACE, and I YIELD TO FATE — CHILDREN FAREWELL FOR EVER.

Musical and sensational elements from the French mingled with material from English and German. The Gothic novel of Horace Walpole and Mrs Radcliffe, full of apparitions, dark secrets, mysterious forests, gloomy castles and dungeons, usurping villains, persecuted heroines and noble heroes, had its stage counterpart in the 1780s and 1790s. These Gothic plays in turn influenced later writers of the Gothic revival as much as *The Castle of Otranto* and *The Mysteries of Udolpho* influenced the stage. In Germany there was also a Gothic school, inspired by English Gothic writers and the earlier English poetry of melancholy. Schiller's *Die Raüber* (1782) added a violent band of robbers to the raw material of melodrama, and all three schools, English, French, and German, merged in the type of English melodrama predominant in the early years of the nineteenth century.

The ancestry of melodramá, however, goes back much further than the last half of the eighteenth century. The sharp distinction between good and evil and the dramatic presentation of conflict between the two may be found in the morality play of the fifteenth century, with characters like Sensual Appetite, Avarice, Penitence, and Good Deeds. Even before this, the ranting Herod in the miracle play is the type of the melodramatic tyrant. Elizabethan and Jacobean tragedy contains many violent scenes and much exaggerated language. Kyd's *The Spanish Tragedy*, Marlowe's *The Massacre of Paris*, and *Titus Andronicus* are wildly melodramatic, and Shakespeare's great tragedies, especially *Hamlet* and *Macbeth*, have a substantial basis of melodrama. Ranting heroes and overwhelming love are features of Restoration heroic tragedy; excesses of pathetic sentiment were supplied by the eighteenth-century sentimental comedy of Steele and Cumberland and their followers, which was also liberally sprinkled with benevolent fathers or guardians, distressed heroines and manly heroes, scheming villains, comic servants, vanished wills, long-lost orphans, and amazing revelations just before the curtain fell. The domestic tragedy of Lillo and Moore

14

provided the same kind of sentiment and a direct clash between virtue and vice.

Of course, hundreds of years of English dramatic history do not converge inevitably to the grand apotheosis of melodrama, nor are all plays in which these characteristics are present melodramas. One can simply point out that by about 1800 all the ingredients were ready to hand, and the special way in which they were combined became the form this book illustrates. Although melodrama altered and developed throughout the century, its fundamental attributes – as just described – remained the same.

The reasons for the enormous popularity of melodrama in England and America in the nineteenth century are not hard to find. In both countries rapid industrial expansion (occurring later in America than in England) created huge urban working classes living in conditions of the utmost drabness and squalor, who demanded entertainment as relief from the long working day. Their level of literacy and taste was low, and the entertainment of melodrama with its combination of cheap sentiment, violent incident, and scenic thrills, was just what they required. Furthermore, the times in which they lived were times of political and military excitement; both countries had an immediate background of war and violence. The French Revolution, the American War of Independence, the Napoleonic War, the War of 1812 – all produced conditions favourable for the reception of melodrama, and, of course, countless melodramas themselves. More generally, the Victorian public enjoyed less sophisticated artistic pleasures than we do today, and thrived on the sensationalism, and the extremes of pathos, nobility, virtue and vice that novels and melodramas alike supplied.

When the metropolitan audiences came into the entertainment market there was nothing for them to buy. Serious drama was sadly out of touch with the new masses. In tragedy, the exhausted Augustan and pseudo-classical plays of the previous century were not at all to their taste. Shakespeare was too literary, and the important writers of the day either refused to participate in the (to them) degrading rough-and-tumble of the contemporary theatre, or were simply more interested in poetry and the novel. Those who did write serious plays were heavily under Elizabethan influence and heedless of the modern world. (The successful plays of serious dramatists like Bulwer-Lytton are strongly melodramatic.) Into this vacuum rushed the melodramatists, who knew what their audiences liked and gave it to them. No matter how crudely presented, there was much material from contemporary life. Pathetic stories of domestic woe in city and country, violent stories of modern crime, patriotic stories of naval and military conflict – these were closer to their hearts than dreary dramas of events hundreds of years ago with Italian or Greek settings and long speeches. And when the melodramatist did deal with history, he at least made it thrilling. With farce and scenic spectacle thrown in for good measure, melodrama offered a lot for one's money.

The popular nature of melodrama obviously influenced its tone and development. Although in England many well-known melodramas were first played at Drury Lane and Covent Garden, and although the patent theatres found melodrama good for the box office, the form bloomed most luxuriantly at the smaller theatres. Its invasion of the large theatres brought lower-class audiences with it, and was one of the reasons for the abandonment of theatre-going as a social habit on the part of the upper classes. Until about 1870 they preferred the opera, and when they came back to the theatre melodrama necessarily underwent some refinement. Thus melodrama's class attitudes, for the greater part of a century, are strongly anti-aristocratic. Villains tend to be wealthy employers and noblemen, heroes workmen and peasants.

The absence of the upper classes from the popular theatre was one of a complex of factors contributing to the poor artistic quality of nineteenth-century drama. Another was low remuneration for dramatists. Fees from managers were small, and in order to make a living from the theatre it was necessary to write and adapt with great speed. Not until authors began to demand a percentage of the profits did they benefit in the slightest from long runs of their plays. To make things worse, there was no copyright protection. If a dramatist's plays were printed, they could be played anywhere without a penny's recompense. If they were not printed, they could still be pirated during performances. Either way the dramatist lost. And as it was much cheaper to pay an author a few pounds to adapt a French piece than a lot more to write his own, original work was not encouraged. As a result there was a great flood of adaptations from the French right through the century. The passage of international copyright agreements followed well behind domestic protection; English writers plundered French and American drama without payment, and the Americans did the same with English and French drama.

Logically, then, authors preferred to make a living from journalism and the novel, and the writing of plays was left to theatrical hacks. It was under these conditions that thousands of melodramas were ground out to satisfy the insatiable public demand. The plays and novels of Victor Hugo and Dumas *père* and *fils* were melodramatic enough for English adaptation (in fact the French romantic drama of which Hugo and Dumas *père* were leaders grew out of the earlier boulevard melodrama, which both enjoyed). *Le Comte de Monte Cristo* and *La Dame aux Camélias* provided America with two of its most popular melodramas, and towards the end of the century Victorien Sardou climaxed a long line of important French writers who had supplied melodrama to the English stage. English and American novels were melodramatized as fast as they were written. Bulwer-Lytton, Ainsworth, Collins, Reade, Scott, Dickens, Cooper, Mrs Stowe, Mrs Wood, Miss Braddon – the list is endless. Scott and Dickens were particularly suitable: Scott for his theatrical approach to history, romantic Gothic settings, and stirring adventure; Dickens for his sensationalism and domestic pathos. The work of both men is full of great acting parts, and they were eagerly seized on; sometimes several versions of one of their novels would appear on the stage within a few months of each other. The whole question of the relation of the novel to the stage in the nineteenth century is a large one; suffice to say here that hundreds of melodramas were taken from novels. The nineteenth century also saw the growth of the mass circulation newspaper, and melodramatists found a treasure trove of plots in police court news and crime reporting. They were always ready to dramatize the latest crime, and the more sensational the crime the more versions of it. This, of course, was nothing new: from *Arden of Faversham* through *The London Merchant* to *The Mousetrap* the history of crime on the stage has been a long and colourful one, and the melodramatic thriller still thrives, especially in England.

Full-blooded English melodrama made its first appearance in the large London patent houses, Drury Lane and Covent Garden, and the spectacle and circus theatres, Astley's and the Royal Circus, at about the same time in the 1790s. While Drury Lane and Covent Garden continued to play melodrama, it found its main home at the minor theatres which grew up to cope with the demand for entertainment created by the growth of London's population; the same growth and the same demand occurred all over industrial England. By law, these theatres were not permitted to play what was called the 'legitimate' drama – regular tragedy and comedy – and in the early days even spoken dialogue was not allowed, which is why the useful scrolls were produced at the Royal Circus. In a sense illegitimate drama (the term was hazily understood, but theoretically the illegitimate was differentiated from the legitimate by a certain number of songs in each act, and musical accompaniment) was forced on the minor theatres, although their fare did not significantly change when the patent theatres' privileges were abolished in 1843. By that time the minors knew their audience vastly preferred illegitimate to legitimate. In America there was no Licensing Act, but in the large cities of both countries melodrama settled comfortably into theatres catering mainly for the lower strata of society. In London there were many in the East End, two or three on the south side of the Thames, and others here and there in unfashionable areas. In New York melodrama established itself chiefly in the Bowery Theatre on the East Side. However, throughout the century both cities saw a great deal of melodrama at the more elegant theatres, and it was part of the repertory almost everywhere. Like any other kind of theatrical entertainment, melodrama was taken into small towns and villages by touring groups with booth theatres, tent shows, and showboats. Indeed, melodrama lived longer outside the big cities.

Because melodrama, especially the cruder sort, appealed mainly to the lower middle and working classes, it created a special audience. West End and West Side melodrama attracted more civilized audiences – though its gallery patrons could never be accused of sophistication – but melodrama in the East End and East Side was patronized by intensely loyal people whose local theatre might have been run for years by the same management, with the same playwrights churning out melodramas and the same actors playing in them. The Britannia, for example, one of London's largest East End theatres, was run by the Lane family for sixty years, and generations of authors and actors grew old in its service. The distinctive character of audiences at this type of theatre was a subject for fascinated comment from the visitor in search of colourful material. Dickens describes the Victoria gallery – which could take 1,500 people – as 'overflowing with occupants . . . rising above one another to the very door in the roof, and squeezed and jammed in, regardless of all discomfort'. The pit audience, neither clean nor sweet-smelling, contained so many mothers and babies that the pit seemed a 'perfect nursery'.

> No effect made on the stage was quite so curious as the looking down on the quiet faces of the babies fast asleep, after looking up at the staring sea of faces in the gallery. There were a good many cold fried soles in the pit, besides; and a variety of flat stone bottles; of all portable sizes. The audience in the boxes was of much the same character (babies and fish excepted) as the audience in the pit.[1]

Melodrama audiences constantly shouted approval, disapproval and advice at the stage, and their reactions could be marked, to say the least. One account of positive audience reaction, to a

[1] 'The Amusements of the People', *Household Words*, 30 March 1850.

19

performance of *Oliver Twist* in the Victoria, also tells us something about melodramatic acting:

> Nancy was always dragged round the stage by her hair, and
> after this effort Sikes always looked up defiantly at the gallery,
> as he was doubtless told to do in the marked prompt copy. He
> was always answered by one loud and fearful curse, yelled by
> the whole mass like a Handel Festival chorus. The curse was
> answered by Sikes dragging Nancy twice round the stage, and
> then, like Ajax, defying the lightning. The simultaneous yell
> then became louder and more blasphemous. Finally when
> Sikes, working up to a well-rehearsed climax, smeared Nancy
> with red-ochre, and taking her by the hair (a most powerful
> wig) seemed to dash her brains out on the stage, no explosion
> of dynamite invented by the modern anarchist, no language
> ever dreamt of in Bedlam could equal the outburst. A thousand
> enraged voices, which sounded like ten thousand, with the
> roar of a dozen escaped menageries, filled the theatre and
> deafened the audience, and when the smiling ruffian came for-
> ward and bowed, their voices, in thorough plain English, ex-
> pressed a fierce determination to tear his sanguinary entrails
> from his sanguinary body.[1]

One can do no justice at all to the immensely interesting subject of melodramatic acting in a short introduction. As might be
expected, it was as exaggerated and unnatural in relation to what
we consider today to be good acting as is melodrama itself in relation to modern serious drama. Yet we must remember that
acting style should always be suited to, and appropriately express, dramatic content. To act melodrama *naturally*, as we
understand the term, would be an absurd contradiction. The
sources of melodramatic acting are numerous: eighteenth-century theories of tragic acting, which elevated and dignified it
beyond all other kinds of acting; the grand declamatory school of
Kemble and Mrs Siddons, the exemplar of these theories; the
exaggeration necessary to make effects without speech in melodramatic dumb show; the intense, strongly physical acting of

[1] John Hollingshead, *My Lifetime*, 1895, I, pp. 189–90.

Edmund Kean and his imitators; the correspondence of speech
and action with music in early melodrama, and the influence of
French melodramatic and romantic acting. The acting of melodrama influenced the acting of Shakespeare, and *vice versa*, and
there were considerable differences between the acting of cruder
melodrama in the popular theatres and before more civilized
audiences. The sentiments and characters and physical action of
melodrama inescapably demanded a particular acting style;
ordinary modes of acting, as we understand them now, would
have been irrelevant.

The nineteenth-century theatre's techniques of production
played an important part in the development and popularity of
melodrama. The nature of melodrama, with a series of climaxes,
swift transitions from violence and pathos to farce, and visual
sensationalism, required speedy production, rapid scene changes,
and ever more spectacular scenic effects. All this the nineteenth-
century theatre became increasingly well equipped to do. Con-
ventionalized scenery – wings, flats, and drops that could be
quickly and easily changed, and on which were painted forests,
prisons, castles, and cottages – were quite adequate to represent
the symbolic world of melodrama, and the more grandiose naval
battles and military pageants called for the full ingenuity of the
stage carpenter. In fact, carpenter, scene painter, and lighting
man assumed positions of immense importance in the theatre,
which was very much dependent on their abilities for success.
The manipulation of spectacular effects was enormously en-
hanced by controlled use of gaslight, limelight, and electric light.
New inventions in stage fire, trapdoors, and trick effects made
the explosions, conflagrations, and spectres of melodrama possible, for this was an age that first saw in the theatre blue and
red fire, the Vampire Trap, the Corsican Trap, and Pepper's
Ghost. As the century wore on, effects in the bigger theatres
became more elaborate as melodrama became more sensational,
and the curious paradox was achieved of an increasing stage
realism being used to present an essentially unrealistic form.
However, the setting and striking of ponderous and expensive
sets in every act for a full display of shipwrecks, train disasters,

horse races, and earthquakes, required greater use of the curtain and more and longer intervals, generally slowing down production. The complete resources of actor, producer, theatre designer, painter, carpenter, lighting man, and a huge army of stagehands, expended on romantic or sensational melodrama, were combined magnificently in Irving's productions at the Lyceum, the Drury Lane sensation dramas, the work of Steele Mackaye, particularly at the Madison Square Theatre, and David Belasco's staging before and after he settled at the Belasco Theatre.

Finally, the retention of the stock company until late in the century strongly influenced the writing of melodrama and kept it along traditional lines. In the stock company each performer had his own line of business and played no other; once an old man or a villain, always an old man or a villain. The stock company had at least its leading man and woman, heavy man, juvenile lead, comic man, comic woman or soubrette, old man, and old woman. These corresponded exactly with the stock characters of melodrama already described. As late as the 1890s the Adelphi, the principal theatre for melodrama in London at that time, had a stock company organized in the traditional manner, and the same performers – William Terriss (hero), Jessie Millward (heroine), Lionel Rignold (villain), Clara Jecks (soubrette) – played the same typed roles for play after play. Parts had to be written to suit the stock company, and much of melodrama's repetitiveness of character and plot is therefore understandable.

Looking now at the content of melodrama, as distinct from its origins and social and theatrical background, we find that it falls into several main categories.

In England, the spectacle melodrama that predominated at Astley's, the Royal Circus, and Sadler's Wells, coexisted with the Gothic melodrama appearing at Covent Garden and Drury Lane as well as with dumb show on the south side of the river. The first kind patriotically depicted victories on land and sea over the French, and for the rest of the century soldiers and sailors were the heroes of incredible feats of arms against the dastardly foe. This type of drama was much more closely in touch with the realities of modern life than the legitimate drama, for it did express the patriotic fervour of the age of Nelson and Wellington, of Trafalgar and Waterloo, of intensely proud national feeling and hatred and contempt for the enemy. Mounted in a circus ring with the thunder of horses' hooves, the roar of cannon, and the shouts of contending armies, these battle spectacles were popular from the Napoleonic to the Boer War. *The Siege, Storming and Taking of Badajoz, The Battle of Waterloo, The Battle of Agincourt, The Burmese War, The Battle of the Alma* were all produced at Astley's.[1] Later in the century other circuses and theatres presented *The War in Turkey, The War in Zululand*, several dramatizations of Boer War battles, and scores of similar military dramas. Sadler's Wells in the first decade of the nineteenth century called itself the Aquatic Theatre, and put on *The Battle of Trafalgar, The Battle of the Nile*, and other marine spectacles. For these a water tank a hundred by forty feet was constructed, and models of hundred-gun ships cannonaded one another, burned, and sank, with satisfying effect. As might be imagined, such spectacles were staged with maximum sound and action, even in small theatres. A manager of a fit-up company remembers that in *The Fall of Sebastopol* he appeared as an English sergeant, 'and defended myself, amid shot and shell, against six of the enemy at one time'. No opportunity for noise was neglected:

> During the siege there would be some fifty persons upon the stage blazing away at each other, and so filling the booth with smoke with their red-hot shot and shells, that the audience had to hopelessly abandon itself to coughing and sneezing for fully ten minutes after the ramparts of Sebastopol had been destroyed.[2]

---

[1] Non-military equestrian melodrama was also popular at Astley's, especially under Andrew Ducrow, the greatest equestrian of his time. Ducrow and his horses also performed at the patent theatres. The most notable of all equestrian melodramas was *Mazeppa*, in which the American, Adah Isaacs Menken, who had no mean figure, created a sensation bound in flesh-coloured tights to the back of a 'wild' horse.

[2] *The Original, Complete, and Only Authentic Story of 'Old Wild's'*, 1888, pp. 123–4.

The Gothic melodrama presented some elements of spectacle, though in a different manner. This sort of melodrama, as has been pointed out, is characterized by bandits, dark forests (where the heroine often gets lost), secret caverns (in which hero and heroine are often imprisoned), woodmen's cottages (the home of innocence and oppressed poverty), and crumbling castles occupied by mysterious tyrants, full of dungeons, concealed passages, and dreadful apparitions. The Gothic melodrama is represented here by *The Miller and His Men**[1] (the most popular of all plays for children's toy theatres), which concentrates on bandits, humble cottage, and dangerous forest, omitting castles and ghosts. Gothic trappings appear extensively in the popular *Castle Spectre* (1797) of Matthew Gregory Lewis, already the author of a lurid Gothic novel, *The Monk*. The play has an agonized villain, Osmond, who *'walks with his arms folded and eyes bent upon the ground . . . he appears lost in thought; then suddenly rises, and again traverses the room with disordered steps'*. Osmond has abducted the heroine, Angela, and her lover Percy comes to the castle to save her. It transpires that Osmond had stabbed his brother and his brother's wife years before, and Angela is their child. The brother languishes in Osmond's dungeons, and the wife's ghost makes two noteworthy appearances, once to Angela:

> *The folding-doors unclose, and the oratory is seen illuminated. In its centre stands a tall female figure, her white and flowing garments spotted with blood; her veil is thrown back and discovers a pale and melancholy countenance; her eyes are lifted upwards, her arms extended towards heaven, and a large wound appears upon her bosom.*

> ANGELA. Stay, lovely spirit! Ah! Stay yet one moment!

> *The Spectre waves her hand, as if bidding her farewell. Instantly the organ's swell is heard; a full chorus of female voices chant 'Jubilate!' a blaze of light flashes through the oratory, and the folding-doors close with a loud noise.*

[1] Throughout this Introduction the plays included in the present collection have been marked with an asterisk at their first mention.

24

And the second to save her husband from the usurper's sword:

> *At the moment that* OSMOND *lifts his arm to stab him,* EVELINA'S *ghost throws herself between them:* OSMOND *starts back and drops his sword.*

OSMOND. Horror! What form is this?
ANGELA. Die! (*She springs suddenly forward, and plunges her dagger in* OSMOND'S *bosom.*)

Lewis himself wrote nine other Gothic dramas, all with similar spectacular elements. The settings and supernaturalism of Gothic melodrama were carefully calculated to excite feelings of horror and foreboding in the audience. *The Castle Spectre* has a '*gloomy subterraneous dungeon, wide and lofty*'; William Dimond's *The Foundling of the Forest* (1809) loses the hero, without his pistols, of course, in '*another part of the forest more entangled and intricate – the tempest becomes more violent – alternate lightning and utter darkness*'. J. C. Cross' *Rinaldo Rinaldini, or The Secret Avengers* (1801) shows the

> *Inside of a vaulted subterraneous dome – over a Gothic throne, a transparent blood-red cross, and radiated eye – near it a Gothic table, on which is a large book, which is lettered with '*BOOK OF BLOOD*' – at the upper end of the stage a half obscured cell which is inscribed,* 'CONDEMNED BY THE SECRET AVENGERS', *and which discovers an opening, skeletons, &c.*

The castle-dungeon-spectre Gothic and the bandit-forest-cottage Gothic, their characteristics frequently mingled in the same play, remained popular until the middle of the century. After that the form declined.[1] Through these melodramas

---

[1] One of the last ghosts in melodrama is that of Louis dei Franchi in Boucicault's *The Corsican Brothers* (1852), which, as late as Irving in the 1890s and Martin-Harvey in 1915, glided wraith-like across the stage to the famous Ghost Melody. Ghosts are not the property of Gothic melodrama only; they appear in all kinds. The 'vision' scene, a vision of past, present or future was often employed; notable examples are Mrs Marten's vision of the murder of her daughter in *Maria Marten*, Fabien's vision of the death of his brother in *The Corsican Brothers*, and Mathias' vision of his own crime in *The Bells*.

moved heroes declaiming speeches like 'Withered be the arm that hesitates to strike against a treacherous, remorseless tyrant', and heroines like Amelia in Samuel Arnold's *The Woodman's Hut* (1814), *'pale, her hair in disorder, and running across the stage'*, crying out in the deathless, timeless utterance of a thousand heroines of melodrama, 'Oh heaven, what will become of me? I die with fatigue! Merciful providence! Abandon me not! Restore me to safety, or end my sufferings at once! Ha! My pursuers approach! I see them! Whither can I fly?'

The Gothic melodrama predominant for some years after 1800 gradually gave way to other types. One of these was nautical melodrama – illustrated in this book by *My Poll and My Partner Joe** – arising out of the naval spectacles at Sadler's Wells, war patriotism, and the long popularity on stage and in song of the British tar. A simple but shrewd man, the sailor of melodrama is ready to die for his country at sea and for his little Sal or Susie on shore. He speaks with a peculiar vocabulary full of sea metaphors, and is liable to break without warning into a hornpipe or merry ballad. Patriotism is a marked feature of many nautical melodramas. In Cross' *Blackbeard* (1798), the dreaded pirate quails in fear when a scroll is held up to him proclaiming that THE ENEMY IS BRITISH AND WILL DIE OR CONQUER. In *Sir Francis Drake* (1800), also by Cross, the villainous Iron Arm is overcome in a terrible combat with Drake's men, and 'with his death, the CURTAIN FALLS to the huzzas of the gallant and victorious British Fleet'. Edward Fitzball, a prolific writer of nautical melodrama, dramatized Cooper's novel, *The Pilot* (1825), in which Lieutenant Barnstable, refusing to surrender his sword, declares, 'Surrender up my sword! never, Sir; from His Majesty of England I received it, to wield in defiance of his enemies and my own, and never would I calmly resign it, except to place it at the feet of my own sovereign.' Jack Junks, the jolly tar in Fitzball's *The Floating Beacon* (1824), says: 'There never yet was a true Englishmen that thought of his own danger, when he could save another in the hour of distress.' Such sentiments, vigorously expressed, were always received with thunderous applause. Many sailor parts were played by T. P. Cooke, who had actually been in the navy. His most famous role was William, in Douglas Jerrold's *Black-Eyed Susan* (1829). William, returning home after a long stretch at sea, rescues his faithful Susan from the importunities of smugglers, and strikes down his own captain, who is bent on Susan's seduction. After a court-martial and pathetic last interview with Susan and his messmates, William goes bravely to death by hanging at the yard-arm – from which he is saved at the last moment by the intervention of his contrite captain.

The subject matter of nautical melodrama covers piracy, shipwreck, smuggling, combat with the foe, the activities of Cornish wreckers, and a broad variety of material relating only incidentally to the sea. Fitzball's *The Floating Beacon, Tom Cringle* (1834) and J. B. Buckstone's *The Dream at Sea* (1835) contain villains who prey on the shipwrecked; lightship keepers in the first, wreckers in the other two. George Dibdin Pitt's *The Eddystone Elf* (1833) is about a monster dwelling in the Eddystone Light. In *The Pilot* and *The Red Rover* (1829), both by Fitzball, the glorious British navy triumphs over Americans and pirates respectively.[1] (Of course, the villainous smugglers, wreckers, and pirates who creep furtively along rocks or meet secretly in caves are merely the bandits of Gothic melodrama in another guise.) For the whole century plays with sailor-heroes and stirring maritime incident were as popular as dramas with soldier heroes and battles. William Terriss was the handsome sailor-hero of Adelphi dramas, notably Sims' *The Harbour Lights* (1885); the English fleet was glorified in *The Armada* (1888), by Augustus Harris and Henry Hamilton; sensation drama, like Dion Boucicault's *After Dark* (1868) and *Lost at Sea* (1869), and Harris and Paul Merritt's *The World* (1880), was cluttered with shipwrecks.

The inclusion of non-nautical matter in nautical melodrama leads us to another category, the domestic.[2] Generally, melo-

---

[1] American dramatizations of Cooper's sea novels revert to their originals: it is the *American* tar who is heroically victorious.

[2] It is artificial to divide melodramas into categories such as spectacle, Gothic, nautical, and domestic, and it is done here simply for convenience.

dramas of this kind were written about the humble home, the sufferings of the family, the farmer, the workman, the employer, the squire, the factory, drink, crime, life in the big city, and so on. *Lost in London** is a remarkably pure domestic melodrama with a classic pattern of noble and virtuous workman, suffering heroine, villainous employer, eccentric comic man and woman. Nelly's death is typical of a period when heroines and villainesses died of sin, such as Lady Audley in *Lady Audley's Secret* (1863) and Lady Isabel in *East Lynne* (1866). Domestic melodrama could be romantically and historically coloured, as for instance Buckstone's *The Flowers of the Forest* (1847), with its mysterious gypsies, or the same author's *The Green Bushes* (1845), with settings of the 1745 rebellion in Ireland and primitive life by the Mississippi.

The most vivid domestic melodrama concerns crime and drink. Then as now the public were avid followers of murder cases, the bloodier the better. The sensational element in crime suited it ideally to the melodramatic stage, and the exploits of William Corder (who murdered Maria Marten), Burke and Hare, Jack the Ripper, and innumerable real-life criminals were luridly adapted, some of them, like *Maria Marten*, with realistic execution scenes. The criminal is usually the villain, but there is a body of melodrama featuring the most desperate criminals as heroes, like Jack Sheppard, Dick Turpin, Paul Clifford, and Claude Duval.[1] This would seem to be a reversal of the strict moral law of melodrama. However, in such plays the criminal-

---

Actually the types overlapped considerably; melodramatists were not purists of form. Just to take two examples, there is an evicting landlord – a domestic character type – in *Black-Eyed Susan*, and a jolly sailor who foils villainy in Buckstone's *Luke the Labourer* (1826), otherwise a purely domestic melodrama. Some of the subject matter of domestic melodrama was available in the Gothic; the distressed poverty and lowly cottage of Kelmar in *The Miller and His Men* turns up in scores of domestic melodramas, and a slight transformation turns the menacing Grindoff into the seducing squire or persecuting landlord.

[1] H. M. Milner's *Dick Turpin's Ride to York* (1841) is one of the more famous equestrian melodramas. The final scene shows Turpin, who consistently outwits the law, defending the body of Black Bess.

heroes represent the idealized common man, brave and clever and humane, rebelling against the forces of society – 'them', as personified by the law. The officers of law and authority become the villains. In the rebel, audiences found a romantic and vicarious satisfaction for instinctive feelings of social discontent and rebellion against a harsh, profiteering social order. The emotional speeches of Richard Parker, the mutineer-hero of Jerrold's *The Mutiny of the Nore* (1830), must have been sympathetically and enthusiastically received:

> I have seen old men, husbands and fathers, men with venerable grey hairs, tied up, exposed, and lash'd like basest beasts: scourg'd, whilst every stroke of the blood-bringing cat may cut upon a scar received in honourable fight. . . . Where shall we see your mercies, Captain Arlington? Shall we see them in the worn ankles of your fettered sailors? Shall we read them in their scarred and lacerated backs? Mercies! by heavens! an eye of stone would melt, to look upon your mercies.

The hero of John Walker's *The Factory Lad* (1832), which is about automation, helps to smash the new machines and fire the factory in revenge against his employer's severity (the employer, after firing his men, exits *'into factory, sneeringly'*). Such manifestations are a part of the class bitterness of much nineteenth-century melodrama. In many ways, melodrama is a true social reflection of its times.

The melodrama of crime is represented in this book by *The Bells**, in which Henry Irving became an overnight star. *The Bells* is less lurid than most plays of this type. Without real comic relief or a suffering heroine, it is an unconventional melodrama, and, with a sympathetic psychological study of the villain-hero, far in advance of its time. Yet its morality and use of elaborate scenic devices for sensational effect is truly melodramatic. Mathias kills his victim (though in narration) nearly as horribly as Corder batters Maria Marten around the red barn, or as Sweeney Todd polishes off his customers in the tipping barber's chair. His agony is more artistic but no less vivid than the agony of the villains of criminal melodrama. Here is Macraisy, the killer in Fitzball's *Jonathan Bradford, or The Murder at the Roadside Inn* (1833), hiding in a vault as the funeral procession of his victim approaches:

> Powers! they are bringing hither the body of Hayes; it's into this vault they are about to deposit it. Sure, shan't I escape at all? Ah! (*The anthem of the dead is faintly heard above.*) They are singing the anthem of the dead! I'll not hear it. Horror! they are lowering the coffin into this vault! I here enclosed – the murderer wid the murdered – alone, shut up! I cannot bear it – no; rather than that I'll die – I'll die – die! (*Stabs himself.*) Ha, ha, ha, die! Ha, ha, ha! (*Music. He falls.*)

A few moments later he staggers on to the stage, confesses his guilt, and dies, just as the innocent hero is about to be hung. The melodrama of crime is anything but dull.

The problem of drunkenness and the growth of temperance movements in both England and America are evident in domestic melodrama. *Ten Nights in a Bar-Room** was perhaps the most popular of all, but there were others: *The Drunkard, or The Fallen Saved, The Bottle, Fifteen Years of a Drunkard's Life, Aunt Dinah's Pledge, Drink,* and many more. Some of these plays were actively sponsored by temperance organizations well into the twentieth century. During the run of *The Drunkard* at Barnum's Museum, Philadelphia, thousands signed temperance pledges in the theatre lobby. Dramas of drink are very moral indeed. The hero goes to ruin and degradation and his wife and children to poverty and despair through his drunkenness; and if he does not die wretchedly, recovers his senses (aided by a kindly temperance spokesman), swears off liquor forever, and becomes happy and prosperous. Before final bliss, however, there are frightful scenes of *delirium tremens* (which terrified audiences), and admirable sentiments like 'By the memory of my sainted mother, I vow never to taste intoxicating drink' and 'Louisa, hear me while I swear ne'er again to pollute my lips with this accursed fluid that has brought this misery on us both'.

The subject matter of melodrama, with changes already noted, repeated itself for the remainder of the century. In the bigger theatres the two-act melodrama disappeared and the full-length 'drama' formed the evening's sole entertainment. The dialogue of the better plays became less exaggerated, the characterization more credible, and the construction more skilful, but essentially melodrama stayed the same. It is almost impossible to separate melodrama from the 'drama'; almost all serious nineteenth-century plays are to a greater or lesser extent melodramatic. Writers who tried to break away from current dramatic modes were unable to free themselves completely. Henry Arthur Jones, who had much to say against melodrama, wrote one of the best, *The Silver King* (1882), and preserved a melodramatic framework in many later plays. There are strong elements of melodrama in Pinero. Even W. S. Gilbert, the last person one would normally associate with melodrama, wrote *Charity* (1874), *Dan'l Druce, Blacksmith* (1876), and, most melodramatic of the three, *Brantinghame Hall* (1888).

The main development in the last half of the century, and one that differentiated melodrama of that period from the earlier variety, was the 'sensation' scene. As stage mechanics improved, effects grew more startling and spectacular, and the success of a play might be ensured by a really good earthquake, train crash, or shipwreck. The sensation scene, or scenes, did not alter the content of melodrama, but made it more exciting. *Under the Gaslight** is an ordinary domestic melodrama, but the 'big scene', where the train thunders down on the helpless victim, makes it an excellent example of a type that appealed strongly to a public demanding ever bigger and better thrills.[1]

The spectacular scene was really nothing new. There are many burning buildings, explosions, and shipwrecks in the earlier melodrama, but now they were staged more realistically and elaborately. Boucicault seems to have invented the term 'sensation drama' and applied it to his *Colleen Bawn* (1860),

[1] The train in *Under the Gaslight* was probably the first to appear on the stage. On the opening night it unfortunately broke down and failed to arrive at the critical moment, but after that created the utmost audience excitement. One of the troubles with sensation drama was that its machinery was so elaborate that it periodically and disastrously went wrong.

whose sensation scene is the rescue of Eily O'Connor from drowning in a lake cave, where blue gauze simulated water and Eily and her saviour could actually be seen beneath the surface. Earlier, he added the two vision scenes and the gliding ghost to the French *Corsican Brothers*, and launched an avalanche in *Pauvrette* (1858). In addition to saving his hero by telegraph in *The Long Strike* (1866), he trapped his villain by camera in *The Octoroon* (1859), blew up a steamboat in the same play, ran the Oxford-Cambridge boat race in *Formosa* (1869) and the Derby in *The Flying Scud* (1866) – the stage's first horse-race.

From the sensation drama of Boucicault and his imitators, with one big scene in each play, it was a simple step to put one big scene in every act, and that scene more spectacular than the one before it. In Robert Buchanan and Harris' *A Sailor and His Lass* (1883), the blowing up of a whole street is followed by the scuttling of a ship, and the play concludes with the hero being led to the scaffold and stood on the trap (he is, naturally, innocent, and of course saved at the very last moment). In *Pluck* (1882), by Harris and Pettitt, *two* trains are wrecked in the same scene, a mob attacks a bank, and a child is found in a great snow-storm.[1] The characters of late nineteenth-century sensation drama tended to come from 'society', and the plays have many balls and peerages and villains in evening dress. One must remember, however, that these expensive settings and vast stage spectacles could only be mounted at the bigger and well-equipped metropolitan theatres, and in the smaller ones melodrama went on much the same as before.

To make a similar survey of the development of American melodrama in the nineteenth century would be largely repetitive. Gothic, nauti-al, and domestic melodramas of the same kind as the English were written, and melodramas were imported from England free of copyright restrictions. In general, Americans preferred their drama from England rather than from native authors.

---

[1] The love of stage spectacle was just as apparent in the immensely lavish Shakespearean productions of Irving and Tree, and the increasingly elaborate pantomimes.

The patriotic spectacle play had a great vogue, and stories of the Revolution, the War of 1812, the Mexican War and the Civil War found their way to the melodramatic stage. One of the earliest was John Burk's *Bunker Hill* (1797), with a battle scene between English and American soldiers lasting fifteen minutes, and

> Charlestown on fire, the breastwork of wood, the Americans appearing over the works and the muzzles of their guns, the English and the American music, the attack of the hill, the falling of the English troops, Warren's half descending the hill and animating the Americans, the smoak and confusion.[1]

The American flag waved triumphantly at the end of many war melodramas, and plays such as *The Siege of Monterey, Horse Shoe Robinson, or the Battle of King's Mountain, Putnam, the Iron Son of '76, The Boy Martyr of September 12, 1814, Bull Run,* and *Mabel, Child of the Battlefield* colourfully adapted American history. The American sailor in melodrama was as jingoistic and loyal as his British counterpart, and battled Algerian pirates or His Britannic Majesty's navy with lusty vigour. John Paul Jones became a stage hero as well as a national one.

A distinctive type of melodrama treats of Indian and pioneer life. The first play about the American Indian was Robert Rogers' *Ponteach* (1766), and with J. A. Stone's *Metamora* (1829) the theme reached melodramatic fruition. Edmund Forrest as the storming, fearless Indian warrior, spoke like this throughout the play:

> I started to my feet and shouted the shrill battle cry of the Wampanoags. The high hills sent back the echo, and rock, hill and ocean, earth and air, opened their giant throats and cried with me, 'Red man, arouse! Freedom! Revenge or death!' (*Thunder and lightning. All quail but* METAMORA.)

The most vivid Indian melodrama is *Nick of the Woods* (1838), a dramatization by Louisa Medina of Robert Montgomery Bird's novel. Its characters include the Jibberainosay, who kills wicked

[1] William Dunlap, *A History of the American Theatre*, 1832, p. 162.

Indians and places his horrible mark on their breasts. His appearance, *'precipitated down the cataract in a canoe of fire'*, causes the villainous Indians to fall on their faces in terror and leads to a *'tableau of astonishment'*. At the climax he seizes on the Indian chief:

> Die! thou human wolf! infuriate tiger! die! die! (*Hurry; grapples with* WENONGA, *wrests hatchet from him and kills him.*) And with thy dying glance behold the fearful fiend, the Jibberainosay, in Reginald Ashburn! Ha, ha, ha! Mother, sister, wife, at last ye are revenged! (*Laughs wildly and exit, dragging the body.*)

The movement westward brought the frontier and the gold country into melodrama. Frank Murdoch's *Davy Crockett* (1872) presents on stage the courage and simple love of this archetype of American folklore. The best scene shows Crockett saving the life of the heroine and her worthless lover by barring the cabin door with his arm – and staying there all night – against the ferocious wolves outside. Daly's *Horizon* (1871) brings white man into conflict with Indian and shows life in a small frontier town. The contrast between the sophisticated East and the primitive West, a favourite subject for nineteenth-century American writers, turns up in this and other plays. Joaquin Miller treats the theme of Mormon vengeance in *The Danites of the Sierras* (1877), in which Mormon assassins pursue a girl who lives disguised as a boy in the mountains to escape them. Miller's next play, *Forty-Nine* (1881), is about a Californian gold camp and the flotsam and jetsam of mining life. The heroine, Carrots, is a lost heiress sought for her family by Charlie Devine, the hero, whose drinking and gambling proclivities are cured by love of Carrots. The villain, Tom Gully, becomes chief of the merciless Vigilantes, and tries to get the heiress for himself. Scenes are laid in a gambling saloon and outside a *'cabin, old, moss grown'*, with mining tools lying around and *'sunset on snow-capped mountains in distance'*. Stolen papers and sudden revelations add to the melodrama, but Miller creates a living human figure in Forty-Nine, the wreck of a miner who came to California full of hope, and who toils on hopelessly in the search for gold. For him Miller writes genuinely moving dialogue:

> All along the long and lonely road of my hard life, I see, as I look back, little grassy mounds – they are the brave miners' graves. I am the last man left. In a few years more the grass will grow over that door-sill; and long, strong, and untrodden it will grow in my trail there; the squirrels will chatter in these boughs, and none will frighten them away – for Forty-Nine will be no more.

Another Californian gold-rush melodrama which infuses warmth and vitality into a character stereotype is Bartley Campbell's *My Partner* (1879), whose hero, Joe Saunders, is a rough miner with a gentle heart and great natural dignity. There is, however, no departure from melodrama; the hero is noble and pure, the heroine betrayed by another (who is conveniently stabbed by the villain), the comic man a Chinaman whose timely discovery saves the hero from execution and exposes the villain. At times American melodrama rises far above English melodrama in the artistic worth of its treatment of certain themes in American life and character. When this happens, it passes from melodrama into another realm, for depth of dramatic character is out of place in the canon of melodrama. Yet such moments are rare, and otherwise the essential structure of melodrama is preserved.

Much later drama dealing with native historical material is essentially melodramatic. Bronson Howard's *Shenandoah* (1888) is a Civil War play with a stirring battle scene, a wounded hero, a despicable yet polished villain, and the usual misunderstandings and discoveries. William Gillette's *Held by the Enemy* (1886) and *Secret Service* (1895) are Civil War spy dramas. Augustus Thomas' *Arizona* (1899), and Belasco's *The Girl I Left Behind Me* (1893) and *The Girl of The Golden West* (1905) are thorough-going Westerns, but like other plays of the historical type frequently rise above melodrama into real feeling and genuine conflict. *Arizona* is concerned with cowboys and Mexicans and the army; *The Girl I Left Behind Me* contains an

Indian uprising, a besieged stockade, and rescuing cavalry; *The Girl of the Golden West* is set in a gold camp dominated by a heroine whom all the miners worship and through whose love a desperate bandit reforms. The scene where the concealed bandit's blood drips on to the searching sheriff's hand, and where the girl gambles with him for her own freedom and her lover's life, are familiar in the work of another lover of melodrama, Puccini.[1] Belasco also wrote *The Heart of Maryland* (1895), another Civil War melodrama, in which the heroine saves her lover by swinging perilously from the clapper of a bell, thus preventing it from ringing to give warning of his escape.

Another aspect of American melodrama is the subject of slavery. There are several versions of Harriet Beecher Stowe's *Uncle Tom's Cabin*, the most popular being George Aikin's (1852), which was played everywhere for at least seventy years by scores of so-called Tom Shows. Mrs Stowe's *Dred*, another novel of slave life, was dramatized by C. W. Taylor in 1856, but the two best slavery melodramas, apart from *Uncle Tom's Cabin*, are Boucicault's *The Octoroon* and Campbell's *The White Slave* (1882), the latter containing the famous lines spoken by Liza, the supposed octoroon, to her cruel owner, 'Rags are royal raiment when worn for virtue's sake, and rather a hoe in my hands than self-contempt in my heart.'

On the whole the best American melodramas of the last half of the century are superior to the best English ones, although sometimes their superiority is achieved by the sacrifice of the spirit of melodrama. No doubt their merit is owing to the inspirational value of contemporary American history, far more epic and colourful than English history of the same period. The westward drive of the pioneer, the conflict with Indians, the frenzied rush for gold, the grimness of slavery, the fury of the Civil War – these themes lent themselves admirably to melodrama. Life lived on the frontier or in a gold camp *was* melodramatic.

The cheaper sensation drama also prospered. Boucicault produced several of his plays in New York before taking them to

---

[1] The whole nineteenth-century Italian opera tradition, especially that of Verdi and Puccini, is heavily dependent on melodrama for its plots.

England. Daly was also a leading sensation dramatist. In *A Flash of Lightning* (1868), the heroine, chained to her bed in the stateroom of a burning steamboat, is rescued, it hardly seems necessary to add, just in time. In *The Red Scarf* (1869), the villain ties the hero to a log in a sawmill, starts the saw going, and sets fire to the mill. The heroine turns up to save him (one must apologize for the repetition) in the nick of time. This sort of thing was common to sensation drama everywhere.

A kind of domestic melodrama that long endured in the popular theatre was the 10–20–30 melodrama, so known because prices of admission were only ten, twenty, and thirty cents. Beginning around 1900, it was packed with the extreme violence and agonies of pathos that marked early English melodrama. The chief writers of this school, like Owen Davis and Theodore Kremer, wrote hundreds of plays with titles like *Nellie, the Beautiful Cloak Model, Bertha, the Sewing Machine Girl, Convict 999, The Fatal Wedding, The Queen of the Opium Den, Chinatown Charlie, The Child Wife*, and *No Mother to Guide Her*. The sentiments of these plays were appropriate to the titles. The hero of Charles Taylor's *From Rags to Riches* (1903) hurls the villain's money back at him with the cry, 'Mother and I battle the world day and night to support our home in poverty. But if we are compelled to purchase riches at the cost of my sister's honour, we'll remain in rags all the rest of our lives. Go!' (He winds up with the riches anyway.)[1] Something of the working methods of the 10–20–30 writers emerges from Owen Davis' recollections of his producer, Al Woods:

Once he had a title, he'd discuss scenes that would make good lithographs – things like the burning of Brooklyn Bridge or the blowing up of the Capitol. Even before I'd begun to write a play, Al would have the lithographs illustrating it ready for the billboards, sometimes twenty or thirty thousand dollars

[1] The English equivalent of 10–20–30 melodrama is the work of Walter and Frederick Melville, who specialized in vice-ridden villainesses. *The Worst Woman in London* (1899), *The Girl Who Wrecked His Home* (1907), and *The Bad Girl of the Family* (1909) are typical titles.

worth. . . . I worked two or three formulas, and could outline a plot in a couple of hours.[1]

All the dramatist had to do was fill in sensations and situations with dialogue; characters were ready-made. The 10–20–30 school represents the climax and the glory of American melodrama. Its material is classically true to the form, and it was enormously popular. 'The American people,' said George Jean Nathan, 'love, honour, and obey melodrama above every other form of dramatic art. . . . The natural impulse of American taste is toward melodrama.'[2]

The date of the decline of stage melodrama cannot be given precisely. It slowly withered away after the First War, and signs of disintegration were evident a good twenty or thirty years before. The question is confused by the fact that melodrama on tour lingered on long after it had ceased playing in cities, in some instances until years after the Second World War. Now, however, melodrama is only revived either as a form of burlesque or as a conscious archaism.[3] As we have defined it, melodrama is no longer written. This is not to deny that there are melodramatic elements in modern plays, such as the thriller, but the pure form does not exist, and would not find audiences in its own spirit if it did.

The reasons for decline, both theatrical and socio-philosophical, are numerous. In the theatre, the growing tendency to realism in acting finally caught up with realistic staging methods; there was no place left for the old extravagance of the melodramatic actor. Many of the noted actors of melodrama died or retired between 1900 and 1910, and the young ones had a different training. The old repertory stock system, long the stronghold of acting tradition, disappeared, and the new acting schools did not teach melodramatic acting. The gradual return to the theatre of fashionable and more sophisticated audiences

---

[1] *The New Yorker*, 15 February 1949.

[2] *Another Book on the Theatre*, 1915, pp. 307–8.

[3] Burlesques of melodrama were written from earliest days, and most of the famous melodramas were burlesqued sooner or later. Strangely enough, burlesque never affected the popularity of melodrama.

led to a change in the content of melodrama and finally to its ultimate disappearance. In the meanwhile the mainstay of popular melodrama, the working and lower middle-class audiences, were increasingly catered for by music-hall and variety houses, where melodrama was reduced to an occasional thirty-minute spot in the bill. Apart from the theatre, however, the twentieth century is not favourable to melodrama. The form was built on moral absolutes; there was and could be no confusion between virtue and vice, between right and wrong, between the hero and the villain. This idealized world was simple and the rules were plain; one knew exactly where one stood. But to the twentieth century the world is not simple; twentieth-century man does not know where he stands and has faith in neither absolutes nor ideals. Furthermore, he is psychologically interested in probing human motives and the deepest recesses of the human mind, in interior rather than external action. Twentieth-century art reflects this inward turning and the absorbing interest in discordance and confusion, in the anti-hero, the fragmented man who lives in a fragmented world and cannot even comprehend himself. Since Freud, we have deserted externals for what lies hidden within, and to this trend melodrama is irrelevant. No doubt the First World War helped to complete the process of disorientation and loss of faith; the tinsel of melodrama must have looked pretty tawdry after 1918, for what price then violence and sensation on the stage?

Yet melodrama is still with us, and in one form or another probably always will be, as long as there is human interest in thrilling stories and tender emotions, and as long as people want to lose themselves in a world which is not their own. What happened was that popular melodrama and its audiences were taken over by the cinema (and, later, television); it was the cinema that dealt the real death blow to stage melodrama. We have already seen how necessary speed is to melodrama: a rapid series of short scenes and quick scene changes. This the cinema was far better equipped to do than the stage, and the ponderously elaborate realism of the sensation drama of the 1880s and 1890s cried out for cinematic rather than theatrical techniques. There was really nowhere for this sort of melodrama to go but film. The success of the cinema was immediate and widespread. By 1915 many notable melodramas had been filmed, and the sensation play was effectively killed by transference to the screen. A public that loved realism on the stage found motion-picture photography infinitely more satisfying. Since then, the screen has tightened its hold on melodrama. Dialogue, techniques, and effects may be subtler than on the stage, but essentially melodrama has not changed. Music reinforces emotion and incident even more emphatically than before. Character types and sentiments are basically the same. The lavish biblical and historical spectacle film is merely an extension of early nineteenth-century spectacle melodrama, and the idealized world where pattern and character are instantly familiar to the audience – and are loved because they *are* familiar – exists most notably in the Western film, a virtually untouched example of classically perfect melodrama.

The popularity of melodrama is not difficult to understand. Presenting its public with a world of fulfilled dreams in contrast to a miserable monotonous reality in which virtue did not necessarily prosper, nor villainy suffer, melodrama nullified distress and danger by directing them to the ultimate happy ending. It would be as irrelevant to criticize melodrama for improbability of situation and unnaturalness of character and dialogue as it would be to criticize a farmhand for not being a ballet dancer. An ideal world is never a probable one, and cannot be judged by standards of realism. If melodrama was plausible, its characters richly human and its situations and dialogue natural, it would not be melodrama. It is easy to laugh at it, but when inclined to scorn one must remember that melodrama was a genuinely popular art form commanding the support and affection of millions of people for over a century of theatrical history. This in itself is not contemptible.

A NOTE ON THE TEXT

The texts of the plays in this book are a collation of nineteenth-century acting editions; in the case of *The Miller and His Men*, the 1813 second edition was also used. I have, where necessary for clarity, attempted some improvement of the sometimes chaotic punctuation of the acting editions. As this collection of melodramas is intended to be read rather than acted, I have eliminated stage directions relating only to particular exit and entrance doors, and to the sort of stage movement necessary for blocking and variety. My reason for doing this is that they interrupt reading with irritating frequency; but, if desired, they can easily be worked out, as any producer knows. I have left scene descriptions unchanged (except, again, for the omission of doors) and kept in all directions essential for a picture of the stage action, as well as those that are emotionally expressive.

M.R.B.

The Miller and His Men

A MELO-DRAMA IN TWO ACTS

by Isaac Pocock

First performed at Covent Garden Theatre, 21 October 1813

CAST

KELMAR, an old cottager	*Mr Chapman*
CLAUDINE, his daughter	*Miss Booth*
LOTHAIR, a young peasant	*Mr Abbott*
GRINDOFF, the miller, later WOLF, robber chief	*Mr Farley*
RAVINA, his mistress	*Mrs Egerton*
RIBER ⎫	*Mr Jefferies*
GOLOTZ ⎬ Robbers	*Mr King*
ZINGRA ⎭	*Mr Sladen*
COUNT FREDERICK FRIBERG	*Mr Vining*
KARL, his servant	*Mr Liston*
LAURETTE ⎫ Kelmar's children	*Miss Carew*
KRUITZ ⎭	*Master Gladstanes*

Banditti, Officers of Count Friberg

London J. Fairburn Minories & 44. Barbican.

Mᴿ FARLEY, as *Grindoff* in the MILLER & HIS MEN.

ACT I

SCENE I. – *The Banks of a River. On the right, in the distance, a rocky eminence, on which is a windmill at work – a cottage in front,* R. *– Sunset.*

Music – The MILLER'S MEN *are seen in perspective, descending the eminence – they cross the river in boats, and land near the cottage, with their sacks, singing the following:*

> *Round*
> When the wind blows,
>   When the mill goes,
> Our hearts are all light and merry;
>   When the wind drops,
>   When the mill stops,
> We drink and sing, hey down derry.
>   *Exeunt.*

Enter KELMAR *from the cottage.*

KELMAR. What! more sacks, more grist to the mill! Early and late the miller thrives: he that was my tenant is now my landlord; this hovel, that once sheltered him, is now the only dwelling of bankrupt broken-hearted Kelmar – well, I strove my best against misfortune, and, thanks be to heaven, have fallen respected, even by my enemies.

Enter CLAUDINE *with a basket.*

So, Claudine, you are returned. Where stayed you so long?
CLAUDINE. I was obliged to wait ere I could cross the ferry – there were other passengers.
KELMAR. Amongst whom I suppose was one in whose company time flew so fast – the sun had set before you had observed it.

47

CLAUDINE. No, indeed, father: since you desired me not to meet Lothair – and I told him what you had desired – I have never seen him but in the cottage here, when you were present.

KELMAR. You are a good girl – a dutiful child, and I believe you – you never yet deceived me.

CLAUDINE. Nor ever will, dear father – but –

KELMAR. But what?

CLAUDINE. I – I find it very lonely passing the borders of the forest without – without –

KELMAR. Without Lothair.

CLAUDINE. You know 'tis dangerous, father.

KELMAR. Not half so dangerous as love – subdue it, child, in time.

CLAUDINE. But the robbers?

KELMAR. Robbers! what then? – they cannot injure thee or thy father – alas! we have no more to lose – yet thou hast one treasure left, innocence! – guard well thy heart, for should the fatal passion there take root, 'twill rob thee of thy peace.

CLAUDINE. You told me once, love's impulse could not be resisted.

KELMAR. When the object is worthless, it should not be indulged.

CLAUDINE. Is Lothair worthless?

KELMAR. No; but he is poor, almost as you are.

CLAUDINE. Do riches without love give happiness?

KELMER. Never.

CLAUDINE. Then I must be unhappy if I wed the miller Grindoff.

KELMAR. Not so – not so; – independence gives comfort, but love without competence is endless misery. You can never wed Lothair.

CLAUDINE (sighing). I can never love the miller.

KELMAR. Then you shall never marry him – though to see you Grindoff's wife be the last wish of your old father's heart. Go in, child; go in, Claudine. (CLAUDINE kisses his hand, and exit into cottage.) 'Tis plain her heart is riveted to Lothair, and honest Grindoff yet must sue in vain.

Enter LOTHAIR.

LOTHAIR. Ah! Kelmar, and alone! – where is Claudine?

KELMAR. At home, in her father's house – where should she be?

LOTHAIR. Then she has escaped – she is safe, and I am happy –
I did not accompany her in vain.

KELMAR. Accompany! – accompany! – has she then told me a
falsehood? Were you with her, Lothair?

LOTHAIR. No – ye – yes. (*Aside.*) I must not alarm him.

KELMAR. What mean these contradictions?

LOTHAIR. She knew not I was near her – you have denied our
meeting, but you cannot prevent my loving her – I have
watched her daily through the village and along the borders
of the forest.

KELMAR. I thank you, but she needs no guard; her poverty will
protect her from a thief.

LOTHAIR. Will her beauty protect her from a libertine?

KELMAR. Her virtue will.

LOTHAIR. I doubt it: – what can her resistance avail against the
powerful arm of villainy?

KELMAR. Is there such a wretch?

LOTHAIR. There is.

KELMAR. Lothair, Lothair! I fear you glance at the miller Grindoff. This is not well; this is not just.

LOTHAIR. Kelmar, you wrong me; 'tis true, he is my enemy, for
he bars my road to happiness. Yet I respect his character;
the riches that industry has gained him he employs in assisting the unfortunate – he has protected you and your child,
and I honour him.

KELMAR. If not to Grindoff, to whom did you allude?

LOTHAIR. Listen: – as I crossed the hollow way in the forest, I
heard a rustling in the copse. Claudine had reached the bank
above. As I was following, voices, subdued and whispering,
struck my ear. Her name was distinctly pronounced: 'She
comes,' said one; 'Now! now we may secure her,' cried the
second; and instantly two men advanced. A sudden exclamation burst from my lips, and arrested their intent; they

turned to seek me, and with dreadful imprecations vowed death to the intruder. Stretched beneath a bush of holly, I lay concealed; they passed within my reach. I scarcely breathed, while I observed them to be ruffians, uncouth and savage – they were banditti.

KELMAR. Banditti! Are they not yet content? All that I had – all that the hand of Providence had spared, they have deprived me of; and would they take my child?

LOTHAIR. 'Tis plain they would. Now, Kelmar, hear the last proposal of him you have rejected. Without Claudine my life is but a blank – useless to others and wretched to myself; it shall be risked to avenge the wrongs you have suffered. I'll seek these robbers! If I should fall, your daughter will more readily obey your wish, and become the wife of Grindoff. If I should succeed, promise her to me. The reward I shall receive will secure our future comfort, and thus your fears and your objections both are satisfied.

KELMAR (*affected*). Lothair, thou art a good lad, a noble lad, and worthy my daughter's love; she had been freely thine, but that by sad experience I know how keen the pangs of penury are to a parent's heart. My sorrows may descend to her when I am gone, but I have nothing to bequeath her else.

LOTHAIR. Then you consent?

KELMAR. I do, I do; but pray be careful. I fear 'tis a rash attempt; you must have help.

LOTHAIR. Then, indeed, I fail as others have before me. No, Kelmar, I must go alone, pennyless, unarmed, and secretly. None but yourself must know my purpose, or my person.

KELMAR. Be it as you will; but pray be careful. Come, thou shalt see her. (*The mill stops.*)

LOTHAIR. I'll follow; it may be my last farewell.

KELMAR. Come in – I see the mill has stopped. Grindoff will be here anon; he always visits me at nightfall, when labour ceases. Come.

Exit KELMAR *into the cottage.*

LOTHAIR. Yes, at the peril of my life, I'll seek them. With the

50

juice of herbs my face shall be discoloured, and, in the garb of misery, I'll throw myself within their power – the rest I leave to Providence. (*Music.*) But the miller comes.

Exit to the cottage – the Miller appears in perspective coming from the crag in the rock – the boat disappears on the opposite side.

Enter the two Robbers, RIBER *and* GOLOTZ, *hastily – they rush up to the cottage and peep in at the window.*

RIBER (*retiring from the window*). We are too late – she has reached the cottage.

GOLOTZ. Curse on the interruption that detained us; we shall be rated for this failure.

RIBER. Hush! not so loud. (*Goes again cautiously to the window of the cottage.*) Ha! Lothair.

GOLOTZ. Lothair! 'twas he, then, that marred our purpose; he shall smart for't.

RIBER. Back! back! he comes. On his return he dies; he cannot pass us both.

Music – They retire behind a tree – a boat passes in the distance from the mouth of the cavern in the rocks beneath the mill; then draws up to the bank.

Enter GRINDOFF, THE MILLER, *in the boat, who jumps ashore. Re-enter* LOTHAIR, *at the same moment, from the cottage.*

GRINDOFF (*disconcerted*). Lothair!

LOTHAIR. Ay, my visit here displeases you, no doubt.

GRINDOFF. Nay, we are rivals, but not enemies, I trust. We love the same girl; we strive the best we can to gain her. If you are fortunate, I'll wish you joy with all my heart; if I should have the luck on't, you'll do the same by me, I hope.

LOTHAIR. You have little fear; I am poor, you are rich. He needn't look far that would see the end on't.

GRINDOFF. But you are young and likely. I am honest and rough; the chances are as much yours as mine.

LOTHAIR. Well, time will show. I bear you no enmity. Farewell!

GRINDOFF (*aside*). He must not pass the forest. (*To* LOTHAIR.) Whither go you?

LOTHAIR. To the village; I must haste, or 'twill be late ere I reach the ferry. (*It begins to grow dark.*)

RIBER (*who with* GOLOTZ *is watching them*). He will escape us yet.

GRINDOFF. Stay, my boat shall put you across the river. Besides, the evening looks stormy – come, it will save your journey half a league.

RIBER (*aside*). It will save his life.

LOTHAIR. Well, I accept your offer, and I thank you.

GRINDOFF. Your hand.

LOTHAIR. Farewell! (*He goes into the boat, and pushes off.*)

GRINDOFF. So, I am rid of him; if he had met Claudine! – But she is safe – now, then, for Kelmar.

Exit into the cottage.

Re-enter RIBER *and* GOLOTZ.

RIBER. Curse on this chance! we have lost him!

GOLOTZ. But a time may come.

RIBER. A time shall come, and shortly, too.

Exeunt.

SCENE II. – *The Forest – distant thunder – stage dark.*

Enter KARL, *dragging after him a portmanteau.*

KARL. Here's a pretty mess! here's a precious spot of work! – Pleasant upon my soul – lost in a labyrinth, without love or liquor – the sun gone down, a storm got up, and no getting out of this vile forest, turn which way you will.

COUNT (*calling without*). Halloo! Karl! Karl!

KARL. Ah, you may call and bawl, master of mine; you'll not disturb anything here but a wild boar or two, and a wolf, perhaps.

Enter COUNT FREDERICK FRIBERG.

COUNT. Karl, where are you?

KARL. Where am I! that's what I want to know – this cursed wood has a thousand turnings, and not one that turns right.

COUNT. Careless coxcomb! said you not you could remember the track?

KARL. So I should, sir, if I could find the path – but trees will grow, and since I was here last, the place has got so bushy and briery, that – that I have lost my way.

COUNT. You have lost your senses.

KARL. No, sir, I wish I had; unfortunately, my senses are all in the highest state of perfection.

COUNT. Why not use them to more effect?

KARL. I wish I'd the opportunity; my poor stomach can testify that I taste –

COUNT. What?

KARL. Nothing; it's as empty as my head; but I see danger, smell a tempest, hear the cry of wild beasts, and feel –

COUNT. How?

KARL. Particularly unpleasant. (*Thunder and rain.*) Oh, we are in for it; do you hear, sir?

COUNT. We must be near the river; could we but reach the ferry 'tis but a short league to the Château Friberg.

KARL. Ah, sir, I wish we were there, and I seated in the old arm-chair in the servant's hall, talking of – holloa!

COUNT. What now?

KARL. I felt a spot of rain on my nose as big as a bullet. (*Thunder and rain.*) There, there, it's coming on again – seek some shelter, sir; some hollow tree, whilst I, for my sins, endeavour once more to find the way, and endure another curry-combing among these cursed brambles. Come sir. (*The storm increases.*) Lor', how it rumbles – this way, sir – this way.

Exeunt.

SCENE III. – *A Room in the Cottage – a door*, R. *flat – a window*, L. *flat – a fire*, R. *– tables*, R. *and* L. *– chairs*, &c.

GRINDOFF *and* KELMAR *discovered sitting at the table – thunder and rain.*

KELMAR. 'Tis a rough night, miller: the thunder roars, and, by the murmuring of the flood, the mountain torrents have descended. Poor Lothair! he'll scarcely have crossed the ferry.

GRINDOFF. Lothair by this is safe at home, old friend; before the storm commenced I passed him in my boat across the river. (*Aside.*) He seems less anxious for his daughter than for this bold stripling.

KELMAR. Worthy man! you'll be rewarded for all such deeds hereafter. Thank heaven, Claudine is safe! Hark!

(*Thunder heard.*)

GRINDOFF (*aside*). She is safe by this time, or I am much mistaken.

KELMAR. She will be here anon.

GRINDOFF (*aside*). I doubt that. (*To* KELMAR.) Come, here's to her health, old Kelmar – would I could once call you father!

KELMAR. You may do soon; but even your protection would now, I fear, be insufficient to –

GRINDOFF. What mean you? Insufficient!

KELMAR. The robbers – this evening in the forest –

GRINDOFF (*rising*). Ha!

KELMAR (*rising*). Did not Lothair, then, tell you?

GRINDOFF. Lothair?

KELMAR. Yes; but all's well; be not alarmed – see, she is here.

GRINDOFF. Here!

Enter CLAUDINE – GRINDOFF *endeavours to suppress his surprise.*

GRINDOFF. Claudine! Curse on them both!

KELMAR. Both! how knew you there were two?

GRINDOFF. 'Sdeath! – you – you said robbers, did you not? They never have appeared singly; therefore, I thought you meant two.

KELMAR. You are right. But for Lothair they had deprived me of my child.

GRINDOFF. How! – Did Lothair – humph! he's a courageous youth.

CLAUDINE. That he is; but he's gentle, too. What has happened?

KELMAR. Nothing, child, nothing. (*Aside to* GRINDOFF.) Do not speak on't, 'twill terrify her. Come, Claudine, now for supper. What have you brought us?

CLAUDINE. Thanks to the miller's bounty, plenty.

KELMAR. The storm increases!

KARL (*calling without*). Holloa! holloa!

KELMAR. And hark! I hear a voice – listen!

KARL (*calling again without*). Holloa!

CLAUDINE. The cry of some bewildered traveller.

(*The cry repeated, and a violent knock at the door.*)

KELMAR. Open the door.

GRINDOFF. Not so; it may be dangerous.

KELMAR. Danger comes in silence and in secret; my door was never shut against the wretched while I knew prosperity, nor shall it be closed now to my fellows in misfortune. (*To* CLAUDINE.) Open the door, I say.

(*The knock is repeated, and* CLAUDINE *opens the door.*)

Enter KARL *with a portmanteau.*

KARL. Why, in the name of dark nights and tempests, didn't you open the door at first? Have you no charity?

KELMAR. In our hearts plenty, in our gift but little; yet all we have is yours.

KARL. Then I'll share all you have with my master. Thank you, old gentleman; you won't fare the worse for sheltering honest Karl and Count Frederick Friberg.

GRINDOFF. Friberg!

KARL. Ay, I'll soon fetch him; he's waiting now, looking as melancholy as a mourning coach in a snow-storm, at the foot of a tree, wet as a drowned rat; so stir up the fire, bless you!

clap on the kettle, give us the best eatables and drinkables you have, a clean table-cloth, a couple of warm beds, and don't stand upon ceremony. We'll accept every civility and comfort you can bestow upon us without scruple.

(*Throws down the portmanteau and exit.*)

GRINDOFF. Friberg, did he say?

CLAUDINE. 'Tis the young count, so long expected.

KELMAR. Can it be possible? Without attendants, and at such a time, too?

GRINDOFF(*looking at the portmanteau, on which is the name in brass nails*). It must be the same! – Kelmar, good night.

KELMAR. Nay, not yet – the storm rages.

GRINDOFF. I fear it may increase; besides, your visitors may not like my company; good night.

Enter COUNT FREDERICK FRIBERG, *followed by* KARL – *he stops suddenly, and eyes the* MILLER, *as if recollecting him* – GRINDOFF *appears to avoid his scrutiny.*

COUNT. Your kindness is well timed; we might have perished. Accept my thanks. (*Aside.*) I should know that face.

GRINDOFF. To me your thanks are not due.

COUNT. That voice, too!

GRINDOFF. This house is Kelmar's.

(KARL *places the portmanteau on the table.*)

COUNT. Kelmar's!

KELMAR. Ay, my dear master; my fortunes have deserted me, but my attachment to your family still remains.

COUNT. Worthy old man. How happens this: the richest tenant of my late father's land – the honest, the faithful Kelmar, in a hovel?

KELMAR. It will chill your hearts to hear.

KARL (*at the fire, drying and warming himself*). Then don't tell us, pray, for our bodies are cramped with cold already.

KELMAR. 'Tis a terrible tale.

KARL (*advancing*). Then, for the love of a good appetite and a dry skin, don't tell it, for I've been terrified enough in the forest tonight to last me my life.

COUNT. Be silent, Karl. (*Retires to fire with* KELMAR.)

GRINDOFF. In – in the forest?

KARL. Ay.

GRINDOFF. What should alarm you there?

KARL. What should alarm me there? come, that's a good one. Why, first, I lost my way; trying to find that, I lost the horses; then I tumbled into a quagmire, and nearly lost my life.

GRINDOFF. Psha! this is of no consequence.

KARL. Isn't it? I have endured more hardships since morning than a knight-errant. My head's broken; my body's bruised, and my joints are dislocated. I haven't three square inches about me but what are scarified with briers and brambles; and, above all, I have not tasted a morsel of food since sunrise. Egad! instead of my making a meal of anything, I've been in constant expectation of the wolves making a meal of me.

GRINDOFF. Is this all?

KARL. All! – No, it's not all; pretty well, too, I think. When I recovered the path, I met two polite gentlemen with long knives in their hands.

GRINDOFF. Hey!

KARL. And because I refused a kind invitation of theirs, they were affronted, and were just on the point of ending all my troubles when up came my master.

GRINDOFF. Well!

KARL. Well! yes, it was well indeed, for after a struggle they made off. One of them left his sting behind, though; look, here's a poker to stir up a man's courage with! (*Showing a poniard.*)

GRINDOFF. A poniard!

KARL. Ay.

GRINDOFF (*snatching at it*). Give it me.

KARL (*retaining the dagger*). For what? It's lawful spoil – didn't

I win it in battle? No! I'll keep it as a trophy of my victory.

(*During this time,* KELMAR *and* CLAUDINE *have taken and hung up the* COUNT's *cloak, handed him a chair, and are conversing.*)

GRINDOFF. It will be safer in my possession: it may lead to a discovery of him who wore it – and –

KARL. It may – you are right – therefore I'll deliver it into the hands of Count Frederick: he'll soon ferret the rascals out; set a reward on their heads – five thousand crowns, dead or alive! that's the way to manoeuvre 'em. (*Poking* GRINDOFF *in the ribs.*)

GRINDOFF. Indeed! humph! (*Turns up.*)

KARL. Humph! don't half like that chap – never saw such a ferocious black muzzle in my life – that miller's a rogue in grain.

COUNT (*advancing*). Nay, nay, speak of it no more. I will not take an old man's bed to ease my youthful limbs; I have slept soundly on a ruder couch – and that chair shall be my resting-place.

CLAUDINE. The miller's man, Riber, perhaps can entertain his excellency better – he keeps the Flask here, on the hill, sir.

GRINDOFF. His house contains but one bed.

KARL. Only one?

GRINDOFF. And that is occupied.

KARL. The devil it is!

COUNT. It matters not; I am contented here.

KARL. That's more than I am.

GRINDOFF. But stay; perchance his guest has left it; if so, 'tis at Count Frederick's service. I'll go directly and bring you word. (*Aside.*) I may now prevent surprise – the storm has ceased; I will return immediately.

(*Unseen he drops the sheath of a dagger and exit.*)

COUNT (*eagerly*). Kelmar, tell me, who is that man?

KELMAR. The richest tenant, sir, you have; what Kelmar was when you departed from Bohemia, Grindoff now is.

COUNT. Grindoff! – I remember in my youth a favoured servant of my father's, who resembled him in countenance and voice – the recollection is strong upon my memory but I hope deceives me, for he was a villain who betrayed his trust.

KELMAR. I have heard the circumstance; it happened just before I entered your good father's service – his name was Wolf.

COUNT. The same.

KARL. And if this is not the same, I suspect he is a very near relation.

KELMAR (*angrily*). Nay, sir, you mistake – Grindoff is my friend. Come, Claudine, is all ready?

KARL. Oh, it's a sore subject is it?

Exeunt KELMAR *and* CLAUDINE.

Your friend, is he, old gentleman? – Sir – sir –

COUNT (*who has become thoughtful*). Well! what say you?

KARL. I don't like our quarters, sir; we are in a bad neighbour-hood.

COUNT. I fear we are; Kelmar's extreme poverty may have tempted him to league with – yet his daughter?

KARL. His daughter – a decoy! – nothing but a trap; don't believe her, sir; we are betrayed, murdered, if we stay here. I'll endure anything, everything, if you will but depart, sir. Dark nights, bad roads, hail, rain, assassins, and – hey! what's this? (*Sees and picks up the scabbard dropped by* GRINDOFF.) Oh, Lord, what's the matter with me? My mind misgives me; and here – (*he sheathes the dagger in it and finds it fits*) fits to a hair – we are in the lion's den!

COUNT. 'Tis evident we are snared, caught.

KARL. Oh, lord! don't say so.

Re-enter KELMAR *and* CLAUDINE, *followed by* LAURETTE *and* KRUITZ *with supper things, &c.*

KELMAR. Come, come, youngsters, bestir – spread the cloth, and –

COUNT. Kelmar, I have bethought me; at every peril, I must on tonight.

KELMAR. Tonight!

CLAUDINE. Not tonight, I beseech you; you know not half your danger. (*Goes to the table and places her hand carelessly on the portmanteau.*)

KARL. Danger! (*Aside.*) Cockatrice! (*To* CLAUDINE.) I'll thank you for that portmanteau.

COUNT. Let it remain – it may be an object to them, 'tis none to me – it will be safer here with honest Kelmar.

KELMAR. But why so sudden?

KARL. My master has recollected something that must be done tonight – or tomorrow it may be out of his power.

CLAUDINE. Stay till the miller returns.

KARL. Till he returns! (*Aside.*) Ah, the fellow's gone to get assistance, and if he comes before we escape, we shall be cut and hashed to mincemeat.

COUNT. Away! (*Advancing to the door.*)

Enter GRINDOFF, *suddenly.*

KARL. It's all over with us.

KELMAR. Well, friend, what success?

GRINDOFF. Bad enough – the count must remain here.

COUNT. Must remain!

GRINDOFF. There is no resource.

KARL. I thought so.

GRINDOFF. Tomorrow Riber can dispose of you both.

KARL. Dispose of us! (*Aside.*) Ay, put us to bed with a spade – that fellow's a gravedigger.

COUNT. Then I must cross the ford tonight.

GRINDOFF. Impossible; the torrent has swept the ferry barge from the shore, and driven it down the stream.

COUNT. Perhaps your boat –

GRINDOFF. Mine! 'twould be madness to resist the current now – and in the dark, too.

COUNT. What reward may tempt you?

GRINDOFF. Not all you are worth, sir, until tomorrow.

KARL. Tomorrow! (*Aside.*) Ah! we are crow's meat to a certainty.

GRINDOFF (*aside, looking askance around the room*). All is right: they have got the scabbard, and their suspicions now must fall on Kelmar.

Exit GRINDOFF, *bidding them all good night.*

COUNT. Well, we must submit to circumstances. (*Aside to* KARL.) Do not appear alarmed; when all is still, we may escape.

KARL. Why not now? There are only two of 'em.

COUNT. There may be others near.

Sestette.

CLAUDINE. Stay, prithee, stay – the night is dark,
    The cold wind whistles – hark! hark! hark!

COUNT.⎫ (*Together.*) ⎧We must away.
KARL. ⎭   ⎩Pray, come away.

CLAUDINE.   The night is dark,
    The cold wind whistles.

ALL.   Hark! hark! hark!

CLAUDINE. Stay, prithee, stay – the way is lone,
    The ford is deep – the boat is gone.

KELMAR. And mountain torrents swell the flood,
    And robbers lurk within the wood.

ALL.   Here ⎰you⎱ must stay till morning bright
       ⎱we⎰
    Breaks through the dark and dismal night,
    And merry sings the rising lark,
    And hush'd the night bird – hark! hark! hark!

CLAUDINE *tenderly detains the* COUNT – KELMAR *detains* KARL –
tableau closed in by next scene.

SCENE IV. – *The Depth of the Forest – stage dark.*

Enter LOTHAIR, *with his dress and complexion entirely changed; his appearance is extremely wretched.*

LOTHAIR. This way, this – in the moaning of the blast, at intervals, I heard the tread of feet – and as the moon's light burst
from the stormy clouds, I saw two figures glide like departed
spirits to this deep glen. Now, heaven prosper me, for my
attempt is desperate! (*Looking off.*) Ah, they come! (*Retires.*)

Music – Enter RIBER, GOLOTZ *follows; they look around cautiously,
then advance to a particular rock,* L. C., *which is nearly concealed by
underwood and roots of trees.*

LOTHAIR (*advancing*). Hold! (*The* ROBBERS *start, and eye him
with ferocious surprise.*) So, my purpose is accomplished – at
last I have discovered you.

RIBER. Indeed! it will cost you dear.

LOTHAIR. It has already – I have been hunted through the
country, but now my life is safe.

RIBER. Safe!

LOTHAIR. Ay, is it not? Would you destroy a comrade? Look
at me, search me – I am unarmed, defenceless!

GOLOTZ. Why come you hither?

LOTHAIR. To join your brave band – the terror of Bohemia.

RIBER. How knew you our retreat?

LOTHAIR. No matter. In the service of Count Friberg I have
been disgraced – and fly from punishment to seek revenge.

GOLOTZ (*to* RIBER). How say you?

LOTHAIR (*aside*). They hesitate – the young Count is far from
home, and his name I may use without danger. (*To the*
ROBBERS.) Lead me to your chief.

RIBER. We will – not so fast; your sight must be concealed.
(*Offering to bind his forehead.*)

LOTHAIR. Ah! (*Hesitates.*) May I trust you?

GOLOTZ. Do you doubt?

RIBER. Might we not despatch you as you are?

LOTHAIR. Enough; bind me, and lead on.

Music – They conceal his sight, take each a hand, and lead LOTHAIR *round the stage, interposing their swords to cause him to raise his feet and stoop his head, so that he may have no idea of their path –* GOLOTZ *leads* LOTHAIR *to the rock, pushes the brushwood aside, and both exeunt, followed by* RIBER, *watching that they are not observed.*

SCENE V. – *A Cavern.*

BANDITTI *discovered variously employed, chiefly sitting carousing around tables on which are flasks of wine, &c. – steps rudely cut in the rock, in the background, leading to an elevated recess,* C., *on which is inscribed:* 'Powder Magazine' *– other steps leading to an opening in the cave – a grated door,* R. *– stage light.*

Chorus. – BANDITTI.
Fill, boys, and drink about, –
Wine will banish sorrow;
Come, drain the goblet out,
We'll have more tomorrow.

(*The* ROBBERS *all rise and come forward.*)

Slow Movement.
We live free from fear,
In harmony here,
Combin'd, just like brother and brother;
And this be our toast,
The free-booter's boast,
Success and good-will to each other!
Chorus   Fill, boys, &c.

63

Enter RAVINA *through the grated door, as they conclude.*

RAVINA. What, carousing yet – sotting yet!

ZINGRA. How now, Ravina; why so churlish?

RAVINA. To sleep, I say – or wait upon yourselves. I'll stay no longer from my couch to please you. Is it not enough that I toil from daybreak, but you must disturb me ever with your midnight revelry?

ZINGRA. You were not wont to be so savage, woman.

RAVINA. Nor you so insolent. Look you repent it not!

FIRST ROBBER. Psha! heed her no more. Jealousy hath soured her.

ZINGRA. I forgive her railing.

RAVINA. Forgive!

ZINGRA. Ay! our leader seeks another mistress! and 'tis rather hard upon thee, I confess, after five year's captivity, hard service too, and now that you are accustomed to our way of life – we pity thee.

RAVINA. Pity me! I am indeed an object of compassion: five long years a captive, hopeless still of liberty. Habit has almost made my heart cold as these rude rocks that screen me from the light of heaven. Miserable lost Ravina! by dire necessity become an agent in their wickedness; yet I pine for virtue and for freedom.

ZINGRA. Leave us to our wine. Come, boys, fill all, fill full, 'to our captain's bride'.

ROBBERS. To our captain's bride!

A single note on the bugle is heard from below.

ZINGRA. Hark! 'tis from the lower cave. (*Bugle note repeated.*) She comes! Ravina, look you receive her as becomes the companion of our chief – remember!

RAVINA. I shall remember. So, another victim to hypocrisy and guilt. Poor wretch! she loves perhaps, as I did, the miller Grindoff; but, as I do, may live to execrate the outlaw and the robber!

Music – the trap in the floor is thrown open.

Enter RIBER *through the floor, followed by* GOLOTZ *and* LOTHAIR.

ROBBERS. Hail to our new companion!
RAVINA. A man!
LOTHAIR *tears the bandage from his eyes as he arrives in the cave –*
the ROBBERS *start back on perceiving a man.*

LOTHAIR. Thanks for your welcome!
ZINGRA. Who have we here? – Speak!
RIBER. A recruit. Where is the captain?
ZINGRA. Where is the captain's bride?
RIBER. Of her hereafter. (*A bugle is heard above.*)
ROBBERS. Wolf! Wolf!

Enter GRINDOFF *in robber's apparel – he descends the opening, and*
advances.

ZINGRA. ⎫
⎬ Welcome, noble captain!
ROBBERS. ⎭
GRINDOFF (*starts at seeing* LOTHAIR). A stranger!
LOTHAIR (*aside*). Grindoff!

The ROBBERS *lay hands on their swords, &c.*

GRINDOFF. Ha! betrayed! Who has done this?
RIBER. I brought him hither, to –
GRINDOFF. Riber! humph! You have executed my orders well,
    have you not? Where is Claudine?
LOTHAIR. Claudine! (*Aside.*) Villain! hypocrite!
GRINDOFF. Know you Claudine likewise?
RIBER. She escaped us in the forest. Some meddling fool thwarted
    our intent, and –
GRINDOFF. Silence; I know it all. A word with you presently.
    Now, stranger – but I mistake; we should be old acquain-
    tance – my name is so familiar to you. What is your purpose
    here?
LOTHAIR. Revenge!
GRINDOFF. On whom?
LOTHAIR. On one whose cruelty and oppression well deserve it.
GRINDOFF. His name?

LOTHAIR (*aside*). Would I dare mention it!

GRINDOFF. His name, I say?

RIBER. He complains of Count Friberg.

GRINDOFF. Indeed! then your purpose will soon be accomplished: he arrived this night, and shelters at old Kelmar's cottage. He shall never pass the river; should he once reach the Château Friberg, it would be fatal to our band.

LOTHAIR. Arrived! (*Aside.*) What have I done! My fatal indiscretion has destroyed him. (*To* GRINDOFF.) Let him fall by my hand.

GRINDOFF. It may tremble – it trembles now. The firmest of our band have failed. (*Looking at* RIBER.) Henceforth the enterprise shall be my own.

LOTHAIR. Let me accompany you.

GRINDOFF. Not tonight.

LOTHAIR. Tonight.

GRINDOFF. Ay, before the dawn appears, he dies! Riber!

LOTHAIR *clasps his hands in agony.*

RAVINA. What, more blood! must Friberg's life be added to the list?

GRINDOFF. It must; our safety claims it.

RAVINA. Short-sighted man! Will not his death doubly arouse the sluggish arm of justice? The whole country, hitherto kept in awe by dissension and selfish fear, will join; reflect in time; beware their retribution!

GRINDOFF. When I need a woman's help and counsel, I'll seek it of the compassionate Ravina. Begone! (*Exit* RAVINA.) Riber, I say!

RIBER. I await your orders.

GRINDOFF. Look you execute them better than the last – look to't! The Count and his companion rest at Kelmar's; it must be done within an hour: arm, and attend me – at the same time I will secure Claudine – and should Kelmar's vigilance interpose to mar us, he henceforth shall be an inmate here.

LOTHAIR. Oh, villain!

GRINDOFF (*rushing towards* LOTHAIR). How mean you?

LOTHAIR. Friberg – let me go with you.

GRINDOFF. You are too eager; I will not trust thy inexperience: trust you! what surety have we of your faith?

LOTHAIR. My oath.

GRINDOFF. Swear, then, never to desert the object, never to betray the cause for which you sought our band – revenge on –

LOTHAIR. On him who has deeply, basely injured me, I swear it.

GRINDOFF. 'Tis well – your name?

LOTHAIR. Spiller!

GRINDOFF (*to* RIBER). Quick! arm and attend me. (RIBER *retires.*) Are those sacks in the mill disposed of as I ordered?

ZINGRA. They are, captain.

GRINDOFF. Return with the flour tomorrow, and be careful that all assume the calmness of industry and content. With such appearance, suspicion itself is blind; 'tis the safeguard of our band. Fill me a horn, and then to business. (*A* ROBBER *hands him a horn of wine; he drinks.*) The Miller and his Men!

ROBBERS (*drinking*). The Miller and his Men!

GRINDOFF *and* ROBBERS *laugh heartily* – GRINDOFF *puts on his miller's frock, hat, &c.* – RIBER, *armed with pistols in his belt, advances with a dark lantern, and exeunt with* GRINDOFF *through the rocks.*

Chorus. – BANDITTI.
Now to the forest we repair,
Awhile like spirits wander there;
In darkness we secure our prey,
And vanish at the dawn of day.

Count Friberg.

Count Friberg.

Grindoff.

Grindoff.

Claudine.

Banditti Carousing.

Grindoff.

Sold by J.REDINGTON, 208, Hoxton old Town.

London Pub. Nov. 1.1853 by J.K.GREEN, 3 George Street Walworth New Town.

Price Halfpenny.

ACT II

SCENE I. – *The Interior of* KELMAR'S *Cottage, as before.*

COUNT FREDERICK FRIBERG *discovered asleep in a chair, reclining on a table, and at the opposite side, near the fire,* KARL *is likewise seen asleep,* R. – *the Count's sword lies on the table,* L. – *the fire is nearly extinguished – stage dark – music as the curtain rises. Enter* CLAUDINE, *with a lamp, down the stairs.*

CLAUDINE. All still, all silent! The Count and his companions are undisturbed! What can it mean? My father wanders from his bed, restless as myself. Alas! the infirmities of age and sorrow afflict him sorely. Night after night I throw myself upon a sleepless couch, ready to fly to his assistance, and – hush – hush! (CLAUDINE *extinguishes the light, and conceals herself.*)

Enter KELMAR.

KELMAR. They sleep – sleep soundly – ere they wake I may return from my inquiry. If Grindoff's story was correct, I still may trust him – still may the Count confide in him; but his behaviour last night, unusual and mysterious, hangs like a fearful dream upon my mind – his anxiety to leave the cottage, his agitation at the appearance of Count Friberg – but above all, his assertion that the ferry-barge was lost, disturbs me. My doubts shall soon be ended. At this lone hour I may pass the borders unperceived, and the grey dawn that now glimmers in the east will direct my path.

Looks about him fearful of disturbing the sleepers, and exit.

CLAUDINE. My father appears unusually agitated. Ah, it may be! sometimes he wanders on the river's brink, watching the

69

bright orb of day bursting from the dark trees, and breathes a prayer, a blessing for his child; yet 'tis early, very early – yet it may be – Oh, father, my dear – dear father! (*Exit.*)

KARL. Yaw! (*Snoring.*) Damn the rats! Yaw, what a noise they keep up! Hey, where am I? Oh, in this infernal hovel; the night-mare has rode me into a jelly; then such horrible dreams, yaw! (*A light from the dark lantern borne by* RIBER *is seen passing the window.*) And such a swarm of rats – damn the rats! (*Lays his hand on his poniard.*) They'd better keep off, for I'm hungry enough to eat one. Bew – eu. (*Shivering.*) I wish it were morning. (*Music.*)

Enter RIBER; *he suddenly retires, observing a light occasioned by* KARL'S *stirring the fire with his dagger.*

KARL. What's that? (*Listens.*) Nothing but odd noises all night; wonder how my master can sleep for such a – yaw – aw! Damn the rats! (*Lies down.*)

Music – Enter RIBER *cautiously, holding forward the lantern –* GRINDOFF *follows.* RIBER, *on seeing the* COUNT, *draws a poniard – he raises his arm,* GRINDOFF *catches it, and prevents the blow. Appropriate music.*

GRINDOFF. Not yet; first secure my prize, Claudine; these are safe.

KARL. How the varmint swarm!

GRINDOFF. Hush! he dreams.

RIBER. It shall be his last.

KARL. Rats, rats!

RIBER. What says he?

KARL. Rats! – they all come from the mill.

RIBER. Do they so?

KARL. Ay, set traps for 'em, poison 'em.

(RIBER, *again attempting to advance, is detained by* GRINDOFF.)

GRINDOFF. Again so rash – remember!

KARL. I shall never forget that fellow in the forest.

RIBER. Ha! do you mark?

GRINDOFF. Fear them not; be still till I return. He is sound; none sleep so hard as those that babble in their dreams. Stir not, I charge you; yet, should Kelmar – ay – should you hear a noise without, instantly despatch.

Exit GRINDOFF *up the stairs.*

RIBER. Enough! (KARL *wakes again – he observes* RIBER, *grasps his dagger, and, watching the motion of the* ROBBER, *acts accordingly.*) This delay is madness, but I must obey. (*Looking at the priming of his pistol, then towards the table –* KARL *drops to his position.*) Hey, a sword! (*Advancing to the table and removing the sword.*) Now, all is safe – Hark! (*A noise without, as of something falling.*) 'Tis time! if this should fail, my poniard will secure him.

Music – RIBER *advances hastily, and, in the act of bringing his pistol to the level against the* COUNT, *is stabbed by* KARL, *who has arisen and closely followed his every movement; at the same moment enter* GRINDOFF *– the* COUNT, *rushing from the chair at the noise of the pistol, seizes him by the collar – the group stand amazed. – Tableau.*

COUNT. Speak! What means this?
KARL. They've caught a tartar, sir, that's all. Hey, the miller!
GRINDOFF. Ay!
COUNT. How came you here?
GRINDOFF. To – to do you service.
COUNT. At such an hour!
GRINDOFF. 'Tis never too late to do good.
COUNT. Good!
GRINDOFF. Yes; you have been in danger.
KARL. Have we? Thank you for your news.
GRINDOFF. You have been watched by the Banditti.
COUNT. So it appears.
KARL. But how did you know it?
GRINDOFF (*confused*). There is my proof. (*Pointing to the body of* RIBER.)

71

KARL. But how the plague got you into the house? – Through a rat-hole?

COUNT. Explain.

GRINDOFF. Few words will do that: – on my return to the mill, I found you might repose there better than in this house; at all events, I knew you would be safer in my care.

COUNT. Safer! Proceed! what mean you?

KARL (*aside*). Safer!

GRINDOFF. Kelmar –

COUNT. Hah!

GRINDOFF. Had you no suspicion of him? – no mistrust of his wish to – to detain you?

COUNT. I confess, I –

GRINDOFF (*to* KARL). The poniard you obtained in the forest, that you refused to give me –

KARL. This?

GRINDOFF. Is Kelmar's.

COUNT. Wretch!

KARL. I thought so; I found the sheath here.

GRINDOFF. I knew it instantly; my suspicions were aroused – now they are confirmed; Kelmar is in league with these marauders; I found the door open – you still slept. I searched the house for him; he is no where to be found – he and his daughter have absconded. Now, sir, are you satisfied?

COUNT. I am.

KARL. I am not; I wish we were safe at home. I'm no coward by daylight, but I hate adventures of this kind in the dark. Lord, how a man may be deceived! I took you for a great rogue; but I now find you are a good Christian enough, though you are a very ill-looking man.

GRINDOFF. Indeed; we can't all be as handsome as you are, you know.

KARL (*pertly*). No; nor as witty as you are, you know.

GRINDOFF. Come, sir; follow me. You can't mistake; see, 'tis day-break; at the cottage close to the narrow bridge that passes the ravine you will find repose.

COUNT. We'll follow you. (*Exit* GRINDOFF.)

KARL. I don't half like that fellow yet. (*Gets the portmanteau from table.*) Now, the sooner we are off the better, sir. As for this fellow, the rats may take care of him. (CLAUDINE *shrieks.*)

COUNT (*drawing his sword*). Ha! a woman's voice! Karl, follow me!

KARL. What, more adventures! (*Drawing his sword.*) I'm ready. I say, (*to the body of* RIBER) take care of the portmanteau, will you? (*Exit, closed in by next scene.*)

SCENE II. – *The Forest* (1st grooves) – *Stage partly dark.*

Music – Enter GRINDOFF, *with* CLAUDINE *in his arms.*

COUNT (*without*). Karl! Karl! follow, this way!

GRINDOFF (*resting*). Ha, so closely pursued! – Nay, then –

Going hastily, he pushes aside the leaves of the secret pass, and they disappear.

Enter COUNT FREDERICK FRIBERG, *hastily.*

COUNT. Gone! vanished! Can it be possible? Sure 'tis witchcraft. I was close upon him – Karl! The cries of her he dragged with him, too, have ceased, and not the faintest echo of his retiring footsteps can be heard – Karl!

Enter KARL.

KARL. Oh, Lord! Pho! that hill's a breather! Why, where is he? Didn't you overtake him?

COUNT. No! in this spot he disappeared, and sunk, as it should seem, ghost-like, into the very earth. Follow!

KARL. Follow! – Follow a will-o'-the-wisp!

COUNT. Quick – aid me to search!

KARL. Search out a ghost! Mercy on us! I'll follow you through the world, fight for you the best cock-giant robber of 'em all, but, if you're for hunting goblins, I'm off. Hey! where the devil's the woman, though? If she was a spirit, she made more noise than any lady alive.

COUNT. Perchance the villain, so closely pursued, has destroyed his victim.

KARL. No doubt on't; he's killed her to a certainty; nothing but death can stop a woman's tongue.

COUNT (*having searched in vain*). From the miller we may gain assistance: Grindoff, no doubt, is acquainted with every turn and outlet of the forest; quick, attend me to the mill. (*Exit.*)

KARL. Rat me if I'll run after the girl; why should I? girls never run after me. I know the tricks on 'em; they are all deceptions and full of mischief, like a barrel of gunpowder. They are like – they are like a lawsuit, and a lawsuit's like a devil's kettle, in which everything that's disagreeable is all boiled up together. None on 'em ever took delight in me, except it was to vex and jilt me. Ever since Wilhelmina slighted my passion, I have forsworn the sex, and all alone by myself have struggled through life, like a fly in treacle. (*Exit* KARL.)

SCENE III. – *The Cavern.*

Music – ROBBERS *discovered asleep in different parts,* (R. *and* L.) – LOTHAIR *on guard, with a carbine, stands beneath the magazine – stage partly light.*

LOTHAIR. Ere this it must be daylight – yet Grindoff returns not – perchance their foul intent has failed – the fatal blow designed for Friberg may have fallen upon himself. How tedious drags the time, when fear, suspense, and doubt thus weigh upon the heart. Oh, Kelmar, beloved Claudine, you little know my peril. (*Looks at the various groups of* BANDITTI, *and carefully rests his carbine at the foot of the rugged steps leading to the magazine.*) While yet this drunken stupor makes their sleep most death-like, let me secure a terrible but just revenge. If their infernal purpose be accomplished, this is their reward. (*Draws a coil of fuse from his bosom.*) These caverns, that spread beneath the mill, have various outlets, and in the fissures of the rock the train will lie unnoticed. Could I but reach the magazine.

Music – LOTHAIR *retires cautiously up* – *he places his foot over the body of a* ROBBER, *who is seen asleep on the steps leading to the magazine* – *by accident he touches the carbine, which slips down* – *the* ROBBER, *being disturbed, alters his position, while* LOTHAIR *stands over him, and again reposes* – LOTHAIR *advances up the steps* – *as he arrives at the magazine,* WOLF'S *signal, the bugle, is heard from above* – *the* ROBBERS *instantly start up, and* LOTHAIR, *at the same moment, springs from the steps, and, seizing his carbine, stands in his previous attitude.*

Enter WOLF (GRINDOFF) *descending the steps of the opening, with* CLAUDINE *senseless in his arms.*

ROBBERS. The signal!

GOLOTZ. Wolf, we rejoice with you.

LOTHAIR. Have you been successful?

WOLF (*setting down* CLAUDINE). So far, at least, I have.

LOTHAIR (*aside*). Claudine – merciful powers! (*To* WOLF.) But Kelmar –

WOLF. Shall not long escape me – Kelmar once secure, his favourite, my redoubted rival, young Lothair, may next require attention – bear her in, Golotz. (GOLOTZ *bears* CLAUDINE *off.*) Where is Ravina?

Enter RAVINA.

Oh, you are come!

RAVINA. I am; what is your will?

WOLF. That you attend Claudine; treat her as you would treat me.

RAVINA. I will, be sure on't.

WOLF. Look you, fail not. I cannot wait her recovery – danger surrounds us.

ROBBERS. Danger!

WOLF. Ay, everyone must be vigilant, every heart resolved – Riber has been stabbed.

LOTHAIR. Then Friberg –

WOLF. Has escaped.

LOTHAIR. Thank heaven!

WOLF. How?

LOTHAIR. Friberg is still reserved for me.

WOLF. Be it so – your firmness shall be proved.

RAVINA. So – one act of villainy is spared you; pursue your fate no farther – desist, be warned in time.

WOLF. Fool! could woman's weakness urge me to retreat, my duty to our band would now make such repentance treachery.

ROBBERS. Noble captain!

WOLF. Mark you, my comrades: Kelmar has fled; left his house – no doubt for the Château Friberg. The suspicions of the Count are upon *him*. All mistrust of me is banished from his mind, and I have lured him and his companion to the cottage of our lost comrade, Riber.

LOTHAIR. How came Claudine to fall into your power?

WOLF. I encountered her alone, as I left Kelmar's cottage. She had been to seek her father; I seized the opportunity, and conveyed her to the secret pass in the forest. Her cries caused me to be pursued, and one instant later I had fallen into their hands – by this time they have recovered the pathway to the mill. Spiller shall supply Riber's place – be prepared to meet them at the Flask, and prove yourself –

LOTHAIR. The man I am; I swear it.

WOLF. Enough – I am content!

RAVINA. Content! such guilt as thine can never feel content. Never will thy corroded heart have rest – years of security have made you rash, incautious – wanton in thy cruelty – and you will never rest until your mistaken policy destroys your band.

76

WOLF. No more of this – her discontent is dangerous. – Spiller! when you are prepared to leave the cavern, make fast the door; Ravina shall remain here confined until our work above is finished. (*Aside to him.*)

LOTHAIR. I understand –

WOLF. Golotz and the rest – who are wont to cheer our revels with your music – be in waiting at the Flask, as travellers, wandering Savoyards, till the Count and his followers are safe within our toils; the delusion may spare us trouble. I know them resolute and fierce; and, should they once suspect, though our numbers overpower them, the purchase may cost us dear. Away – time presses – Spiller – remember –

LOTHAIR. Fear me not – you soon shall know me.

Exit WOLF *and* ROBBERS *up the steps –* LOTHAIR *immediately runs up the steps to the magazine, and places the fuse within, closes the door and directs it towards the trap by which he first entered the cave.*

RAVINA. Now, then, hold firm, my heart and hand; one act of vengeance, one dreadful triumph, and I meet henceforth the hatred, the contempt of Wolf, without a sigh.

In great agitation she advances to the table, and taking a vial from her bosom pours the contents into a cup, and goes cautiously across to where CLAUDINE *has been conducted.*

RAVINA. As she revives – ere yet her bewildered senses proclaim her situation, she will drink – and –

LOTHAIR, *who has watched the conduct of* RAVINA, *seizes her arm, takes away the cup, and throws it off.*

LOTHAIR. Hold, mistaken woman! Is this your pity for the unfortunate – of your own sex, too? Are you the advocate of justice and of mercy – who dare condemn the cruelty of Wolf, yet with your own hand would destroy an innocent fellow-creature, broken-hearted, helpless, and forlorn? Oh, shame! shame!

RAVINA. And who is he that dares to school me thus?

LOTHAIR. Who am I?

RAVINA. Ay! that talk of justice and of mercy, yet pant to shed the blood of Friberg!

LOTHAIR (*aside*). Now, dared I trust her – I must, there is no resource, for they'll be left together. (*To* RAVINA.) Ravina – say what motive urged you to attempt an act that I must believe is hateful to your nature?

RAVINA. Have I not cause – ample cause?

LOTHAIR. I may remove it.

RAVINA. Can you remove the pangs of jealousy?

LOTHAIR. I can – Claudine will never be the bride of Wolf.

RAVINA. Who can prevent it?

LOTHAIR. Her husband.

RAVINA. Is it possible?

LOTHAIR. Be convinced. Claudine, Claudine! (*Music.*)

CLAUDINE (*without*). Ha! that voice!

LOTHAIR. Claudine!

CLAUDINE (*entering*). 'Tis he! 'tis he! then I am safe! Ah! who are these, and in what dreadful place am I?

LOTHAIR. Beloved Claudine, can this disguise conceal me?

CLAUDINE. Lothair! I was not deceived.

(*Falls into his arms.*)

RAVINA. Lothair!

LOTHAIR. Ay, her affianced husband. Ravina, our lives are in your power; preserve them and save yourself; one act of glorious repentance, and the blessings of the surrounding country are yours. Observe!

Music – LOTHAIR *points to the magazine – shows the train to* RAVINA, *and explains the intention – then gives a phosphorous bottle, which he shows the purpose of – she comprehends him –* CLAUDINE'S *action expresses astonishment and terror –* LOTHAIR *opens the trap up the stage.*

RAVINA. Enough, I understand.

78

LOTHAIR. Be careful, be cautious, I implore you; – convey the
train where I may distinctly see you from without the mill;
and, above all, let no anxiety of mind, no fear of failure,
urge you to fire the train till I give the signal. Remember,
Claudine might be the victim of such fatal indiscretion.

RAVINA. But Wolf.

Re-enter WOLF, *who hearing his name, halts at the back of the
cavern.*

LOTHAIR. Wolf, with his guilty companions, shall fall despised
and execrated. (*Seeing* WOLF.) Ah! (*Aside to* CLAUDINE.)
Remove the train..

WOLF. Villain! (*Levels a pistol at* LOTHAIR – RAVINA *utters an
exclamation of horror* – CLAUDINE *retreats, and removes the
train to the foot of the steps.*)

LOTHAIR. Hold! – you are deceived.

WOLF. Do you acknowledge it? – But 'tis the last time. (*Seizing*
LOTHAIR *by the collar.*)

LOTHAIR. One moment.

WOLF. What further deception?

LOTHAIR. I have used none – hear the facts.

WOLF. What are they?

LOTHAIR. Hatred to thee – jealousy of the fair Claudine urged
this woman to attempt her life.

WOLF. Indeed! – for what purpose was that pass disclosed?
(*Pointing to the trap.*)

LOTHAIR. I dared not leave them together.

WOLF. Vain subterfuge – your threat of destruction on me and
my companions –

LOTHAIR. Was a mere trick, a forgery, a fabrication to appease
her disappointed spirit – induce her to quit the cave, and
leave Claudine in safety.

WOLF (*going up to, and closely observing* RAVINA). Plausible
hypocrite, Ravina has no weapon of destruction – how then?
(*Crossing back to* LOTHAIR.)

LOTHAIR (*looking towards* RAVINA, *who holds up the vial, unseen
by* WOLF). Ah! (*Aside.*) We are saved. (*Crossing and*

snatching the vial, which she had retained in her hand.) Behold, let conviction satisfy your utmost doubts.

WOLF (*looking on the label*). Poison! – you then are honest, Wolf unjust – I can doubt no longer. (*Seizes* RAVINA *by the arm.*) Fiend! descend instantly, in darkness and despair anticipate a dreadful punishment.

Music – RAVINA *clasps her hands in entreaty, and descends the trap, which is closed violently by* WOLF.

WOLF. Now, Spiller, follow me to the Flask. (*Music.*) Be sure, make fast yon upper door.

He takes his broad miller's hat, for which he had returned – exit up steps, LOTHAIR *following, and looking back significantly at* CLAUDINE, *who then advances cautiously, opens the trap, and gives the train to* RAVINA *– appropriate music –* RAVINA *and* CLAUDINE *remain in attitude, the latter watching* LOTHAIR, *with uplifted hands.*

SCENE IV. – *The Cottage of Riber – The sign of 'The Flask' at the door,* L. *in flat.*

Enter COUNT FREDERICK FRIBERG *and* KARL.

COUNT. This must be the house!

KARL. Clear as daylight; look, sir, 'The Flask!' Oh, and there stands the mill! I suppose old rough-and-tough, master Grindoff, will be here presently. Well, I'm glad we are in the right road at last; for such ins and outs, and ups and downs, and circumbendibuses in that forest, I never –

COUNT. True; we may now obtain guides and assistance to pursue that ruffian!

KARL (*aside*). Pursue again! – not to save all the she sex! – flesh and blood can't stand this.

COUNT (*abstracted*). Yet, after so long an absence, delay is doubly irksome – could I but see her my heart doats on!

KARL. Ah! could *I* but see what my heart doats on.

COUNT. My sweet Laurette!

KARL. A dish of saur-kraut!

COUNT. Fool!

KARL. Fool! so I mustn't enjoy a good dinner even in imagination.

COUNT. Still complaining!

KARL. How can I help it, sir? I can't live upon air, as you do.

COUNT. You had plenty last night.

KARL. So I had last Christmas, sir; and what sort of a supper was it, after all? – One apple, two pears, three bunches of sour grapes, and a bowl of milk; one of your forest meals – I can't abide such a cruel cold diet – oh, for a bumper of brandy! But, unfortunately, my digestion keeps pace with my appetite – I'm always hungry. Oh, for a bumper of brandy!

Music heard within the Flask.

COUNT. Hush!

KARL. What's that? Somebody tickling a guitar into fits; soft music always makes me doleful.

COUNT. Go into the house – stay; remember, I would be private.

KARL. Private – in a public-house. Oh, I understand, incog. But the miller knows you, sir.

COUNT. That's no reason all his people should.

KARL. I smoke – they'd be awed by our dignity and importance – poor things, I pity 'em – they are not used to polished society. Holloa! house! landlord! Mr Flask.

Enter LOTHAIR *as landlord.*

KARL. Good entertainment here for man and beast, I'm told.

LOTHAIR. You are right.

KARL. Well, here am I, and there's my master!

LOTHAIR. You are welcome. (*Aside.*) I dare not say otherwise; Wolf is on the watch.

(GRINDOFF *appears, watching at a window.*)

KARL. Have you got anything ready? (*Smacking his lips.*)

LOTHAIR. Too much, I fear.

KARL. Not a bit, I'll warrant. I'm devilish sharp set.

LOTHAIR. Well, you are just in time.

KARL. Pudding-time, I hope! Have you got any meat?

LOTHAIR. I must ask him. (*Aside and looking round anxiously.*) Won't your master –

KARL. No! he lives upon love; but don't be alarmed, I'll make it worth your while; I'm six meals in arrear, and can swallow enough for both of us.

Exit KARL, *with* LOTHAIR, *to the Flask* – WOLF *closes the window.*

COUNT. Yes, I'm resolved – the necessity for passing the river must by this time have urged the peasantry to re-establish the ferry – delay is needless. I'll away instantly to the Château Friberg, and with my own people return to redress the wrongs of my oppressed and suffering tenantry.

Enter KARL.

COUNT. Well, your news?

KARL. Glorious! – The landlord, Mr Flask, is a man after my own heart, a fellow of five meals a day.

COUNT. Psha! who are the musicians?

KARL. Ill-looking dogs, truly; – Savoyards, I take it; one plays on a thing like a frying-pan, the other turns something that sounds like a young grindstone.

COUNT. What else?

KARL. As fine an imitation of a shoulder of mutton as ever I clapp'd my eyes on.

Enter KELMAR, *exhausted by haste and fatigue.*

COUNT. Kelmar!

KELMAR. Ah, the Count and his companion! – Thank heaven, I am arrived in time! my master will be saved, though Claudine, my poor unhappy child, is lost. Fly, I beseech you, fly from this spot! Do not question me; this is no time for explanations; one moment longer, and you are betrayed – your lives irrecoverably sacrificed.

COUNT. Would you again deceive us?

KELMAR. I have been myself deceived – fatally deceived! Let an old man's prayers prevail with you! Leave, oh leave this accursed place, and –

Enter WOLF, *in his miller's dress.*

KELMAR. Ah, the miller! then has hope forsaken me – Yet one ray, one effort more, and –

WOLF. Thy treachery is known. (*He seizes* KELMAR *by the collar.*)

KELMAR. One successful effort more, and death is welcome.

WOLF. Villain!

KELMAR. Thou art the villain – see – behold!

With a violent effort of strength, the old man suddenly turns upon WOLF *and tears open his vest, beneath which he appears armed –* WOLF, *at the same instant, dashes* KELMAR *from him, who is caught by the* COUNT *– the* COUNT *draws his sword –* WOLF *draws pistols in each hand from his belt, and his hat falls off at the same instant – tableau – appropriate music.*

COUNT. 'Tis he! the same! 'tis Wolf.

WOLF. Spiller! Golotz! (*Rushes out.*)

KARL. Is it Wolf? Damn his pistols! This shall reach him. (*Draws his sword, and hastens after* WOLF *– the report of a pistol is immediately heard.*)

Exit COUNT FRIBERG *and* KELMAR *– At the same moment,* GOLOTZ *and another* ROBBER, *disguised as minstrels, followed by* LOTHAIR, *burst from the house.*

GOLOTZ. We are called; Wolf called us! – Ah, they have dis-covered him!

LOTHAIR. 'Tis too late to follow him; he has reached the bridge.

GOLOTZ. Then he is safe; but see, at the foot of the hill, armed men in the Friberg uniform press forward to the mill.

LOTHAIR. This way we must meet them, then; in, to the subterranean pass! (*Exeunt* GOLOTZ *and* ROBBER *to house.*) Now, Claudine, thy sufferings shall cease, and thy father's wrongs shall be revenged. (*Exit to house.*)

SCENE V. – *A near View of the Mill,* C., *standing on an elevated projection – from the stage a narrow bridge, to rise and fall, passes to the rock,* R. C., *on the platform of which stands the mill.*

Music – Enter RAVINA, *ascending the ravine with the fuse, which she places carefully in the crannies of the rock.*

RAVINA. My toil is over; the train is safe. From this spot I may receive the signal from Lothair, and, at one blow, the hapless victims of captivity and insult are amply, dreadfully avenged. (*Music – a pistol is fired without.*) Ah, Wolf! (*She retires.*)

Enter WOLF *pursued, and turning, fires his remaining pistol off; then hurries across the bridge, which he instantly draws up –* KARL *rushes on.*

WOLF (*with a shout of great exultation*). Ha, ha! you strive in vain!

KARL. Cowardly rascal! you'll be caught at last. (*Shaking his sword at* WOLF.)

WOLF. By whom?

KARL. Your only friend, Beelzebub: run as fast as you will, he'll trip up your heels at last.

WOLF. Fool-hardy slave, I have sworn never to descend from this spot alive, unless with liberty.

KARL. Oh, we'll accommodate you; you shall have *liberty* to *ascend* from it; the wings of your own mill shall be the gallows, and fly with every rascal of you into the other world.

WOLF. Golotz! – Golotz, I say!

Enter COUNT FRIBERG, *with* KELMAR *and the* ATTENDANTS *from the Château Friberg, in uniform, and armed.*

COUNT. Wretch! your escape is now impossible. Surrender to the injured laws of your country.

WOLF. Never! the brave band that now await my commands within the mill double your number. Golotz!

Enter GOLOTZ *from a small door in the mill.*

WOLF. Quick! let my bride appear.

Exit GOLOTZ.

Enter RAVINA – WOLF *starts.*

RAVINA. She is here! What would you?

WOLF. Ravina! – Traitress!

RAVINA. Traitress! What, then, art thou? But I come not here to parley; ere it be too late, make one atonement for thy injuries – restore this old man's child.

KELMAR. Does she still live?

WOLF. She does; but not for thee, or for the youth Lothair.

RAVINA. Obdurate man! Then do I know my course.

Re-enter LOTHAIR, *conducting* CLAUDINE *from the mill, a cloak concealing him.*

CLAUDINE. Oh, my dear father!

KELMAR. My child – Claudine! Oh, spare, in pity spare her!

WOLF. Now mark me, Count: unless you instantly withdraw your followers, and let my troop pass free, by my hand she dies!

KELMAR. Oh, mercy!

COUNT. Hold yet a moment!

WOLF. Withdraw your followers.

COUNT. Till thou art yielded up to justice, they never shall depart.

WOLF. For that threat, be this your recompense!

LOTHAIR (*throwing aside his cloak*). And this my triumph!

Music – LOTHAIR *places himself before* CLAUDINE *and receives* WOLF'S *attack – the* ROBBER *is wounded, staggers back, sounds his bugle, and the mill is crowded with* BANDITTI *–* LOTHAIR *throws back the bridge, and crosses it with* CLAUDINE *in his arms.*

Ravina, fire the train.

RAVINA *instantly sets fire to the fuse, the flash of which is seen to run down the side of the rock into the gully under the bridge, and the explosion immediately takes place –* KELMAR, *rushing forward, catches* CLAUDINE *in his arms.*

CURTAIN

My Poll and My Partner Joe

A NAUTICAL DRAMA IN THREE ACTS

———•◉•———

by John Thomas Haines

First performed at the Surrey Theatre, 31 August 1835

CAST

HARRY HALLYARD, a waterman	*Mr T. P. Cooke*
JOE TILLER, his partner	*Mr R. Honner*
MARY MAYBUD, his sweetheart	*Miss Macarthey*
WATCHFUL WAXEND, a cobbler	*Mr W. Smith*
WILL WALL-IT, landlord of the Crown and Crozier	*Mr Young*
OLD SAM SCULLER, a waterman	*Mr Mortimer*
DAME HALLYARD	*Mrs Stickney*
BLACK BRANDON, captain of a slaver	*Mr Dillon*
BEN BOWSE, his mate	*Mr Cullen*
SAM SNATCHEM, a bailiff	*Mr Asbury*
CAPTAIN OAKHEART ⎱ of HMS	*Mr Bannister*
LIEUTENANT MANLY ⎰ Polyphemus	*Mr Norman*
ZINGA, a slave	*Mr C. Pitt*
ZAMBA, his wife	*Miss Cross*
SENTINEL	*Mr Maynard*
ABIGAIL HOLDFORTH, a shoebinder	*Miss Martin*

Sailors, Pirates, Slaves, Watermen, Lasses, Jews

Mr. T. P. COOKE AS HARRY HALLYARD, 2nd DRESS.

IN MY POLL & MY PARTNER JOE.

Printed & Sold by M & M, SKELT, 11, Swan St. Minories, London.

N.º 106.

ACT I

SCENE I. – *Interior of the Crown and Crozier Public House at Battersea; the Hard, or landing place, seen at the back, and the opposite shore visible through the large window; boats passing and re-passing as the curtain ascends.*

WATERMEN *discovered seated, smoking and drinking –* OLD SAM SCULLER *reading a newspaper –* WATCHFUL WAXEND *seated near him, tipsy –* WILL WALL-IT, *the landlord, attending – the company laughing.*

WAXEND. You may laugh, you profane scoffers, but I stick like wax to my religious spirit.

WALL-IT. That you do, Master Waxend, and to my full proof spirit, too! (*They all laugh.*)

WAXEND. You're all going by steam to the diabolical oven – drinking and sotting from morning till night! (*To* WALL-IT.) Fill my pot! You'll be thirsty enough in the next world, and no beer; there they allows none to be drunk on the premises.

WALL-IT. Your beer, Master Watchful. Money!

WAXEND. Oh, stick it up. (*Turning to the* WATERMEN.) Don't trust me, but read the Commen – Com-en-tatories of Julius Caesar. (*They all laugh.*)

Enter JOE TILLER *from the Hard.*

JOE. Harry Hallyard not here yet!

Then I must forth again to wander by the river,
To see if I my par-tener and kind friend can diskiver.

WAXEND. Ah, Master Joe, you're a poet; why don't you turn your thoughts to holy subjects? Why don't you do as somebody did – write a legacy in a country churchyard?

JOE. An elegy, you mean.

91

WAXEND. Well, I know; some people call 'em t'other way. (*Drinking.*) All the world's a sot! (*Drinking again.*) Ah, you little think how drinking wears out the soul.

JOE. So much the better for you cobblers.

> If drinking wears the soul away,
>> Why add a little leather;
> For, till our welting does decay.
>> We'll drink and stick together.

ALL. Bravo! capital, Joe! hurra!

WAXEND. That would make a capital psalm. I'll uplift my voice. (*Singing loudly.*) 'If drinking wears . . .'

SCULLER. Hold your tongue, Master Waxend. I've got athwart of the account of the great battle of late; here's a full list of the killed and wounded.

ALL. Oh, let us hear – let us hear.

WALL-IT. Is Dan Deadeye there?

SCULLER. No.

WALL-IT. Or Sam Scupper? or Charley Coil? or Mike Marline?

SCULLER. No, no!

WALL-IT. I'm glad of that – they left a long score unpaid. Now, I shouldn't mind if Ben Binnacle was popped off; he was the only one as paid his shot afore he sailed; and I've got his shore togs in keeping.

SCULLER (*starting*). What's this? Harry Heartly dead! Harry! Poor fellow! poor fellow!

JOE. What! Harry that you were bound for? – That's bad news, Master Sculler; he'll never come back to pay his debt.

SCULLER. No, Joe; and if they come upon the poor old waterman, why, they must e'en sell his boat, and make a beggar of him at once.

JOE. That'll be hard; let's hope better; no one would be Philistine enough to rob a poor white-headed old man of his last crust.

WAXEND. Philistine! – Ha! the Philistines were common robbers – all Dick Turpins, every one of them!

JOE. You're too learned for us, Master Watchful; but I will say it's a hard law:

> For if a man is taken to prison,
> And stripped of everything that's his'n,
> 'Twere better far to stop his wizzen.

ALL. Capital! capital!

WALL-IT. Bravo, Master Joe! Why, you're quite the Byron of Battersea!

JOE (*modestly*). I does a little poetical poetry; it comes natural to me.

WAXEND (*standing on a chair, and drinking*). Yes, the spirit naturally gets over us. Hear me preach.

ALL (*pushing him off the chair*). No, no! No preaching!

JOE. Come, don't be cast down, Master Sculler. Where's Harry Hallyard? I've got a little present for him – something as I've been writing about his pretty Poll – his Poll. Well, he deserves her, or a better lad with a truer heart never feathered an oar.

SCULLER. Right, lad; Harry's the pride of the Hard, and Mary's the prettiest, aye, and the most industrious wench on either side of the river. It's a pleasure to see her little fingers go – stitch, stitch, hem, hem, from morning till night. She's been a daughter to me since her father died. Poor fellow, his was a brave end. Well, as I was saying, she's looked up to me because I was his friend; and a neater cabin than old Sam Sculler's ain't to be found near the Thames – all her work. And now, if these harpies come for poor Heartly's debt, they'll sell up all the sticks, and leave the old man without a rag of canvas to weather out his days. (*Sighing.*) Well, well!

JOE. But they won't do that, Master Sculler; come, come, keep a good heart. But as I was telling you, I've written a something about Mary.

ALL. Let us hear.

JOE (*taking out a paper*). Here it is. I –

WAXEND. Them charity schools is a good thing. (*All laugh.*)

JOE. Ah, laugh away – they are a good thing. How many children

they save from depravity! How many do they teach the
difference between a brute and a man! I learnt in one; and I
should think I was unworthy the charity shewn to me, if I
ever stooped to deny it: for, mark ye, my lads –

When the mountains so high are kiver'd with snows,
What a very cold wind from the top of 'em blows!
But when great ones and rich ones are kind all the while,
What a very warm sun's for the poor in their smile!

SCULLER. Good lad! good lad!
WAXEND (*tipsy, singing loudly*). 'When them mountains so
high' – common time – 'when – '
ALL. Silence! silence! – Let's hear Joe's verses.
JOE. Now, lads. (*Reading.*)

'Near Putney bridge there lived a maid,
More bright than Mayday morn'.

WAXEND. Oh, stop! stop! – I've heard something like that in a
hymn – long metre. (*Singing.*)

'On Richmond Hill there lived a lass,
More bright than Mayday morn'.

WATERMEN. Oh, fie! oh!
JOE (*offended*). Well, I'll never write no more. I'm no pirate –
I never steals another man's ideas; at all events, *you* can
never be robbed.

Enter BLACK BRANDON – *the* LANDLORD *bows to him – he advances
sullenly, and takes a seat, eyeing the company.*

BRANDON. This is the Crown and Crozier?
WALL-IT. It is, sir; the best house above bridge for comfort and
respectable company.
BRANDON (*sneeringly*). So I perceive. Bring me some rum; I
have business in this neighbourhood.
WALL-IT. Can I assist you in –
BRANDON (*surlily*). You can – bring the rum, and be hanged to
you! (*Exit* WALL-IT, *muttering.*)

WAXEND (*drawing his seat near* BRANDON). Sir, were you ever among the niggers?

BRANDON (*starting and looking fiercely at him*). Why do you ask?

WAXEND. You'd make a capital slave-driver.

BRANDON. Dare you insult me?

WAXEND. Don't wax wrath, or I shall bristle up myself – hear me preach!

BRANDON. Psha! fool!

He thrusts WAXEND *back, who falls over his seat – the* WATERMEN *rise tumultuously.*

JOE (*interposing*). Come, come sir; you are forgetting yourself, and insulting the clergy. This is the Bishop of Battersea; and –

If the church is knocked down with such gaiety,
Why there'll be pretty pickings for the laity.

BRANDON. Am I among madmen here? Oh, here's the rum.

Re-enter WALL-IT.

Hark ye, landlord: is there one Sculler, a waterman, living in these parts?

SCULLER. My name's Sculler – Old Sam Sculler.

BRANDON. You had a friend named Heartly?

SCULLER. Ah, poor fellow! – I have just read of his death.

BRANDON. Then you must be aware he can't pay a certain debt he owed, and that you are bound for it – here's the agreement, and so old gentleman, hand over the rhino.

SCULLER. Great Heaven! I'm a ruined man!

BRANDON (*drinking*). This rum's not so bad.

SCULLER. You will give me time to look about me?

BRANDON. I want the money! (*Going and beckoning off.*) You must talk to this gentleman about time.

Enter SAM SNATCHEM.

BRANDON (*pointing to* SCULLER). There's your prisoner!

WAXEND. Oh, my lapstone! what a *gentleman!* Baalam and his ass! Oh, ye captivators of corpusses! hear my voice.

BRANDON (*to* WAXEND). Silence! or I'll spoil your voice for a month to come. (*To* SCULLER.) Where's the rhino?

SCULLER. If you insist on your demand, I am a beggar.

BRANDON. Away with him!

SNATCHEM. You see, my old cove, here's the parchment – no gammon about it – all reg'lar. So you'd better out with the yellow 'uns, and stash all patter.

SCULLER. I must sell my boat.

SNATCHEM. To be sure; you must put up the floater. Take my adwice; I'm the honestest chap as is – has a feeling for the misfortunate. Never resist the law; if a man claims your vestcoat, let him have it, or you'll lose your kicksies in trying the argument.

BRANDON. Away with him!

JOE. This is too bad. What, lads, will you see Old Sam Sculler, a man whose hairs are grown white in honesty and industry, dragged like a dog to a gaol? Let go your hold!

SNATCHEM. Don't resist the law. Take my advice; if a man kicks you, rub the place; for if you strike agin, ten to one if you has witnesses as to who was the degressor.

WATERMEN. Down with them! down with them!

BRANDON. Look to your prisoner. Stand back, I say!

He thrusts SCULLER *over to* SNATCHEM, *throws himself between them and the approaching* WATERMEN, *and levels a pistol at them.*

WAXEND (*running behind, and jumping on a chair*). I'm a man of peace – hear me preach!

BRANDON. Quick! quick! away!

SNATCHEM *is dragging* SCULLER *towards the door, when* HARRY HALLYARD *enters suddenly – he darts forward hastily, and knocks* SNATCHEM'S *hat over his eyes, seizes* BRANDON'S *pistol, throws him round to the corner, and points it at him.*

HARRY. Ahoy! what boats are foul here? An old wherry run down by a coal-barge! Damme! stand back!

A loud shout, and a momentary picture of consternation and surprise.

BRANDON. Who the devil are you, that board strangers like a red squall, without leave or notice!

HARRY. Who am I? I'm the happiest dog on the Thames; got the best craft, and the prettiest sweetheart; will pull a match with any man between bridges; know how to serve a friend, 'specially an old one; always pay my rent; can wash my own shirts; and hate lawyers. – Now, who the devil are you?

SNATCHEM (*pushing up the hat from his eyes*). Don't resist the law – take my advice.

HARRY. So I will, lad. (*Knocking his hat over his eyes again – the* WATERMEN *follow* HARRY'S *example, and hustle him from one to the other.*)

SCULLER (*interposing*). Don't, lads, don't! Hark ye, Harry; you are a fine fellow, and I know will listen to reason. This is Harry Heartly's debt; he, poor fellow, is dead, and –

HARRY. Harry dead! – Poor Harry! Well, but who's this gentleman that's come to shoot us all?

BRANDON. I demand payment of the debt.

WAXEND. When the devil demands his due, then look out; you'll be saying you knew me, but I'll send notice that I never kept such company.

BRANDON. A truce to this foolery! Am I to be paid, or must the man go to prison?

HARRY. Why, look ye, sir; if your demand be a just one, it would be folly to resist.

SNATCHEM. That's right – take my advice! –

HARRY. It would be vain to resist, as I've said; but you would never be so stone-hearted as to strip an old man of the hard earnings of sixty years of weary toil, and that, too, for a debt not his own. To pay your demand, he must sell his boat; then what remains for him? He must go to the workhouse; the winter of his days must be passed at the fireless hearth of charity, after having honestly toiled away his summer to build himself a home of independence. You wouldn't break the old man's heart? – Or, if you would, your own must be of stone so hard, that all the paviours of London couldn't break it up to macadamize one foot of road to the poorhouse, the last resting place you would send him to.

BRANDON. All the preaching in the world won't talk me out of my debt; my money, or a prison for him.

ALL. Shame! shame!

HARRY. Hold, friends! Here, I will be bail for him, and Will Wall-it here will be bound with me.

WALL-IT. That I will!

SCULLER. Thank you, lads, thank you!

HARRY (*to* BRANDON). And, do you hear? do you and your devil's imp beat down to the old man's house in half an hour; and if my Poll is what I think her, we'll board you in the smoke of a salute you little expect. Lead the way, landlord. (*To* SCULLER.) Cheerly, old heart! – 'Tisn't every squall that capsizes a boat. – Cheerly! cheerly!

ALL. Hurra! hurra!

Exeunt HARRY, SCULLER *and the rest, shouting* – SNATCHEM *is following, when* WAXEND, *who is sitting at the back, knocks his hat over his eyes, and the scene closes.*

SCENE II. – *A Room in* SCULLER'S *House.*

Enter MARY MAYBUD, *with needle-work, followed by* ABIGAIL HOLDFORTH.

ABIGAIL. And so, seeing you at work, you see, ma'am, I thought I'd make bold to ask you.

MARY. Well, but my good girl, London is a large place and the industrious never need starve in it. What trade are you?

ABIGAIL. I'm a shoe-binder, ma'am, from Bullock Smithy. I'm a girl of moral perpensities, can sing a psalm, or beat a carpet; and, as for turning a corner in the binding-way, leave me alone for neatness.

MARY. But what made you come away from your own town?

ABIGAIL. There it is: one of my moral perpensities got the better of me – I fell in love.

MARY. And not being able to meet a return, you ran away from the object?

ABIGAIL. No, I runned *after* the object; he was obliged to emigrate through a misfortune – a wicked hussy swore a filiation to him.

MARY. Then you should endeavour to forget him.

ABIGAIL. I can't forget him; and I thought it was best to come away, for fear they should swear something of that sort to me.

MARY. I am sorry I cannot serve you; I am an orphan, and obliged to work for every meal. I am content to do so, because I think, somehow, that the bread we have earned must eat the sweeter. I am a stranger, too, to London; I never travel farther from Putney than just down the river in Harry's boat to Westminster Bridge – yes, once I made a voyage to Hungerford Market. So, you see, my good girl, I could direct you but badly; but if you had written to this lover of yours –

ABIGAIL. I did, bless you!

MARY. Then you know his direction?

ABIGAIL. Oh, yes; the girl at the huckster's shop wrote three times for me, and I saw the letters carefully directed, 'Mr Watchful Waxend, London'.

MARY (*aside*). So, so, Mr Watchful! (*Aloud.*) You had better look in again towards evening; I have an old friend here who can, perhaps, advise you.

ABIGAIL. I'm much obliged to you. Be so good as to say that I can turn my hand to anything: I can hem and seam, and trundle a mop, nurse the baby, or turn a mangle; I can bind shoes, and make hay, milk a cow, or sing a psalm; and don't forget to say, that I'm a girl of strong moral perpensities.

Curtseys and exit.

MARY. So, so; here's a discovery for the Bishop of Battersea, as

99

my Harry calls Waxend. Oh, dear! I wish our marriage was over! – And yet, I'm sure, if Harry was to ask me, I should put it off for another year. Harry's to row for another wherry in a month. La! if he was to win that, as he did the last! – that might alter affairs. Mr and Mrs Hallyard, with two boats of their own! – I'd have one, with a white awning all fringed round, and a flag at the stern, for Richmond parties, and t'other for everyday work – Joe should row that. I like Joe, because he's Harry's friend, and he's so good natured and poetical, and because he's so kind to me; – yes, he should row the everyday one, and my Harry should sit like a king in the other; and then, when there happened to be no company, he should just pull me and the little ones down to . . . La! what am I thinking of? We've neither got the boat nor the little ones yet.

JOE (*singing without*).

> Poll, dang it; how d'ye do? &c.

Enter JOE TILLER.

JOE. Ah, my pretty Mary! I've been longing all the day to have a peep at your blue eyes. Why, what's the matter?

MARY (*pouting*). I don't like your singing about Poll this, and Poll that. My name's Mary.

JOE. I mean no disrespect, Mary; but aren't you called Pretty Poll of Putney?

MARY. Oh, yes; and there's a parrot at the public-house – she calls herself Pretty Poll of the King's Arms.

JOE. Well, well, forgive me.

> Oh, kill not my heart with a frown from your eyes,
> For if you look angry, the poor flutterer dies.
> Men may talk as they like, each pretends he's a wise 'un, –
> A frown from a woman to true love is pison.

MARY (*mildly*). Well, I'm sure I don't frown – I'm not angry, Joe; only, you see, Harry is in a fair way to be a most respectable proprietor of boats; and he wouldn't like his wife to be

called Poll Hallyard this, and Poll Hallyard that. Decent
people must have decent comportment.

JOE. Very true, Mary; every word you say is wisdom:

There's some folks speaks wisdom and sense every
    minute,
Some, when they opens their mouth, always puts their
    foot in it.

But here, Mary, I've brought you a present. (*Taking a ring
from a paper.*) Here's a ring – a keeper: when Harry gives
you a plainer ring, but of more value – ha! – then, Mary, put
this on – his friend's present as a guard to protect his own.
Harry loves you dearly, Mary, but not more than Joe loves
you – as – as a friend.

MARY. Yes, Joe, I know you do; and I'll wear your ring, and
dance with you at our wedding.

JOE. Will you, though?

HARRY (*without*). Yo ho! the pretty Mary, there!

MARY. Oh, here he comes! (*Imitating.*) Yo ho! there, the saucy
Harry! yo ho!

HARRY (*without*). Yo ho! – Now, a long pull, old one!

JOE. I forgot to tell you – don't be alarmed – Harry sent me
forward that you mightn't be alarmed – but poor old
Sculler –

MARY. What – what of the old man?

JOE. Is going – to – to prison.

MARY. To prison!

Enter HARRY HALLYARD.

MARY (*running to him*). Oh, Harry! the old man – my dear
Harry –

Enter OLD SCULLER.

Ha! (*Rushing to* SCULLER, *and embracing him.*) You are not
gone, then! What – what is the meaning of this?

Enter BLACK BRANDON, SAM SNATCHEM, *and several* WATER-MEN.

What men are those? Is it true, is it true?

HARRY. Come, cheer up, lass! – Why, you're as troubled as Chelsea Reach in a gale. Only shipped a little of the bilge water of misfortune: you and I must lend him a hand to bale him dry. Hark ye, lass – come here. (*They retire up.*)

SNATCHEM. She's a pretty little 'un, an't she?

BRANDON. Silence!

SNATCHEM. Got a nice little vaist, and a neat article of a foot; not like a pick-axe – as much behind as before.

BRANDON. Fool! Hold your tongue!

HARRY (*coming forward with* MARY). Go and fetch it, then, Mary – will you? – There's a little queen; and I'll talk a bit to these visitors. (*Exit* MARY.) Come, old heart, we're on the right track; now just listen to me. (*Crossing to and eyeing* BRANDON, *who meets his gaze with ferocious defiance.*) Hark ye, my black-looking friend, it strikes me that, after all, you're a sort of a kind of a pirate. The paper you've brought is right, but how the devil did you run foul of it? Come, show your reckoning, as they say at sea. Who are you?

BRANDON. Who am I? I am one who thinks the frog of the river looks well when he questions the shark of the sea.

HARRY. That observation's true in your log – shark, indeed; but when we get the shark in the shallows, let him look out.

BRANDON (*significantly*). The frog would look pretty in the Atlantic. – I never forget an insult.

HARRY. Tell us how I may insult a callous heart like yours, and I'll do it, that your memory may last for ever. Ah! here comes the best girl in the world, with a load of ammunition that shall founder your cockleshell.

Enter MARY *with a canvas bag.*

Give it me, my lass. Look at that girl: she's life and all the world to me; even your iron soul must tell you I'm a happy

102

fellow, for she loves me. Bless her blue eyes! they are heaven's stars to me.

MARY. Harry – Harry! remember –

HARRY. I must talk to 'em, lass; and just now my heart feels like a Member of Parliament – it could speechify till a dissolution; but, hang it, girl, I hope to more purpose. (*To* BRANDON.) Well, as I say, we love each other; we were both poor; I won a wherry; it enabled me to earn and to save money; she worked hard, too; we agreed to marry when we had saved thirty pounds; there's the sum. (*Throwing the bag at the feet of* BRANDON.) Your debt is thirty-two; will you take it? – No! – There's the black demon of avarice grinning in every wrinkle of your ugly phis-og. But there, sir, (*throwing down another bag*) I have earned a pound today – that makes thirty-one; and if you don't take that, and discharge the old man, damme, I'll give you both a pound's worth of drubbing to get a full receipt. (*Throwing off his jacket.*)

MARY (*interposing*). Stay, Harry, stay! It were a pity a humble and honest man should ever foul his hands by a contest with either a tyrant or a rogue. I don't mean to say, sir, you are the one or the other; but there's another pound, earned by honest labour; take your full demand, and quit the house before this gallant spirit (*pointing to* HARRY) bursts through the bonds of prudence, and makes you do it by the window.

BRANDON (*taking up the money, and laying down the paper*). This is all I want; you can talk about honesty when I'm gone; it's not a saleable commodity, and I know nothing about it. But hark you, sir (*turning fiercely to* HARRY) – I've already told you I never forget an insult; we shall meet again. (*To* SNATCHEM.) Come, sir.

SNATCHEM. She's a werry pretty one, for all that, though there is a bit of the brimstone, too.

HARRY *turns and moves towards him – he darts off.*

HARRY. Why, old man, the tears are in your eyes; give us your hand. Poll and I have only to wait another year or two, and you are happy.

SCULLER. But I have prevented *your* being so.

JOE. Pshaw, never mind that; Harry, you're a noble fellow – Mary, you're a queen. I'll help you, I'll never go to the Crown and Crozier; but every farthing I can save, you shall have; we'll soon have the thirty pounds.

> With a long pull and a strong pull, we'll shoot the
>   bridge in style,
> And we'll have the thirty pounds, yet be merry all
>   the while.

HARRY. What a happy man I am, old heart, though the shark has sheered off with the gold. Hang the mopusses! – what care I for the world's ups and downs, while I've my Poll and my partner Joe?

SCULLER. You were made for each other, and I am the cause of a continued separation.

MARY. Not so; the money we have paid was Harry's, my earnings were trifling; and I love him more for sacrificing the means of our marriage, than I did for earning them; for that sacrifice was for you, my second father. (*Turning to* HARRY.) Why should we not struggle together as man and wife, as singly; if you think my hand a reward for your noble devotion, take it – I will be yours, even tomorrow.

HARRY (*mad with joy, and kissing her*). Eh, what, mine – tomorrow – my dear Mary; run, Joe, run down to Tommy Teazepsalm, the parish clerk; tell him I'm to be married tomorrow – run, old man, run to Will Wall-it, tell him to send me in a store of grog, we'll be merry tonight, my dear Mary. Bless that fellow's black-looking ugly mug, if he hadn't come I shouldn't – oh, my eyes, married tomorrow; Mary mine – what will old dame say? Married tomorrow! Cut and run; my dear Mary – bear a hand, bear a hand. (*Exit in ecstasies.*)

SCENE III. – *Outside of* HARRY'S *House, with a Garden looking over the River – the opposite shore seen – boats passing – oars leaning against the door, &c.*

DAME HALLYARD *discovered bringing on a table –* WATCHFUL WAXEND *seated on a stool near the table, smoking.*

DAME. And so Harry said I was to welcome some friends.

WAXEND. Yea, welcome them with a joyous spirit. (*Drinking.*) I feel that thou hast made me welcome; I should like a little heeltap, a little more wax on the thread. (*Offering the glass.*)

DAME (*rising*). You shall have it, though you're rather shaky now.

WAXEND. The struggling of the spirit is mighty within me; I want to preach, and I can't till I've finished my pipe.

DAME. And so, my boy – bless him – is going to have a merry-making; well, well, I suppose Mary and he have made up the match. Some mothers wouldn't like a young wife coming home, and turning them out of office, but I know the wench – a better doesn't breathe by the old river.

WAXEND. Ah, women are troublesome spirits.

DAME. What do you mean? you never suffered by them.

WAXEND. Haven't I, though; their love has been my ruin. I looked too much after the flesh; I worked very hard at my trade, but I couldn't help leaving a few Waxends about.

DAME. Pooh, you should have got married, as my Harry means to do: there's everything ready for him; there's his pipe, and Mary's favourite mug, and old Sam Sculler's backey-box. Oh, what a happy old woman I am to have two such children.

HARRY (*without*). Mother – Dame Hallyard – hoy, there!

DAME. Here they come.

Enter HARRY, MARY, JOE, OLD SAM SCULLER, *and* WATERMEN.

Oh, my dear boy, welcome all of you. Mary, my lass, give us a buss; well – Eh, where is it to be? Have you agreed – Um! can I have a new cap made? Hark ye, old Sam, you and I'll dance a jig at the wedding.

SCULLER. That we will, old lass; ah, you don't know.

DAME. Why, what's the matter?

SCULLER. Come here. (*They go up.*)

HARRY. Well, Mary, here's the Bishop all ready to marry us. How does your reverence feel today? Is the spirit strong within you – for we've news, news that will shake it.

WAXEND (*very drunk, looking at his glass*). Thanks to your good mother, it's pretty strong; I had it waxed a little more.

MARY. Master Watchful, were you ever in love.

WAXEND. Twenty-seven times.

MARY. Oh, shameful.

HARRY. Do you know a place called Bullock Smithy?

WAXEND (*staggered*). I've heard of it.

JOE. Were you ever in love there?

WAXEND. The spirit was strong.

HARRY. Did a girl ever swear –

WAXEND (*interrupting*). Don't mention it.

HARRY. A girl from Bullock Smithy is here.

WAXEND (*alarmed*). Here – then I must fly.

JOE. But she will see you.

WAXEND. She shan't – it's not mine; mine are like wax-dolls, with hair like bristles, and eyes as sharp as an awl. I'll fly – I'll not be made a victim; one more sup (*drinking*) and I'll exile myself as far as Tuttle Street. Farewell, Battersea – I'll – I'll not be sacrificed.

Falls, and tumbles off in great terror – they all laugh – DAME HALLYARD *and* SCULLER *come forward.*

DAME. Boy, you've done a noble action; hang the pence, Mary and I will soon save it up again. There's a grunter yet in the stye; the wherry's tight and light; you are strong and willing, and Mary's active and industrious. As for me, I shan't, I suppose, be able to reckon much on myself after a little time. Baby's clothes are tedious things for an old woman – Eh, boy! eh, Mary. (*Laughing.*)

HARRY. Come, let us be merry; take a seat, dad. (*They all sit round the table.*) Joe, run yourself ashore; Mary and I moor together. Mother, what matters it which way the wind blows, so that our hearts are true, and we have no leaks in our conscience; fill out a bumper – let's drink a health to Mary – I'm so happy we're to be married tomorrow.

DAME. Fill, fill – I'll drink that – I'll drink that.

While they are busy regaling, a boat rolls on, filled with SAILORS.

Enter BEN BOWSE *and* PRESSGANG, *landing quietly from the boat* – BLACK BRANDON *comes forward.*

BRANDON (*points to* HARRY). Those are the men – fine young fellows. (*Retires.*)

BOWSE. Aye, aye.

The SAILORS *approach silently –* HARRY *snatches a kiss from* MARY *– raises his glass, and is about to drink her health when* BOWSE *taps him on the shoulder.*

BOWSE. You must come with me.

HARRY (*rising*). Who are you?

BOWSE. The king wants men.

HARRY. What do you mean?

BOWSE. You'll make a devilish good sailor, and must serve him.

HARRY AND JOE. Pressed!

MARY. Pressed! – Oh! no, no!

BOWSE. He'll come back an officer, my girl; and he'll have his friend with him.

JOE. No, you're out of your reckoning there. I serve a fire-office – here's my protection.

BOWSE (*looking at the paper*). All's right – you're safe.

MARY. And must he go! oh, sir, for pity –

BOWSE. Pity aren't among the articles of the press service, my pretty dear.

HARRY. Right. Fiends incapable of pity first gave birth to the idea, and by fiends only is it advocated. What! force a man from his happy home, to defend a country whose laws deprive him of his liberty? But I must submit; yet, oh, proud lordlings and rulers of the land, do ye think my arm will fall as heavily on the foe as though I were a volunteer? No! – I shall strike for the hearts I leave weeping for my absence, without one thought of the green hills or the flowing rivers of a country that treats me as a slave!

BOWSE. Duty is duty, and must be done.

JOE. So says the thief when he serves the devil,
And does it the readier 'cause it is evil.

HARRY. Come, Mary, lass, (*she is almost fainting*) cheer up; I'll return an admiral – be faithful to you in every clime. This little lock of hair shall be the sheet-anchor of our constancy. Bless you, mother! I must go.

DAME (*drying her tears, and stifling her sobs*). You must, boy. I know you will do your duty as a man; but for the sake of the young lass, and for the old lass, too, don't be rash, my Harry: be a hero – I know you will – bless you, my son – bless you!

HARRY. Dear mother! – Mary, bid me good bye – a kiss, lass! – You will be true to me? (MARY *points upwards.*) All's over. – I'm ready, lads. – Joe, you are my friend: take care of the wherry – protect Mary and my mother – be to them as I would! Bless you, Mary! (*Kissing her.*) I have your promise, Joe?

JOE. You have.

HARRY (*wringing his hands*). Farewell! – Mother – Mary. Heaven bless you all!

Enter BLACK BRANDON.

BRANDON (*to* BOWSE). Seize him! (*To* HARRY, *sneeringly.*) You see I never forget an insult!

HARRY. Ah, villain! art thou here? (*He darts fiercely at* BRANDON, *but is dragged away and the act-drop falls – Tableau.*)

MISS MACARTHY as MARY MAYBUD.   N.º 104.

IN MY POLL & MY PARTNER JOE.

Pub. by M & M SKELT, 11, Swan S.ᵗ Minories, London.

ACT II

[A period of Four Years is supposed to elapse between the First and Second Acts.]

SCENE I. – *The Quarter-Deck of the Polyphemus.*

Enter CAPTAIN OAKHEART, LIEUTENANT MANLY, *and* OFFICERS, *from the cabin.*

OAKHEART. Gentlemen, the duty for the performance of which we are assembled, though a painful, is an imperative one. To preserve the necessary discipline, we are compelled to reprimand a brave man for an act that confers honour on the British flag; yet, while obliged to condemn, we shall applaud and honour in our hearts one of the best seamen that ever trod a plank – one of the most fearless spirits that ever handled a cutlass: his very courage must be restricted with severity, or his example and extraordinary success will banish subordination from the fleet.

Enter a MIDSHIPMAN *with a* GUARD OF MARINES, *conducting* HARRY HALLYARD *prisoner – he bows respectfully to the* OFFICERS.

OAKHEART. You have been four years aboard the Polyphemus?
HARRY. Ay, your honour.
OAKHEART. You were a volunteer?
HARRY. No, your honour; I was a pressed man, pressed on the day before I was to be married to the prettiest and best lass in the world. (*Taking a lock of hair out of his bosom, and kissing it.*)
OAKHEART. You are a brave fellow, Hallyard.
HARRY. Thank your honour: there's no scarcity of 'em aboard this craft.

OAKHEART. Right: I am proud of my crew, but brave men should never forget obedience to their superiors. You have forgotten your duty; you have been promoted since you came on board; you are a petty officer, and Mr Manly has ever been your friend; yet you have proved yourself ungrateful.

HARRY. Oh, your honour! don't say that – it cuts me to the soul! Do you think I can ever forget that Mr Manly did all that he could to get me my pretty Poll's letter that was lying for me at Trieste, when we were up the Mediterranean? And he would have got it, too, but sudden orders came for us to join the fleet in the West Ingees. – My log wouldn't be worth keeping, if I hadn't got that in large letters. And then your honour's been so kind to me since I've been aboard, that you've almost made me forget the cruel law that took me from a young bride; so, what with your goodness, and the ship (bless her!) being called the Polly – Polyphemus, keeping me always in mind of somebody at home: I've begun to be almost happy. Ingratitude! May I spring a leak, and go down in the black sea of contempt, if ever I take such a villainous cargo on board!

OAKHEART. And yet, Hallyard, you have dared to disobey orders. Mr Manly, state your charges against him.

MANLY. I must first preface, that, in thus complaining of him, I am performing an imperative duty, with which no private feeling dare to interfere. He will respect me the more for a conscientious discharge of it, when I publicly avow that he has twice saved my life.

HARRY. Oh, your honour! say no more of that. I'd have done it even for sulky Sam, the cook's mate, though he is the most disagreeable swab in the whole crew.

OAKHEART. Proceed, Manly, with your charges.

MANLY. After orders had been passed to lie close, (we, having in the night crept in, and anchored under the enemy's guns) he secretly persuaded twelve of the crew to a breach of discipline. They lowered themselves over the side into the ship's boat, and, at the imminent hazard of the lives of all, and the destruction of the commodore's plans, they attempted

111

the cutting out of an armed store-ship, loaded with ammunition and supplies.

HARRY. Avast there, your honour! There's a bit of an error in your charge. We *did* cut her out, and brought her clear off, in spite of the fire of all their batteries, and the bellowing and blazing of their flotilla to boot; and if your honour only remembers the prisoners we brought in – there were just two to a man – six-and-twenty Spaniards, and we without a scratch, excepting Georgy Gunnel, who would be so venturesome as to fight six –

OAKHEART. Still you were wrong.

HARRY. Wrong, your honour! Begging your honour's pardon, a great deal of it was your own fault.

OAKHEART. Mine?

HARRY. Aye, your honour, with respect be it spoken. – Don't you remember when you had me on the quarter to give me a little jobation, because, in the action of the day before, I took the trouble to go and fetch the enemy's flag to tie round Mr Manly's wound – don't you remember that, as I was standing by, you pointed out where the store-ship lay, and said it would be a glorious thing to disappoint the enemy of all the powder and stores on board? Ah, I see your honour recollects; and you said, too, it was an impossibility. Now comes my fault. Says I, to myself, I don't think so; I knows about a dozen as would do it, and, as our chaplain says, 'damme! if I don't try'. And so I axed 'em, and they said 'yes'; and we tried it, and we did it; and that's all I can say about it, your honour.

OAKHEART. Now, mark what might have been the consequences had you failed. We were in the presence of an enemy of superior strength; the policy of the commodore was to hem them with their heavy vessels in shore. Day by day we had been creeping on them, till, on the night in question, we had taken up a position which, with every advantage on our side, must have brought them to a battle. Now, as I before observed, had you failed, our resources and position would have been known, and the prospects of the war totally destroyed in consequence.

HARRY. But as it was, your honour, they thought the devil was among them, and, standing at all hazards out to sea, dropped like pigeons into the commodore's hands. – Your honour will admit that, although you punish the cause –

Enter a MIDSHIPMAN.

MIDDY. Sail on the larboard quarter, your honour.

OAKHEART. What is she?

MIDDY. Can't yet make her out. (*They all listen eagerly.*)

OAKHEART. Jump aloft, Hallyard: take my glass; you've a quick eye – report her build.

HARRY. I'm a prisoner, your honour.

OAKHEART. We'll take your parole for the present.

HARRY. Thank your honour. I suppose, your honour, I mustn't board this craft, whatever she is, till – till I can lay my grappling irons on her. (*Exit bowing.*)

OAKHEART. Gentlemen, each to his quarters; we will resume when this business is over.

Re-enter a MIDSHIPMAN.

MIDDY. Hallyard reports a brig, armed – black hull – a good sailer – no colours.

OAKHEART. My life on it, he is right. Be brisk, gentlemen; we may have warm work in store; to your quarters – quick! quick! (*Exeunt – shouts from forward, &c.*)

SCENE II. – *Between decks of a Slave Ship – the ports open – the hatchway seen,* C. – *a large cask,* L.

SLAVES *discovered chained to the floor – a* SEAMAN *walking to and fro, heavily armed, and carrying a whip – other* SEAMEN *hastily passing with powder, &c. –* BLACK BRANDON, *with a glass, at the port.*

113

BRANDON. Curses on her! she walks the water like a witch! Are all the black cattle safe aboard?

SEAMAN. Ay, ay.

BRANDON. Where in the name of the fiend is Bowse? She keeps the weather gage in spite of us, and yet the Black Bet is no skulker on a wind. Hark ye, ye nigger animals, if I hear the least noise, or see the least sign of grumbling among ye, I'll make sharks meat of every devil of you! (*Looking out of the port with his glass.*) Her sails rise above the waters as fast as the cloud of a white squall.

Enter ZINGA *from the hold, heavily manacled – he creeps close to* BRANDON, *and falls on his knees.*

What the devil do you want?

ZINGA. I would ask mercy, master; poor Zinga begs his wife.

BRANDON. Your wife, fool! – She's in my cabin; had she been kinder, you might now have had your arms and legs at liberty.

ZINGA. I'll wear your fetters, master; see – they eat into my flesh; yet I will be happy. Let me have my wife – my Zamba!

BRANDON. You thought to escape me, did you?

ZINGA. I followed but the impulses of nature. Three years ago you tore me from my country – from the presence of my parents, and the arms of the maid who is now my wife. Regardless of my shrieks and cries, you dragged me away to slavery; my heart was broken; and, if I murmured, the lash was my only answer. Yet, master, I did not seek revenge; I could have had it. Yes, one night, when you were sleeping, my knife was at your throat; but I thought of the words the good white man said to me at my own home, when he taught us his religion, and I conquered the temptation. Well, I served you faithfully; you again sought my country to make more slaves; I fled to join my Zamba. Was it a crime? Oh! give her to me, and I will be your slave for ever! In pity to my agony, spare her! give her to my arms unharmed!

BRANDON (*striking him*). Back, beast!

114

ZINGA *staggers, then making a weapon of his chain he rushes to strike* BRANDON, *who presents his sword – the* SEAMAN *draws a pistol, cocks it, and is about to fire.*

BRANDON (*preventing him*). Stop! – If we throw him overboard his carcase may betray us to those bull-dogs. Give him the whip, and keep an eye upon him. Let us get clear of this hell-cat in chase, and his hours are numbered.

The SEAMAN *strikes* ZINGA *with the whip, till, overcome by pain, he crouches piteously at the feet of* BRANDON, *who fells him with a blow –* BRANDON *bursts into a loud laugh, while the* SEAMAN *thrusts* ZINGA *among the rest of the* SLAVES.

Enter BEN BOWSE, *with a glass in his hand.*

BRANDON. What news?

BOWSE. I've made her out, though her hull isn't above the water, for I know the cut of her jib. 'Tis the Polyphemus sloop, she that I was boatswain of, and deserted from, when I fell in with you. We must make more way than we do now, or she'll walk over us; 'tis the fastest craft in the service.

BRANDON (*looking out*). She's a flying devil! (*Distant report of a gun heard.*) Boom! – She's begun to talk; we must lighten the Bet. (*Gun.*) Boom again! – Ah! chatter away! – If we can keep out of the reach of her long speechifyers for another hour, we may double her in the dark. Some of our heavy metal must go over. (*Exit.*)

BOWSE. It'll be all of no use, Master Brandon. (*Looking out.*) See, her sails flap – she is about to take a longer reach. (*Gun.*)

Enter WATCHFUL WAXEND, *his dress half-sailor, half-cobbler.*

WAXEND. Oh, lord! oh, lord! I wish I was at Battersea! I'd better have fathered all the children of Bullock Smithy than been kidnapped here, and treated like a white nigger; and now I shall be shot at like a piece of wax stuck in the middle of a target! (*A shout and noise heard on deck.*)

BOWSE. There goes Black Tommy overboard.

115

WAXEND (*to the negroes*). Oh, Lord! they'll be coming down for
some of your black Tommies soon. (*Shouts and noise again.*)

BOWSE. There goes his brother Bill.

WAXEND. My spirit sinks; when they've settled all the bills
they will dot and carry one with me. Oh, Mr Bowse, who is
it they are throwing overboard – how many is there before it
comes to my turn?

BOWSE. Pshaw, fool! It's the two guns, our heavy thirty-two
pounders. Ha! she feels it, but not enough. (*Noise again.*)
Right, Brandon, better lose our metal than our lives.

WAXEND. Very right, I'll lose anything rather than my life.
(*Gun.*)

Enter BLACK BRANDON, *hastily.*

BRANDON. She nears us fast; will it never be night? Curses on
her! I've ordered Rasper to cut eight inches into her ribs;
let her shake a bit, so that we can run under the rock of
Martinique – damn the repairs. (*Looking out.*)

WAXEND. Oh! if he was to cut eight inches into my ribs!

BRANDON. Bravo, Bet! she'll bother them yet. (*Crash heard,
followed by a gun.*) It's all over with us! no, curse it, no – the
black cattle shall feed the fishes first, every mother's son of
them. Ah! hark ye, Bowse, do you take charge of the papers;
tie a shot to them, and if we're spoke to, let the fishes read
'em. (*Crash and gun.*)

Enter a SAILOR.

What now?

SAILOR. They've carried away the quarter bulwarks – shall we
heave to?

BRANDON. The first man that speaks of surrender, I'll scatter his
brains about the deck. (*Exit* SAILOR.)

WAXEND. I'll hide myself, for I'm sure to speak of it. (*Gets into
the cask, and stoops down to conceal himself.*)

BRANDON. Stay, a thought strikes me; it's getting dark. Pick
me out one of those niggers – we'll give him a floating-bath;

116

if they shorten sail to pick him up, we gain time; if they don't, the sharks will get him.

WAXEND (*peeping out of the cask*). Oh, Lord! they'll be mistaking me for a nigger.

BRANDON. Bowse, I have it; bring me the woman from my cabin. (*Exit* BOWSE.)

ZINGA (*darting forward, and kneeling*). Master, you will give me my wife – oh, master, mercy, master!

BRANDON (*laughing*). Ay, ay!

ZINGA (*mad with joy*). Master, good master!

Enter SAILORS, *with* ZAMBA – *she rushes into the arms of* ZINGA.

BRANDON. Tear them asunder! (*The* SAILORS *separate them.*)

ZINGA (*piteously*). No, no; you mistake: master captain has given me my dear wife, my own Zamba; master will make Zinga happy.

BRANDON. Tie her in an empty hogshead; let her gently over the side; they'll hear her shrieks.

They seize her – she screams – ZINGA *breaks from the* SAILORS *and embraces her – she is dragged off,* ZINGA *clinging to her, and shrieking – he is pulled back by the* SAILORS.

ZINGA (*turning to* BRANDON). You are a white man, can your own God forgive you? (*Falls fainting –* BRANDON *looks out.*)

Enter BEN BOWSE *with papers – shrieks of* ZAMBA *heard in the shouts – they grow fainter and fainter as she is seen through the port-holes floating away – they listen.*

BRANDON. 'Tis done.

BOWSE. 'Tis a bad act.

BRANDON. 'Tis good policy; see, they shorten sail to pick her up. Now's our time; one or two more, and we defy them. Are all the papers there?

BOWSE. They are.

BRANDON. We gain upon them; yes, they are changing their course to snap at my black bait: I'll upon deck; have the

117

husband ready for the gudgeons, and, d'ye hear, if it comes to the worst, you know what to do with the papers.

BOWSE. Ay, ay.

Exit BRANDON – BOWSE *runs and looks out.*

All right, the poor thing will be saved – ah, them Polyphemus lads are of the right sort; what a fool have I been to leave her – no matter, I mustn't live to be found out.

ZINGA (*recovering from his swoon, and rushing to the port*). Ha, she is there! I see her arms raised for help, and as the wind comes I hear her wild shrieks – my brain will burst. Ha! the ship is shortening sail – they put out a boat – they near her – one moment more and – oh, misery! the cask is filling – they will be too late – my eyes will start – she sinks – she is lost! – no, no; a sailor plunges into the waves. I cannot see them now; yes, he rises; she is in his arms; they take her into the boat. (*Rushing forward, and falling on his knees.*) She is saved! thanks, oh, heaven! thanks! thanks!

A momentary pause – a terrific crash heard – a report of cannon, and then a loud shout and lamentations – part of a sail drops before the ports, and gives the effect of the vessel being violently shaken.

BOWSE (*tying the papers to a ball, and laying them near the hatches.*) The game's up; they've shot away her mast.

Exit with the SAILORS, *rushing off to go upon deck.*

WAXEND (*creeping out of the cask*). Oh, lord, how hot I am! my flesh melteth and my spirit waxeth faint. They've shot away the mast; I wish they had shot away the master. (*Guns.*) There, they're at it again – what a row they're kicking up about these papers – they seem of consequence; I'll take one or two for my own private reading when I'm at home at Battersea – don't mention Battersea, I'm likely to be battered at sea, here. (*He takes out some of the papers and hides them in his bosom – gun, and noise.*)

Re-enter BOWSE, *hastily.*

BOWSE. It's all over; another minute, and they'll board us.
(*Snatching up the papers and throwing them through the port
into the sea.*) Now, then, to die like a man. (*Exit.*)
WAXEND (*hiding in the barrel*). Now, then, to live like a man.
(*Guns – crash.*) There seems to be a deal of welting going
on; I hope one side will get leathered. Oh, Bullock Smithy,
Battersea, anywhere but here.

Music – noise continued – SAILORS *cross hurriedly –* ZINGA *rises,
looks round, and tries in vain to force his chains – the Polyphemus is
seen through the ports of the Black Bet – a tremendous crash heard
– loud shouts, firing and clashing of swords.*

Enter SLAVERS *with* SAILORS *of the Polyphemus fighting –*
BOWSE *and* MANLY, HARRY *and* BRANDON – BOWSE *is disarmed
after a furious conflict, and, rushing past desperately, jumps through
the port into the sea –* BRANDON *is cut down by* HARRY, *who turns
from him, when* BRANDON *fires a pistol, which knocks off his hat.*

HARRY (*turning upon him*). Missed, you black-looking piratical
robber! you'll swing for this. (*To* MANLY, *pointing to the*
NEGROES.) There, your honour, there they are, poor souls,
chained all of a row like so many bullocks at Smithfield.
(*Pointing his sword at* BRANDON.) May six of my week days
be banyan days, if I aren't as great a mind to let your ugly
soul adrift on its downward voyage as – but no, I'll leave
you to the gallows.
MANLY. Let the hold be searched, and the manacles struck off
these poor creatures.

HARRY *goes to the hatchway and looks down, while the* SAILORS
are releasing the SLAVES – BLACK BRANDON, *making an effort,
rises, and with a small dirk is about to stab* HARRY *in the back, when*
WAXEND, *peeping from the barrel, snatches a pistol from the belt of
a passing sailor, and shoots him in the head –* BRANDON *shrieks and
falls.*

119

WAXEND (*looking knowingly from the cask*). There's a ball of wax for you, my boy. (*He jumps out of the cask, and runs into the corner, as if afraid of the pistol he has fired* – HARRY *turns his head, and looks significantly at* BRANDON.)

BRANDON (*raising himself*). It's all over – run down at last by a Peter-boat! – Well, well! no hanging this time! – Hallyard, you don't recollect me; but I remember you! I never forget an insult!

HARRY (*approaching him*). I recollect that voice – those words! (*Recognizing him.*) Is it possible?

BRANDON. Ay, ay; I did a good thing in getting you pressed – made a neat rod for my own hide. Well, it's all over – the Black Bet and her captain will go to Davy Jones together. Put me over to the sharks – Ha! ha! – I never forget an insult! (*Hysterically.*) Ha, ha, ha! (*Dies.*)

MANLY. Let the ship be cleared of the dead – turn all hands upon deck.

HARRY. But the poor woman, your honour, that we picked up, she may have a friend or a brother among these ebony gentlemen.

MANLY. Right: pass the word for the negro woman.

Music – ZAMBA'S *voice is heard without.*

ZINGA (*coming forward and looking anxiously at* HARRY). Zamba! my wife.

HARRY (*eagerly*). Your wife?

ZINGA *nods assent* – HARRY *rushes off* – *re-enters with* ZAMBA, *and throws her into the arms of her husband.* – *In an ecstasy of gratitude, they prostrate themselves at the feet of* MANLY *and* HARRY.

HARRY. Lord love my eyes, the poor creeturs are lovyers – she's the Poll of his heart. Tip us your black fin, my honest fellow; there's one at home I'd give the world to hug in my arms as you do your brown fair one here. Here's a bit of her silky hair – it's my breast-plate in the day of battle, and my library of comfort in the dark hours of the night-watch.

My Poll and My Partner Joe:
Watchful Waxend kills Black Brandon

MANLY. Hallyard, I shall leave you as prize-master while I return to report to the captain. (*Introducing* WAXEND.) This poor fellow saved your life – you must look to him. Come, bear a hand, lads. (*Exit.*)

HARRY. Ay, ay, your honour. Follow me, my lad, we'll overhaul your log. And, do you hear, boys? Let the wounded be looked to – let the poor niggers go free upon deck. Dance, you black angels, no more captivity; the British flag flies over your head, and the very rustling of its folds knocks every fetter from the limbs of the poor slave. (*Exit.*)

SCENE III. – *Cabin of the Slaver.*

Enter HARRY HALLYARD, *followed by* WATCHFUL WAXEND.

HARRY. Now, my lad, who are you? – you saved my life and I thank you; I'll do the same for you another time. But – why, there's something about the build of your figurehead as strikes me – did you ever cross my latitude afore?

WAXEND. I don't know what you mean by your latitude, but I've crossed your door-way at Battersea many a time to see the old dame – capital punch she used to make – haven't had a drop since.

HARRY. Why, surely, no – it can't be the Bishop – what, Master Watchful Waxend turned pioneer and slaver!

WAXEND. I was a slave myself – they made a white nigger of me; I was kidnapped on board one night when the spirit had mastered me, and I fell asleep at Wapping, and I've had nothing but wopping ever since.

HARRY. Give us your hand; it does one's heart good to see any one from the dear home. Well, and how was my Poll, pretty and constant, eh? and the old lass, old mother, and Joe, eh? how are they? speak lad, speak. (*Shaking hands violently with* WAXEND.)

WAXEND. So I – I – I will when you've done joggling so.

HARRY. Why don't you give fire, then? my heart's up in my mouth. My dear Mary! (*Looking at the lock of hair.*) Let out a reef of your jawing tackle, my lord bishop, or you'll get monkey's allowance. (*Impatiently.*) How are they all? how's Poll?

WAXEND. I can't tell you; I've been away these three years.

HARRY. Oh, lord! oh, lord! no news any way; not one letter have I had, and I've wrote a dozen.

WAXEND. Oh, yes, stop a bit; I've got one for you.

HARRY. Eh, from Mary? where is it, lad, where is it? How did you get it?

WAXEND. Why she gave it to me to take to the Admiralty the night before I was kidnapped; and I popped it into my portmantle, and stuck it in with a ball of wax, and so I've kept it ever since. (*Untying his neckerchief, taking out the letter, and giving it to* HARRY.) Here it is.

HARRY (*snatching and kissing it*). Bless her little fingers! How it smells of cobbler's wax! – never mind – let's see what she says. (*Opening and reading it.*) 'My dearest, dear Harry' – Bless her! – 'we haven't none of us never had no letter from you' – Why, I'd writ a matter of four before this was writ – 'and I do nothing but cry for fear of some accident.' Bless her pretty eyes, my poor Mary! 'Oh, Harry, you aren't unconstant, sure?' I'll be damn'd if I am. 'Your poor mother asks the letter-man every day whether he expects one from you tomorrow. Joe's very kind, and works like a good one for the old dame.' Bless him! 'She's crying over my shoulder now. Do write – I can't see the paper – excuse blottings, my dear Harry – I must give over. My heart will break if you don't write – do, soon, my dear, dear own Harry, and God bless you. – Mary Maybud. P.S. – Mother's and Joe's love, and mine a million times.' Thank you, lad, for bringing this; thank you, thank you; bless them all. (*Sinks his head on* WAXEND'S *shoulder and weeps.*)

WAXEND. Why, Harry, Harry.

HARRY. Oh, I aren't ashamed of these drops; when the heart's

123

brim full of love and happiness, it must run over somewhere, and where and why shouldn't it at the eyes? – I don't think a man has less fire and courage in him for having a little of the water of affection.

WAXEND (*giving* BRANDON's *paper*). Here's something may serve to brighten you up a bit; may serve, as I say, to put a little more wax on the thread.

HARRY (*looking with ecstacy on the papers*). Where! eh! what! correspondence with the enemy! – Umph – map of a secret cove or harbour beneath the Rock of Martinique – plan of the communication with the fort – list of pirate signals – all's right.

Enter ZINGA.

ZINGA. It was you, sir, who saved my Zamba's life; I owe you my gratitude. The object dearest to your heart is glory – I can put the pirate's horde into your hands. I have been his messenger to the rock for near two years; do you prepare a strong cable by which you can ascend; put me ashore. I will enter the fort as if from him; I will lower a rope from above, and – you understand?

HARRY. I do, my brave fellow; the rock's ours; you shall be made a general for this, and (*turning to* WAXEND) you an archbishop. Not a moment must be lost – we are right off the rock now; the enemy will know this vessel. Here we have the signals, and let British courage do the rest, huzza! Damme, I'll plant the British flag on their fort before the moon sinks. Bear ahead, lads; old England for ever! (*Exeunt.*)

SCENE IV. – *Moonlight – the Slaver's Fort and Stronghold on a high rock at the back,* L., *approached by a flight of steps cut out of the rock – a rampart running across from the steps to* R. – *a pole on the rampart with a lamp near the bottom, with a cord attached to it, the whole having the appearance of immense height.*

An armed SENTINEL *discovered patrolling.*

SENTINEL. The Black Bet has taken a long sweep this time; it's my turn for a cruise next – better than being cooped up in this dog-hole. I thought I made her out this afternoon; if so, she'll be for running under the rock tonight. Let me see, this is four hundred feet above the sea, yet I can almost fancy I feel the spray. (*Yawning.*) Yaw, aw; and by the booming of the cave beneath, in spite of the moon's smiling, I should say it will be a rough night. Yaw – I'm devilish sleepy. (*A signal like a boatswain's call is heard.*) What devil's bird is that chirruping. (*The signal repeated twice – he runs and looks over the rampart.*) 'Tis Brandon – there's the signal light of the Black Bet under the rock; I must show the lamp for 'em to hoist the portcullis in the path below. (*Raises the lamp by a cord to the top of the pole.*) There's a wind rising, and Brandon's not the man to hug the shore. We shall lose our supplies. (*Yawning.*) Yaw – I'd rather turn in than be prowling here with a storm brewing – yaw. (*A knock heard – he opens the door.*)

Enter ZINGA *with a wallet.*

Oh, it's you, Master Nigger, is it; well, what luck this trip?
ZINGA. Good, Master Beargruel, good. Here, (*giving a bottle*) here's a drop of the good; drink, while I deliver my message.

Music, piano – while the SENTINEL *drinks,* ZINGA *draws a rope from his wallet and makes fast the end to a stanchion, and drops it over the rock.*

SENTINEL. I was glad to see that light below as if I'd had a fortune aboard.
ZINGA (*looking over the rampart*). 'Tis a fearful height.
SENTINEL (*still drinking*). It is.
ZINGA. Hark how the wind howls. (*Aside.*) If their hearts should fail – 'tis too much for mortal courage to contemplate.
SENTINEL (*turning to* ZINGA). Here's your bottle – yaw, aw.
ZINGA. No, keep it till my return.

SENTINEL. Yaw – right. (*Exit* ZINGA.) That black's got a white soul. I – I'm very sleepy; another pull at the bottle may wake me. (*Drinking.*) I wish I was aboard the brig. (*Walking about hastily to keep awake.*) I – yaw, aw. (*Laying down on the steps.*) Capital; yes, I – yaw. (*Goes to sleep.*)

Re-enter ZINGA *cautiously.*

ZINGA (*watching*). The opiate in the brandy has taken effect; now to my task. (*Music – he pulls up the cord he had lowered, and secures the cable which is attached to it with sticks run through it, and fastens it securely to the stanchion – a pause – stooping and looking anxiously over the rock.*) The rope is pulled; they will make the attempt; 'tis a fearful peril. I see by the torch in the boat, which the preserver of my Zamba holds, that they have begun to mount; he is the last, to cut off all retreat; each has his cutlass in his mouth, and with a raging sea beneath them, five-and-twenty souls are trusted to a single rope. The howling wind below dashes them against the rock; I can gaze no longer; my heart sickens at their danger; yet, like the basilisk, it fascinates me to the spot. They pause – does one heart shrink? – the word is passed from man to man. What do I see? Hallyard is mounting over the shoulders of those above him; the wind almost extinguishes his torch. Ha! he with his cutlass compels the men to mount. Ha! they fall – no, 'tis but the torch; they are in darkness – still they mount; should the rope give way – it has worn with their weight upon the rocks – should it break – no, no, they are here!

Music – HARRY *is seen on the cable waving the Union Jack – he springs over the battlements followed by* SAILORS, *and shakes hands with* ZINGA, *who points to the* SENTINEL, *whom one of the* SAILORS *has raised his sword to strike.*

HARRY (*preventing him*). No, no, the poor fellow sleeps; all fair and above board. (*Securing the arms of the* SENTINEL, *and placing them against the rampart, then trying the door of the fort.*) So, fastened – perhaps this fellow has the keys. (*Search-*

ing him.) What's to be done? I have it. (*He shakes the* SENTINEL, *and the* SAILORS *retire.*)

SENTINEL (*waking*). Hollo! who the devil are you?

HARRY. Silence; I am from Brandon.

SENTINEL. Oh, good; I'll inform Sebastian and the rest.

HARRY. Do so.

Music – the SENTINEL *goes up the steps and gives three knocks at the door of the fort – a* GUARD *puts his head from above, the* SENTINEL *gives the pass-word,* 'Brandon and the Black Bet' – *the* GUARD *retires –* HARRY *motions his men forward – they range on each side of the door.*

SENTINEL. What does this mean?

HARRY (*seizing him, and putting a pistol to his head*). That you are in our power; one word, and you die.

SENTINEL. I don't fear death.

The door is thrown open, and the PIRATES *rush out – the* SENTINEL *calls out* 'Treachery!' *but too late –* HARRY *snatches up the* SENTINEL'S *fire-lock, and discharges it at the* PIRATES *– one of them is seen on the top of the fort bearing a tri-coloured flag – the* SAILORS *dash into the fort – a general conflict ensues – a shell is thrown from the ship below – it falls among the combatants –* HARRY *seizes it and hurls it into the fort – an explosion takes place – the fort is blown up – torches are brought on –* HARRY *attacks and disarms the Commandant, whom he conquers – the* PIRATES *are subdued – the fort bursts into flames –* HARRY *dashes through the fire, rushes to the top of the fort, seizes the* PIRATE *with the tri-coloured flag, hurls him into the sea, and hoists the British Standard, amidst enthusiastic cheers – tableau.*

ACT III

SCENE I. – *The Interior of the Seamen's Friend Inn, Portsmouth
– a large bow window*, c. *flat, through which is seen the road and
quay beyond, with the docks, vessels, &c. – a fireplace*, R. – *the bar,
with a glass partition, through which the people are seen serving,* L.
– tables, forms, &c. – the church bells ringing a joyful peal.

A FIDDLER *discovered on a high chair – another outside the window,
in the street, playing different nautical tunes –* SAILORS *and* GIRLS
dancing – other SAILORS *with their* GIRLS *on their knees – some
intoxicated, sitting on the ground, examining a Jew duffer's slops
and trinkets, and buying handkerchiefs, with which they decorate the*
GIRLS *– others they put in their pockets, which are immediately
stolen, and re-sold to the* JEW *by the* GIRLS *– a party of* SEAMEN,
*quite drunk, round the fireplace with a frying-pan and a pack of
cards – they pour spirits into the pan, and, amidst uproarious
laughter, fry the cards and their watches –* WATCHFUL WAXEND,
fresh rigged out as a SAILOR, *sitting with a* GIRL *on each knee, and
a long pipe in his mouth.*

CHORUS OF SAILORS.
Sailors lead a jolly, jolly life,
    While roving on the ocean;
In every port they have a wife;
    Of every girl a notion.
            Tol de rol, &c.

WAXEND. Yes, my loves, to be sure you shall have as much grog
    as you can swim in; but as for the rings and things you want,
    I'll give you them the next time we come to Portsmouth.
    (*The* GIRLS *get up, disappointed, and go to those* SAILORS *who
    are buying off the* JEW.) Oh, dear! Yes, they'd soon bring the
    cobblers all to an end. (*To a* SAILOR, *who is frying his watch.*)

128

Hollo, Jack! If you hadn't kept your watch better at sea, you wouldn't have been able to make so free with your time ashore.

SAILORS (*laughing and shouting*). Bravo, Bishop of Battersea!

WAXEND (*turning to the fiddler*). Come, strike up a tune, old Rosin! give me a hornpipe – common time. (*A dance.*)

HARRY (*without*). Yo! ho!

Enter HARRY HALLYARD – *they all cheer him and retire up, except* WAXEND.

HARRY. Yo! ho! lads! – Here I find you. Rather queerish anchorage, though (*pointing to the girls*) – lots of rocks and quicksands – eh! (*pointing to the duffer*) and swarming with sharks, too. When I landed I could have knelt down, but everyone was looking; my heart kept tittuping – tittuping, and the tears of a whole lifetime seemed swelled into a large lump just here. So I pressed Mary's lock of hair, with the iron grip of a seaman, to my heart, crowded all sail, and, without seeing a single landmark, made this harbour; but how the devil I managed to steer clear of the chaisesses and the postesses, I'm jiggered if I can reckon.

WAXEND. I've seen two or three London-looking chaps about here; and so I –

HARRY (*eagerly*). Eh? – Did you ask 'em about Mary, and Joe, and the old house?

WAXEND. I was just going to do it, when one of 'em says to the other, (*mimicking*) 'Demme! what a 'orrid smell of tah! – I never could abide the wo-tah, demme!' So, you see, after that, I thought it was no use axing 'em about a waterman's home; for their manners convinced me they were no better nor lords or linen-drapers, or some such people!

HARRY. Well, well – have you made soundings about the coach?

WAXEND. Ay, ay.

HARRY. And secured the berths?

WAXEND. Ay.

HARRY. Then I'll only just beat about here till the captain bears down with a few gimcracks that want stowage, and then crowd all sail for London. What's the name of the craft we're to go by?

WAXEND. The Nonpareil.

HARRY. The Nonpareil! I wish it had been the Polly, or the Polly-phemus; but never mind, the Nonpareil will answer for my Mary. So, do you hear? heave ahead, and just make a minute of the exact time they say they'll weigh anchor.

WAXEND. To be sure I will, and ask all about her rate of sailing: there's a fair wind – we shall soon be at Battersea. (*Exit.*)

HARRY. I'm there now: I can see the old mother, with the bellows in her lap, listening to Mary, as she reads my last letter about coming home; I can see the tears standing in the wrinkles of her dear old cheeks; and I can hear Mary's voice quivering a bit, as she comes to the part where I tell her that I love her more than ever – Joe, in the corner, with his pipe, fancying he's shaking hands with his old friend, Harry, and puffing out the smoke to hide his quivering lips – I can see 'em all three, and the old wherry, and Sculler picking gooseberries in the garden, and the old clock behind the door, ticking louder as if to welcome me; I can see 'em – I can hear 'em! What a fool I am! I'm crying like a boy!

JEW. Von't you puy noting for de pretty tears?

HARRY. No, I'll buy nothing; I'll take her home no wisheywashey trinkum-trankums, no base metal covered with a little finery, like the ugly figurehead of the Saracen's phisog with a gold beard, but I'll take her the pure coin of an unaltered affection, and the hard earnings of five years of toil and glory.

JEW. Very nice, put you'd petter take dem de earrings or de shoe puckles, ma tear. (*Goes up and sits with the* GIRLS.)

HARRY. Mary would give all the finery in the world for one word of love. My eyes! I'm so happy! my heart is as merry as a newly-made middy, and I feel running before the wind of joy with all the sails of content filled to bursting.

Re-enter WATCHFUL WAXEND.

WAXEND. All right! In half an hour they'll take the peg out of the last! Pooh! I mean to say, weigh anchor, or, vulgarly speaking, be ready to start in that time.

HARRY. Hurrah! eh – here, shipmates. (*The* SAILORS *and* LASSES *come forward.*) Some of us have been five years together; let our parting be a merry one. Order some punch, I'll pay for all; let us have a dance, drink success to our ship, and then home to our sweethearts and wives. (WAXEND *orders liquor at the bar.*) The Polyphemus sloop! The pretty Polyphemus! (*All shout and drink – aside.*) The pretty Polly! Fill again – I wish the captain would bear down. Now, my lads, Captain Oakheart and the memory of the brave Manly. (*They drink.*)

Enter CAPTAIN OAKHEART – *they all shout.*

OAKHEART. Thanks, my brave fellows; I'll give you a toast anon. Hallyard.

HARRY. Your honour.

OAKHEART. I shall see you in London soon; if you call at my bankers you will find that your friend, Lieutenant Manly, has made you his heir; you saved his life twice, Harry, but your arm couldn't save him from the grim tyrant in the last action; and as he had no relatives, you will now come into possession of three hundred a year.

HARRY. Oh, gemini! three hundred a year! Was there ever such a sum?

OAKHEART. Don't let wealth spoil you and your pretty Poll, but tell her that your captain, who admires your honest integrity, will be her father on the day of marriage, and give her, too, the best protection – a good husband.

HARRY. Oh, your honour, I'm all over gratitude! Won't Poll be proud, not of the money, though I thank and bless the good lieutenant for it! (heaven rest his brave soul!) but to think that your honour, a captain just posted, should – Oh! my heart, what a jolly day we will have!

OAKHEART. Come, my lads! fill me a glass of punch! (*To* WAXEND.) In the meantime, my good fellow, here is a purse of fifty guineas for the papers you furnished us in the slaver.

WAXEND (*taking the purse and bowing awkwardly*). Oh, thank your honour. (*Aside.*) My eye! won't I buy a stock of leather and wax. (*Retires –* HARRY *gives* CAPTAIN OAKHEART *a glass of punch.*)

OAKHEART. Here's our country, and may she always have sons as brave in battle, and as humane in victory, as the lads of the Polyphemus. (*Drinking.*)

Great shouting without, during which OAKHEART *takes leave, and exit – a coach is seen through the window –* PEOPLE *enter –* HARRY *and* WAXEND *take leave, and exit – they are seen through the window to mount the coach – the confusion recommences, the horn blowing, fiddling, &c. – a* SAILOR *commences a hornpipe on the roof of a coach, which gives way, and he falls through amidst great laughter, hurraing, and waving of hats, as the scene closes.*

SCENE II. – *Interior of Joe's House.*

Enter JOE TILLER, *with his jacket on his arm, and a crape round his hat, followed by* OLD SAM SCULLER.

JOE. And so we are to pull the gentleman down to the wharf, eh?

Where the timber from the Swedish coast is floating,
There the gentleman would go a-boating.

SCULLER. Ay, and we must make haste, too; he said he would be ready in a few minutes, so come along.

JOE. No, I can't go out without seeing Mary; there's no persuading her out of her melancholy –

All day she sits in tears, as sure as my name's Tiller,
Like a crying cherry-bum, or else a weeping willer.

I'll be bound, now, she's gone down to the church-yard to sit by the side of old Dame Hallyard's grave; she's almost always there, and as for a smile on her face –

They're as scarce to be met with as oysters in June weather,
And as difficult as strawberries in winter time to gather.

SCULLER. Ah, the old dame was a mother to her; and how she
used to watch the poor old woman as she faded day by day!
Why, you might see her sink inch by inch into the grave.

JOE (*melancholy*). Yes; and Mary got as pale as a winding-
sheet; bless her, I *must* see her for a moment, then I'll go to
work; work's my comfort. I don't know how it is, but I feel
a sort of a something hanging over me – it's very foolish, I
know, but –

When the blue devils is wexing your brain,
You may drive them away, but they come back again.

SCULLER. Well, then, run down to the church-yard and look for
her; I'll go to the Hard and prepare the boat.

JOE. Agreed. Ha, here she comes! Look at her dear eyes, they're
quite red; yet she endeavours to hide them from me as if my
own symphonies didn't inform me.

Enter MARY, *very pale, in a plain neat half-mourning dress.*

MARY (*advancing with a melancholy smile, and giving her hand to*
JOE). Did you want me, Joseph?

JOE. I was just waiting to say a word to you before I went down
to the Hard; you are still fretting; you shouldn't take on so,
Mary, it's breaking my heart.

MARY. I won't then, Joe, for you're very kind to me. I will
endeavour to be cheerful; it is my duty to be so, but I've had
a dream, and I've been down to mother's grave, and I
couldn't look upon the blue flowers I've planted there without crying a little – they seemed so like her own dear bright
old eyes! Besides, there's a strange flower grown up among
them – I didn't put it there, it came up of itself, like a message
from the dead! It's a – yes, Joe, it's a Forget-me-Not! (*Sobbing.*) A Forget-me-Not!

JOE (*with emotion*). Well, well, we never can forget her.

MARY. Oh, never! I hope it will not die; pretty bud, to come of
itself! I'll water it every day. Do you know, as I looked at

it, I heard her dead voice say the words as sure as I stand here, so you must forgive me for being a little melancholy.

JOE. Yes, Mary, I'm rather low myself today; I had a dream – I thought my boat was run down, and I had a narrow escape of my life.

MARY (*anxiously*). Heaven forbid! you are my best friend.

JOE. I was a fool to let it annoy me –

But if we dream of one thing, it's sure to come con-tra-ry,
Because it is a maxim, you see, my dearest Mary.

SCULLER. There's one thing I'm dreaming of that won't come contrary: if we don't go down to the boat, the gentleman will hire somebody else to row him down to the wharves, and it's a guinea job.

JOE. Right.

And if we lose a guinea,
I know who'll be a ninny.

I don't know when I shall be home, Mary, but Sculler will come with me. Come, cheer up a bit; go out and buy a few trinkums; call on Mrs Strop, the barber's wife; she'll talk you into spirits. God bless you!

Come along, my old chap, and let us diskiver,
If the customer's ready to go down the river.

(*Going but returns.*) Goodbye, Mary! goodbye! (*Exit with* SCULLER.)

MARY. I have called on Mrs Strop already, and I have seen a newspaper: the ship of my poor Harry has come home; but, ah, where is he? (*With great agony.*) Stay – stay, Mary! you mustn't think in this way now; yet there can be no crime in loving the dead. I loved Harry living, and I can't do wrong in loving his memory. I passed by the Hard, and I saw the wherry. Joe hasn't taken out his name, for I could see it through the bit of crape he has nailed over it. I looked and looked till I couldn't see boat or river; my head swam, and my heart beat. I'm a silly – silly girl! I ought to have died with his mother; but I feel I'm burning away. Ha! ha! I'm strong, but it won't last for ever; no – no! (ABIGAIL HOLD-FORTH *heard singing without*.) Oh, here comes this silly girl to annoy me; I have no spirits for her prattle.

Enter ABIGAIL HOLDFORTH, *dressed in the height of vulgar fashion*.

ABIGAIL (*speaking rapidly*). Just comed up to Battersea for a breath of hair; Lunnun is so smoky! We who gets our livelihood in the fashionable quarters, to be sure, is better off than them as vegetates in the purloins of the Mansion House; but to me, a native of the delightful city of Bullock Smithy, it's all very condense and mistificatory. So I took advantage of having to measure Mrs Fubsey, the great maltster's wife (who lives within a short distance), for a new Parisian corset, to rustificate for a day, or, rather, half a day; for I've got to take home Miss Jemima Jumper's, the dancing-master's daughter's new yeller silk frock, and there aren't a stitch done; but I would come to see you, for, you know, you first recommended me, and though my own talons have exasperated me into a first-rate Magazin des Modes, I never forgets that to your good nature I'm indebted from the first. But you don't look well: as Mrs Cackle, the poulterer's wife, says, there's a melancholy conglomerification about you. (*A pause*.) What's the matter?

MARY. I am not well. (*Aside*.) She'll kill me with talk!

ABIGAIL (*twirling round, and shewing off*). Do you like this dress? – Pretty taste, isn't it? – You can't think how the fellers did stare at me! one sailor-gentleman, in particular: it struck me I'd seen his face afore – at first I thought it was your Harry, but –

MARY (*starting at the name*). Oh, do not – do not! – This is cruel!

ABIGAIL. I beg your pardon – I didn't think – But I must go to Mrs Fubsey's: la! she is such a perdigious size round! Oh, now I think of it, there was somebody with the sailor-gentleman very like Watchful Waxend; but I was on the coach, and it couldn't be he. (*Going*.) Well, good morning.

(*Returning.*) I must go, or Miss Jumper won't have the yeller frock, and the Magazin des Modes will lose its charackter for punctualarity. (*Going.*) Good morning, my dear! (*Returning.*) Remember me to all; goodbye! – Comment vous portez vous to you! – Mrs Fubsey will be in such a way! – Bye, bye.

Curtseying, and talking as she goes off.

MARY. The sailor-gentleman she saw! – That's like my dream. In my sleep I thought Harry had come back. There he was with his manly face tanned by the sun, but looking better than ever; and his mother was crying with joy; and he was dressed like an officer, and opened his arms to me; and I tried and tried, but I couldn't move near him. Yet I saw him, and I heard him speak my name, and I felt sure that he loved me – and this was dreaming! Oh! I wish the sleep had lasted! yes – how I wish I could have died in that dream! – But I awoke, and I – (*Overcome with emotion.*) Oh, my heart! – Harry! Harry! (*Exit in an agony of tears.*)

SCENE III. – *The Banks of the Thames, and the opposite shore in the distance – the House of* DAME HALLYARD, *with the shutters closed,* R. *– another house,* L.

Enter WATCHFUL WAXEND *from behind the house,* R., *in the dress of a sailor, and smoking his pipe.*

WAXEND (*surveying* DAME HALLYARD'S *house*). Well, this is all very odd! – I've been 'round the house, and round the house,' as the riddle says; but every window is as close as a clicker's seam, and Harry is waiting for me all this while in the road; he wouldn't come for fear of frightening the old dame and Mary. – He needn't have been afeared; they've gone out for some frolic on the water. I haven't seen a soul I know. –

Well, I'll go down to the Crown and Crozier; old Wall-it will remember me, for I owes him two-and-ninepence. But, first, to find Harry, and then –

Enter HARRY HALLYARD *hurriedly.*

HARRY. Avast, lad! – Why didn't you come? – You don't know how my heart has been keeping reckoning of all the time you've stayed. Have you seen 'em? May I go in? – (*Looking at the house.*) Belay, there! I'm taken right aback! – What's the meaning of all these dead-lights being hung out? – Have they shifted their anchorage? – Have they fallen foul of any misfortune? – Where's my Poll? where – where's the old mother? – Speak! say out what intelligence you've got, or I shall founder with the trembles!

WAXEND. The house is shut up.

HARRY. I see – I see!

WAXEND. I've been round it, and can't find a hole to peep in at.

HARRY. Well – well!

WAXEND. So I conclude –

HARRY. What – what?

WAXEND. That Joe's giving 'em a bit of a nautical discursion on the river.

HARRY. Right, lad! that's it! – My heart was up in my throat! – There's no harm happened to the old craft, that the young one has been obliged to sail from her moorings? No! no! – Joe would take care of that – I know him. Joe's a true heart! – It's hard, though, within sight of port, to be blown out to sea again in this fashion. What's to be done?

WAXEND. I know what I shall do: I shall bear down to the Crown and Crozier, and old Sculler's.

HARRY. Good – they'll spin you a yarn. Crowd all sail, while I tack about these latitudes. I can't leave the old spot. (*Hurrying him off.*) Come, lad, bear a hand, and be back in the turning of a handspike!

WAXEND. I'll be back before you can wax a thread. You stay here, my boy: I'll hoist a signal that shall put a sparable in your heel, and I'll stick to you like wax!

HARRY (*impatiently*). Ay! ay! (*Exit* WAXEND.) No, I can't leave the old house, though there is nobody to welcome me. I thought I should have been scrunched up with kissings and huggings, and hard shakings before now; and here, after five years of danger, no one knows me. The old house shuts its doors against me, and there's no Polly – no mother – no friend! Well, well! They didn't expect me. My eyes! How glad they will be to see me when they do come! – What a fool I am! (*Crossing to the house,* L.) I don't know who lives here. But they'll give me some chart to steer by. I'll knock and ax a question or two. (*Knocking, and coming forward.*) Yes, there's the old garden, and the little dock where I used to launch all the small craft I cut out of the bits of wood I got from Charley Chips, the carpenter! Ah! my pretty Polly was a young one then! – Law! how she used to laugh to see 'em sail away lop-sided down the river! – Bless her!

Enter MARY *from the house,* L.

MARY. Was it you that knocked at our –
HARRY (*starting suddenly*). Ha! that voice! (*Turning and seeing her.*) Mary! (*Advancing a step or two – she recedes, gazing at him.*) Mary! my own Polly! – Don't you know me? – Harry, my girl! – Harry!
MARY (*as if awaking from a dream*). Alive! (*Screaming with joy.*) Harry! my Harry! (*She springs into his arms, and instantly faints.*)
HARRY. Gently, my little tender one! But I hardly know myself whether *my* senses won't desert the flag. Lord love her pretty pale face! – Joy's colours I see are white. (*Kissing her.*) Polly, lass, cheerly – cheerly! – Come, don't shut the port of your pretty peepers to give your sailor his welcome, like the old mother's house there. Mary – my precious Mary! Ha! her recollection's heaving to; there – there!
MARY (*partially reviving, and looking vacantly around, as if striving to recollect*). I thought that –
HARRY. Mary!
MARY. 'Tis he! – 'Tis so, then; my dear Harry, you are alive,

and – (*Rushing into his arms, but recollecting herself, and screaming.*) No! (*Shuddering back.*) No! Don't come near me – don't touch me, Harry! – don't touch me, I say! – It is past! – Oh, cruel deceit! – Don't touch me! I dare not – I – Oh! my brain is bursting!

HARRY (*seizing her arm*). What does this mean?

MARY. Oh, for mercy's sake! unhand me! you must not come near me! I am – I cannot speak the word! Let go – let go! (*Struggling wildly.*) I shall go mad! (*Breaking from him.*) There – there! Oh, pity me! When you know all, pity me! (*Rushes distractedly into the house, L.*)

HARRY (*thunderstruck*). When I know all! What all? Is this my fond Mary, that – Oh, I'm dreaming! (*Rubbing his eyes.*) Not come near her!

Enter OLD SAM SCULLER, *hastily and agitated – he crosses as if going to the house, L.*

HARRY (*catching his arm*). Avast heaving, old man! A word or two with you.

SCULLER. Don't stay me: I'm on business of life and death!

HARRY. Your answer is life or death to me. Don't you know me, old boy? Why, you aren't altered a bit.

SCULLER (*in astonishment*). Why, no! – What! can it be Harry Hallyard?

HARRY. It is.

SCULLER. We thought you dead.

HARRY (*eagerly*). Why's the old house shut up? Where's my mother? – Why does Mary fly from me? – Tell me quick, old man: my brain's on fire!

SCULLER (*half aside*). Oh, unhappy business! When he knows all –

HARRY. When I know all! – What is there for me to know? Out with the worst. My mother –

SCULLER. Lies in yonder churchyard.

HARRY (*staggering*). Dead! – Poor old mother! and I not here to close her eyes! (*A pause.*) Mary –

SCULLER. Mary is – I – I can't tell you.

HARRY. Oh, do, old man! If you have any mercy – if you have any recollection of your green days, when your heart loved, and – speak! speak!

SCULLER. It must be told. Mary is – Mary is married!

HARRY (*paralysed*). God! married? Mary, that I have loved so truly, married! Oh! (*Laughing hysterically.*) Ha! ha! ha! – It's a lie! (*Wildly.*) You may as well trifle with a hungry shark! – Come, tell the truth! – Yet she wouldn't come near me. I'm surely going mad! – Who's her – her – you know what I mean.

SCULLER. Her husband. Joe – your partner Joe.

HARRY (*nearly falling*). Oh, is – is this –

He tries in vain to speak; at length bursts into a passion of tears, and throws himself upon the shoulders of SCULLER.

SCULLER (*supporting him*). My poor noble Harry! I won't attempt to comfort you – words would be in vain! But they were not to blame – I am their witness.

HARRY (*with sarcastic energy*). Not to blame? – Oh, no! Falsehood isn't a fault, treachery isn't a crime. I have been five years away, but I have never for a moment forgotten her. I have worn this lock of hair upon my heart day and night, in the battle, the storm, and the calm, ever since, and her name, my old mother's, and his, have been oftener on my lips than my prayers, and dearer to me than the life I ventured. Well, I come back; I – I – find her false – the friend I loved a villain – and my poor mother cold and dead! And all through their treachery – no! oh, no! – they are not to blame! I – I – Curse it! I wish the tears didn't come up in this way – they are fire! Here, here, take my money – take my watch – take all! (*Putting them into the hands of* SCULLER.) I earned all for their sake, and now I have lost them. (*Going.*)

SCULLER (*detaining him*). Stay, you shall see Joe; I have just come from him, poor fellow! He was well an hour ago, but he has little life in him now – I am going to tell Mary – they are bringing him here.

HARRY (*anxiously*). Why, what's the matter?

SCULLER. In helping to unload a barge, the crane-chain snapped; it fell on him, and he is all but dead.

HARRY. Um – hark ye: break it to her gently – she'll suffer much; she'll be able to guess what my heart feels; tell her gently, and quickly, too. (*Aside.*) She must not founder on the banks of poverty! Oh, my brain! (*To* SCULLER.) I'll wait for you. Now, be gentle, old man; she's but a tender thing. Come, come. (*Exit into the house,* L.)

SCENE IV. – *An Apartment, with a large opening,* C. *in flat, covered by a chequered curtain, which, when withdrawn, shows a neatly furnished room, with a glass door,* C. *standing open, discovering the garden, the river, and opposite shore.*

Enter MARY, *in excessive agitation, dragging a chair after her, and holding an old newspaper in her hand – her manner is wild and hurried in the extreme – she seats herself.*

MARY (*with trembling eagerness*). I can't see, my eyes flash fire – I wish that I could cry! I did see it here – no, no! (*Searching the paper.*) Ha! there, dead! dead! and yet I have seen him – I have heard him call me his Mary, and I have lived to know myself another's! Oh! if I could but sink into his mother's grave, and he never know – but he will know, and he will loathe me – he will curse me! Oh – do not, do not, Harry, curse me! no, no! the old woman begged it with tears in her dying eyes – he won't believe me – I – would I could die at your feet, Harry, that you might see my heart! I was true; I – oh, don't spurn – I –

Enter OLD SAM SCULLER – *she falls insensibly from the chair.*

SCULLER Poor broken-hearted girl! She breathes! (*He goes up, pulls back the curtain, discovering the room, and* HARRY

HALLYARD *anxiously peeping in at the glass door, and supporting himself by the door-post – beckoning him.*) Look here, Harry, the poor thing's fainted!

Enter HARRY *– he advances and gazes for a moment on her –* SCULLER *is going to raise her.*

HARRY (*preventing him*). No, no, let her lie still; I hear a noise of voices – they are bringing him – she must be told first.

SCULLER. Right! (*Exit cautiously, on tip-toe.*)

HARRY (*gazing sorrowfully on her*). There she lies in her pale beauty, like a moon-beam on the stilled waters of the ocean! What a pity she should be as cold as the one and as fickle as the other! All my world is on that little spot of earth! Oh! if she could conceive how I love her! even *her* changing heart would weep for me; but she can't – no, no! she knows nothing of the holy hopes and the sweet longings of a real love – even now false to me – another's! My soul is pouring out of my eyes in adoration! I will raise her off the ground; 'tis a coarse bed for so tender a flower. (*Raising her.*) I cannot resist the impulse! She will not know that I have stolen that which is now another's – 'twill be the last – (*kissing her*) the last, the last, and for ever!

Re-enter OLD SAM SCULLER.

SCULLER. I don't see them yet; has she recovered?

HARRY (*raising her*). I think her recollection's heaving to. Here, take her, old man, take her.

SCULLER *receives her in his arms –* HARRY, *overpowered with emotion, leans on the chair, and weeps.*

MARY (*recovering*). It is true! He is dead, and – mother, don't cry so! I – oh, my brain! (*Looking round wildly, and seeing* HARRY.) Oh, I remember now! (*She rushes to the paper, holds it up to* HARRY, *pointing in agony to the place, and throws herself on her knees.*)

SCULLER. 'Tis the paper with the account of your death.

HARRY. What of that? Had she loved, she would have hoped it
was false, she would have gone down to – to her grave as –
(*overpowered with emotion*).

MARY (*still kneeling to him*). Would to heaven I had, Harry!
How did I prove my love? though 'tis sin in me to speak of
it now. Two, three, four years elapsed, and no letters from
you, but I never doubted – I tried to prove my love for you
by performing all the duties of a daughter to your mother.
Still time went on; at last the news came that you were
killed – we saw it in the newspaper – Joe got the list from
the Admiralty – there we saw it again – I won't say how my
heart was bleeding as I watched your poor old mother dying
with the news – she and I wept together, and prayed for the
Peace. I saw she was sinking too; she trembled to leave me.
For your sake she pointed to Joe as a protector – for your
sake she begged, and to let her die in peace, for your sake,
Harry, I consented – I became a wife, but I still loved, I still
wept in secret, though duty made me silent. Go! It is a
broken heart now, and my hand is another's, but it is yours
till the grave – till – oh, pity! oh, pity and forgive! (*She sinks
exhausted, and is supported by* SCULLER.)

HARRY. I do! I do! but can't believe that you – no – I have
stayed to tell you that there is money – I have earned it for
your sake, and if you wish to – not quite to kill me, you will
use it.

MARY. No, oh, no!

HARRY. You will, Mary!

MARY. Oh, spare me!

HARRY. You will obey me, if you wish me to forget – forget!
oh! that's as impossible as that I should ever cease to love.
But you may have need of it; the shoals of adversity aren't
always to be avoided; even now you are among the breakers.
There it is. (*Putting it on the table.*) And now – the old man
there will explain; I forgive you, but I don't wish to curse
him. God bless you! (*Going.*)

MARY (*on her knees, clinging to him*). Oh, pity!

HARRY. I do! I do! and do you pity me!

He breaks from her, and rushing up is met by WATERMEN, *&c.,
bearing in* JOE, *wounded –* MARY *shrieks, and runs to him –* HARRY
comes down.

MARY (*attending*). He is my husband!

HARRY (*covering his eyes with his hands and standing immovable*).
Right! right!

JOE (*faintly*). Bless you, Mary! I hoped to see you again, for –
I – I had heard of Harry's return, and I wished to say something before I died, to prove that you were innocent of falsehood to him.

MARY. Don't speak – you are bleeding.

JOE. I am, but I must speak. Harry thinks I am a villain, but do
explain. I'm faint!

MARY. I have told him – I –

JOE. And is he convinced?

HARRY. Joe, I grieve to see you thus, but unless my mother's
voice from the grave assured me of –

JOE. Hold; here – here – here's your mother's will, where she
leaves the sticks in the cottage, and the wherry, and all to
me, to marry Mary. You'll see how she urges it for your
sake. Read, Harry, read! – That is her voice from the grave!

HARRY (*looking at the will*). Poor old mother! (*Kisses it and
weeps.*)

JOE. Do you forgive her – forgive Mary?

HARRY (*dropping on his knees by his side*). I do.

MARY. And Joe?

HARRY. Yes, yes!

JOE. Then I'm happy. – I'm dying! Harry! Mary!

He pulls their hands together, joins them and dies across them.

HARRY. He is dead! – Mary!

MARY. Harry! Harry!

*They rush into each other's arms, recollect themselves, and kneel in
prayer by the side of* JOE – *the others take off their hats, and surround
him, and the curtain slowly descends.*

CURTAIN

Ten Nights in a Bar-Room

A TEMPERANCE DRAMA IN FIVE ACTS

———————●◦●———————

by William W. Pratt

*First performed at the National Theatre, New York,
23 August 1858*

CAST

MR ROMAINE, a temperance
    philanthropist   *Mr J. Nunan*

SIMON SLADE, landlord of the
    'Sickle and Sheaf'   *Mr A. W. Young*

MRS SLADE, his wife   *Miss Colbourne*

FRANK SLADE, his son   *Mr G. Edeson*

WILLIE HAMMOND, a young man *Mr R. S. Meldrum*

HARVEY GREEN, a gambler   *Mr J. M. Ward*

JOE MORGAN, a drunkard   *Mr A. Fitzgerald*

MRS MORGAN, his wife   *Mrs J. J. Prior*

MARY MORGAN, his daughter   *Miss Plunkett*

SAMPLE SWICHEL, a Yankee   *Mr Yankee Locke*

MEHITABLE CARTWRIGHT, his
    sweetheart   *Miss Rosa Cline*

HOME OF DRUNKENNESS

HOME OF SOBRIETY

Ten Nights in a Bar-Room: Stock posters

ACT I

SCENE I. – *Exterior of the 'Sickle and Sheaf'*

ROMAINE *enters.*

ROMAINE. After a long and tedious ride in the stage-coach,
here I am in the quiet village of Cedarville. How pleasant
is the sight of an inn to the weary traveller, and this, too,
looks inviting. There is an air of neatness and comfort, at
least, about its external appearance, and if the landlord
proves agreeable, I shall pass a social night at his house –
who have we coming this way? (SWICHEL *is heard singing off.*)
One of those happy, good-natured fellows, evidently, by his
appearance, that are found in almost every New England
village. (SWICHEL *enters.*) Good-day. Can you tell me who
is the landlord of this hotel?

SWICHEL. Of this hotel? Landlord? Why, where have you been
travelling all your life, not to know Simon Slade! He's the
landlord, to be sure, and he's got the smartest wife, the
pootiest darter, and the cutest son, and sells the most
powerful liquor in the county.

ROMAINE. Indeed!

SWICHEL. Yes indeed, and you'll say so yourself arter you've
had an interview with him. But I say, Squire, you seem to
be a stranger round here?

ROMAINE. Somewhat so.

SWICHEL. Collecting taxes, I reckon?

ROMAINE. Not exactly.

SWICHEL. Surveyin' for the Cedarville Grand Trunk Carpet-
Bag and Valise Railroad?

ROMAINE. You're wrong again.

SWICHEL. You ain't a corn-doctor?

149

ROMAINE. No, sir. I'm not.

SWICHEL. Maybe you're distributin' tracts around here?

ROMAINE. You're still in the wrong.

SWICHEL. P'r'aps it's none o' my business.

ROMAINE. Now you are right.

SWICHEL. So I s'posed.

ROMAINE. Well, my good fellow, you seem to be well disposed, and so I will tell you what I am doing.

SWICHEL. Well disposed! You just ask Judge Hammond if I didn't get the premium for being the smartest disposition child in the county; that's the reason they gave me the name of Sample, because I was weaned on gin and bitters.

ROMAINE. And I suppose you still love that exhilarating beverage?

SWICHEL. Well, Squire, I guess I do. You ask Simon Slade or his son Frank if there's a man in the county that takes his regulars more constant than I do, and I'll defy sin to say that I ever neglected my work any more than I do my liquor.

ROMAINE. You appeared anxious, a few moments since, to know who and what I was, and I promised to tell you, but your love for liquor seems to have swallowed up all other desires.

SWICHEL. Well, you see, Squire, I don't want to pry into anyone's business in particular, only I like to keep a running idea of what's going on in general. You see I keep myself pooty considerable busy up to the big house yonder – Squire Hammond, as fine a man as natur' ever made, and as for his son Willie, there's nothin' proud about him, even if his father is a judge, and rich into the bargain. He's always high-spirited and honourable, and I know he'd lose his right hand, rather than be guilty of a mean action. Well, Squire, I can't stand talking here any longer, 'cause you see it's 'most time for young Hammond to come home. I have to look after that boy, just as careful as I do the judge's old grey mare, and she's so darned contrary lately that I'd give ten dollars for the horse secret to tame her down with. Say,

Squire, you wouldn't mind putting up for the drinks before
you go, would you?

ROMAINE. No, sir, I never use intoxicating drinks.

SWICHEL. You don't! Get eout! I don't want to be rude, but
I'll be darned if I'd trust any liquor in your hands, any more
than I would a cat over a dish of cream. I'll be darned if I
would. Good day, Squire. (*Exit.*)

ROMAINE. Thus it is. Go where you will, the love for drink,
that destroys all the heart's best energies, prevails.

Enter SLADE *with market-basket.*

SLADE. I flatter myself everything is in apple-pie order; my
marketing for the week is now attended to, and what with
my wife in the kitchen and Frank behind the bar, I feel
provided to meet the wishes of all who may visit the 'Sickle
and Sheaf'. Ah! a customer. Good day, sir.

ROMAINE. Good day – are you the landlord of this hotel?

SLADE. Yes, sir – I have that happiness. We've only been open
about a month, and we are not yet in thorough working
order. It takes time, you know, to bring everything into the
right shape. Have you dined yet?

ROMAINE. No, I have not. Everything looked so dirty where the
cars stopped for dinner that I could not venture upon the
experiment of eating. How long before your supper will be
ready?

SLADE. In an hour, sir.

ROMAINE. That will do. Let me have a piece of tender steak,
and the loss of a dinner will be forgotten.

SLADE. You shall have that cooked fit for an alderman. I call
my wife the best cook in Cedarville, and as for my son and
daughter, they are the two smartest children in the county,
though I do say it myself.

ROMAINE. You ought to be a happy man.

SLADE. I am so; I have always been, and always expect to be.
Simon Slade takes the world as it comes, and takes it easy.
I have now everything handy about me. I can leave my
house at any time in Frank's care, for he understands how

to wait upon the customers, and can mix a toddy or a punch as well as I can.

ROMAINE. But are you not a little afraid of placing one so young in the way of temptation?

SLADE. No, sir. Temptation! No, sir. The till is safer under his care than it would be in that of nine in ten. That boy, sir, comes of honest parents. Simon Slade never wronged anyone out of a farthing.

ROMAINE. You altogether misapprehend me. I had no reference to the till, but to the bottle.

SLADE. Is that all? Nothing to fear there, I assure you. Frank has no taste for liquor, and might for months pour it out without a drop finding its way to his lips. But come, sir, walk into the house; you will find considerable life indoors. This way, sir, this way. (ROMAINE *follows* SLADE.)

SCENE II. – *Interior of the 'Sickle and Sheaf'*. GREEN *discovered at table*. FRANK *behind the bar, arranging bottles*.

Enter SLADE *with basket and* ROMAINE.

SLADE. Here we are, sir, and everything, you see, inside and outside of my house, is in apple-pie order. Will you have a glass of wine and a cigar to amuse yourself until supper is ready?

ROMAINE. No, sir. I'm obliged to you. The evening paper will serve me until tea is prepared. (*Sits at table*.)

SLADE. Here, Frank. Bring the evening paper for this gentleman.

FRANK. Yes, sir, as soon as I mix this toddy for Mr Green.

SLADE. Well, be lively. There, sir, is a boy worth having.

FRANK. Here you are, sir.

GREEN. And here's the cash, my lad.

FRANK. Newspaper, sir. (*Hands it to* ROMAINE.)

WILLIE (*outside*). Landlord!

SLADE. Coming! The house is full of customers tonight. (*To* ROMAINE.) Will you excuse me, sir? (*Exit.*)

Enter WILLIE.

WILLIE. Ah, Frank, my lad! Busy as usual, eh? That's right. Industry must prosper. Ah – my friend Green; how are you tonight? (*Sits at table with* GREEN.)

GREEN. Quite well, thank you. You're just in time – will you have a drink? Here, Frank – a brandy toddy; he's first-rate at it; I never drank a better in my life. He beats his father, that's certain.

WILLIE. I believe he does. Here, Frank, don't belie our praises – do your handsomest!

FRANK. Two brandy toddies, did you say, gentlemen?

WILLIE. Exactly; and let them be equal to Jove's nectar.

GREEN. Any news stirring tonight?

WILLIE. No; nothing special – only I have to be a little careful about my visits here, lately. The old governor has got his eyes on me.

GREEN. Well, that's clever; just as if you wasn't old enough to go alone – come, that's devilish good! – ha, ha!

WILLIE. Yes – devilish good! – ha, ha!

FRANK. Yes, and here's your drinks, and if you don't find them devilish good I'm no judge.

GREEN. Say, Will, what do you say to a game at seven-up?

WILLIE. I'm ready. Frank, give us a pack of cards. (*They play.*)

Enter SLADE.

SLADE (*to* ROMAINE). Supper is nearly ready, sir – we do things on the two-forty principle here. I like to do everything well. I wasn't just raised to tavern-keeping, you must know; but I am one who can turn my hand to almost anything.

ROMAINE. What was your former business?

SLADE. I am a miller by trade; and a better miller (though I say it myself) is not to be found in Bolton county. I got tired of hard work, and determined to lead an easier life; so I sold my mill, bought this house with the money, and I find it an easy life, and, if rightly seen after, one in which a man is sure to make money.

ROMAINE. You were still doing a fair business with your mill?

SLADE. Oh, yes; whatever I do, I do well. Last year I put by a thousand dollars above all expenses – which was not bad, I can assure you, for a mere grist-mill.

ROMAINE. That certainly ought to have satisfied you.

SLADE. There you and I differ. Every man desires to make as much money as possible, and with the least labour. Now, I hope to make two or three thousand dollars a year above all expenses at tavern-keeping. A man with a wife and children tries to do as well by them as possible.

ROMAINE. True; but will this be doing as well by them as if you had kept on at the mill?

SLADE. Two or three thousand a year against one thousand! – where are your figures, man?

ROMAINE. Consider the different callings and influences; the trades – that of the miller and that of the tavern-keeper; will your children be as safe from temptation here as in their former home?

SLADE. Just as safe – why not? I don't see why a tavern-keeper is not just as respectable as a miller – in fact, more so. The very people who used to call me 'Simon', or 'Dusty Coat', now say 'Mr Slade', or 'Landlord', and treat me in every way more as if I were an equal than ever they did before.

ROMAINE. The change may be due to the fact of your giving evidence of possessing means. Men are apt to be courteous to those who have property.

SLADE. That is not it – it is because I am advancing the interests of Cedarville.

ROMAINE. In what way are you advancing the interests?

SLADE. Why, in every way. Since I opened this hotel the property has advanced thirty per cent all along the whole street. No longer ago than yesterday Judge Hammond – who is the father of one of my very best customers, who is sitting yonder with Mr Harvey Green – told me that the opening of the 'Sickle and Sheaf' had increased the value of his property at least ten thousand dollars.

ROMAINE. Who is this Mr Harvey Green you speak of?

SLADE. Well, you see, I never inquire much about the business of my guests. He is a visitor here in Cedarville, and seems to like my house. He has plenty of money, and is not at all niggardly in spending it. He says his health is better here than in the South, so he has engaged one of my best rooms for a year. He seems to be deeply interested in all that is going on in Cedarville.

ROMAINE. What is his business?

SLADE. I don't know that, any more than I do yours. When I was a miller, I never asked a customer whether he bought, stole, or raised his wheat. It was my business to grind it – beyond that, it was all his own affair; and so it is here – I mind my own business, and keep my own place.

Enter MRS SLADE.

MRS SLADE. Husband, the gentleman's supper is ready.

SLADE. Frank, my boy, show the gentleman to the dining-room.

FRANK. Yes, sir. This way, sir. This way. (*Exit* FRANK *and* ROMAINE.)

SLADE. That seems to be a nice kind of a man, wife, only I think he's a little too cranky in his ideas. Why, do you know he appeared as anxious about Frank's being led into the temptation of drinking as if he was his own son?

MRS SLADE. If he was concerned about him, and an entire stranger too, judge, then, how I must feel. I do not believe we are as happy as when we were at the old mill. You yourself seem different. You assume a cheerfulness that, in reality, I fear you feel not. Do you not think the habits of these men will exert a bad influence over our dear boy?

SLADE. Well, you might as well turn temperance lecturer at once; you're worse than old Parson Slowman. He said last Sunday that rum-sellers had no souls; what's come over you all of a sudden?

MRS SLADE. Forgive me, Simon, I meant not to offend you; I only spoke for your good and the welfare of our family.

SLADE. Well, we won't talk any more on this disagreeable subject just now. There, go and see to the wants of our guests.

MRS SLADE. Ah, husband, we shall never be as happy again as we were at the old mill. (*Exit.*)

SLADE. Old mill! blow the mill! what the devil is the matter with me? I've got a touch of the blue devils coming on: I'll just mix me a nice drop that will soon drive them away.

Enter SWICHEL.

SWICHEL. I'm pooty certain that I had a half-dollar piece, and I can't find it anywhere; couldn't have slipt through my pockets, 'cause there ain't a hole bigger than a half-dollar in 'em. Hallo, neighbour Slade, how do you endure?

SLADE. Ah, Sample, is that you?

SWICHEL. I should say it was. Say, Simon, you are a pooty lucky fellow; I should like to throw the dice with you for tew drinks.

SLADE. Well, I'm agreeable.

SWICHEL. First throw, or best out of three?

SLADE. First throw; time's precious.

SWICHEL. Yes, 'tis to me; I'm dryer than a sap-tree in August. Give me the bones. Well, throw first yourself.

SLADE. Fifteen. Good throw.

SWICHEL. I should say so. Well, here's at you. Eighteen. How do you like that? Give me a touch of whisky.

SLADE. You are a lucky fellow, Sample. (*Hands whisky bottle and glass.*)

SWICHEL. Slightly inclined that way, I think myself. Hallo! I swow if there ain't young Squire Hammond. Say, Willie, ain't you going home pooty soon?

WILLIE. Not quite yet, Sample. You need not wait for me.

SWICHEL. All right, Squire. It's getting so dark out of doors you can't see your hand before your face, so I'll be trudging home. (*Aside.*) I kinder think I shall watch about here a little while, though, for I don't like the looks of that chap that is playing cards with the young squire. I'll lay low, and if he comes any of his blarney over Willie it will trouble the tailor to mend the hole I shall make in the seat of his pants. (*Exit.*)

SLADE. Come, gentlemen, will you drink with the landlord this time?

GREEN. To be sure we will. I say, Mr Hammond, I give our host here the credit of being a shrewd, far-seeing man, and in ten years, mark my word, he will be the richest man in town.

SLADE. You forget Judge Hammond, this young gentleman's father.

GREEN. No, I do not forget him, nor will I except him, with all deference to young Squire Hammond.

Enter MORGAN *during last speech.*

MORGAN. If Slade gets richer, somebody will get poorer.

GREEN. If our excellent friend, Mr Slade, is not the richest man in Cedarville in ten years, he will have the satisfaction of knowing that he has made the town richer.

WILLIE. A true word that, as true a word as was ever spoken. What a dead-alive place this has been within the past few months; all vigorous growth had stopped, and we were actually going to seed.

MORGAN. And the graveyard too! (GREEN *and* WILLIE *sit at table;* MORGAN *goes to bar.*) Come, landlord, mix me a good whisky-punch, and do it right, and there's a dime towards the fortune you are bound to make. It's the last one left, not a cent more in my pocket; there, take it; I send it to keep company in your till with four others that have found their way into that snug place since morning. They will be lonesome without their little friend.

SLADE. Joe, I'll give you another drink, but it's time you were at home. Why can't you be good-natured, and behave like the rest of my company?

MORGAN. You are a good man to give advice, you are, Simon Slade. Now you've got my last dime, no more use for me tonight. How apt a scholar is our good friend Dusty Coat in this new school! Well, he was a good miller – no one ever doubted that – and it is plain to see that he is going to make a good landlord. I thought his heart was a little soft, but the hardening process has begun, and in ten years if it isn't as hard as one of his old millstones, Joe Morgan is no prophet. Oh, you needn't knit your brows so, friend Slade. We are old friends, you know, and friends are privileged to speak plainly.

SLADE. You know one thing, Joe Morgan, if your senses are not wholly gone, and that is, I have been a friend to you in days gone by.

MORGAN. That was before you turned landlord. You know, Simon Slade, that my father owned the mill, where, as boys, we worked together. After the old man's death, when the property came into my possession, you were in my employ. I left all my business in your hands. Bad associates led me into scenes of dissipation. I neglected my business, while you, in your eager thirst for gain, watched every chance to enrich yourself at my expense. Time rolled on, and, not content with wretchedness myself, I must get married, and cause another fond, devoted heart to suffer. I contracted debts, and I knew not how it was, but at the end of ten years Joe Morgan was no longer the owner of the mill. It came into the hands of his *friend*, Simon Slade. Dark days then came upon my loving wife and child. Yet, in all the misery of my earthly lot, that wife has never been anything but a loving, forbearing, self-denying angel, and Joe Morgan, fallen as he is, and powerless in the grasp of the demon, has never hurt her with a cruel word. (*Sobs.*)

SLADE. Well, well, Joe, don't talk about old times. Let bygones be bygones. Maybe my heart is growing harder. I have heard you say, Joe, that one of my weaknesses was being too woman-hearted.

MORGAN. No danger of that now. I've known a good many *land-*

lords in my time, but can't remember one that was troubled with the disease that once *afflicted* you.

MARY (*outside*). Father! father! where is my father?

Enter MARY – *runs to* MORGAN.

Oh, I've found you, at last! Now won't you come home with me?

MORGAN. Blessings on thee, my little one! Darkly shadowed is the sky that hangs gloomily over thy young head.

MARY. Come, father, mother has been waiting a long time, and I left her crying so sadly. Now do come home, and make us all so happy.

(*The well-known song* 'Father, dear Father, Come Home with Me Now,' *may be introduced with effect.*)

MORGAN. Yes, my child, I'll go. (*Kisses her.*) You have robbed me of my last penny, Simon Slade, but this treasure still remains. Farewell, *friend* Slade. Come, dear one, come. I'll go home! Come, come! I'll go, yes, I'll go! (*Exit* MORGAN *and* MARY.)

GREEN. If I was in your place, landlord, I'd pitch that fellow into the street the next time he came here. He's no business here in the first place, and in the second place he don't know how to behave himself. There's no telling how much a vagabond like him injures a respectable house.

SLADE. I wish he *would* stay away.

GREEN. I'd *make* him stay away!

WILLIE. That may be easier said than done. Our friend here keeps a public house, and can't say who shall or shall not come into it.

GREEN. But such a fellow has no business here. He's nothing but a sot. If I kept a tavern I should refuse to sell him any liquor.

WILLIE. That you might do. But still he will have liquor as long as he can get a cent to buy it with. He is not a bad fellow, by any means. True, he talks a little too freely, but no one can say that he is quarrelsome. You've got to take him as he is, that's all.

GREEN. I am one who is never disposed to take people as they are, when they choose to render themselves disagreeable. If I were Mr Slade, I'd kick him into the street the next time he came here. He is a good-for-nothing drunken sot.

WILLIE. That would be cruel, and if I was here it should not be done.

GREEN. What's that, sir?

WILLIE. I presume you heard my words. They were spoken distinctly.

GREEN. Do you mean to insult me?

SLADE. Gentlemen! gentlemen!

WILLIE. You can construe my remarks any way you may think proper.

GREEN. I have only one answer for such striplings as you – this.

Rushes at WILLIE, *struggles, throws him into corner.* SWICHEL *rushes in, knocks* GREEN *down.*

SWICHEL. Lay there until the cows come home. Say, Squire, I was looking. (GREEN *tries to get up.*) You lay still. You attempt to get up, and I'll make you remember Swichel as long as breath is left in your rotten carcase. (*Tableau.*)

ACT II

SCENE I. – *Exterior of 'Sickle and Sheaf'*.

Enter MEHITABLE *with letter*.

MEHITABLE. I've been to the post-office for Mrs Hammond, and, instead of getting a letter for *her*, I've got one for myself! Who would write *me* a letter, now, I wonder? I shouldn't be surprised if it was some of them saucy fellows I saw last night, smoking, near the hotel. Let me see. 'To the most beautiful woman in Cedarville – To gaze on you is but to love you. Will you share my lot? Will you be willing to leave these rural districts and fly far away where we can revel in the bliss of love together? Answer at once, and relieve your devoted admirer. – H. G.' There now, isn't that beautiful? Who knows but some rich landlord wants me to run away with him? Oh, dear! – I shall be stolen away at night – I know I shall! And the fierce banditti will force me to marry one of their number – and I shall be obliged to do it – I know I shall! (*Cries.*) Oh, dear! oh, oh, oh!

Enter SWICHEL.

SWICHEL. Hallo! what's broke? What's the matter with you, Mehitable? Your eyes sprung a leak – or have you broken something you can't mend?

MEHITABLE. Oh, Sample! Sample!

SWICHEL. Well, what of it? Spit it eout! – what is it?

MEHITABLE. Sample, Sample! The Black Knight is coming to carry me to his Enchanted Castle!

SWICHEL. Is he? Well, I'll lick him, I reckon, before anyone can come to his assistance!

MEHITABLE. With his deep blue eyes –

SWICHEL. Blue? Well, I calculate they'll be black afore we part!

MEHITABLE. And his sabre in his hand –

SWICHEL. Yes; he'll find a cudgel about his head afore I get through with him!

MEHITABLE. He will bear me to his cavern –

SWICHEL. I'll bet ten dollars he don't carry you to a tavern!

MEHITABLE. And there the holy priest –

SWICHEL. Now, look here, Miss Cartwright – I just want to know what in the name of heaven you are talking about!

MEHITABLE. Read that, you lunkhead! and tell me if I have no cause for tears!

SWICHEL. Hallo! Got a letter, ain't you? 'To the most beautiful woman in Cedarville – To gaze on you is but to love you! Will you share my lot?' – Hallo! he's got a lot! Wonder if it's a corner lot? – 'Will you be willing to leave these rural districts and fly far away, where we can revel in the bliss of love together? Answer at once, and relieve your devoted admirer. – H. G.' H. G., H. G. – Holland Gin. No, that ain't it. H. G., H. G., H. G. – Let me think. (*Pauses.*) H. G. – oh, now I've got it! See here, Miss Cartwright: that ain't no 'Black Knight', as you call him; it's that darned skunk, Harvey Green; and I'll fix him a dose that will relieve him suddenly!

MEHITABLE. Don't harm Alphonso!

SWICHEL. Who in thunder said anything about 'Alphonso'? I'm talking about Harvey Green.

MEHITABLE. See that not a hair of his head is injured, and I am yours forever!

SWICHEL. You are? – all right! Go right along home – Mrs Hammond may want you! I'll take care of this letter – don't you fret about the matter.

MEHITABLE. Generous man! I fly! – Adieu! (*Exit.*)

SWICHEL. Oh, you git, with your story-book talk! Arter I've made a bonfire of all her yaller novels, she'll talk as sensible as any of them decent gals! Young Squire Hammond wants me not to pitch into that Green ag'in; but, if he meddles with my pasture ag'in, he'll find himself planted so far in the ground that his friend Rural Districts can't find him in a hurry! (*Exit.*)

Enter ROMAINE.

ROMAINE. A year has rolled on in its flight since first I saw this spot. How many times I've thought of the different individuals I met here! I could not forbear paying another visit to ascertain if the landlord and his interesting family were still alive. I shudder when I think of the dangers to which he exposed his children; yet I cannot but believe there is a basis of good in his character, which will lead him to remove as far as possible those soul-destroying sins that attach themselves to almost every house of entertainment.

Enter SWICHEL.

SWICHEL. Well, how du do, Squire? I'll be hanged if the saying ain't true – thinking of the devil you'll be sure to see his second cousin! It's about a year ago since I met you on this very spot. You recollect, don't you? – time I took you for a corn-doctor?

ROMAINE. Yes, my good friend, I remember, and I am glad to see you are still alive.

SWICHEL. Alive! I guess you'd thought I was alive if you'd seen me lick that high-low-jack fellow – Green.

ROMAINE. What did you do that for?

SWICHEL. Do it for! why, for nothing, I guess, and I wouldn't mind paying a trifle next time to do it ag'in. You see he undertook to strike young Willie, but before he finished, he concluded to let the job out.

ROMAINE. What became of this Green?

SWICHEL. He's round here yet, cuss him, drinkin' up all the good liquor intended for hard-working people. I've got my eye on him, and if he don't let my young master alone, I'll give him a second dose of Swichel that will operate more powerful than the first.

ROMAINE. Do you still entertain the same opinion in regard to strong drink that you did a year since?

SWICHEL. Well, to tell you the truth, I don't like to see young Squire Willie swillin' it down so, 'cause I don't think he can hold out as well as I can. As near as my judgment goes, I feel a darned sight smarter arter drinkin' four or five good horns, than I do without them, and the most of it is, Squire, if a feller wanted to leave off he couldn't do it nohow. It's under your nose and eyes here in Cedarville all the time, and if I don't think of it myself, somebody will for me, and will say, 'Come, Sample, let's take something' – so you see, situated as I am, there isn't much help for it.

ROMAINE. But just now you expressed your fears for your young master's safety. Are you not afraid for yourself – can't you see where it will end?

SWICHEL. End! That's what starts me sometimes a leetle, for I'm afraid it may make an end.

ROMAINE. Why don't you avoid the temptation?

SWICHEL. It's easy enough to ask that, but how in thunder are you going to do it? Where are you going nowadays, where they don't sell liquor? It comes so natural to drop in and take a social smile, that it's darned hard to break off. Why! arter I licked that sarpent Green, old Slade mixed me a drink that made me wish that my throat was a yard long, it felt so good all the way going down.

ROMAINE. My good friend, you are not yet fully aware of your danger. Habitual intoxication is the epitome of every crime; all the vices that stain our nature germinate within it, waiting but for a moment to spout forth in pestilential rankness. When the Roman Stoic sought to fix a damning stigma on the author of his sister's shame, he called him neither rebel, bloodshedder, nor villain – no! he wreaked every odium within one word, and that was – drunkard,

SWICHEL. Say, Squire, I'm worried about you. I wish I knew what you was, right out and out; I'll be darned if you don't talk pootier than a pictur'-book – you don't mean to say there is any danger of my becoming a regular guzzler, do you?

ROMAINE. I would have you be cautious, both for yourself and your employer's sake, for I tell you when a man stoops to continual intoxication, 'tis only to drench him well with what he loves, and you may cause him to commit any crime.

SWICHEL. I don't know but what you are about half right. P'r'aps you have been through the mill?

ROMAINE. I have.

SWICHEL. Jest as I s'posed – you come out pooty bright.

ROMAINE. Yes, I escaped almost by a miracle; the exertion of friends, after years of suffering, at last caused me to see the danger in time and fly from it.

SWICHEL. Well, Squire, all people ain't built just alike. Now what upset you jest as like as not wouldn't start me one peg. I've been in the habit of taking my regulars ever since I was weaned, as I told you before. I remember, years ago, when uncle Kreosote Swichel used to bring home the communion wine, taking the tumbler, after he had tasted it to ascertain its quality, and worrying it down just as natural as ever old Slade could in his life. Since that time, I've had the most awful pain in my interior organs reg'lar about three times a day, and nothin' in natur' ever touches the right spot so quick as a leetle of that selfsame medicine. It comes hard to take, but, as the old woman told the eels as she skinned them, you must grin and bear it. Well, Squire, I must be off – I'll manage to see you ag'in. If that darned skunk Green, or any of his gang, offer to insult you, I'll fight for you as long as there is any cornjuice left in old Slade's tavern. Good day, Squire. (*Exit.*)

ROMAINE. How true it is that experience is the only teacher mankind will believe. I'll enter the house and see what changes a year has made in its occupants. (*Exit.*)

SCENE II. – *Interior of* SLADE'S *inn.* SLADE *discovered at bar.*

SLADE. This is a dull day, sure enough – nothing going on. I
thought Willie Hammond would have been in before this
time. I had a hard time of it to get him and Harvey Green to
become reconciled. The fact is, Willie is a stubborn little
fellow. He's not half so easy to persuade as Green is. As I
live, here comes my stranger friend who was here a year ago.

Enter ROMAINE.

Ah! Good day, my friend! It is about a year since you were
here?
ROMAINE. Yes. How is the 'Sickle and Sheaf' flourishing? As
well as you expected?
SLADE. Better.
ROMAINE. You are satisfied with your experiment?
SLADE. Perfectly. You couldn't get me back to the old mill if
you were to make me a present of it!
ROMAINE. How does the present owner come on?
SLADE. Not doing very well. How could it be expected? Why,
he didn't know enough of the milling business to grind a peck
of wheat right. He lost half of the custom I transferred to
him in less than three months; then he broke his main shaft,
and it took three months to put in a new one. Half of his
remaining customers discovered by this time that they could
get far better meal from their grain down to Harvey's mill,
so they didn't care to trouble him any more. The upshot of
the whole matter is – he broke down next, and had to sell the
mill at a heavy loss.
ROMAINE. Who has it now?
SLADE. Judge Hammond is the purchaser.
ROMAINE. He is going to rent it, I suppose?
SLADE. No; I believe he intends turning it into a distillery. He'll
make a fine thing of it. Grain has been too low in this section
for years, and there is altogether too much of it wasted for
bread. The advantages of the mill for grinding corn will be a

mere song compared with the profits resulting from an extensive distillery.

ROMAINE. That is your opinion, and I'll not attempt, at this moment, to dispute it. This Judge Hammond is one of your richest men, is he not?

SLADE. Yes; the richest man in the county – and what is more he's a shrewd man, and knows how to multiply his riches.

ROMAINE. How is his son, Willie, coming on?

SLADE. Oh, first-rate, I believe.

ROMAINE. What is his age now?

SLADE. About twenty.

ROMAINE. A critical age, landlord.

SLADE. So people say – but I didn't find it so.

ROMAINE. At his age you were, no doubt, daily employed in hard work?

SLADE. You are right; I was, and no mistake.

ROMAINE. It might not be with you as it is now, if leisure and freedom to go in and out when you pleased had been offered at the age of nineteen.

SLADE. I can't tell as to that. But I don't see as Willie Hammond is in any special danger. He's a young man with many good qualities, and has wit enough, I take it, to keep out of harm's way.

GREEN (*outside*). Landlord!

SLADE. Ah, there's Mr Green's voice! He's one of my best customers; you must excuse me.

ROMAINE. Certainly; and, as I am in no humour for company, if you will show me to my room, I will retire.

SLADE. With pleasure. This way, sir. (*Exit* ROMAINE *and* SLADE.)

Enter GREEN, *with* WILLIE.

GREEN. So, then, that ends all animosity between us.

WILLIE. To be sure. I'm the last man to bear malice. Here, Frank! Frank!

Enter FRANK.

Frank, mix us a couple of cocktails, will you?

FRANK. Yes, sir, in a twinkling.

WILLIE. I say, Green, my boy, I'm deuced dry. How much wine do you suppose myself and three jolly fellows murdered last night? You can't guess? Well, we sat down to a cool two dozen.

GREEN. The deuce you did. Well, as you sat down gentlemen, under what character did you arise? Ha, ha, ha!

WILLIE. Come, that's good! But I say, Green, I am beginning to go it a little too steep. I'll reform; I'll give it up! That's what I said last night at the conclusion of the fifth bottle. Says I, 'Gentlemen, this is too bad; I'm afraid we're getting drunk; and this must be the last.' But we'll give it up; yes, Green, I forswear it!

FRANK. Drinks ready for you, gentlemen.

WILLIE. Yes, and we're ready for the drinks.

GREEN. You are! Why, you this instant forswore wine!

WILLIE. So I did. That is, wine *as* wine; but this I (*drinks*) take as medicine.

GREEN. Drink hearty, old boy. I say, Frank, fine girl that sister of yours – fine girl.

FRANK. Yes, sir.

GREEN. I must try and find her a good husband. I wonder if she wouldn't have *me?*

FRANK. You had better ask her.

GREEN. I would if I thought there was any chance for me.

FRANK. Nothing like trying – 'Faint heart never won fair lady.'

GREEN. You're a fast boy, Frank. I shall have to speak to your father about you. You're getting on too fast. You must be put back to your lessons.

FRANK. I guess I'll do.

GREEN. Yes, I think you will! (WILLIE *and* GREEN *play cards.*)

Enter MORGAN.

MORGAN. Here I am. In spite of my good resolutions, I find myself once more in the 'Sickle and Sheaf'. What hope is there left for poor Joe Morgan? Every dime I get only makes me the more anxious to reach this house to obtain that which will keep me from thinking of my miserable home – my heart-broken wife and angel child. Here, Frank, give me some rum. There – there is more money for you – take it!

FRANK. Father told me not to let you have any more liquor unless you keep quiet.

MORGAN. Well, I'll keep quiet. I'll not disturb the *gentlemen* yonder. Give me my glass; I'll sit here by myself. Yes, yes; so it is: let a man once fall – no matter when, no matter where, no matter how much he may have suffered – the *good* people of this world raise their hands, set up the long, loud cry, and the poor inebriate dies – when a timely hand might have saved him. No matter – no matter!

FRANK. I forgot to tell you, Mr Hammond, that your father was here this evening to inquire for you.

WILLIE. Indeed! The old governor needn't have troubled himself. Neighbour Green and myself were enjoying a social game of cards in his room. There was no gambling.

MORGAN. No gambling – of course not – no danger. Oh, no – only a glass of wine and a game of cards; but it doesn't stop there, and well your father knows.

WILLIE. Perhaps he does; I remember he has warned me often about gaming. But I think I am now capable of taking care of myself.

MORGAN. So I thought once myself. But your father is a good man, and knows well the lurking snares that beset all who visit this place. He himself has had woeful experience in the past.

WILLIE. That's true, and I don't see as it has done him much harm. He sowed his wild oats, got married, settled down into a good, substantial citizen. He had his pleasures in early life; why not let his son taste of the same agreeable fruit? If I had met my old dad after me here, I should decidedly have told him to go about his business.

GREEN. Good blood, Willie – good blood! You would have served him right. (*Aside.*) What an ass he is! (*Exit* FRANK.)

Enter SLADE.

SLADE (*to* GREEN *and* WILLIE). Good-evening, gentlemen. I am glad to see you all looking so sociable this evening. (*Sees* JOE MORGAN.) Joe Morgan, what the devil brings you here, like an evil star, to mar our happiness?

MORGAN. Oh, yes; I know I am an unwelcome guest! My presence displeases the refined miller – I beg your pardon – *landlord.* He has become ashamed of his old friend!

SLADE. Off with you, Joe Morgan! I won't put up with your insolence any longer! Leave my house and never show your face here again. I won't have such low vagabonds as you here. If you can't keep decent, and stay decent, don't intrude yourself here.

MORGAN. You talk of decency! – a rumseller's decency. Poh! You were a decent man once, and a good miller into the bargain, but that time is past and gone. Decency died out when you exchanged the pick and facing-hammer for the glass and shaker. Decency – poh! How like a fool you talk; as if it were any more decent to sell rum than to drink it!

SLADE. I've heard enough from you. (*Goes to bar – takes up a glass.*) Now, leave my house!

MORGAN. I won't!

SLADE. Won't you? – take that, then!

Throws glass – it passes MORGAN – *glass crashes off* – MARY *screams – runs in, forehead bloody – falls.*

MARY. Father! dear father! They have killed me!

Enter MRS SLADE.

MRS SLADE. It's Joe Morgan's child. Oh, Simon! Simon! Has it come to this already? Who struck her?

MORGAN. Who? – curse him! – Simon Slade! Villain, your career of landlord shall be short; for here I swear, by the side of my murdered child, you shall die the death of a dog!

Soft music. MORGAN *seizes* SLADE – *they struggle; at last* MORGAN *throws him into corner – rushes to get stool, and raises it to strike* SLADE – *is held back by* WILLIE *and* GREEN. *Tableau.*

ACT III

SCENE I. – *Exterior of the Inn. Landscape.*

Enter SWICHEL.

SWICHEL. I've been looking for young Squire Hammond everywhere and can't find him; maybe he's down to the hotel along with that skunk Green. I do wish he'd drop him; speaking of dropping – I dropped him once, and I'll do it again, and heavy too, if he troubles my calico doings any more. That fellow hain't got any more principle about him than old Josiah Wilkins, and he was so all-fired mean that he took his wife's coffin out of the window, for fear he'd rub the paint off the banisters. Wal, I do believe he's coming – 'tis he, by chowder! Now, if he don't tell me where Willie Hammond is, he'll wish he'd never been introduced to the oldest surviving member of the Swichel family. (*Enter* GREEN.) Say neow, don't be in such a hurry, I want to talk to you.

GREEN. I've no time to waste on fools.

(*Attempts to pass on.* SWICHEL *intercepts him.*)

SWICHEL. Fools! Shew! You don't say so. Wal, since you are so darned wise, I want to get a little information from you.

GREEN. Some other time; I've business to attend to.

SWICHEL. Pshaw! You don't tell; I thought you'd retired from business long ago, and set up swindling on your own account.

GREEN. What's that you say?

SWICHEL. Oh, you needn't swell up as though you were going to bust; you can't frighten me any more than you could uncle Josh's bull. Talking of uncle Josh's bull, now I look at you I'll be darned if you don't resemble him – wa'n't any relation, was you?

GREEN. How dare you insult a gentleman!

SWICHEL. A gentleman! Do you call yourself a gentleman? Old uncle Kreosote used to say that a gentleman was a man of money, wit, and manners. Now I don't think you have got either. Say, what did you write that letter to my Mehitable for?

GREEN. I didn't write any letter to your Mehitable.

SWICHEL. Yes, you did; you and that other fellow there, Rural Districts. Say, where's my young master – Willie Hammond?

GREEN. I don't know; I ain't seen him in a couple of hours.

SWICHEL. That's a lie, I know.

GREEN. What! Do you mean to tell me I lie?

SWICHEL. To be sure I do – you've seen him within half an hour, I'll bet. Now, if you don't want to get yourself into trouble, you had better tell the truth for once in your life.

GREEN. I can tell you one thing – if you don't go about your business, and cease to interfere with mine, you will be sorry for it.

SWICHEL. So I hear you say. Say, Green, I don't know whether you believe in a hot place, that's kept up in good shape, waiting for the arrival of such no-souled critters as you, but I do, and if old clubfoot don't treat you to a brimstone bath before long, he will neglect his business most confoundedly.

GREEN. I give you timely warning – from this time forth, if you ever cross my path again, I'll level you to the earth, and *spit* upon you as a debased, degraded menial, beneath the notice of a gentleman. (*Exit.*)

SWICHEL. Sheow! You get. Well, you'd better get a spittoon big enough to hold the whole of your miserable carcase, for you'll find yourself stuck up in the middle of it, an awful warning to tobacco-chewers. I wish I could find the young squire – I must hunt him up somewhere. Now, friend Green, he worries me a leetle about his future accommodations. If there was any way of telegraphing to a certain friend of his that I've read about, he should have the hottest corner in the lowest part of his house that could be found, whenever he made his final journey in that direction. He should, by thunder! (*Exit.*)

SCENE II. – *Room in* MORGAN'S *house* – MORGAN *discovered putting on his coat* – MARY *on couch, head bound up* – MRS MORGAN *trying to restrain* MORGAN *from going out.*

MRS MORGAN. Don't go out tonight, Joe. Please don't go.

MARY. Father! father! Don't leave little Mary and poor mother alone tonight, will you? You know I can't come after you now.

MORGAN. Well, well, I won't go out.

MARY. Come and sit near me, dear father.

MORGAN (*goes to couch*). Yes, dear Mary.

MARY. I am so glad you won't go out tonight.

MRS MORGAN. How very hot your hand is! Does your head ache?

MARY. A little, but it will soon be better. Dear father –

MORGAN. Well, love?

MARY. I wish you would promise me something.

MORGAN. What is it?

MARY. That you will never go into Simon Slade's bar-room any more.

MORGAN. I won't go there tonight, dear; so let your heart be at rest.

MARY. Oh, thank you! I'll be well enough to get out in two or three days. You know the doctor said I must keep very still.

MRS MORGAN. Yes, my dear. That is to avoid your having a fever. Husband, you feel better for the promise you have given our darling child, I know you do.

MORGAN. Yes, Fanny. But my constitution is broken, as well as my heart. I feel now each moment, as I stand near that suffering child, as though my reason was leaving me. It is now five hours since I have tasted liquor, and I have been the slave so long of unnatural stimulants, that all vitality is lost without them.

MRS MORGAN (*takes cup from table*). Here – here – drink this. It is coffee. I cannot, dare not give you rum, even though you should die for the want of it! (*Gives him cup – his hand trembles as he drinks.*)

MORGAN. Thank you, dear one! O God, what a wretched slave

173

have I become! Fanny, I could not blame you were you to leave me to die alone!

MRS MORGAN. Leave you – no! Though you have banished relatives and friends from your door, though you have drawn the contempt of the world upon your wretched head, though you are a mark for the good to grieve at, and the vain to scoff at, still, still I will never desert you. The name of husband is not lost, though it be coupled with that of –

MORGAN. Drunkard! Yes, end the sentence – 'tis too true.

MRS MORGAN. Oh, think how I have suffered, to see you day by day sink from your once exalted station, until you have reached the wretched footing of the outcast, your temper broken by that infatuation which my heart sickens to think of and my lips refuse to name. (*Knock.*) Try and compose your feelings, Joe. Come in!

Enter MRS SLADE.

MRS SLADE. Fanny, how are you this evening, and how is little Mary?

MRS MORGAN. She is not so well, I fear, tonight.

MRS SLADE. Indeed! Oh, I am sorry! What a dreadful thing it was! You don't know how it has troubled me.

MRS MORGAN. It came near killing her.

MRS SLADE. The very thought makes me shudder.

MARY (*sitting up and pointing off*). Mother, I see him! there he is now!

MRS MORGAN. Her mind at times wanders. Lie down again dear. What is it, my child?

MRS SLADE. Has the doctor seen her today?

MRS MORGAN. No, he has not.

MRS SLADE. He should see her at once. I will go for him, and should you need my services, pray send for me. I will do anything in my power to assist you. (*Exit.*)

MARY (*delirious*). Remember, you have promised me, father. I'm not well yet, you know. Oh, don't go! – don't! There, he has gone! (*Sits up again.*) Well, I'll go after him again! I'll

try and walk there! I can sit down and rest by the way! Oh
dear, how tired I am! Father, father! Oh dear!

MORGAN. Here I am. Lie down, my child. I have not gone and
left you.

MARY. Oh, I know you, now! It is my father! Stoop down to me.
I want to whisper something to you – not to mother. I don't
want her to hear it – it will make her feel so bad.

MORGAN. Well, what is it, my child?

MARY. I shall never get well, father; I am going to die.

MRS MORGAN. What does she say, husband?

MARY. Hush, father! Don't tell her; I only said it to *you*. There,
mother; you go away – you've got trouble enough. I only
told him, because he promised not to go to the tavern any
more until I got well – and I'm not going to get well. Oh!
Mr Slade threw it so hard; but it didn't strike father, and
I'm so glad! How it would have hurt him! But he'll never go
there any more, and that will be so good, won't it, mother?
(*Sleeps.*)

MRS MORGAN. Do you hear what she says, Joe?

MORGAN. Yes. Her mind wanders; and yet she may have spoken
the truth.

MRS MORGAN. If she should die, Joe?

MORGAN. Don't! oh, don't talk so, Fanny! She's not going to
die; it's only because she's a little light-headed.

MRS MORGAN. Yes; why is she light-headed? It was the cruel
blow that caused this delirium. I'm afraid, husband, the
worst is before us. I've borne and suffered much. I pray
Heaven to give me strength to bear this trial, also. She is
better fitted for Heaven than for earth. She has been a great
comfort to me and to you, Joe, too – more like an angel than
a child. Joe, if Mary should die, you cannot forget the cause
of her death, nor the hand that struck the cruel blow?

MORGAN. Forget it? – never! And if I ever forgive Simon Slade –
(*Excitedly.*)

MRS MORGAN. You'll not forget where the blow was struck, nor
your promise given to our dying child?

MORGAN (*in delirium*). No, no! Wife, wife! My brain is on fire!

175

Hideous visions are before my eyes! Look! look! – see! – what's there? – there – in the corner? (*Points.*)

MRS MORGAN. Oh, heavens! 'Tis another symptom of that terrible mania from which he has twice escaped. There's nothing there, Joe.

MORGAN. There is, I tell you! I can see as well as you. Look – a huge snake is twining himself around my arms! Take him off! Take him off! – quick! quick!

MRS MORGAN. It's only fancy, Joe. Try and lie down and get some rest; I will get you a cup of strong tea; you're only a little nervous. Mary's trouble has disturbed you – there – I'll return in a minute. (*Exit.*)

MORGAN. There! look for yourself! Don't go! – don't go! Oh, you've come for me, have you? Well, I'm ready! Quick! quick! How bright they look! – their eyes are glaring at me! And now they are leaping, dancing, and shouting with joy to think the drunkard's hour has come. Keep them off! keep them off! Oh, horror! horror! (*Rushes; throws himself behind couch.*)

MARY (*awaking*). Oh, father! is it you? I'm so glad you're here.

Enter MRS MORGAN, *hastily, with cup.*

MRS MORGAN. Not here? Gone? Joe! husband! – where are you?

MARY. Here he is, dear mother.

MORGAN. Keep them off, I say! Keep them off! You won't let them hurt me, will you? (*Clings to* MARY.) There they are, creeping along the floor! Quick! jump out of bed, Mary! See, now – there – right over your head!

MARY. Nothing can hurt you here, dear father.

MORGAN. No, no; that's true. Pray for me, my child; they can't come in here, for this is your room. Yes, this is my Mary's room, and she is an angel. There – I knew you wouldn't dare to come in here. Keep off! keep off! Ha! ha! ha! ha!

Falls. MRS MORGAN *kneels over him.* MARY *sits in bed with her hands raised in prayer. Soft music. Tableau.*

Ten Nights in a Bar-Room: The Fight. Stock Poster

ACT IV

SCENE I. – *Interior of 'Sickle and Sheaf'*.

Enter SLADE.

SLADE. It does seem to me as though I had the devil's own luck lately. That's just the way, when a man tries all in his power to get an honest living, something is sure to turn up to injure him.

Enter GREEN.

GREEN. Ah! Landlord! how are you, tonight? Well and jolly as ever, I suppose. Your particular friend, Joe Morgan, hasn't given you his usual call yet.

SLADE. No; and if he'll just keep away from here, he may go to the devil on a hard-trotting horse, as fast as he pleases. He's tried my patience beyond endurance, and my mind is made up that he gets no more liquor at my bar. I've borne his vile tongue and seen my company annoyed by him just as long as I mean to stand it. Last night decided me. Suppose I had killed that child?

GREEN. You'd have had trouble, and no mistake.

SLADE. Wouldn't I? Blast her little picture; what business has she creeping in here every night?

GREEN. True enough. She must have a queer kind of a mother.

SLADE. I don't know what she is now – heartbroken, I suppose. But there was a time when Fanny Morgan was the loveliest woman in Cedarville. What a life her miserable husband has caused her to lead!

GREEN. Better he were dead and out of the way.

SLADE. Better; yes, a thousand times better. If he'd only fall down some night and break his drunken neck, it would be a blessing to his family.

178

GREEN. Yes, and to you in particular.

SLADE. You may be sure it wouldn't cost me a large sum for mourning, ha! ha! ha!

Enter FRANK, *dressed gaily, cane, and smoking.*

Ah! Frank, that you? Where's your mother?

FRANK (*swaggering*). I don't know. Gone out somewhere.

SLADE. Where?

FRANK. I don't know.

SLADE. How long has she been away?

FRANK. I don't know, I tell you. I've been gunning with Tom Wilkins. I ain't seen her these three hours.

SLADE. Didn't she say where she was going?

FRANK. No, she didn't. I asked her no questions, and so of course she told me no lies.

SLADE. Didn't she? Hark you, Mr Frank! You've become mighty impudent lately. Don't let me hear any more from your mouth. Go and fix up the bar; I expect customers here every minute.

FRANK. Oh, you dry up. (*Drinks with* GREEN. *Exit.*)

Enter MRS SLADE.

SLADE. Here comes wife at last. Ann, where have you been?

MRS SLADE. Where I wish you had been with me.

SLADE. Where was that?

MRS SLADE. At Joe Morgan's.

SLADE. The devil you have.

MRS SLADE. Ah, Simon! If you don't have this child's blood clinging through life to your garments, you may be thankful.

SLADE. What do you mean by that?

MRS SLADE. All that my words indicate. Little Mary is very ill. The doctor says she is in danger. Oh, Simon, if you had heard what I did! She talked about you so pitiful, told how good you used to be to her when she came to the mill; how you took her on your knee, stroked her hair and kissed her. I shall never forget her pale frightened face, nor her cry of fear when she spoke of you. Simon! Simon! if she should die!

SLADE (*alarmed*). Die!

MRS SLADE. If we were only back to the old mill.

SLADE. There, now, I don't want to hear that again. I've made a fool of myself long enough listening to such talk. One would think, by the way you talk, I had broken every commandment in the Decalogue.

MRS SLADE. You will break hearts as well as commandments if you keep on for a few years as you have done, and ruin souls as well as fortunes. *Do* think of this, Simon, before it is too late, and let us go back to our old calling. I will work night and day, and stare poverty boldly in the face – will live content on one meal a day, to see you *once more a man!* (*Exit.*)

SLADE. What the devil's the matter with everybody? Grumble, grumble! A woman is never contented. When I was a miller she grumbled because I worked too hard; now she grumbles because I don't work hard enough. Well, her mind, like all the rest of her sex, changes every ten minutes, so that's some comfort.

Enter WILLIE *and* SWICHEL, *somewhat intoxicated.*

WILLIE. Here we are, my jolly old trump! here we are! I say, Sample, what's the matter with you? You don't stand steady.

SWICHEL (*staggering*). Stand stea – hic – dy! It's tough work for me – hic – to stand anyhow.

WILLIE. Ah, Green, my boy, how are you? Glad to see you; here is Sample. I know you don't agree very well; but I've been telling him what a tiptop fellow you are, and how we have been arranging our business matters together; so you'll find him all right now.

SWICHEL. Say, Green, I forgive you for all the compliments you bestowed on me at our last meeting, 'cause Squire Hammond told me you sold him that fast horse dirt-cheap. (*Staggers.*)

WILLIE. Slade, have you heard the news? The man with the poker is after one of your customers.

SWICHEL. Yes, shovel, poker, tongs and – hic – all.

SLADE. What do you mean?

WILLIE. Who? Why, Joe Morgan. It's the second or third chase, and he'll be likely to catch him this time.

SWICHEL. He may catch Joe Morgan, but I kalkelate *I* could outrun him.

GREEN. Don't you be too sure of that.

SWICHEL (*staggers; crosses to* GREEN). Who said anything to you?

WILLIE. Sample! remember, we are all friends here now.

SWICHEL. All right, Squire. (*Staggers and crosses back to former place.*)

WILLIE. I say, Simon, that was a devilish unlucky thing for you. They say the child is going to die.

SLADE. Who says so?

WILLIE. Dr Green.

SLADE. What! he wasn't in earnest?

WILLIE. Yes, he was. They had an awful time there last night. Joe had the delirium tremens, and I don't know but what he is dead by this time.

SWICHEL. Poor fellow. I'll be darned if I don't pity him.

GREEN. I don't see anything to pity about such a miserable wretch as he is. But I pity his family.

SWICHEL. (*staggers across to* GREEN). You be blowed. You don't know what pity is.

WILLIE (*warningly*). Sample!

SWICHEL (*staggering back behind* WILLIE *to position*). All right, Squire, I'll give him my idee of what pity is at some future time.

WILLIE. I heard some strong suggestions over to Lawyer Philip's office today, and if that child dies, you'll probably have to stand trial for manslaughter.

GREEN. No, he won't. Girl-slaughter! Ha! ha! ha!

SWICHEL (*staggers across to* GREEN). Shut up, you miserable skunk, or I'll –

WILLIE. Sample! Sample!

SWICHEL (*crossing back as before*). Jest as you say, Squire.

SLADE. It was only an accident, and all the lawyers in Christendom couldn't make anything more of it.

WILLIE. Hardly an accident, for our worthy landlord did throw
a heavy tumbler at her father's head. The intention was to do
an injury, and the law will not stop to make any nice dis-
crimination in regard to the individual upon whom the injury
was wrought.

SLADE. Anyone who intimates that I meant to harm that girl is
a liar.

SWICHEL (*staggers; crosses to* SLADE). What's that? You call
Squire Willie a liar? Now, look here, old Slade, throwing
tumblers, I kalkelate, is about the meanest kind of business
ever invented, though it appears to be a favourite sport of
yours. But if you call Willie Hammond a liar again, I'll
embellish that ugly demijohn-looking countenance of yours
with more cuts than you can find in the illustrated weekly.

WILLIE. Keep cool, Sample.

SWICHEL. Keep cool! You jest let me have my own way – I'll
fix him so they'll have to pack him in ice, to keep *him* cool
anyhow.

SLADE. Come, gentlemen, we're old friends here, you know –
don't let's have any hard feelings – come, drink with me.

WILLIE. Yes! We'll drink with the landlord.

SWICHEL. Jest as you say, Squire – I'll be darned if my throat
don't feel as if a leetle corn-juice would ease it. I hain't been
so dry since Noah sent round notices for the cattle to hurry
up and get into the ark.

SLADE. Prosperity – gentlemen – prosperity. (*All drink.*)

GREEN. Now, Mr Hammond, if you are agreeable we will finish
that little game of amusement we were at last evening.

They sit at table and play cards.

WILLIE. Just as you say – I'm agreeable.

SLADE. I hope you are not offended with me for my remarks – I
had no intention of insulting young Willie. He is a young
man for whom I entertain a great respect – come, fill up
again.

SWICHEL (*drinks*). Sartin. I don't bear no malice. (*Getting
drunk.*) I say – that's rare old white-eye, ain't it?

SLADE. Yes; I don't mean to keep anything but the best. But I have had to suffer a good deal lately on account of the stringent laws in regard to the sale of liquor. Where are our liberties, I should like to know, if all guarantees are gone? Why, the next thing you know, we shall have laws to fine a man if he takes a chew of tobacco! Come, take another drink!

SWICHEL. Jest so! Yes, I guess I will. (*Aside.*) I swow! old Slade's a first-rate fellow – hic – arter all – hic. (*Aloud.*) You're right there – hic – there, neighbour Slade, if you never was before in your life! There's no telling what – what – telling – what they will do; now, there's old uncle Josh Wilkins, who's been keeper of the almshouse these ten years. Well, these darned temp'rance skunks are going to turn him out if ever they get the upper hand in Bolton county.

SLADE. 'If'; – that word means a good deal. We must not let them get the upper hand. Every man has a duty to perform to his country in the matter, and every one must do his duty. What have they got against your uncle Josh?

SWICHEL. Nothin' in natur'; only they say they're not going to have any poorhouse in the county.

SLADE. Going to turn the poor wretches out of doors, I suppose?

SWICHEL. No, not that; these temp'rance people say if they carry the day there'll be no need of poorhouses, and I'll be cursed if I don't believe there's something in it; for I never knew a man to go to the almshouse that he hadn't rum to blame for his poverty. You see, I'm interested in this matter. I go in for keeping a poorhouse, for I think I'm travelling that road at a mighty good gait myself, and I shouldn't like to reach the last mile-stone and find no uncle Josh there to greet me. Hurra for the rummies! Hurra for uncle Josh! He's safe for one vote, anyhow. Hurra! hurra! (*Flourishes his glass.*)

GREEN (*at table*). That's my trick!

WILLIE. No, sir – mine! You've tried that bluff on me before and it won't hold this time.

GREEN. You are a cheating scoundrel!

Rushes down – WILLIE *rushes down.*

WILLIE. Call me a cheating scoundrel! Me, whom you have followed like a bloodhound? Me, whom you have robbed, cheated, and debased from the beginning? Oh, for a pistol, to rid the earth of the blackest-hearted villain that walks its surface! I have lost all I possessed with you. I have nothing left to care for; disgraced and ruined, I dare not return to my home. Let me do society the service of ridding the earth of this monster before I die!

Music, forte – seizes GREEN – *they struggle –* GREEN *draws knife, stabs* WILLIE, *and rushes out.* WILLIE *falls in* SLADE'S *arms;* SWICHEL *slaps his hat on his head, and staggers out after* GREEN.

SCENE II. – *Landscape – Wood.*

Enter GREEN *hurriedly.*

GREEN. What shall I do? Escape seems impossible. Already they are on my track. Could I but once manage to elude their vigilance, I would leave this accursed spot and never again return. Fool, to let my passion get the better of my reason! His money was already mine, and he himself so completely the slave of habit that he was wholly in my power.

SWICHEL (*outside*). Where is the darned skunk? Where is he? Let me find him, and he'll see thunder and rain!

GREEN. Ah! someone comes – I must manage to conceal myself. (*Retires.*)

Enter SWICHEL *running – falls.*

SWICHEL. I'm here, I guess, at last! I thought I should fetch up somewhere and I have! My head feels as if it had apartments to let! Wonder if I've the nightmare, and fallen out of bed? No; I remember all about it, now. That darned skunk, Slade, filled me up fuller than a Medford rum barrel! And poor Willie Hammond killed by that darned blackleg, Green. (*Tries to get up; fails two or three times; at last succeeds.*) Only let me find him, and I'll hug him closer than a western b'ar ever did a Kentucky hunter! (*Noise.*) Hallo! what's that creeping around there?

GREEN (*rushes in*). Ah! Discovered! Die!

Snaps pistol at SWICHEL.

SWICHEL (*catches his arm*). Couldn't think of such a thing, no-how; you'd better go home and load up fust!

GREEN. Let go of me, or you'll follow your master!

SWICHEL. I rather guess you'll see him afore I shall! Your game is about up, so you'd better pass in your checks!

GREEN. Release me, I say! (*Struggles.*)

SWICHEL. Guess not! I shan't never let go my hold of you until I've locked you safe in your room and given the key to the sheriff! 'Tain't safe to let you go round loose any longer. If I had my own way, I'd make something exhibiting you; but now I've got my fingers on you, and about ten quarts of genuine rum-strength added to my nateral heft, I kinder kalkelate I'm fire-proof! (GREEN *struggles*.) Oh, you needn't kick round here; you've got to dance a dance without any music pooty soon, and if I don't have a crowd to see you double-shuffle off your mortal coil I ain't no judge of Italian fandancy, I can tell you! (GREEN *struggles*.) Keep quiet; we ain't quite ready for the jig yet! You'll have due notice, and I've got your quarters ready to receive you when you arrive – come along! (*Pulls* GREEN.) You needn't hold back, for there won't be any fun going on until you get there! Come along, I say! Come along!

Exit, pulling GREEN.

SCENE III. – MORGAN's *house* – MORGAN *on floor* – MARY *on couch asleep* – MRS MORGAN *watching her. Slow music.*

MRS MORGAN. Throughout the long, long night have I watched my suffering ones. Heaven only knows what is in store for me; yet I cannot bring my mind to believe that all that is truly noble, truly deserving in his nature should be destroyed. My poor child; how anxiously have I watched every movement of that sweet face! How I have longed for the morning sun to usher in its beams, and bring a gleam of joy to this almost broken heart!

MARY (*waking*). Mother! Oh, how long I've been asleep! See if father's awake.

MRS MORGAN. He is still asleep, dear.

MARY. Oh, I wish he was awake – I want to see him so much. Won't you try and wake him, mother?

MRS MORGAN. My dear child, father has suffered very much, and I was obliged to give him opium.

MARY. I'm sure he's been asleep a long time. Father!

MORGAN. That voice! Where am I? (*Awakes.*)

MRS MORGAN. You have been very ill, husband.

MARY. Oh, father, I'm so glad you're awake. I was afraid you were never going to wake up again.

MORGAN. What can I do for you, my dear child?

MARY. Nothing. I don't wish for anything, I only wanted to see you. You've always been good to little Mary.

MORGAN. Oh, no! I've never been good to anyone.

MARY. You haven't been good to yourself, but you have always been good to me. Yes; and to poor mother too.

MORGAN. Don't Mary! Don't say anything about that – say that I've been very bad. I only wish that I were as good as you are; I'd like to die then, and go right away from this wicked world. I wish there was no liquor to drink – no taverns – no bar-rooms – I wish I were dead.

MARY. Father! I want to tell you something more.

MORGAN. What is it, Mary?

MARY. There will be no one to go after you any more.

MORGAN. Don't talk about that, Mary – I'm not going out in the evening any more until you get well. Don't you remember, I promised?

MARY. Yes, I know, but –

MORGAN. What, dear?

MARY. I'm going away to leave you and mother; our Heavenly Father has called me.

MORGAN. What shall we do when you are gone? Let me die too.

MARY. You are not ready to go with me yet – you will live longer, that you may get ready. Haven't I tried to help you – oh, so many times, but it wasn't any use. You *would* go out. You *would* go to the tavern. It seemed almost as if you could not help it – maybe I can help you better, father, after I die. I love you so much that I'm sure the good angels will let me come to you, and watch over you always. Don't you think so, mother?

MRS MORGAN. My dear child, you are not going to leave us?

MARY. Oh, yes, I am! I dreamed something about pa while I slept. I thought it was night, and I was still sick – you promised not to go out again until I was well, but you did go out, and I thought you went over to Mr Slade's tavern. When I knew this, I felt as strong as when I was well, and I got up and dressed myself, and started out after you. At last I came to Mr Slade's tavern, and there you stood, father, in the door, and you were dressed so nice. You had on a new hat, and a new coat, and your boots were new, and shined ever so bright; I said, 'Oh! father, is this you?' and then you took me up in your arms and kissed me, and said, 'Yes, Mary, this is your real father, not old Joe Morgan, but Mr Morgan now.' It seemed all so strange; for there wasn't any bar-room there any longer, but a store full of goods, and over the door I read your name, father. Oh, I was ever so glad that I awoke, and then I cried all to myself, for it was only a dream.

MORGAN. That dream, my dear child, shall become a reality; for here I promise that, God helping me, I will never go out at night again for a bad purpose!

MRS MORGAN. Do you indeed promise that, Joe?

MORGAN. Yes, and more.

MARY. What?

MORGAN. I'll never go into a bar-room again!

MARY. Never?

MRS MORGAN. Do you indeed promise that?

MORGAN. Yes; and what is still more, I will never drink another drop of liquor as long as I live.

MRS MORGAN. Oh, husband, this is indeed happiness! (*Kneels by* MARY's *side.*) Look! look at our dear child! Her eyes are fixed – she is dying!

MARY. Yes, mother; your Mary has lived long enough – the angels have heard little Mary's prayer! Father won't want anyone to follow him, for he will be good, and sometime we shall all be together. Don't you remember the little hymn you taught me? It all comes in my mind now, although I had not thought of it before for a long time. Everything looks so beautiful around me. I don't feel any pain now. Good-bye, father; I shan't have to ask you to be good to mother now. (*Kisses him.*) Good-bye, mother. (*Kisses her. Sings.*)

We shall meet in the land where spring is eternal,
　　Where darkness ne'er cometh – no sorrow nor pain;
Where the flowers never fade – in that clime ever vernal
　　We shall meet, and our parting be never again.

MARY *dies;* MORGAN *falls on the couch.* MRS MORGAN *sobs over the body. Slow music. Tableau.*

ACT V

SCENE I. – *Exterior of the Inn.*

Enter ROMAINE.

ROMAINE. Ten years have elapsed since I visited this spot. Ten years have passed away and are numbered with the things that were. Curiosity has again led me into this locality. The acquaintances that I formed during my different visits here have created a desire to learn more of their history.

Enter SWICHEL.

SWICHEL. Wal, I guess I've got down about as fur towards the foot of the ladder as I intend a-goin'. Why! How do you do, Squire?

ROMAINE. Can this be possible! Is your name Swichel?

SWICHEL. 'Tain't nothin' else. Say, Squire, you look jest as you did ten years ago when I took you for a corn-doctor.

ROMAINE. I'm sorry I can't return the compliment.

SWICHEL. No, you couldn't very well, unless you lied some, could you?

ROMAINE. Have you had all the experience in dram-drinking yet that you desire?

SWICHEL. I should say I had. I knocked off the critter, Squire.

ROMAINE. How long since?

SWICHEL. Well, 'tain't a great while, that's a fact. But long enough to brush up my idees and see where I am. I'll be darned if I touch another drop of liquor as long as I live. I gave that promise to Squire Morgan not more than half an hour ago.

ROMAINE. And who is this Squire Morgan?

189

SWICHEL. Who is he? Why, he's one of the most likely men we've got in Cedarville.

ROMAINE. I don't remember such a fellow. There was a poor degraded wretch here, on my former visit, by that name, but he –

SWICHEL. That's the same critter. Arter his child died, he came out right side up, and he never drank a drop since.

ROMAINE. What became of Green?

SWICHEL. He played a game of seven-up with the law and as soon as he found out the sheriff held the ace and deuce, he dealt from the bottom, turned up jack and shot himself – died game.

ROMAINE. And Slade, the tavern-keeper, where is he?

SWICHEL. Where's he? Where he always is, nowadays, by the side of a barrel of new rum from morning till night. They tried him for killing Joe Morgan's child, but most of the jury was old Slade's customers, so they couldn't agree on a verdict, and they let him off. Since that time he's been pooty busy tryin' to kill me, but I guess he'll have to let the job out on a venture, for I've made up my mind to stop it. Mr Morgan has given out orders for me to have a new suit of clothes, and I'm going to work for him in the mill.

ROMAINE. That's right; you are on the right road now, and you'll be sure to prosper.

SWICHEL. I believe so myself, Squire. Things are altered a little since you came around here, I can tell you! You wouldn't hardly know old Slade now; and as for his son, Frank, he takes to drink just as nateral as can be. Between the two of them they've broke the old woman's heart and sent her up to the lunatic asylum. They had another room there waiting for me, but I gin orders to let it if they could get a week's pay in advance.

ROMAINE. I have a great curiosity to make one more visit to the 'Sickle and Sheaf' before I leave the county.

SWICHEL. Well, you can if you choose. I have discontinued my visits, unless I have some special business, and then I go in and out jest like a telegraph dispatch! The fact is, every time

I look at old Slade, I'm afraid of spontaneous combustion,
and I don't want to be around when he delivers up his papers!

ROMAINE. You have only to remain firm in the good resolutions
you have formed, and you can defy temptation. I must leave
you now to make the call I spoke of, but shall endeavour to
see you again before I leave the village. Good day. (*Exit.*)

SWICHEL. Good day. That's a fust-rate chap, anyhow! I wish I'd
minded what he said ten years ago; I should not have
looked so cussed shabby as I do now. No matter – when I
get that new suit of clothes I'll shine out brighter than a
pewter spoon! I'll be darned if Mehitable Cartwright ain't
comin' this way. I should like to ascertain if she's inclined to
Swichel herself into the matrimonial noose – I'm in the
market now! I've knocked off rum, and as it's the nature of
the Swichels to be in some mischief, I might as well spread
myself and get married as quick as possible! Ah! here she
comes.

Enter MEHITABLE.

MEHITABLE. Sample! Sample! where have you been? I've been
looking all over the world for you!

SWICHEL. You travel faster than the telegraph, then, for it ain't
more than an hour since I left you peelin' onions, and cryin'
as if you'd lost your aunt!

MEHITABLE. Mr Morgan sent me after you. He wants you to go
and find that man – you know who I mean – the one that has
been round here two or three times; the man Mr Morgan
saw down to the 'Sickle and Sheaf' years ago. He has heard
that he is again in the village, and he wants you to go and
find him, and invite him to stay at his house while he remains
in Cedarville.

SWICHEL. I've given up going to the tavern, but I shall du jest
as Mr Morgan says. Say, Mehitable, you know what I was
hinting to you about, last night?

MEHITABLE. Yes, I do; and much good may it do you! What
have you done with all my books? Where's my *Fair One
of the Golden Locks*?

191

SWICHEL. I spread her all over with strengthening plaster, and put her on the back of Mr Morgan's one-horned cow!

MEHITABLE. So, you great clumsy brute, you've destroyed that lovely book, have you?

SWICHEL. Say, Mehitable – what's the use of your making such a cussed fool of yourself? Why can't you take example by me, and be something?

MEHITABLE. Be something! You're a nice one to talk! You are drinking rum from morning to night! You're a disgrace to everybody!

SWICHEL. No such thing; I've knocked off. Now, jest give up all your old novels, and I'll give up all the rum, and we shall be better able to come to some mutual understanding. You see, I want you to assist me in a little enterprise I'm goin' into.

MEHITABLE. What is it, Sample?

SWICHEL. I've been talking to old Justice Smith a good deal lately about improving the stock in this vicinity. Old Slade has managed to kill off about two-thirds of the population. Now I'm goin' to do my share towards building up the town, and I want you tew go into a joint-stock partnership with me.

MEHITABLE. Pshaw – how foolish you talk!

SWICHEL. That's your opinion, is it? Well, you needn't fret about it. 'Tain't no matter. I've fooled away my time about long enough, and I've made up my mind to get married; and if you won't have me I'll go down to Sam Walker's house, and make love to his old black cook. I've got to stay at home nights now, and (*emphatically*) I'll be cussed if I'm goin' to stay alone.

MEHITABLE (*coyly*). I didn't say I wouldn't have you.

SWICHEL. No, and you didn't say you would. What's the use tormenting a poor fellow to death before you get spliced? I should like to know where you could get a better, hand-somer, and more durable article than I am, warranted to wear, rum-proof, and will stick to you through life, closer than a bee to a honeycomb. Spit it eout – will you become Mrs Swichel, or not?

MEHITABLE. Beloved Alphonso! – but this is so sudden –

SWICHEL. Oh! stow that!

MEHITABLE. Well, Sample, you know I couldn't refuse.

SWICHEL. That's the talk. Let's cut off a remnant to bind the bargain. (*Kisses her.*) Hold on a minute. A remnant ain't enough. I'll take a half a yard. (*Kisses her.*) By chowder! I should like to measure off a whole cotton factory in the same way.

MEHITABLE. Now, Sample, I must return. Mrs Morgan is to have a party at her house tonight, and you know I shall be busy. You go and do your errand, and return.

SWICHEL. Hold on a minute – you've forgot something.

MEHITABLE. What is it?

SWICHEL. A skein of thread to match that remnant. (*Kisses her.*)

MEHITABLE (*slaps his face*). Take that for your impudence. (*Exit.*)

SWICHEL. If her breath ain't sweeter than eau de cologne, I ain't no judge of liquor, that's all. I should like to have six yards more of that same piece of calico. I feel a darned sight better since I settled matters with her, and better since I've bid farewell to brandy, gin, and toddies. 'Twas hard work to part with 'em. I've written a few lines, and as we seem to be all alone I don't mind stretching my lungs a little.

SONG

AIR – '*Yankee Doodle*'

I

Farewell! farewell! a long farewell
   To brandy, rum and toddy;
Old Slade may buy, old Slade may sell,
   And ruin soul and body.
Of brandy tods I've had my fill,
   Of whisky, rum and gin, sirs;
I leave them all with right good will,
   And a temperance life begin, sirs.

II

The best advice I give to all
    Of every clime and nation,
Is take a wife, yes, short or tall;
    'Twill prove your sure salvation.
Leave brandy toddies, rum and gin,
    And be sure that you start right, sirs;
Commence at once, this night begin,
    With me and Miss Cartwright, sirs.

III

When time rolls on, pray call around,
    And happen in to meet me;
Some little Swichels will be found
    To straighten up to greet ye.
And now I bid a. fond adieu
    To all good topers frisky;
I hope when next again we meet
    I'll find you've sworn off whisky.   (*Exit.*)

SCENE II. – *Interior of 'Sickle and Sheaf'. Everything in a dilapidated state.* SLADE, *in this scene, is bloated, and one eye gone,
clothes much worn.* FRANK *is seedy, beard uncut, dirty shirt on, and
is smoking.*

Enter SLADE.

SLADE. Frank! Frank! Where the devil is that boy – he's turned
    out just like everything else – all gone to ruin together.
    There never lived a man that has tried harder to get an
    honest living than I have, and yet everything has worked
    against me. What the devil's the use of trying to be honest

– it's all humbug. If I had my life to live over again, I'd cheat, steal, lie, do anything that would better my condition.

Enter ROMAINE.

ROMAINE. Ah, landlord! You're still alive.

SLADE. Yes, I'm alive, and that's about all – I'm glad to see you once more, although I'm not just – not just – well, how are you, anyhow?

ROMAINE. I am well, I thank you. Can I get accommodations here for a day or two?

SLADE. I suppose so – Frank will be in soon. Since his mother died, you see, he's attended to everything himself.

ROMAINE. Things look dull with you here.

SLADE. Yes, rather.

ROMAINE. Not doing as well as you were?

SLADE. No, these 'ere blamed temp'rance folks have ruined everything.

ROMAINE. Indeed!

SLADE. Yes, Cedarville ain't what it was when you first came to the 'Sickle and Sheaf'. I – I – you see – cuss the temp'rance people, they've ruined me. Here's my son, he'll wait upon you.

Enter FRANK, *smoking*.

FRANK. Look here, old man, what are you loafing about here for? Go and cut some wood – I want to build a fire in the front room. (*Sees* ROMAINE.) Hallo! I remember you. How do you flourish?

ROMAINE. I am well, I thank you. I intend remaining two or three days with you. Your father recommended me to you.

FRANK. Well, you'll have to put up with such as you can get these dull times; they won't let us get a living, nohow. Old Squire Hargrove was here this evening, and threatened to prosecute us if we sold his son any more liquor.

ROMAINE. Well, then, I should refuse to sell him any, and thus avoid the prosecution.

SLADE. That would be smart; why, it's *my trade* to sell liquor.

ROMAINE. I wish, with all my heart, you had a more honourable calling.

FRANK. Look out, old covey; if you insult my father I'll knock you down!

ROMAINE. I respect filial devotion, meet it where I will; I only wish it had a better foundation.

FRANK. What! Do you think you can come here and insult us without provocation? Take that! (*Rushes to hit* ROMAINE.)

Enter SWICHEL *quickly, as* FRANK *goes towards* ROMAINE, *and throws him round into corner.*

SWICHEL. No, you don't! Now you jest take two steps to the rear – double-quick, open order, march! You lay your hand on that gentleman, and I'll wring your neck off quicker than you can make a gin cocktail!

FRANK. Damnation!

SWICHEL. Oh, you can swear to your heart's content – it won't hurt anyone but yourself. You'll spoil soon enough without swearing.

ROMAINE. I thank you, Sample, for this manly interference. It is no more than I should have expected from you.

SWICHEL. I never suffer a young man to strike an older one, anyhow; apart from that, I like you, Squire; and when I told Mr Morgan you were here, he sent me right arter you. He's going to have a little sociability up to his house tonight, and he wants you to come up and stay with him jest as long as you stop in the village.

ROMAINE. He is very kind, and I shall accept his hospitality.

SLADE. Yes, that's it; if I get a customer, some miserable drunkard like Joe Morgan is sure to invite him to his house, and away he goes. A respectable man has no chance here to get a living. It's just as I told you; everyone for himself, and the devil for us all!

SWICHEL. Wal, I guess you can have my share of the devil, old Slade. I have dissolved partnership with you, and your amiable son here don't amount to a piece of fiddler's rosin, in my estimation! (FRANK *takes up a chair.*) Now, jest you drop that! Oh, it's no use, Mr Frank, of your puttin' on any of your big looks to me! Your old daddy's rum has been oozing out through my veins long enough. My nateral strength has come back, and with it a large assortment of genuine Yankee courage, which would soon knock that Dutch spunk of yours further than five glasses of your father's fifty-cent rum! Squire, I'm going up to Mr Morgan's, so do you follow on. Don't stay here any longer with these two demijohns! Good-bye, old Rum and Brandy! You're a splendid specimen of the march of improvement, ain't you? You look more like a portable beer-barrel! Come along, Squire. (*Exit.*)

SLADE. I hope you are not offended at Frank – he means well enough.

FRANK. Who cares whether he's offended or not? – I don't! You needn't put in your oar, old man.

SLADE. Come, come – none of your insolence to me; I won't put up with it!

FRANK. Well then, don't interfere with my affairs, and I won't with yours – that's all! (*Takes up bottle.*)

SLADE. You have drunk enough already today. Put up that brandy-bottle!

FRANK. I can't do it, my amiable friend.

SLADE. Put it up, I say!

FRANK. I won't!

SLADE. Put it up, I say! You're drunk as a fool now. Put it up.

Goes to FRANK.

FRANK. Keep off, I say! Keep off, or I'll knock you down!

SLADE *seizes him –* FRANK *throws him into corner –* SLADE *starts towards him –* FRANK *throws him off, and hits him on the head with the bottle –* SLADE *falls –* FRANK *appalled. Music.*

ROMAINE. Frank Slade, you have killed your own father!

SCENE III. – *Exterior of 'Sickle and Sheaf'*.

Enter ROMAINE.

ROMAINE. Yes, after I call at Mr Morgan's house, I will at once leave this part of the country. The contemplation of such scenes as I have just witnessed is enough to sadden the stoutest heart. Who now could enter yonder tavern, and see the misery that there exists, and not use all his efforts to redeem those who have lost all control of themselves? I will hasten to Mr Morgan's and inform him of the terrible calamity that has befallen the wretched Simon Slade. (*Exit.*)

SCENE IV. – *A parlour in* MR MORGAN'S *house* – MORGAN *and* MRS MORGAN *discovered seated on lounge.*

MORGAN. Dear wife – have I not faithfully kept the promise given to our angel child?

Enter ROMAINE.

MRS MORGAN. Yes, you have, and the years that have passed since she was taken from us have rolled by like some sweet dream, adding every day some new joy to our happy home.

MORGAN (*to* ROMAINE). You are welcome, sir. It is some time since we met. This, sir, is my wife. Believing you would be more comfortable during your stay in our village here than at the 'Sickle and Sheaf', I sent Sample to invite you here. Pray be seated, sir.

ROMAINE. You were very kind, for an event has happened which is the anticipated end that I so long feared of Simon Slade.

MRS MORGAN. What has happened?

ROMAINE. Murdered – by his son Frank.

MORGAN. Can it be possible?

ROMAINE. It is too true.

MORGAN. Wife! wife! I shudder when I think of the dangers to which I have been exposed. Ten years ago there was not a happier spot in Bolton county than Cedarville. Ten years ago there was a kind-hearted miller in Cedarville, liked by everyone, and as harmless as a little child; now his bloated corpse lies in a lonely room in a house that he himself has made wretched. Ten years ago Judge Hammond was accounted the richest man in Cedarville – today he is the unmourned occupant of a pauper's grave. What is the cause of all this? A direful pestilence is in the air – it walketh at night and wasteth at noonday – it is slaying the first-born in our houses, and the cry of anguish is swelling on every gale. Is there no remedy?

Enter SWICHEL *with* MEHITABLE.

SWICHEL. I should say yes – sartin there was.

ROMAINE. You are right – there is, Sample, a remedy. But you must cut off the fountain if you would dry up the stream. If we would save the young, the innocent, we must cover them from the tempter, for they can no more resist his assaults than the lamb can resist the wolf. They are helpless if you abandon them to the powers of evil. Let us, then, one and all, resolve this night that the traffic shall cease in Bolton county. A large majority of the people, I am convinced, will vote in favour of such a measure. Look at Simon Slade, the happy, kind-hearted miller, and Simon Slade, the tavern-keeper. Was he benefited by the liberty to work harm to his neighbour? In heaven's name, then, let the traffic cease.

SWICHEL. That's just my opinion exactly. I've formed myself into a committee of one to put down the trade all that's in my power. 'Tain't long ago, Squire, since I was arguing with you on the subject. I thought moderate drinking was all right. Wal, I s'pose it was all well enough until I got to swillin' the stuff down for a livin', then I found it pooty tough. I tried to get rid of all the liquor I could, to prevent any further mischief; but as fast as I managed to empty one barrel, old Slade would fill up another. I worked faithfully for seven years to worry it down, and I've found there was always a little left, so I concluded to knock off and call it square.

MORGAN. Sample, you, like myself, have been freed from a terrible curse. I have lived to see and suffer all the evils that cling round the drunkard's home. I have lived to see hearthstones deserted, men shorn of their manliness, women from whose white cheeks sorrow has crushed the roses, children across the golden thresholds of whose lives trails the black shadow of a parent's shame. I have seen frightful death-bed scenes, where the frothing lip and the bloodshot eye, the distorted features and the delirious shrieks, told the fierce agony of the departing soul, and as my shuddering glance takes in but a feeble outline of the revolting spectacle, I know how much of the great sea of human crime, and want, and woe, pour through the slender channel of that one word 'Drunkard'.

MRS MORGAN. Words cannot describe the joy I feel to see you thus redeemed. I could have knelt above your grave and blessed Him who took you from me, rather than had you continue in your old habits. How day by day have I looked forward, with a shuddering and dread at my soul, as I have seen you sinking day by day away from me! But that is past. You are now free once more, and able manfully to stand up and breast the temptation with which the coming years are crowded. There will be no more hindrances, no more hands stretched out to drag you down. If love can shield you, you are safe; for my heart will, for your sake, ever prove constant.

ROMAINE. Yes, years in happiness are in store for us all. And the results of the past few years will serve always as a beacon to warn us of the dangers and temptations that constantly beset the pilgrim on his voyage through life.

MORGAN. Restored once more to happiness, let us hope that others may learn a useful lesson from our past experience, and that none will regret deducting from the calendar of their lives the

TEN NIGHTS IN A BAR-ROOM

As some poor stranger wrecked upon the coast,
With fear and wonder views the dangers past,
So I with dreadful apprehensions stand,
And thank the powers that brought me safe to land;
A drunkard now no longer – that is o'er.
Free, disenthralled, I stand a man once more.

MRS MORGAN

A wife's fond heart with grateful prayers ascend
To Him who proved the drunkard's only friend;
Our angel child, sweet spirit hovering near,
Will bless this hour – this hour to all so dear –
While friends beholding this, our happy home,
Greet us with smiles, and with kind wishes come.

MEHITABLE

Please, ma'am, may I now you've spoke your spoke
Say just one word? Nay, 'tis no joke;
To see you happy fills my heart with glee,
And Sample's happy too, as well as me;
He's named the day when he'll be mine.
Then, *goodness* gracious, won't we shine?

ROMAINE

Our Drama's ended, but the lessons taught
Are with truthful warnings deeply fraught,
So wisely ponder and try while you can –

SWICHEL

Hole on a minnit, Squire, till I try my hand:

While all who are around us will rejoice,
Shall not Sample meet with one encouraging voice

To cheer him while the road is dark and misty,
And help to keep his emancipation from bad whisky?
Who'll jine my cause? Will you? – or you?
You will? – 'nuff sed; we'll put her through.
I'll raise my standard – spread it bold and high:
Down with rummies – 'root, hog, or die!'

CURTAIN

Lost in London

A NEW AND ORIGINAL DRAMA
IN THREE ACTS

———•◉•———

by Watts Phillips

First performed at the Adelphi Theatre, 16 March 1867

CAST

JOB ARMROYD, a miner	*Mr H. Neville*
NELLY ARMROYD, his wife	*Miss Neilson*
GILBERT FEATHERSTONE, owner of the Bleakmoor Mine	*Mr Ashley*
SIR RICHARD LOADER, his friend	*Mr Branscombe*
TIDDY DRAGGLETHORPE, Nelly's friend	*Mrs A. Mellon*
JACK LONGBONES ⎫	*Mr Paul Bedford*
DICK RAINE ⎬ miners	*Mr Aldridge*
NOAH MOORHEAD ⎭	*Mr Tomlin*
BENJAMIN BLINKER, a Cockney servant	*Mr J. L. Toole*
TOPS, a post-boy	*Mr C. J. Smith*
THOMAS ⎱ servants	*Mr W. H. Eburne*
FLOUNCE ⎰	*Miss A. Seaman*

Miners, Guests, Opera singer, Man with lantern

Lost in London: Stock Poster of the Mine Scene

ACT I

SCENE I. – *Interior of* JOB ARMROYD's *cottage. At back, a large latticed window and door. Another door,* R. *Same side, further up stage, a huge fireplace. To* L., *a press; beside it a beer barrel on stand. In window, a wicker cage, containing a blackbird. Between door and window at back, and against wall, hang a variety of mining implements and a safety lamp; in another part of room, a Dutch clock. On window sill, a pot filled with heath in blossom. There is no ceiling, but from crossbeams that support roof are suspended a couple of flitches of bacon, and several ropes of onions. The other furniture of the room very homely and rough. On table, which is covered by a white cloth,* (coarse) NELLY ARMROYD *is arranging* JOB's *breakfast, consisting of bread, cold boiled bacon, and cheese. The clock strikes six.*

NELLY. Six o'clock! Job's late this morning. It'll be the first time these four months he's seen the sun rise. There's no change of season for the poor miner. Summer or winter, it's one endless night. (*While speaking she fills a huge black jack, or tankard, with ale from barrel, and places it on table.*) It's a dreary life – a miner's! (*She sighs.*) And it's a dreary life to be a miner's wife – to sit o' nights a-listening to the wind wailing out o' doors, or rumbling i' the chimney, or to go a-wandering i' the day ow'r the bleak moorland, which even the birds seem to shun. (*She seats herself, or rather sinks into a chair.*) And yet a word of mine can change all this into a life as gay, as bright, and as full of happiness, as this is dreary and desolate. But that word I cannot speak! I *dare* not speak it! (*She rests her arm on table, covering her face with her hands.* JOB *heard singing in inner room. She hurriedly wipes her eyes and looks up.*) He is so happy, too – happy in his love for me – for me. (*The singing inside room strikes into a louder and merrier key –* NELLY *rises.*) Job! Job! my husband! save me from this man! Save me from myself! (*As she makes a step or two towards door a loud tapping is heard at cottage window. She pauses with a gesture of alarm.*)

VOICE (*outside window*). Nelly! Nelly!

NELLY. Heaven help me! He is here! (*The lattice is opened, and* GILBERT FEATHERSTONE *is seen leaning upon window sill. His appearance that of the town bred man of fashion. He is young and handsome, wears a blonde moustache and beard, carefully trimmed à la mode.*)

GILBERT. Is the coast clear? Can I enter?

NELLY (*with a gesture of alarm, and approaching window*). Mr Featherstone, sir, I entreat you.

GILBERT. What's the matter? Have you seen anything of my rascal, Blinker? I sent him to – (*The singing, which had ceased, is renewed, and heavy footsteps heard in room to* L. GILBERT, *who has been leaning into room, draws back, half closing lattice.*) Who's that?

NELLY (*in much agitation*). My husband!

GILBERT. King Coal not gone yet! The devil! (*He hastily closes window as* JOB ARMROYD *lifts the latch of door to left, and puts head into room, while* NELLY, *to hide her agitation, bends over the flowers in window as if arranging them, singing the while with a strained assumption of carelessness.*)

JOB. Sing away, lass! sing away! (*He laughs and shakes his head with an expression of broad good humour.*) I allays say o' thee an' Billy th' blackbird, that there is'na another two such pipes to be found in th' county, an' my heart allays beats time to the music o' thy tongue. (*He pushes door open, and enters, still laughing. He is a fine rough-looking specimen of his class. His face is full of frankness and good humour, and his general appearance that of a hale, strong man in his fiftieth year. He holds in his hand a clumsy looking razor, and in the other a towel – with the latter he, while speaking, wipes off the soap lather from his face.*)

JOB (*laughing and holding out razor*). Look'ee here, Nelly! That whirl 'um gig Tiddy a' been chopping wood wi' my razor ag'in. She be 'most as bad as Tom Moorhead's gell, who

opened a hunder o' oysters wi' his'en – but Tom's such a
soft muzzled chap, he never found it out till told on't. (*He
laughs and rubs chin.*) Mine's a rasper! (*He takes coat from
wall, and is putting it on, laughing and chuckling, when looking
up he sees* NELLY'S *face. Struck by its expression his mirth
vanishes, and he crosses quickly to her, his manner marked by
much homely tenderness.*) What's cast thee down, lass? Art
grievin' cos thy old playmate Tiddy Dragglethorpe be goin'
to Lunnon to tek service an' better her'sen?

NELLY (*pettishly, and moving away*). I wasn't thinking o' Tiddy.
I daresay she's happy enough to quit this lonesome life for
London.

JOB. Whoi, Nell, what a lot o' gibberish thee'st talkin'. The lass
were born here, and it ain't natur' for th' bird to scorn th'
nest in which 'twas hatched. (*He takes loaf from table, and
prepares to cut a slice, laughing as he does so.*) The Lunnoners
may try till they're toired, but they'll no more mek one o'
theer foine birds out o' Tiddy Dragglethorpe than ye can
turn a moor hen into a singin' bird by sticken 'un into a
goolden cage, and fiddlin' to't. Whoi, all th' lords and ladies
in Parliament could'na do't.

NELLY (*sighs*). It's a lonesome life, nevertheless, Job.

JOB (*pausing in the middle of cutting the slice, and looking at* NELLY
in open-eyed astonishment). Lonesome! Thee dunna mean it to
be thee that's lonesome, Nelly? Happen I a' done summut to
worrit thee now? I'm but a slow koind o' a blunderin' chap,
as is allays a-stumblin' ower somebody's shins unbeknown
loike, so you must foind head for us both, Nelly, head for us
both. (*He puts down loaf, and looks at her with a sort of
awkward sadness.*) I'm an old chap alongside o' thee, Nelly,
and twenty year wunna allays think loike fifty.

NELLY (*quickly*). Oh! 'tisn't that, Job! indeed, 'tisn't that!
(*Slowly.*) Only I do think sometimes it would be so pleasant
to live in London. (*She looks down, smoothing apron, so as to
conceal her face from* JOB, *whose countenance still wears a blank,
puzzled look.*) To see, and know more o' the world.

JOB (*his face clearing up*). See Lunnon! Bless'ee lass, thee'd'st be

209

glad enough to get away fro't. (*He takes up loaf, and cuts off a huge slice.*) Theer were my feyther, who'd worked in the pit, man and boy, for sixty year, an' should a' known somethin' o' th' world; well, *he* went to Lunnon, an' (*he gives a contemptuous flourish with knife*) thought nothin' o't! (*Cuts bread and eats.*)

NELLY (*eagerly*). What did he say, Job?

JOB (*eating and speaking slowly*). Say! whoi, he said, that arter bein' theer for more nor two weeks – (*He pauses.*)

NELLY. Well, Job?

JOB (*impressively*). He could'na mek head nor tail o't.

NELLY. What did he see, Job?

JOB. Not much. For what wi' th' clatter an' th' jabber, he wur sure to lose his'sen in th' day time, so he niver stirred out till all t' folk were in bed, an' he could walk aboot wi'out a-breakin' something, or a-treadin' on somebody.

NELLY (*half laughing*). He didn't see much then?

JOB. Well, he got a-nigh drownded, for t'were November time, an' as t' fog were prutty thick, he were allays a-walkin' into th' river. Th' third time they pulled un out, he'd enough o' Lunnon, an' started for hoame th' next mornin'. (*He drinks from tankard.*) 'Job,' said he to me, when he found his'sen once more a-workin' quite comfortable down in th' pit, 'Job, dunna thee gi'e no heed to trav'lers lies, better lose thy'sen down here among th' workin's wi'out a lamp, than be adrift in that theer Lunnon, an' no one to gi'e thee a helpin' hand.'

NELLY. But the mine – think o' the dangers o' the mine, Job.

JOB. True, lass, true, the mine has its faults, o' coorse. Theer's the choke damp as blots out a man's life afore he can lift an eyelid to see o' which side th' death's comin'. Then theer's the fire damp, as scorches a stout lad into a cinder. But nothin's perfect, Nelly, so we mun tek the rough wi' th' smooth. (*He approaches her, and places his hand kindly on her arm.*) But thee'st cause to be afeard of the mine, Nelly – it robbed thee of a feyther, a'most afore thou wert old enough to know the vally on 'un.

NELLY (*her eyes fixed on the ground, and face slightly averted*). Ah, Job, it was a sad burden o' trouble he left you in me.

JOB. Trouble! (*He takes both her hands in his, and, with gentle violence, forces her to look into his face.*) What's gotten into thy noddle, lass? Thou'st never made trouble for no one as belonged to 'ee, least of all to Job Armroyd. Dunna cry, my birdy, dunna cry, I love to see thy cheeks red, not thy eyes. (*He leans over her, and kisses her forehead.*)

TIDDY (*heard singing outside, and passing window*).

> Oi've clogs an' a box full o' clo-o-o-as,
> Just sixpence and tuppence in brass,
> A heart for frien's, a fist for fo-o-o-es,
> Loike a farrantly Lancashire lass.

JOB. Here's Tiddy! Come to say good-bye. They'll be in luck as she teks sarvice wi'. There ain't many such to be met in Lunnon, I'm thinkin', big as 'tis. (*The door of cottage opens, and* TIDDY DRAGGLETHORPE *appears on threshold. She is a strapping, red-cheeked, angular specimen of the genuine Lancashire breed. Her hair drawn back from face, and done up in a large and extremely ragged knot. She is dressed in a very large patterned gown, short in the waist, and with shoulder of mutton sleeves. Beneath the gown a portion of the petticoat is visible, and beneath the petticoat her ankles clothed in coarse knitted blue stockings. She wears upon her feet a pair of Lancashire clogs, which she clatters as she walks. A shawl is tied loosely over her shoulders, so as to give free play to her arms, and one end of it is allowed to draggle on the ground behind her. In her hand she carries an umbrella of huge proportions, with a bundle – a band-box is also slung from her arm. She halts on the threshold, crosses her hands over crook of umbrella, and bending nearly double, bursts into an inordinate fit of laughter, in which* JOB, *smiting his hands upon his knees, immediately joins, and even* NELLY, *in a modified degree, catches the infection.*)

TIDDY. Wull, lad! wull, Nelly! I be coom to say good-bye to 'ee! haw! haw!

JOB (*still laughing*). Thee dunna seem like to croi aboot it.

211

TIDDY (*wiping eyes with end of shawl*). Croi! oi croid all naight till my oies were as big as that. (*Making motions with hands*). An' I should a' croid all th' mornin', but Jack Longbones as carried my box croid all the way here, so o' coorse that sot me off laffin, and haw! haw! haw! when once I get on that road I canna stop. If foine feathers make foine birds, I be a rare one. (*Holding arms wide*.) All th' village ha' gotten up an hour earlier to have a look at oi afore I staart, so I ha' promised to show my 'sen at all their houses, poor things. But (*showing bundle, which she places on chair*) I shall come back here, Nelly, to put on th' old gown and shawl afore gettin' on th' coach, or I should be spoilt long afore I got to Lunnon. (*She comes laughing down stage with bonnet box, which she plumps down in centre of stage, between* JOB *and* NELLY; *at the same time looking from one to the other in triumph*.) Guess what I gotten here, Nelly; or no, let Job try.

JOB (*smiling and shaking head*). Some artificials, or fly aways, I be bound,

NELLY (*peeping as* TIDDY *slowly raises the lid*). It's a bonnet.

TIDDY. O' course it is! They told I, if I didn't want foulk to stare I mun wear a bonnet in Lunnon. So Betty Floyd, who's bin a month in service at Shuttleville, an' knows all th' fashions, lent I a hond wi' un. Here it is! (*She draws forth bonnet, which she holds up in triumph. It is a wildly grotesque bit of invention – coal scuttle in shape and gaudily trimmed.* NELLY *laughs behind her hand, but* JOB, *who seems struck by the elegance of the structure, examines the bonnet on every side*.)

JOB (*rubbing his chin with evident admiration, his gaze still riveted*). It be a beauty sure-ly, but, I say, lass, I'm a-thinkin' none but born'd gentlefolks wear such hots as that.

NELLY (*quickly*). Oh! no! the ladies who came to Shuttleville last year wi' old Sir Gilbert wore little bit bonnets as light an' as white as apple blossoms.

TIDDY. Bless 'ee, lass! them sort o' people can wear onything, but a lonesome lass loike I must'na make herself pecooliar 'mong strangers. (*Replaces bonnet in box*.) Thof if I'd such a face as thine, Nelly, oi'd be sure to please everybody, no matter, what I wear'd.

NELLY. For shame, Tiddy!

TIDDY. On'y yesterday I heard Mester Featherstone say to th' manager that Job Armroyd's wife had better reason to perk her'sen afore a lookin' glass than ha'f the foine town ladies.

NELLY (*confused*). Hold your foolish tongue, Tiddy!

JOB (*laughing uproariously and smiting his sides*). Thee'st no call to redden, my lass! thee'st no call to redden. We mun show Mester Featherstone we a'gotten good looks as well as good foulk in t' county.

TIDDY. I met un in th' lane just now, an' thout he'd coom fro' th' cottage.

JOB. He a'na bin here, but he wur here last naight, an' t' naight afore that, a-waitin' for my comin' home. He be main coorious to know 'bout mining matters, be Mester Featherstone. A civil soft spoken lad as knows a mort, tho' he be town born an' bred. (*Bell of the works heard ringing in the distance.*) Theer goes th' first bell! (JOB *takes down lamp and mining implements, then crosses to* NELLY, TIDDY *having gone up stage to look out at door.*) Good-bye, my wench. (*He kisses her, and, placing his hands upon her shoulders, looks lovingly into her face.*) Mester Featherstone was 'na far fro' th' truth, Nelly. Thee'st a face as pleasant to look on as that bit o' heaven I often see shining up o' top o' th' shaft wi' just a glimmer o' stars in it.

TIDDY. Theer be Jack Longbones! a-sittin' on th' box jest wur I left un. (*She laughs.*) Haw! haw! haw! he *do* look miserable, sure-ly. Here be some o' th' lads, Job.

JOB. Hegh! th' bell's rung. I mun be goin'. (*He is moving towards the door when* JACK LONGBONES, DICK RAINE, NOAH MOOR-HEAD, *and several other* MINERS *enter. They all wear the pit-man's costume, with candles (unlighted) in their hat-bands. They are rough, stalwart, hirsute-looking fellows, and enter tumultuously, laughing, and pushing before them* BENJAMIN BLINKER, *a diminutive, but extremely pompous specimen of the*

London tiger. *He is habited in a green laced frock, leather
breeches, and top boots.*)

BLINKER. Now then! now then! do yer want me to do some on
yer an injury? (*He cocks his hat, and puts his arms akimbo –
aside.*) Poor devils! 'tisn't hoften they see a man like me in
these parts. (*He proceeds to arrange his toilette, whistling the
while 'Champagne Charley' with an air of great nonchalance.*)

JOB (*who is regarding* BLINKER *with puzzled astonishment*). What
kind o' thing hast bro't wi' 'ee, Dick Raine? Sure it wur
niver grow'd hereabouts.

RAINE (*removing his hat and scratching his head dubiously*). I
canna rightly guess what 'tis. Happen it be some sort o'
insect; it looks loike one and speaks furrin'.

BLINKER (*aside*). Brubarians! Ain't never seed a gen'l'man in
livery afore? How shall I catch the heye of th' missus? (*He
continues to whistle, and endeavours to attract* NELLY'S *attention
without being seen by the others.*)

LONGBONES. I see it a stannin' on its two legs, a tryin' to peep
into your winder, Job. So, thinks I, happen that poor
creetur's forgotten theer's a door; an' wishing to be polite
to a stranger, I teks 'un gently up by th' scruff o' th' neck
an' brings 'un in wi' me.

TIDDY (*aside to* NELLY). It be that little tooad Blinker, as be
allays a-worrittin' an' a-coortin' o' me! (*Coming forward and
speaking to* MINERS.) This be Mester Featherstone's toiger,
as they call 'un.

BLINKER. 'Ow d'ye do, Miss D? (*Aside.*) Fine grow'd young
woman that!

TIDDY. An' I wish you'd drag 'un thro' th' horse pond.

BLINKER (*aside*). Decided character too.

JOB. Toiger! He be more like a grasshopper. (*All laugh.*)

BLINKER. Bless yer! I ain't a bit hoffended! (*Urbanely.*) 'Appy
to contribute to the amusement o' the lower classes. 'Tain't
your fault you're hignorant, how could it be? You can't dig
up politeness with a pick haxe.

LONGBONES. Ignorant! What do you mean? (*He advances on

214

BLINKER, *who retreats quickly, so as to place* TIDDY *between them.*)

BLINKER. Don't disturb yourself, my man! Miss D.'s friends are priweleged, but I've a huncle who's been in the ring; the P.R., you know, (*doubling fists*) and biceps run in the family. (*He extends right arm, and manipulates muscle, knowingly.*)

JOB. Lave 'un aloon, Jack, theer's nothin' i' th' creetur worse nor his tongue. (BLINKER *takes advantage of the momentary withdrawal of attention from himself to draw a letter from his pocket, and endeavours to pass it to* NELLY. *It falls to the ground; and* NELLY, *whose manner exhibits great agitation, places her foot quickly upon it, without its being seen by the others,* JOB, *seizing* BLINKER *by the arm, and pulling him forward, just as that gentleman is coughing and winking to attract* NELLY'S *attention.*) Now tell us who owns ye? What are ye chowkin' ower? (*Turns and sees* TIDDY.) Is it Tiddy Dragglethorpe?

BLINKER (*aside*). Wonder whether Mrs A.'s picked up the billy! (*To* JOB, *who shakes him roughly by the arm.*) You'd better take care, my man, I don't wish to be rough with you, but —

JOB (*shaking him*). Were it oi ye wanted to see?

BLINKER. No. (*Aside.*) The meeting's quite unexpected.

JOB (*shaking him*). Who were it then?

BLINKER (*aside*). Now for a bouncer! (*Aloud.*) Her! ! ! (*He points to* TIDDY, *who is lifting a box. She drops it with an exclamation of astonishment.*)

TIDDY. Me! ! !

BLINKER (*aside*). Must keep it up! (*Aloud, and sidling over to* TIDDY, *while* NELLY, *unobserved, picks up note, which she thrusts in her bosom.*) We'd an apintment, jist to say goodbye, an' see her hoff, yer know. (*Aside to* TIDDY.) Hush! it's hall right; hintentions 'onorable, I assure you, Miss D.

TIDDY. A 'pintment wi' oi! Why, you little maggot.

BLINKER (*with gratified smile*). Fond creetur'! Can't hide her feelin's. (*Aside to* TIDDY.) It's all right! I hain't hoffended.

TIDDY (*indignantly*). What's all raight? Get away wi' 'ee, blinkin' at me in that fashion, loike an owl i' an ivy tod!

BLINKER (*aside, with fervour*). She's a splendid woman! such a

215

flow! and such muscle! (*She gives him so smart a push, that he reels back and falls with a crash upon the bonnet box, which is crushed to a pancake.*)

TIDDY. My bonnet! ! ! (*She snatches up box.* MINERS *laughing.*)

BLINKER (*rising*). Re-e-markable woman! Great strength o' mind! (*rubbing himself*) and *arm!* (*He retreats before the infuriated* TIDDY, *who still holds box by cord.*) What a biceps! (*He ducks to avoid blow, and bolts out of door pursued by* TIDDY, *who first flings box after him. The* MINERS *crowd up to door, laughing and clapping hands. Bell rings.*)

LONGBONES (*to* JOB). Be aloive, lad! that's the second bell. (MINERS *go out. Bell to continue ringing.* JOB *collects tools, takes down hat, and approaches* NELLY, *who stands leaning against table, her hand pressed tightly upon her bosom, and her eyes bent upon the ground.*)

JOB (*half serious, half laughing*). I dunna know what's come ower me o' late; I used to be th' first down in th' pit, an' now I'm loike to be th' last. Somehow, when thou talk'st o' bein' lonesome loike a sort o' cloud seems to arise atween us. (*He places his hand upon her arm.*) Thee must'na take me unkind, Nelly, if my ways dunna quite fit wi' thine o' times. I be made o' rougher stuff, I know, but theer's a bit o' pure metal here, Nelly, (*he places his hand upon his breast*) as is allays to be found by thee. (*Kisses her on forehead, and is moving towards door.*)

NELLY (*catching him by sleeve*). Job, do not go! Stay with me!

JOB (*laughing*). Stay wi' 'ee? Nay, nay, that munna be. Thee woulds't na a' Job Armroyd's name get a cross to't as a lag behind.

VOICES OF MINERS (*outside window*). Job! Job!

JOB. Comin' lads! comin'! (*He good humouredly releases himself from* NELLY'S *grasp.*)

NELLY. Job! Job! I *must* speak. Let me speak now. (JOB, *who is at door, turns as struck by a something in her voice; at same moment* LONGBONES *appears on threshold.*)

LONGBONES. Job! the bell's stopped!

JOB. Tonaight, Nelly, tonaight! thee shalt tell me all thy

216

troubles tonaight! (*He exits hastily with* LONGBONES. NELLY *stands for a moment, her arms outstretched, as in appeal, then sinks into chair, and covers her face with her hands.*)

CHORUS OF MINERS (*outside house*).

> Down in the depths o' th' darksome mine,
>   We work thro' a changeless night,
> That comfort round English hearths may shine,
>   And the coal blaze warm and bright,
>   And the coal blaze warm and bright.

As their rough voices die away in the distance, NELLY, *who has raised her head to listen, springs to her feet.*

NELLY. Oh! fool! fool! that I have been to listen to the voice of the tempter, and oh! accursed vanity of woman that gave to that voice such power! (*She draws letter from bosom, opens it, and appears to read a few lines – the letter falls from her hands, which she raises for a moment, then presses convulsively to her bosom.*) Leave him! leave him for ever! I cannot! No, I cannot do it! (*Footsteps heard outside door, and the latch is moved as by someone about to enter.*) It is Job! He has returned! Job! Job! my husband! (*She rushes up stage towards door, but recoils with a cry as it opens, and* GILBERT FEATHERSTONE *appears on threshold.*) Gilbert Featherstone!

GILBERT. Nelly! (*As he advances towards her, she hastily retreats, her hands extended to repel, her face full of alarm.*)

NELLY. No, no, not a step further! not a step! I implore! I entreat! (*She staggers as about to swoon;* GILBERT *springs forward, and catches her in his arms.*)

GILBERT. Nelly! dear Nelly! (*He places her in chair, and kneeling at her feet, presses again and again her hand to his lips, as scene closes.*)

SCENE II. – *A Dreary Moorland. Time, sunrise. In distance the works over the pit's mouth, and a few scattered houses. Shouts heard off stage.*

Enter TOPS, *a post-boy, lazily cracking his whip.*

TOPS. Someone's callin'! Well, let 'un call – they'll call long enough 'fore I looks arter 'un. (*Puts whip under arms, and walks up and down, stamping feet and flapping arms as cold.*) Precious out o' the way place this! I've been a boy at the Shuttleville Arms for nigh on eight an' forty year, an' niver got a job on Bleakmoor afore. (*Shouts repeated.*) They're a-murderin' someone! (*He stands still, and flaps body with arms.*) Let un, so long as *I* ain't the one. I've on'y got to look arter my osses; feelin's ain't paid for by the mile, so I can't afford 'em.

BLINKER *rushes on, his clothes plastered with mud, his hat crushed and down over his eyes. He comes full butt against* TOPS, *and both stagger back from the shock.*

TOPS. Hulloh! Where are *you* comin' to?

BLINKER (*pushing hat from eyes*). Comin' *to!* 'Tain't your fault I've had a chance o' comin' to at all!

TOPS. Why it's Mr Blinker!

BLINKER. And I 'ope Mr Blinker will jist be somebody helse when he finds hisself ag'in in sich a sitiwation. (*Angrily.*)

TOPS. If I'd on'y a' known it wur you, Mr Blinker, I'd a' done my best to help yer – (*aside*) to holler. (*Looking at* BLINKER, *who is wiping his clothes, and appears to be out of breath.*) You've had quite a race, Mr Blinker.

BLINKER. Race! Damme! It was likely to have been a dead heat with me. But, oh! Tops! I love her! *Such* a woman – *all* muscle! Wish my huncle could a' seen her.

TOPS. What woman?

BLINKER. She's left her himpression *here*, (*aside*) and here. (*He alters position of hand, and rubs himself with a rueful grimace.*)

TOPS. Who's *she?*

218

BLINKER. Miss Matilda Dragglethorpe. What are you laughin'
at? Do you know her?

TOPS. Bless 'ee! Tiddy be known for more nor thurty mile
round. She bean't a bad 'un.

BLINKER. She's lovely!

TOPS. Well, theer's plenty of her.

BLINKER (*enthusiastically*). There can't be too much. I hadore a
fine woman. I was struck the very fust time I saw her, (*aside*)
and the last.

TOPS (*looking off*). Here comes Mester Featherstone, so just
gi'e oi a leg up in the saddle. I be main toired a-waitin, and
so be th' osses. (*He exits, cracking whip*, BLINKER *slowly
following him.*)

BLINKER. She's goin' to London. So am I. Touching coincidence!
(*Sighs.*) If she'd on'y consent to be a Blinker, my huncle
would rest 'appier in his grave to know we'd such a biceps in
th' fam'ly. (*He pushes out crown of hat, which has been completely crushed in, holding it up as he exits.*) And such un-
common force o' character! (*As* BLINKER *exits* GILBERT
FEATHERSTONE *and* NELLY *enter hastily. She is wrapped in a
shawl, which she also wears after the fashion of the mantilla over
her head.*)

NELLY (*breathless, and grasping* GILBERT'S *arm as he endeavours
to urge her onward*). Gilbert! Gilbert! My heart fails me! I
must return!

GILBERT (*speaking rapidly, his manner very excited throughout the
scene*). Impossible! There is no backward step upon the path
we have chosen.

NELLY. Ah! Cruel! cruel! (*She pushes him away.*) Surely, of all
bad women I am the worst! (*She weeps.*)

GILBERT (*with a momentary impatience which he restrains*). This
weakness is foolish! It is childish! Listen, Nelly! From the
time I visited Shuttleville with my father last year, and saw
you at the *fête*, your face has been engraven on my heart – an
instant had riveted chains, which an eternity cannot break.

NELLY. And yet you left me without a word of farewell.

GILBERT. My departure was a necessity. Dependent upon my

219

father, I was compelled to make his will my law. He died in Brussels, and I returned to England. Ever thinking of the English rose I had seen blossoming on the desolate moor, I found you again, Nelly; but this time, to my misery, to my madness, you were – a wife!

NELLY. I was an orphan, without a soul to love me but Job. *He* loved me – had cherished me with a father's fondness – had educated me as far as his scanty means would permit. Gratitude, my unprotected position, the whisper of cruel tongues, all combined to urge a decision – and I became his wife.

GILBERT (*encircling her waist with his arm*). Why speak of this now? The time for hesitation is past. I take you to a world of brightness and beauty, where, encircled by a myriad of admirers, you will forget that you have ever known this desolate spot.

NELLY. Forget Job! Never!

GILBERT. Be assured he will forget you.

NELLY. Would I could think so, for to remember *must* be to curse.

GILBERT. Tut! Nelly, you do not know these men.

NELLY. Not know Job Armroyd! Miserable girl that I am, I know him but too well – know the kind heart that never beat but with a thought for the happiness of another, that heart in which I might have nestled for ever, but which I am about to leave bleeding and torn. (*She draws back, clasping her hands.*) Oh! Gilbert! Gilbert! have pity on me! I dare not go. (*She makes a movement as to retreat, but* GILBERT, *seizing her somewhat roughly by the wrist, detains her; at the same moment the voice of* TIDDY *is heard off stage.*)

TIDDY. Nelly! Nelly! (NELLY *starts, and throwing back cloak from her head, turns eagerly towards the voice.*)

NELLY (*calls*). Tiddy!

GILBERT (*with a fierce impatience and stamping his foot*). Silence, are you mad? (*Aside, and looking off.*) Thank Heaven! I see the chaise under the trees! (*He lifts her from the ground, and forces her off, her face still turned and her hands distractedly*

220

extended in the direction of voice, which still continues to cry, 'Nelly! Nelly!')

TIDDY (*rushing on – her costume is much more simple than before*). Nelly! dear Nelly! stop! stop! (*There is a loud crackling of postilion's whip, followed by the rolling of wheels as of a chaise departing at full speed.* TIDDY's *arms, which she has raised in her last appealing cry, fall slowly to her sides.*) Lost! lost! (*She staggers back a few paces as if quite exhausted, leans against tree, and holds up a crumpled letter which she has drawn from her pocket.*) I found this on th' floor o' th' cottage, when I run back just now to change my gownd. She knew it, and yet could say good-bye to me, to *him.* Oh, Nelly! Nelly! who shall break this woefu' news to Job? I canna do't! (*With energy.*) I wonna do't! (*With change of manner.*) And yet I must. 'Twould kill th' lad to coom whoam and no find her theer. I'll go! Go weer? Down th' shaft! ! ! P'raps he may feel it less awfu' loike down theer in th' cruel darkness than up here in th' loight which she made doubly broight for him. Yes, it'll coom best fro' me, for – for – (*the voice breaks with emotion*) he knows I loved her well (*she lifts her apron to her eyes, and bursts into an agony of tears as she exits*).

SCENE III. – *Interior of the Bleakmoor Mine. Varied perspective of galleries and workings, in which* MINERS *are seen passing to and fro with their mining implements and safety lamps. Basket seen ascending and descending shaft.*

CHORUS OF MINERS.

Down in th' depths o' th' darksome mine,
   We work thro' a changeless night,
That comfort round English hearths may shine,
   And the coal blaze warm and bright,
   And the coal blaze warm and bright.

LONGBONES, DICK RAINE, NOAH MOORHEAD *and other* MINERS *come down stage.*

LONGBONES (*after cautiously looking round, takes pipe from pocket*). Eh! lads! who's for a smoke?

NOAH. It be agin rules.

LONGBONES. Rules be hanged! Theer wouldn't be no such rules if them as made 'em were down here.

RAINE. Th' overman's up th' shaft (*taking pipe from pocket*). If we on'y had a light.

NOAH (*holding up safety lamp*). They keep the key o' these precious things up above.

LONGBONES. Let 'em! I opens mine wi' this bit o' rusty iron.

He opens lamp with nail, and is about to light pipe, when it is dashed from his mouth, and the lamp snatched from his hand by JOB ARMROYD, *who comes suddenly between.*

JOB. I'm 'shamed on ye, Jack Longbones! and yo', Dick Raine, as a'worked in this pit, man an' boy, for nigh on forty year, to set these younkers up to break rules made for theer benefit.

LONGBONES (*contemptuously*). Benefit! (*He endeavours to wrest lamp from* JOB, *but the latter thrusts him back, holding him at arm's length, yet laughing good humouredly.*)

JOB. Dinna sot up your bristles, lad. 'Tain't a rough tongue, nor a dark look 'ull skear Job Armroyd. (*He releases* LONGBONES, *and turns to* MINERS.) Tell 'ee what it is, lads. I dinna wish to see foulk ower foolhardy, niver sin' I stood, just fifteen year ago, wi' two hundred white-faced women about this pit's mouth, to see each time that basket coom up, a corpse come wi' it. I were stannin' as may be here, a-holdin' my Nelly by the hand – she wur a little five year old gal then, no higher nor my knee – when all of a suddent, she gi'e a shriek as made my heart stan' still. 'Feyther! it's feyther!' ses she; an' sure enough it *was* her feyther, as had gone down th' mine that mornin' a man wi', to all appearance, a good thirty year more life in him, an' now – (JOB *pauses, and covers his face with his hands.*)

RAINE. Were he dead, Job?

JOB. No, lad, he lived long enough to tek my hand i' both o' his, and pray me to watch over his little wench – now my Nelly. (*Turns to* LONGBONES.) I was'na white-livered, Jack, but I croid like a child when I gi'e my promise, an' saw a sorter light grow up in 's face when he heared it, an' I an't ashamed that my eyes get dim when I think o't now.

LONGBONES (*with sudden outburst of feeling*). Gi'e I thy hand, Job! gi'e I thy hand! We all know how thee'st kept they word to Isaac Bradley, an' what'st done for his da-ter. (*Half a dozen hands are stretched forward to* JOB, *who, half-crying, half-laughing, shakes them all. At the same moment* TIDDY *is seen descending.*)

JOB. Nay! nay, lads! but for Nelly, I should be nought better i' the world nor cumber.

TIDDY *has stepped from basket, and now stands at back of stage, speaking earnestly and with an impassioned gesticulation to the* MINERS, *who group around her. Some of them point to the group of which* JOB *forms the centre. They retain their places, stand fixed and motionless as statues, while* TIDDY *comes hesitatingly down stage. Other* MINERS *come out of the various workings or galleries, and join group at back. A whispering follows – all gaiety vanishes, and leaning on their picks, they watch* TIDDY *with the same riveted gaze of anxious expectation, as she slowly approaches* JOB.

JOB (*gaily*). Now, lads! to work! If I ha' put out thy pipe this mornin' ye shall score a gallon to my 'count at the Featherstone Arms tonight. (*As he is turning to go up stage his eyes rest on* TIDDY'S *pale and terrified face. He retreats a step or two with a cry of astonishment.*) Tiddy! why lass, thee'st gi'en me quite a shake. What brings thee doon in t' pit? I tho'ght thee on th' road to Lunnon.

TIDDY (*her eyes bent on the ground, and speaking very slowly*). I ha' coom to speak to thee, Job.

JOB. What's gone amiss, lass? (*As he approaches her the* MINERS *fall back.*) Thee'st gotten a face like a ghaist!

TIDDY. I ha' got summut to tell thee. (*She looks at him for a moment, then averts her face.*) Summut dreadful, Job!

JOB (*seriously*). Nothin' thee'st need to be 'shamed on, I hope? (*He glances round and encounters the anxious and commiserating looks of the* MINERS.) What's amiss, lads? Ye all look at me as if – (*He turns quickly towards* TIDDY.) Happen all's not well at home? Speak, lass! Why dinna thee speak?

TIDDY (*with much feeling*). Oh! Job! dear, good Job! thee know'st nobody loved her better nor I.

JOB. Her!

TIDDY. Nelly! (*Struck by sudden pallor of his face, she pauses, but as he catches her roughly by the arm, and draws her towards him.*) Oh! Job, lad, I canna, canna say it!

JOB (*in a tremulous voice, which he in vain endeavours to render firm*). Happen she's ill? She's been sore changed for days past – not her'sen like.

TIDDY (*with an outburst of grief*). She's gone, Job! She's gone!

JOB (*staggers back as from a blow and drops lamp which he has been holding*). Not dead! She's not dead?

TIDDY. Worse nor that! – far worse – she be gone wi' – wi' –

JOB (*fiercely*). Out wi' it, woman! Speak! and dinna look at me i' that fashion!

TIDDY. Wi' Mester Gilbert! She be gone wi' Mester Featherstone!

JOB (*as speaking to himself, his eyes still riveted on* TIDDY's *face*). Gone! My Nelly! my – (*He turns suddenly towards the* MINERS.) It's a lie. (*He makes a step towards them, pauses, looks from one to the other, and laughs faintly.*) I ain't to be caught wi' your starin' an' gapin'. Ye'd get the laugh agin me 'cos I be one o' th' home birds as like to nestle under th' thack. (*Impatiently.*) Why dunna speak, some o' ye? (*Raises his hand to his throat and tears open his neckerchief, his breast heaving with the endeavour to suppress his emotion.*) I feel as tho' th' choke damp had gotten hold o' me somehow. (*He again forces a laugh and turns to* TIDDY.) It's not true, Tiddy! It's spoort – it be cruel spoort though, but I wunna complain o' that – on'y say it's not true, Tiddy!

TIDDY (*solemnly*). It's Holy truth, Job. (JOB *stands, his eyes fixed on* TIDDY, *his arms for a few moments retaining their imploring gesture. Then he makes a step or two in a wandering and vacant way. He staggers, and* TIDDY *catches him by the arm.*)

JOB (*with a strange, puzzled smile*). Thank'ee, Tiddy, thank'ee – thee were't allays a good gell, allays. (*He raises his hands to his face with the expression of one who has been stunned by a sudden shock.*)

LONGBONES (*aside to* RAINE). He be gone daft, I think.

RAINE. Poor Job! I pity 'un.

JOB (*turning quickly towards them*). Eh! lads! dunna pity me! pity her, poor child, pity *her!* (*He stops, his voice becoming inarticulate from emotion.*)

TIDDY. I doubt she be gone to Lunnon.

JOB. Loike enough! loike enough! (*He again pauses, a gleam of hope for a moment irradiating his face.*) But, Tiddy, art sure that – that – I canna speak his name. Art sure she were wi' un?

TIDDY. I saw 'un lift her into th' chay – an' afore I follered 'em I found this. (*Gives letter.*)

JOB. It be his writin'. I know it, 'cos he were allays scribblin' daan bits o' things when he coomed talking abaat th' mine. (*He glances at the paper, then passes his hand quickly across his eyes.*) I canna fix it no how – I canna read *her* shame. (*He tears letter, and places his foot upon the fragments.*) He's turned her poor head, the villain! wi's fine talk, an' fine clothes – but her heart ain't bad – she niver had a bad heart, my poor Nell.

LONGBONES (*to* MINERS). It be cruel hard to work for such a man.

JOB (*fiercely*). Work! I wunna raise hand for *that* man again 'xcept to be to strike 'un dead!!! (*He moves,* TIDDY *clinging to his arm. In the faces of the* MINERS *there appears an indignant sympathy.*)

TIDDY. What'll ye do, lad? What'll ye do?

JOB (*his head erect, and speaking very firm*). My duty! I've but one road to take, an' that's th' straight one. I know she be a poor lost creetur – to all but me – to all but me. (*He stands in centre of stage,* TIDDY *by his side, the* MINERS *grouped picturesquely about, but all with their eyes on him.*)

LONGBONES (*who has taken* JOB's *hand*). It be a weary way to Lunnon, lad!

JOB (*with much emotion*). The dead a' gotten my word that I'd tak' care o' her, an' I *wull*. I'll find her were the world twice as wide! Coom, lass! croyin' wunna help her. (*He steps into basket followed by* TIDDY.) Let's be goin' up into th' world – th' world! ! ! (*He points up shaft. The* MINERS, *who now crowd scene, all uncover heads as the basket slowly ascends,* JOB *standing erect, and pointing upwards,* TIDDY *kneeling at his feet, her face hidden in her hands. As second basket descends give signal for curtain – slow.*)

Lost in London: Stock poster of the Snow Scene.

ACT II

SCENE I. – *Interior of* GILBERT FEATHERSTONE'S *Villa, Regent's Park. Evening drawing on. A sitting room luxuriously furnished. Windows at back, through which is seen a snow effect. Doors left and right curtained after the French fashion; also, further up the stage,* R., *folding doors, so placed that by cutting off corner of apartment they partly face audience. A fire is burning in the chimney,* L., *which is faced on* R. *side of room by a cabinet piano, open. On right of scene, and near table, a causeuse, fauteuils, and several light and elegant articles of furniture scattered about.* FLOUNCE *arranging flowers in a vase, which she places on piano,* R., *while* BLINKER, *standing near table,* L., *is seen taking up several folded newspapers, one after the other.*

BLINKER (*contemptuously throwing down papers*). Times! bah! Public Opinion! pish! The Pall Mall! pshaw! Hathenaeum! Well, I never! Ah! here it is! (*Joyfully unfolding paper.*) Bell's Life!!! When a chap has been a hexile from Halbion for nigh six months he gets to know the wally of a noospaper. (*He reads.*) 'The Chicken, though his head was now as big as two, and the shutters up to both peepers, looked quite pleasant and lively, and came to the scratch brisk and smiling.' Ah, (*smacking lips*) there's style! When a man reads such writing as *that*, he feels hisself a Henglishman. (*He throws himself back on sofa, and appears lost in enjoyment of paper.*)

FLOUNCE. What do you find so interesting in the paper, Mr Blinker? Is it a murder?

BLINKER (*testily*). No.

FLOUNCE. Something in the Divorce Court, p'r'aps.

BLINKER. Well, it's much the same sort o' thing. (*Reads.*) 'The Ring! Spirited set to! Interposition of the authorities.' This is the reading I like, Mrs Flounce; no sentiment, or that kind o' stuff, but muscle in every line of it. If ever I'm blessed with a little Blinker, or, say, half-a-dozen little Blinkers, they shall be brought up on *Bell's Life* every one of 'em.

FLOUNCE. Lor!

BLINKER. Muscular Christianity – it's all the go, now, Mrs F. Directly a child can move its fists, put the gloves on 'em. (*He strikes a sparring attitude – sighs, and shakes his head.*) The gloves! Ah! I once knew a woman who'd have been a credit to 'em.

FLOUNCE (*laughing*). Was she a muscular Christian?

BLINKER (*enthusiastically*). She were! We met in Lancashire just afore Featherstone and me started for the continent.

FLOUNCE. Why, that's six months ago! What a memory you have, Mr Blinker. Was she in love with you?

BLINKER. She must a'been – she pursued me everywhere. I shall never forget her – never!

FLOUNCE (*coming close to him*). Never? (*She leans upon his shoulder, looking coquettishly into his face.*) Not if you found another such a heart?

BLINKER. Heart! It was her arm! (*Sighs.*) Such a biceps. You see, Mrs Flounce, connected as I am, through my late huncle, with the P.R., muscle's a disideratum: I owe it to the fam'ly. Now, you're but a poor weak thing! Too much of the sex, you know.

FLOUNCE. What do you mean, you Lillyproochin? (*Shaking him by the collar.*) Haven't I muscle enough for such a mite as you? (*She releases him, and he falls back on sofa.*)

BLINKER (*with melancholy approval*). It's something, just a little. But, bless yer, its nothing to *her*. She knew *how* to lay it on. I never shall forget her – never! (THOMAS, *opening folding doors, looks in, and seeing only* FLOUNCE *and* BLINKER, *comes lounging down.*)

THOMAS. Missus wisible?

FLOUNCE. She hasn't left her room all day. What is it, Mr Thomas?

THOMAS. Here's that country gal been ag'in 'bout the 'ouse-maid's place.

FLOUNCE. I'll see her.

THOMAS. But she says she always treats with principals, and must see if the missus suits as well as the sitiwation. She's a rum 'un, reg'lar original. (*Crosses to table.*) Is the *Post* anywheres among them papers, Mr Blinker? Thank 'ee. (*Putting paper in pocket.*) I'll just throw a heye over the fash'nabble hintelligents. (*Thundering double knock heard as from street.*)

BLINKER. That's Featherstone.

FLOUNCE. In a tantrum, as usual.

BLINKER. I always know when anything's gone wrong with the guv'nor, he do so take it out of the knocker. (*Knocking repeated.*)

THOMAS. Drat the knocker! I wish he'd screw it off! (*He exits.*)

BLINKER. Featherstone's been out with Sir Richard Loader all day.

FLOUNCE. And all night. Not that there's much to keep him at home. Missus does nothing but mope. You never come upon her alone but she's tears in her eyes.

BLINKER. My late huncle was a bacheldor, Mrs Flounce; and it was one of his obserwations, that marriage was like a haction at law, there were sure to be one person dissatisfied. But, alking of marriage, can you keep a secret? (*He mysteriously approaches her.*)

FLOUNCE (*eagerly*). Certainly.

BLINKER (*who has made movement to whisper in her ear, stops, looks full in her face, and shakes his head*). No, I see it won't do. You've too much o' the sex about yer.

FLOUNCE (*angrily*). You provoking little – Hush! here's missus! (*They draw back as* NELLY ARMROYD *enters. She is very plainly though richly dressed. Her face is pale, and her general demeanour more subdued than in Act I. As she crosses the stage,* BLINKER *exits;* FLOUNCE *advances.*)

NELLY. You need not wait, Flounce.

FLOUNCE. Can I do anything for you, madam?

NELLY. Thank you, no. (*She seats herself beside table, and takes some work, which she is embroidering, from basket.* FLOUNCE *is about to place her hand on lock of doors when they are flung roughly open, and* GILBERT FEATHERSTONE *enters – his appearance much the same as in Act I – manner somewhat more brusque and careless. His type is that of the half foppish, half blasé man of fashion.*)

GILBERT (*who has nearly stumbled over* FLOUNCE). Deuce take the women! they're always in the way!

FLOUNCE (*bridling*). Well I'm sure, sir, I –

GILBERT. Pshaw! don't talk, but go. (FLOUNCE *sweeps out indignantly.*) Set a woman's tongue once in motion, and stop it who can. (*Comes down stage, stands for a moment in centre looking at* NELLY, *who continues to work. He shrugs his shoulders impatiently, crosses to fireplace, and placing hand upon chimney piece warms one foot, then the other at the blaze – he still keeps on hat – aside.*) Curse this weather! Snow without, and (*glances over shoulder at* NELLY) ice within. (*Shrugs his shoulders again, turns his back to fire, still leaning against chimney piece, and speaks aloud.*) Not a word! Egad! if you're as free from every other fault of your sex as that of over much talking, you only lack wings to be an angel.

NELLY (*laying down work wearily*). What would you have me say?

GILBERT. Say! say! Oh! anything! Say you're glad to see me; it's polite, if not true.

NELLY (*gently*). I am glad you've returned.

GILBERT. Come, that's something. Let's get a little brightness somewhere. Bother these coals! They're hard as a money-lender's heart, and no more warmth in 'em! (*Laughs and lays down poker.*) Mustn't speak against coals, though. But for that Tom Tiddler's Ground at Bleakmoor, Loader and the rest of these fellows would find it difficult to pick up their gold and their silver. (*Takes off hat, and, as he turns in chair to place it on table, sees* NELLY'S *face.*)

GILBERT (*rising*). What's the matter? Are you ill? (*Testily.*) Must the mere mention of that place always affect you thus?

NELLY. It is not that – not altogether that – but (*Rests one hand, as for support, upon table, the other she presses to her bosom convulsively.*)

GILBERT (*gaily*). Nonsense, Nelly. It's time you banished such dismal thoughts; with most women I've known, a six months' absence has been equivalent to an eternity. I'd wager they've forgotten *you* long ago.

NELLY (*clasping her hands with fervour*). Would I could think so. I would not have one thought of me linger in their honest hearts.

GILBERT (*turns away impatiently, and begins tossing over visitors' cards*). Tra! la! la! Always in the same key. A song that never changes is apt to become monotonous. Hilloh! (*Taking up card.*) Signora Simondi! I thought she was in Milan.

NELLY. She called this morning.

GILBERT. 'Signora Marrietta Simondi.' (*Laughs.*) Think of pretty Mary Symonds turning up in this shape. Returned to change her Italian notes into English gold, I suppose. What did the Signora say?

NELLY. I did not see her.

GILBERT (*surprised*). Were you from home?

NELLY. I was indisposed. I – I – did not see her. I did not wish to see her.

GILBERT. Umph! (*Tosses over cards.*) Flora Gauzely, Madame D'Alton, Signora Cavallas. Why, here's a perfect nest of singing birds. We shall have a large gathering tonight.

NELLY. Tonight?

GILBERT. Sorry to put you out, but it was only arranged this morning. I want to have my revenge on Loader for the money I lost in his rooms, and, as it's an off night at the opera, I thought we might kill two birds with one stone by just throwing our doors open for a few hours. The house wants an airing, for, egad! you've kept it hermetically sealed since our return from the Continent. D'Alton promised to let you know all about it this morning, but as you chose to be invisible to all comers, you've only yourself to thank for the shortness of the notice. Nelly, when you are

again asked to take wine, oblige me by not saying that you
don't like it.

NELLY (*forcing smile*). But if I *don't* like it?

GILBERT. Say you do. The true secret of good breeding is to
appear to like everything. (*He lounges across room to piano,
against which* NELLY *is leaning; he runs his fingers carelessly
over keys.*) Why, here's a string broken! Have you observed
it?

NELLY. How should I? You know I cannot play.

GILBERT. I beg your pardon. I had forgotten. (*Turns to* NELLY,
laughing.) That reminds me – you fell asleep at the opera.
By Jove! you did – fast as a church! 'pon my honour! Curious,
isn't it? You don't play, and you hate singing.

NELLY (*with an emotion he does not perceive*). Indeed I do not. I
used to sing once.

GILBERT (*gaily*). Once! and why not now? Ah! here's that thing
which D'Alton sings so well – you should learn it. (*He plays
an air and a few bars of accompaniment; then sings.*)

> As flowers to their stem,
>   As leaves unto the tree,
> He swore to cling like them
>   To thee, poor heart! to thee.
> But flowers soon grow wan,
>   And leaves forsake the tree,
> The false one now is gone
>   From thee, poor heart! from thee;
>   From thee,
>   From thee, poor heart! from thee.

NELLY (*upon whose face has appeared the struggle of her contending
emotions during the singing, utters a stifled cry as of pain, and
presses her hand tightly on her heart*). Oh, my heart is breaking!
(*She makes a few faltering steps from piano, then, with another
low cry, half sob, half sigh, sinks into chair.*)

GILBERT (*who has sprung up in alarm*). What is this? Are you
ill? You are pale as death! (*He stoops over her, but she rises
quickly and gently but firmly repulses him.*)

233

NELLY. It is nothing! – a pain that will pass; but – but I cannot receive your guests tonight.

GILBERT. How! (*With rising anger.*) Are you mad? Loader, Gosling, D'Alton, all of them will be here in a few hours. Postponement is out of the question. It is my wish! Nay, it is my command you receive them.

NELLY. Your command?

GILBERT (*who has been pacing room impatiently, pauses*). Be reasonable, and reflect. These people are asked – I'm sorry for it now – but the thing is done. It is our first reception, and, if you will have it so, it shall be our last; but I should never hear the end of it if these fellows –

NELLY (*coldly*). You have the *power* to command.

GILBERT. Command! No, no – I *entreat!* For an hour – half-an-hour – a few minutes only. The heat of the rooms – a dozen things will furnish an excuse for your abrupt departure.

NELLY. I obey.

GILBERT (*with some awkwardness*). Obey, pshaw! (*Takes up fan which he keeps opening and shutting nervously.*) Use another phrase. I'm no tyrant – nor – (*Clock on chimney-piece strikes the hour.*) By Jove! it's seven o'clock! Well, I've your promise; but remember, our friends are punctual. (*With assumed gaiety.*) You will not fail us, Nelly?

NELLY. I have told you I obey. (*She turns away and sinks in chair;* GILBERT *makes a step or two towards her – the smile has vanished from his face – and he strikes the fan he still holds fiercely upon the palm of the other hand.*)

GILBERT. Be it so; for once, then, I – I – (*outburst of temper*) command! (*Snaps fan in two, and casts fragments in fire; snatches hat from table: pauses; again looks at* NELLY, *then exits hurriedly.*)

NELLY. Oh! I cannot bear this splendid misery. This bitter, bitter burthen of an ever-present past. It kills me; *yes*, it is killing me, I am sure. (*Going towards door.*) Wealth undreamt of – luxury unbounded – yet not a friend in this wide world! Not *one!* (*As she exits, the folding doors at back are opened, and* THOMAS *enters, ushering in* TIDDY DRAGGLE-

234

THORPE. *The costume of the latter is much modified from that in Act I. She has the appearance of a rough maid-of-all-work, with a considerable dash of country in her aspect. She carries an umbrella and pattens.*)

THOMAS (*entering*). Here's the young 'ooman come after the 'ousemaid's place, m'am. (*Looking round.*) There ain't no one! Gone to dress, I s'pose; we've no end o' company a-coming tonight.

TIDDY. Then mine's not wanted.

THOMAS. Stop! I'd better say you're here – they may want you to wait tonight. You can wait, I s'pose?

TIDDY. As I ha' waited ha'f th' day, another hour wunna mak' a difference.

THOMAS. I mean, can you wait at table?

TIDDY. Thank'ee, lad, I'd liefer wait here. (*Seating herself in fauteuil.*) Dunna stan' theer loike a mawkin'. Get off wi' 'ee, an' tell th' missus I'm coom.

THOMAS (*who has watched her movements with an open-mouthed astonishment*). Ha! ha! ha! Well, I never! Ha! ha! ha! (*Exits laughing.*)

TIDDY (*half rising, and looking everywhere about*). What's he laffin' at, the gawk? Haw, haw, haw! It be lucky I dunna see it – on'y set I off, an' I be like Tom Carman's team – there be no pullin' I up in a hurry. (*She is about to place on floor the pattens she holds, and which are covered with mud, when she looks at carpet and shakes her head.*) That be loike I allays goin' to spoil somethin'. (*She claps them down on small gilt table by her side, rises, and leaning on umbrella, again surveys room.*) It be mortal foine here! If th' missus be on'y ha'f as foine she wunna suit. I been in Lunnon six months, an' a' had as many missusses, till I a gotten toired o' cordin' an' uncordin' my box. I think them missusses wur invented to be my tarmint. I canna put up wi' none o' 'em. This be the card they gi'e I at th' office. 'Y. Z., The Ferns, Regent's Park.' I wonder what Y. Z. be loike! I a' been through all the alphabut, and am glad I a' got to the end on't at last. (*She drops card, and is stooping to pick it up, her back towards door, as NELLY re-enters.*

The latter is advancing towards her, when, raising her eyes, she sees TIDDY'S *face reflected in the great chimney glass.*)

NELLY (*aside, and with a gesture of horrified surprise*). Tiddy! ! !
(*She makes a movement as about to retreat, but her strength fails her, and she leans for support against piano, her face averted from* TIDDY.)

TIDDY (*turns and curtseys*). My service to'ee, ma'am.

NELLY (*aside*). I dare not speak!

TIDDY. You're Y. Z., ain't ye, ma'am? The Ferns, Regent's Park. Th' lad at the registry-office sot it all down. (*She curtseys.*) I'm Tiddy Dragglethorpe, o' Bleakmoor, a Lancashire body. (*She has approached* NELLY *while speaking, when, struck by her averted head and drooping attitude, her tone softens into one of kindly anxiety.*) Ye are 'na ill, ma'am? (*In alarm aside.*) She be all a tremblin' as wi' th' aguey fit. (*Aloud.*) Ye *are* ill, ma'am; I'll call someone!

NELLY (*hastily, but in a low voice*). No! no! Call no one! I shall be better soon, better in my room – don't approach me! (*With face still averted* NELLY *moves a few steps towards door, but her strength fails her, and she sinks, after a vain effort to save herself.*)

TIDDY (*who has started with a strange confused look at sound of* NELLY'S *voice, springs forward*). Mercy me, she a' swound! Let me lift ye to th' sofy, ma'am. (*She bends over her, but* NELLY *shrinks from her extended hands.*) Nay, thee must'na stay theer. Be 'na frighted o' me. I be a rough lass, but a' coom o' honest foulk. (*She stoops to raise* NELLY, *but the latter, still shrinking from her, rises hastily to her feet. In rising, she discovers her face to* TIDDY, *who starts back with a cry and uplifted hands.*) Hegh! hegh! It's Nelly! Nelly Armroyd! (*The two women stand some paces apart –* TIDDY *erect, her head lifted up, and her face full of mingled sorrow and indignation.* NELLY, *her head bent, seems to droop under the riveted gaze of the other. Suddenly,* TIDDY, *after drawing a step or two off, moves quickly towards door at back, at the same time fastening bonnet strings tightly. The movement seems to awaken* NELLY *from her stupor.*)

NELLY. Tiddy! Tiddy! would you leave me thus – thus, without a word!

TIDDY. What words can I speak to ye, Nelly Armroyd, that 'ull not be words o' reproach? We a' talked too often together in th' ould happy times for me to trust my'sen to 'ee now.

NELLY (*with an imploring gesture*). Speak as you will! Heap reproach upon reproach – only stay, if but for a few brief moments, that I may hear the old familiar voice yet once again before I die. (*She presses her hand on her breast.*) My heart is breaking, Tiddy!

TIDDY (*coldly, and without moving*). Thee'st broke a better heart nor either thine or mine.

NELLY. Broken! (*She catches* TIDDY's *sleeve as the latter is turning away.*) You must not leave me, and those terrible words unexplained. Tiddy! Tiddy! if only in remembrance of the dear old times, when two happy children we played together – say – is it my – my –

TIDDY (*stopping her by a gesture*). I spoke o' one who be nought to thee – as thee'rt nought to him. I spoke o' Job Armroyd.

NELLY (*removing her grasp from* TIDDY's *sleeve – draws back – she speaks in a voice of plaintive emotion*). Pardon me! I was wrong to detain you. Farewell! and forget that we have met. (*She comes down stage with faltering steps,* TIDDY *watching her with a contracted brow and compressed lips, as* NELLY *reaches fauteuil, upon the back of which she places her hands.* TIDDY *again turns to leave room, when* NELLY, *with a low moan, lets her head sink down, so that her forehead rests upon her clasped hands.* TIDDY *starts, comes a few paces down stage, and pauses irresolutely. Another loud sob from* NELLY, *and her firmness quite deserts her.*)

TIDDY. Nelly! Nelly! my own dear Nelly! I canna part wi' 'ee so. (NELLY *raises her head with a look of wild, eager hope.* TIDDY *essays to speak, but her voice dies away in one word –* TIDDY *extending her arms.*) Nelly! (*With a cry,* NELLY *springs towards her, and the two are locked in each other's arms –* TIDDY *gently smoothing* NELLY's *hair, as the sobbing woman rests her head upon her shoulder.*) Dunna croi so, dearee! Dunna croi!

237

It be but a wearisome world for us all, an' we mun forgi'e as we hope to be forgi'en.

NELLY. Do not leave me, Tiddy! I have prayed to see no one – to be forgotten by all those who, who – but (*grasping her dress*) do not leave me, Tiddy. (*They come down stage and seat themselves on sofa,* NELLY *still clinging to* TIDDY. *It is now quite evening; the stage has darkened gradually.*)

TIDDY (*tenderly, as speaking to a child*). Hush! dearee, hush! You are 'na happy, I know. It's not in natur', for where th' tree war first planted theer th' roots mun be.

NELLY. Happy! My life is one long agony. I have grown to be a fearful thing to myself! (*She raises her head and looks eagerly in* TIDDY's *face, her hands resting on her shoulders.*) You are the same – the same dear Tiddy; while I – it is but six months since we parted – and how changed, how changed, in face and heart.

TIDDY (*after a pause, during which they attentively regard each other – each holding the other's hands*). He be sore changed too.

NELLY (*bending her head*). You have seen him.

TIDDY. Eh, lass! but a few hours ago. (NELLY *starts.*) He a' been in Lunnon these six months – all that weary time he a' sought for thee.

NELLY (*in alarm*). For me! (*She would rise, but* TIDDY *restrains her.*)

TIDDY. He canna forget bygones, Nelly! He seeks thee everywhere – workin' i'th' day for enough to keep life wi', he wanders after naight fall, fur an' wide, seekin' some trace o' thee.

NELLY (*in alarm, with wild energy*). He must find none! I am dead – do you hear? Dead to him, to all! (*She seizes* TIDDY's *hands.*) Promise you will forget that we have met – that you have seen me! I would not have him look upon me again – not alive! Tiddy! Tiddy! I entreat – I implore you! grant me this last request!

TIDDY. I dare'na; I a' niver told a lie to him, an' I would'na look in 'is face, an' know 'im so bowed down wi' care an' sufferin', an' deceive 'im now.

NELLY (*with an almost fierce excitement*). You must not say we have met! (*Seizes* TIDDY's *arm.*) You shall not go! Not a step till you have promised never to speak to him of me! (*Her tone changes into one of great supplication.*) Oh think, Tiddy, it is my last request! In memory of the old bright days, that never, never can return, give me your promise! Nay, you shall not stir! On my knees I ask it! Forget me! and oh! let *him* forget!

TIDDY. Dunna kneel! Oh! dunna kneel to me, dearee! I never contrairied thee in ought (*with a burst of emotion*), an' I wunna contrairy thee now! (*She raises her.*)

NELLY. You will grant me this boon? You will grant it, you must – (*clinging to her almost fiercely*) you *shall!*

TIDDY (*caressingly*). Yes, yes! on'y dunna look so scared – thou'rt white as a sheet, and all of a tremble loike. Come, dearee, canna thee foind one o' thy old smiles for Tiddy? Thee used to laugh at I rarely once – jest for laffin's sake. (NELLY *raises her hand and a faint smile rests for a moment on her lips; it passes away as quickly.*)

NELLY. I cannot smile! (*She bursts into tears, and her head sinks on* TIDDY's *shoulder.*) Oh! Tiddy! Tiddy! my heart is breaking! breaking! breaking! (*The folding doors at back open suddenly, and* THOMAS *appears on threshold, carrying a handsome candellabra, lighted, which illumines scene.* FLOUNCE *appears at same time at door on left, both stand as paralysed by a horrified astonishment at the sight of the two unconscious women seated on sofa and locked in each other's arms – tableau.*)

SCENE II. – *An Ante-room at the Ferns. Window showing trees, &c., laden with snow.*

Enter BLINKER *twisting letter in his hands and peeping inside.*

BLINKER. Another letter for Sir Richard Loader! My master

and him must be very intimate, to judge by the quantity of their correspondings. They're always a-writin' backwards and forrards. Exchange o' notes they call it (*peeping into side of letter*). Notes o' exchange, *I* calls it. An exchange in which, as far as Loader's concerned, there's plenty o' robbery. He's a bad 'un, is Loader – one o' those glow-worm people as shine only by night. Featherstone, now, isn't all bad, though it's equally certain he isn't all good. As my ree-spectable and ree-spected huncle used to say, 'knavery and honesty are both nice things in their way. Like brandy and water, all depends on how you mix 'em. A quantity of the former with a modifying dash of the latter and you go through the world tri-humphant.'

Enter FLOUNCE.

FLOUNCE (*laughing*). Oh! Mr Blinker, come here and help me to laugh! (*She is about to sink on his shoulder.* BLINKER *slips aside and she nearly tumbles.*)

BLINKER. Always 'appy to assist a female in distress, but in your case it's *quite* the contrary. What's the joke?

FLOUNCE. Only think of missus (*ironically and with half curtsey*), my lady! hugging and kissing a vulgar creature in a dress not worth sixpence a yard, and (*with intense disgust*) in pattens.

BLINKER. You don't mean it?

THOMAS (*entering*). She do! It were hawful. My ears stood on end with 'orror.

BLINKER. And they won't go down in a hurry. (*To* FLOUNCE.) Compose yourself. (*To* THOMAS.) Use pheeloosaphy.

THOMAS. I resign my place tomorrow.

FLOUNCE. And I go with Thomas. Pattens, indeed! I hope I've a character to lose.

BLINKER. Do you? do you really? You must be a very sanguine young woman. But I'm hoff with this letter.

THOMAS. While I show out the lady in pattens.

FLOUNCE. And with the gingham umbrella. Ha! ha! ha!

THOMAS. Ha! ha! ha!

BLINKER. Ha! ha! ha! Ah! (*Sighs.*) *I* knew a woman once – a hangel! She wore pattens, too, and also carried a gingham!

FLOUNCE (*sneer*). She must have been charming.

BLINKER (*solemnly*). She were. She'd a heart like butter and a biceps as hard as a flint. (*Sighs.*) She'd have made you laugh t'other side *of your* mouth, Mr Thomas. (*Bell rings.*)

FLOUNCE. That's missus' bell, and clickety-clank, clickety-clank, here's her *friend* coming down stairs.

BLINKER. Then I'm hoff.

THOMAS. Haven't you any curiosity?

BLINKER. Not the least. (*Aside, as he exits.*) Oh, Tiddy! shall we hever meet again? (THOMAS *and* FLOUNCE, *grinning and nudging each other, move up stage a little as* TIDDY *enters.*)

TIDDY (*without at first seeing them and wiping her eyes*). I ha' tried so to harden my heart again th' sights an' sounds o' this cruel Lunnon that I thou't I hand't a good croi left in me. But to help an' comfort my poor Nell, I'd – I'd – Theer, (*dashing hand impatiently across eyes*) I'm at it again. *They* shan't see me croi anyhow, though I chokes my'sen by swallowin' every tear. (*She gives a great gulp and turns on* THOMAS.) Show me out.

THOMAS (*sneering*). Doesn't the place suit?

TIDDY. Noa, nor the company.

FLOUNCE (*bridling*). Well, I'm sure. I'll soon rid you of mine.

TIDDY. 'Twould take a bigger house nor this to hold we three, I'm thinking; (*exit* FLOUNCE) and keep the windows whole and roof entire. (*She puts on pattens, draws shawl about her, and straightens herself suddenly up.*) Which is the way out?

THOMAS. I'll show you, but don't be angry.

TIDDY. Angry! What, angered wi' a thing loike thee? I'd as soon think o' quarrelling wi' a worry crow for flutterin' its rags in a farmer's field. (*Taking out coin and flinging it on ground.*) There's a shillin' for thee. I ain't many to spare, but I would'na be beholden to thee for the turnin' of a lock. Open the door! (*As* THOMAS *is moving to side, she stays him with her umbrella.*) Stop! On second thoughts I'll do't myself. It's not for the loikes o' you to walk afore the loikes o' me. (*She*

241

thrusts him back, still with her umbrella held lengthways, and passes out with a crushing dignity.)

THOMAS (*astounded*). Wul-garity!!! (*Makes a step towards side, stops, returns, stoops, picks up shilling, places it in his pocket with a wink, and exits.*)

SCENE III. – *Exterior of the Ferns.* FEATHERSTONE's *Villa, and picturesque view of other villas in varied perspective. This set should partake of those characteristics which form what is called a realistic and sensational scene. A great snow effect. Scene brightens gradually, as the various windows and distant gas lamps are lighted up. As scene progresses, broughams, &c., can be driven on if necessary, and all the minor out-door details which accompany the giving of a grand evening party.* FEATHERSTONE's *villa has handsome portico, with large practical doors. This portico is placed as to present its front obliquely to audience. Above this portico a window, which remains dark some time after the rest of the house is brightly illuminated. Snow falling in scattered flakes at first, afterwards more thickly.*

BLINKER (*runs on, blowing fingers*). Here's weather! Blessed if I'd send a dog out on a herrand tonight. But Featherstone's no 'art – never had. To hear him speak when he's got on his company manners, you'd think butter wouldn't melt in his mouth. Those hoily, insinuating chaps, they twists and they winds like corkscrews, till once they've got a *hold* and then – pop! – (*imitates drawing cork*) – who likes may 'av the hempty bottle. (*Slips and falls.*) That makes the tenth slide I've been down on 'tween this an' Cumberlan' Gate. (*Rising and rubbing off snow.*) If I didn't come of a strong fam'ly an' hadn't the constatushun of a 'os, I couldn't stand sich a life. If my haunt would only die an' leave me fifty pun, I'd take a public 'ouse, a skittle-ground for the lower horders, an' a rat-pit for the gentry, with a grand set-to every night in the back parlour. (*Throws himself into sparring attitude; as he strikes out, his foot slips, and he nearly falls.*) Keep the pot a-boiling! That makes the eleventh! Another 'll make up the dozen! (*While he is talking,* TIDDY *comes out of house. She stands on step endeavouring to open umbrella, without seeing or being seen by* BLINKER. *As the latter turns to ascend steps, she opens the umbrella with a burst,* BLINKER *starts back, slips, and goes down.*) Com-plete! Twelve exactly.

TIDDY (*peering over rim of umbrella*). Who's theer?

BLINKER (*sitting up*). I say, you, sir! take care what you're about! I shouldn't like to do hanything rash, but a man hasn't had a huncle in the P.R. for nothink! (*Seeing face.*) It's Miss D.! (*Springing to his feet.*) My Miss D.!

TIDDY (*coming from step, and raising umbrella over head*). It be that little tooad, Blinker.

BLINKER. Fond soul, she remembers me! (*To audience.*) Touching fidelity of woman!

TIDDY. What a' ye talkin' aboot, ye poor creatur? Happen ye're hurt somewhere?

BLINKER. A rib or two, – a few compound fractions; but as I subscribe to one o' the haccidental companies, *that's* all profit. You've broke my 'art, Miss D. Act honourable, and pay the damage. The werry fust time I saw you – (*he strikes breast*) it cracked across like a plate – (*sighs*) – one o' the *willer* pattern.

TIDDY (*laughing*). Then ye must get someone else to rivet it. (*Going –* BLINKER *seizes her hand, ludicrous struggle beneath umbrella.*)

BLINKER. I love yer! Be a Blinker!

TIDDY. Lave a lass aloon, will'ee! (*She boxes his ears.*)

BLINKER. Oh! (*Rubbing ear.*) What a woman! If I could only get such a hand as that in the fam'ly, what a legacy to make over to the children!

TIDDY (*going*). A' done wi' your nonsense.

BLINKER (*imploringly*). Mother o' the Blinkers! Think o' posterity! (*He makes another grasp at her hand, but she avoids him, and exits laughing. As he is about to follow her, he runs against* MAN, *who enters with lantern.*)

MAN. I say!

BLINKER. No! don't say anything – I don't want to hear yer. (*He is rushing off again when he comes against footman holding umbrella over a lady in ball dress, opera cloak, &c.*) Don't apologise; I'm used to it. (*He exits. Lady passes into house, at door of which* THOMAS *appears. Sound of carriage wheels off stage. More visitors appear, preceded by* MAN *with lantern, who stands by step as they pass into house; the door closes and he goes off, swinging lantern and clinking money in his hand. Stage left clear for a few seconds. The snow falls more thickly. Lively dance music heard within house. Shadows of* GUESTS *pass and re-pass lower windows.* JOB ARMROYD *enters slowly. He is much changed in appearance; his hair, which is quite grey, hangs nearly to his shoulders; his figure is more bent; his garments are much worn and weather-stained. He leans heavily upon a staff as he walks, and appears weary and footsore. He pauses, listening to the music, his features lighting up with a kindly smile.*)

JOB. That be a merry toon, anyhow! played by laight fingers an' danced to by happy harts. An' tween them an' oi theer be on'y a wee bit bloind an' a pane o' glass. Somehow at times it meks th' sufferin' here (*touches breast*) harder to bear. (*Sighs.*) Six months o' weary wanderin' an' all coom to noght. He be away somewhere's in furrin' parts, they toold me up at th' big house his feyther used to own, an' I are'na been able to foind if he be coom back or no. But I wull! I wull! (*Striking staff firmly on ground.*) I'ull niver gi'e up th' search – niver! till I a' looked on my poor gall's face ag'in. (*Leans against pillar of portico, and taking handkerchief from pocket, unfastens knot in corner, and counts money.*) Nineteen shillin'; theer'd a' been the pund, but I gi'e a shillin' to that poor creatur' I coom upon just now doon yonder by th' water – she looked so skeary and desolate that – (*removes hat as unconscious of the falling snow, and hurriedly wipes forehead*) I feel quite sweltered loike when I think o't. It be a dreadful and a dreary place, this Lunnon, for them as are weak an' wi' no hand to guide 'em. (*More* GUESTS. *The music, which has ceased for a few moments, strikes up the same brisk and lively tune.*) It be a great party, this. (*Sound of carriage wheels off stage.* LADIES &c., *cross stage and group beneath the great portico, laughing.*) Happen I'll skear them if they see me a stannin' here. I'd best be goin'. (*They enter house, door closes.*) Goin'? Where? Whither? (*He is moving slowly across stage, when, on the blind of the window above the great portico, which has for some time been as brightly illuminated as the rest, the shadow of a woman is strongly designed. As* JOB'S *eyes rest upon it he utters a cry, the staff drops from his hand, he staggers back, his hands outstretched, his gaze riveted on the window.*) Merciful powers! (*The shadow moves, the head bending forward on the hands.*) Nelly! (*The head of figure is quickly raised as another shadow, that of* FLOUNCE, *appears on blind; then both disappear.* BLINKER *enters, and is about to ascend steps, when* JOB, *starting forward, seizes him by arm.*) Lad! lad! who owns that house? (*As* BLINKER *turns there is a mutual recognition.*)

JOB (*fiercely, and bringing him down stage*). Thy master! Is he theer? (*Points to house.*)

BLINKER (*alarmed and struggling*). You – you'll s–s–strangle me.

JOB (*more calmly*). I'll do thee no harm, lad, but I wunna loose ye till ye say if that *man* be theer?

VOICE OF MAN (*with lantern*). This way, ladies! This way, gentlemen!

BLINKER (*struggling*). Help, someone!

JOB. I wunna loose ye, till you answer me! (*He grapples with him as more* GUESTS *enter, preceded by* MAN *with lantern; they cross stage laughing, and enter house.* BLINKER, *by a sudden twist, escapes from* JOB, *and rushes into house, closing door.* JOB *pursues him, but utterly exhausted, sinks, face downwards, upon the doorsteps, the man with lantern holding it over him in surprise, as scene closes.*)

SCENE IV. – *Ante-room at the Ferns.*

Enter BLINKER, *pale, breathless, and thoroughly exhausted, like one who has seen a ghost. He leans against side, half fainting; he holds clasped under one arm* TIDDY'S *huge, baggy umbrella.*

BLINKER. I feel as if I'd seen a ghost. A ghost! no that's impossible. There never was a ghost with such a biceps. They seem to grow nothing but biceps in Lancashire. Pity I wasn't born there. There he stands like a statue still looking up at the window. (*Coming down stage with comic contortions of pain.*) What with *he* and what with *she*, I'm black and blue all over. Wearing Miss D.'s colours, I call it. (*Leaning on umbrella and regarding audience.*) Now, I've no doubt there's *some* people as might object to this kind o' thing, but *I* like it. (*Furtively rubbing himself and forcing smile.*) It's in the family. It would have done my huncle's heart good to see the way I'm walloped. 'Allays keep your 'and in,' that were his motto, when arter flooring my aunt, myself, and *all* my cousins, he'd pick us up, one arter t'other, as pleasant as if he'd been playing a game o' skittles. (*Rhapsodically.*) He *was* a man! Take him for all in all – (*pauses, and with sudden change of tone*) – I don't much care to look upon his like again. (*Looking at umbrella.*) And *this*, Miss D., is all that remains to me of thee. I held on to it when you sent me down on that last slide. Touching momentum! it's like yourself, all wire and bone. I'll never part with it! never! It shall be my companion by day, and I'll sleep with it under my piller at night.

Enter FLOUNCE, *with tray and coffee, &c.*

FLOUNCE (*coquettishly*). What are you going to sleep with, Mr Blinker?
BLINKER (*holding out umbrella*). This!
FLOUNCE. That!

Enter THOMAS; *joins* FLOUNCE *in laughing.*

BLINKER. You may laugh; but if ever I conduct Miss Matilda D.
to the high menial haltar 'twill be under this auspicious
gingham. In every rib of it there's poetry. (*Opens umbrella
and sings.*)

> Some time ago a knockdown blow,
>> From Cupid's 'auctioneer',
> Made that there part I calls my heart
>> Feel most intensely queer.
> And though I own she's never shown,
>> The least regard for me,
> I can't conceal the love I feel
>> For dear Matilda D.

THOMAS. Did you ever!

BLINKER (*closing umbrella*).

> Yes, I long for married life,
> With my Tiddy for a wife,
> And a lot of little Blinker chick-a-*biddies.*

FLOUNCE (*bridling*). Well, I'm sure.

BLINKER (*stops her as she is going up, takes liqueur from tray and
drinks.*)

> Let us pledge her in a cup.
> While we make a chorus up,
> Of Re-fol-de-lol de riddy-iddy-Tiddies, &c.

FLOUNCE. Your wife! (*Scornfully, and drawing back as he's about
to fill, as unconsciously, another glass.*) Mr Blinker, indeed!

BLINKER. If I've offended you, Mrs Flounce, it's quite huninten-
tional, and to prove I bear no malice, I accept your humble
apologies. What's in a name? Not much, or you wouldn' be
so anxious to get rid of yours.

> My name, I know, is not the go,
>> And yet, upon my word,
> The name of D. appears to me,
>> A good deal more absurd.
> If I could find that gal inclined,
>> To patronize B. B.,

I'd soon arrange to make a change,
In that there name of D.

(*Chorus*)   Yes, I long for married life.

Loud brisk knocking.

Enter GILBERT FEATHERSTONE *and* LOADER.

GILBERT. Which of you fellows is attending to the door? (*Exit* THOMAS, FLOUNCE *with tray.*)

BLINKER (*aside, hesitating*). Shall I tell him? No. (*With feeling, and watching* FEATHERSTONE *and* LOADER, *as they move down laughing.*) I've given my word, and a word's better than a bond with a Blinker. (*Very merry dance music heard from drawing-room.*)

LOADER. You're in force tonight. Will Simondi sing?

GILBERT. Yes, she keeps her catarrhs for the opera. (*Knock repeated.*) More arrivals! (*Turning to* BLINKER.) Why are you loitering here? Go down to the hall, and help Thomas. (*Aside.*) No signs of Nelly yet. (*Aloud.*) Come, Loader. (*Notes of song heard.*) That's Simondi's voice. (*As they go off, his hand on* LOADER's *shoulder, with forced gaiety.*) We mustn't lose a note of the nightingale. (*Exeunt* GILBERT *and* LOADER.)

BLINKER (*glancing again from window*). There he stands just where I left him! The last carriage is gone, and now he crosses over. (*A loud single knock.*) Oh, lor! that made my heart jump! What a hand! I wouldn't be in Featherstone's shoes for a fiver. (*Exit.*)

SCENE V. –*Handsome suite of rooms in* FEATHERSTONE'S *house. Decorations blue and white, profusely relieved by gilt work. Furniture rich, and elegant mirrors adorn the walls, so as to multiply the reflections of the vases and statuettes placed about; chandelier hangs from ceiling of inner room. The two rooms open into each other by a broad arch, surmounted by a handsome cornice, from which falls velvet curtains, drawn up at sides so as to show table spread with refreshments, wines, fruits, &c., &c., the whole giving idea of elegant but prodigal luxury. Music and laughter as* GUESTS (*all in full toilet*) *come crowding in from inner room.* THE SIGNORA SIMONDI *in centre; on either side of her* GILBERT FEATHERSTONE *and* LOADER – *all hold champagne glasses in hand.*

SONG. (*All raising glasses*)

Bright champagne! bright champagne! bright champagne!
Bright champagne! bright champagne! bright champagne!

> Children of the airy dance,
>   Sweet nightingales of song,
> Advance each one of foaming glass,
>   To speed old care along.
> Night shade hide th' dullard's head,
>   Ivy his brows entwine,
> Gloomy cypress screen his bed,
>   Far, far from the vine.

> > Gaily the mad old world spins round,
> > For care is snugly under ground!
> >   Tra! la! la! Tra! la! la!
> > Life's best fence is a ha! ha! ha!
> >   Tra! la! la! Tra! la! la!
> >   Laugh! laugh! ha! ha! ha!

While the starv'ling miser's seen,
   His treasure hoarding up,
We quaff like Egypt's dusky queen,
   Pearls in every cup.
See! our pearls! sunshine nurst.

(*Holding up glasses.*)

> Upsoaring every one,
> As in life these bubbles burst,
> They shine! break! are gone!

(*Chorus*) Gaily the mad old world, &c.

As chorus ceases THOMAS *advances and speaks aside to* GILBERT FEATHERSTONE.

GILBERT. A man wants to see me! What's his name?
THOMAS. He wouldn't give it.
GILBERT (*impatiently*). Send him away!
THOMAS (*hesitatingly*). He says his business is important.
GILBERT. Pshaw! Let him give his name!

Enter JOB.

JOB. Job Armroyd o' th' Bleakmoor Mine! (GILBERT, *who has recoiled before this sudden apparition, recovers by an effort his composure, and turns with a forced gaiety to* GUESTS *who look with surprise on the weather-stained miner, who, without moving his hat, leans upon staff, his lips firmly compressed, and his eyes fixed on* FEATHERSTONE.)
GILBERT (*to* GUESTS). I must beg you to excuse me for a few minutes. I have some business with this person. (*To* LOADER.) Business connected with the mine. (*He follows* GUESTS *up stage, his manner marked by an exaggerated gaiety. When they have all passed into the inner-room he turns to* JOB *a face which he in vain endeavours to render composed.* JOB *has not changed his position, but still leaning on staff, stands motionless as a statue.* GILBERT, *aside.*) An unexpected guest! (*Aloud, and with hauteur.*) The reason of this intrusion?
JOB (*by a sudden movement placing himself directly in front of* FEATHERSTONE). Where is she?
GILBERT. You have chosen a strange time. Come tomorrow, and I will talk with you.
JOB. I wunna trust ye. Ye are'na worthy o' trust. Where is she?
GILBERT. Suppose I refuse to answer?

JOB (*calmly*). I be prepared for that. (*Taking chair from side.*) I wunna lave this house till ye do. (*Seats himself.*)

GILBERT (*impetuously*). How, fellow! Would you dare! (*Advances, and is about to place hand on* JOB's *shoulder, when the latter, his whole manner undergoing a fierce and sudden change, springs to his feet.*)

JOB. Dunna lay hand on me! (*Speaking with increasing energy.*) For months I ha' battled wi' one idea – I ha' fou't it fro' my pillow by naight – I ha' shrunk fro't as it walked wi' me by day. That idea were to kill ye, Gilbert Featherstone! kill ye, whereiver and wheniver we met.

GILBERT. A murder!

JOB. Man! man! I fou't wi' it wakin' an' sleepin' – prayed agin it on my knees, till I thou't it were conquered. Yet, ha' a care! ha' a care! Let th' touch o' thy hand fall on me, an' I lay thee dead at my feet!

GILBERT (*who has recoiled before the stern face, and shrunk beneath the uplifted hand of the other*). You come to threaten me?

JOB. No! Listen, Mester Featherstone. Had we met on'y a month ago, I'd ha' made no more o' thy life than that o' some stooat or polecat. It be well for thee I ha' sought other guidance nor that o' my own tortured heart, and ha' coom at last to care for but one thing – to save *her*. Where is she?

GILBERT. This is neither the time nor the place for such enquiry.

JOB. Is it for you to speak o' time an' place to me? You, who could lave such a world o' brightness an' beauty as this (*indicates by gesture the luxury around*) to enter a poor man's home an' set your foot on th' bit o' fire you found cheering his lonely hearth? Ah! Mester Featherstone! it be little o' sunshine as comes to th' lot o' men loike me, an' you ha' blotted out mine for iver. (*His voice falters for a moment; by an effort he conquers his emotion.* GILBERT, *with an impatient movement, makes as if he would go up stage, but* JOB *intercepts him. In the eyes of the latter there is a fiercer gleam, and his voice denotes the rising anger.*) Where is she?

GILBERT (*as one who has formed a resolve*). She is not here.

JOB. You lie!

GILBERT. How?

JOB. You lie! Ah! you may frown an' clench your hand. Th' brazen forehead always goes wi' th' hardened heart.

GILBERT (*with passion*). Silence! You shall repent this insolence! (*Merry confusion of voices heard behind curtain.*) Begone! Quit the house!

JOB. Answer me, or before your foine friends I'll – (*He is moving quickly up stage, his hands extended to drag aside curtain, when* GILBERT, *springing forward, grasps his arm.*)

GILBERT. Would you dare?

JOB (*with fierce excitement*). Ha' a care! Dunna raise th' devil in me! Ha' a care! (*As they struggle the curtains are drawn aside from within, and the* GUESTS, *alarmed by the noise, come crowding in, filling up scene with a glittering and animated background. The two men release each other, but retain an attitude of menace.*)

SEVERAL GUESTS. What madman's this?

LOADER (*crossing to* GILBERT). This man! – who is he? What does he want? (*The crowd of guests suddenly divide, and* NELLY, *brilliant in diamonds and lace, enters hurriedly; but, as her eyes rest on* JOB, *she utters a wild cry, and, crouching down as he advances towards her, covers her face with her hands.*)

JOB (*standing erect, his hands stretched above the head of the crouching woman, in protection, gazes round at the glittering crowd*). My wife! (*There is a confused murmur of astonishment and a hurried backward movement among the guests, leaving centre group free, tableau.*)

ACT III

SCENE I. – *Interior of a cottage in the neighbourhood of London. Large chimney-place with fire burning upon hearth. Near chimney, L., an easy-chair of black leather, the covering in a most dilapidated condition, in this particular matching with the other furniture of room. R. an ascent of three steps, small landing with rude balustrade and door leading to sleeping-room. At back of scene a wide window in three divisions, giving an extensive landscape view. River with bridge in middle distance. In extreme distance London. The outline of the great city brought out vividly by a brilliant sunset effect. Close to easy chair a rough deal table. To R. of window the back of cottage forms a deep recess – almost another room – at extremity of which is the door of cottage. This recess has a slanting roof of red tiles – no ceiling. Between it and the long latticed windows stands an antiquated and much decayed folding screen. The whole aspect of the room is one of poverty – such as is seen in labourers' cottages. A line extends across recess to door on R., from which some freshly washed clothes are suspended. In front of scene,* TIDDY DRAGGLETHORPE *is engaged washing linen in a tub on bench – beside her, on the ground, a clothes basket filled with linen.*

TIDDY (*throwing clothes from tub into basket*). That'ull make th' sixth dozen today! (*Wiping arms with apron.*) But lawks! when a lass be workin' for her'sen, or for them as she loikes, it do make all th' differents. I ha' had enow o' missusses for one while. They nearly worritted oi into a skillington. (*Sings.*)

TIDDY DRAGGLETHORPE'S COMPLAINT

> Weary wi' work, I sink to sleep,
> Heavy as lead my eyelids fall,
>> Tra la, la, la, la, la, la, la, la, la, la,

In my dreams th' missusses creep
   And once again I see them all.
        La, la, la, la, la, la, la, la, la,
        La, la, la, la, la, la, la.

Six missus' in ha'f a year,
   Fat an' thin, broad, short, an' tall,
I took on trial, yet dear, oh, dear!
   None o' th' bunch would suit at all.
Tiddy, go theer! Tiddy, come here!
   Upstairs, downstairs, 'Tiddy!' they bawl;
Of all the evils lassies mun bear
   Missusses be the worst of all.
        Weary wi' work, &c.

Slushin', sloshin', fro' morn till naight,
   Out in th' frost, th' snow, th' rain,
Rubbin', scrubbin', an' all becos
   Missus is on the rampage again.
It's 'idler and hussy', if weary an' worn,
   Our brains gets numbed an' to sleep we fall,
They treat us like niggurs, no wonder we groan,
   Bad luck to th' missus! Bad luck to 'em all!
        Weary wi' work, &c.

(*After singing song, she lifts tub, and carries it up stage, placing it on ledge in recess.*) It be more nor a month sin' I ha' set foot in Lunnon, an' iv I'd my will I'd niver see more o't nor I do now. (*She pauses by window, and with a comic anger shakes her first in the direction of the city.*) Ye great black beast! lying theer wi' a *hump* on yer back, as if ye hanna ought but peace an' quietness inside ye! Ugh! I canna abide ye. (*She comes a little down stage, pauses at door, listens, then ascends steps and peeps in.*) Asleep at last. (*She comes softly and quickly down, her finger on her lip.*) A blessed relief for one whose wakin' hours be so full o' pain. 'Now th' fever ha' left her, wi' rest an' carefu' nursing,' the doctor said, 'she might yet be

her'sen ag'in' – moight! (*Shaking head.*) She ha' that here
(*touches breast*) which no doctor's stuff'ull cure. Job
dunna know how ill she be, he arn't looked on her feace sin'
her moind coom back – an' he wonna – but he watches o'er
her, bless'm! as a feyther watches o'er an ailin' child. Ah!
(*She sighs, then passes her hand impatiently across her eyes.*) I
canna think o't all wi'out mekin' a fool o' my'sen. (*As she
stoops to arrange linen in basket,* BENJAMIN BLINKER *is seen
peeping in at window; he disappears to reappear at door.*)

BLINKER. She's alone! 'appy chance. (*He enters, and comes down
stage unperceived by* TIDDY – *tapping her on shoulder.*) Don't
be afeard, Miss D.! It's only me.

TIDDY (*who is lifting basket*). Hegh! (*She turns sharply round,
drops basket on* BLINKER'S *toes.*) If it beant that funny little
chap as is allays a hankering after oi – haw! haw! ye be for
all the world loike a barn-door chick a-roostin' on one leg i'
that fashion.

BLINKER (*with many grimaces, and still rubbing feet alternately*).
Yes, it's me. I – I knew you'd be glad to see me.

TIDDY (*laughing*). Thee be'st a droll one. What's thy arrant?

BLINKER (*with amorous emphasis*). You.

TIDDY (*with menace*). Tell'ee what! If thee dunna let I aloon –

BLINKER (*retreating*). Don't, *don't* hagitate yourself! I comprehend the delicacy of the sitiwation, an' can make allowance
for the weakness o' woman.

TIDDY (*aside*). He be gone clean daft, sure-ly.

BLINKER. Miss D., in all that happertains to the 'ring', I'm an
authority. Having made the requisite deposit o' my haffec-
tions, I can't consent to draw the stakes. Game to the last.
It's the motter o' our fam'ly.

TIDDY (*laughing, and seating herself on bench*). Ha' ye gotten no
frien's to tek care o' ye?

BLINKER (*with solemnity*). Hi'm the last o' the Blinkers at present. Yesterday I buried the relick o' my late huncle, a
charming woman, six feet six in her stockin's. Began her
business life in a caravan, an' closed it in the snuff an' cigar
line. She took to *weeds* when she lost my huncle. (*Approaching*

TIDDY, *and speaking with a slow emphasis*.) She's left me her *H*eir.

TIDDY (*surprised*). What'll thee do wi't?

BLINKER (*with dignity*). *H*eir to her property, 'ouse, shop, an' fixtur's. (*Seating himself on opposite side of bench*.) Say the word, Miss D., and take possession. (*Imploringly*.) Be a fixtur'.

TIDDY. Lave off, will'ee! (*Rises abruptly, bench tips over with* BLINKER.)

BLINKER (*on his knees and seizing her dress*). It's a bony fidy offer! Capital business! Heverythink in tip-top style – a nigger at the door, and a large plantation of cigars on the premises. My haunt always cut them to order. 'If you're only up to *snuff*,' she'd say, 'you may double your own *returns*.'

TIDDY. Loose me!

BLINKER. P'raps you object to the nigger? *Don't* secede on that account! I'll sell him, and buy a Scotchman – he's more hattractive if not so decent.

TIDDY (*with sudden and startling energy*). Mester Benjamin Blinker! ! ! (*Seizing him by collar, pulling him on to his feet*.) Thee serv'st that man, and ha' th' feace to talk o' marriage to me! (*Shaking him*.) What d'ye mean by't?

BLINKER (*as she shakes him*). D-o-o-n'-t h-a-g-g-gitate yourself!

TIDDY. What do ye mean by't? (*She releases him, and snatching up hat, which has fallen on ground, bangs it upon his head in such a manner that it descends over his eyes; then placing her hands on his shoulders, she twists him round, and is hurrying him towards door*.)

BLINKER (*frantically struggling*). Stop! I'll discharge Featherstone tomorrow – I discharge him *now*! (*She releases him, he takes off hat, the crown of which has collapsed, and eyes it ruefully*.) This is the second as you've spoilt, Miss D. You've got such a powerful way of putting things. (*Aside*.) Catch me deliverin' Featherstone's letter! After such an hexhibition o' feelin'. (*Looks at hat*.)

TIDDY (*laughing*). Whattens the good o' hats to thee, who ha' gotten no head – poor creatur'?

BLINKER (*reproachfully*). But I've a *heart*. Don't laugh, my nerves won't stand it!

TIDDY (*kindly*). Coom lad! I ha' been a bit rough wi' ye, an' I be sorry for 't. (*Holding out hand which* BLINKER *shakes.*) Thee bean't th' first honest lad who ha' had a reskel for's mester.

BLINKER (*aside, and touching pocket*). Featherstone may deliver his own letter – I won't. (*Aloud, and approaching* TIDDY.) 'Ow about the pardnership? Blinker and Co. (*Insinuatingly.*) The Co. capable of any hextension. (*Stopping her as she is about to speak.*) Don't be in a hurry – take time to reflect! I'll wait outside. I ain't partick'lar for five minutes.

TIDDY (*stopping him*). I thank thee for thy offer, but (*with emphasis*) it canna be!

BLINKER (*in much distress*). Oh! I say! this won't do. I'll call tomorrow – (*following her down stage*) – or – in a week.

TIDDY (*shaking head*). Noa, lad! it canna be! (*She places hand on* BLINKER'S *shoulder as he stands with a lugubrious expression twirling hat, and gazing on ground.*) Thee'st a heart, an' that understan's better nor th' head sometimes, so thee shalt decide for thy'sen.

BLINKER (*impatiently*). I *have* decided.

TIDDY (*without heeding him*). When I wur a bit gall no higher nor that table, I'd for playmate one o' the prettiest little creatur's eyes iver saw. We were allays together, ate out o' th' same bowl, played the same games, an' shared th' same bed. But wi' years th' diff'rents atween us widened more an' more. She wur one o' natur's fav'rites, getten all t' beauty and grace, whoile oi, like a shepherd's toyke, growed only th' rougher wi'age, but oi'd a warm heart for them as I loved, an' I loved that child wi' *all* my heart. Bless'ee lad! the soight o' her braight face, an' th' soun' o' her merry voice, wur meat an' drink to oi. She seemed to me a koinder queen, not that I'd iver clapped eyes on one, but I mean my darlin' wur differend all around. *That* child be now a woman, an', as I think, a dying one. (*Laying one hand on* BLINKER'S *arm, she points with the other to room.*) She be *theer*, wi' th' whole face o' th' once braight world a darkness to her. The poor birdie who all thou't made for song an' for sunshine, be theer. (*Pointing again.*) Now, lad, where be my pleace?

BLINKER (*with burst of feeling*). Oh, never mind me, Miss D., I can wait.

TIDDY (*with impetuous fervour*). Theer! (*Giving him a sounding kiss.*) Noo get along wi' 'ee. (*Pushing him again towards door.*) Had things been different there's no known' but I moight ha' consented to tek keer o' ye. (*There is a sound as of the movement of some pieces of furniture in inner-room.* TIDDY, *quitting* BLINKER, *crosses hastily to steps – aside.*) She canna ha' 'wakened. (*As she bends her head towards door to listen,* BLINKER *draws note from pocket, and crumpling it up indignantly, throws it, as he believes, in the fire. It falls just within chimney, and near chair, and is visible to audience, but concealed from those on stage.*)

BLINKER. Phew! That's off my mind! When Featherstone hasks if I've left it, I can say yes with a clear conscience. Goodbye, Miss D. This meeting's hadjourned, only hadjourned, you know. (*He exits abruptly, but immediately re-appears, holding the door ajar, as he thrusts in head and arm, and points mysteriously in direction of fire-place.*) It's there, and that's where they'll *all* go, if he don't get another postman. (*He closes door, and immediately re-appears at window, his finger placed to his nose confidentially.*) It's Blinker and Co. I shall buy the Scotchman on spec! (*He closes window and disappears, blowing kisses to* TIDDY, *who crosses to window.*)

TIDDY (*startled, and looking about*). What's theer? I see nought. (*She laughs, shrugs shoulders, and draws curtains across windows.*) He is a funny one, sure-ly. (*She turns to come down stage, when her eyes fall on* NELLY ARMROYD, *who appears at door of room.* NELLY *is much changed; her face is very pale, her whole aspect that of one worn by illness and much suffering.*) Whoi, Nelly, lass, whattens left thy bed for?

NELLY. I've had a long sleep, a very long sleep. (*Comes down stage,* TIDDY *assisting her.*) I shall be better here. (*She glances*

round cottage with a vague, puzzled look.) All appears so new,
so strange to me!

TIDDY (*aside*). Her moind be a-wanderin' ag'in. (*Aloud.*) Indeed, thee munna stay, dearee. Th' naight be comin' on, and
th' wind blows in this ramshackle pleace fro' all th' four
corners at once.

NELLY. I'm better here. (*She leans on chair back, still gazing in
a bewildered way about cottage.*)

TIDDY (*aside — nervously twitching clothes from line and tossing
them into basket*). Job 'na be here soon. He munna meet her
— he *wunna* meet her. He be iron in that.

NELLY (*with a faint smile*). Working! Always working, Tiddy.

TIDDY (*coming down stairs*). Work! bless'ee lass! it do oi good.
We beant all made aloike. Some on us be chaney, and some
on us be delf; oi 'm delf, an' precious hard to break, I can
tell'ee. (*She laughs, and extends her two red arms.*) Look
theer! them's graters, ain't 'em?

NELLY (*pressing hand to forehead*). How long have I been ill,
Tiddy?

TIDDY (*hesitating*). A' nigh a month.

NELLY. So long!

TIDDY. Thee'st been cruel ill, Nelly. Loike to die, we feared, but
that be all passed now.

NELLY. I remember a terrible shock; it seems but yesterday; and
yet — (*There is a pause, during which* NELLY *appears both by
look and gesture to be endeavouring to recall something — suddenly looking up.*) This is not Bleakmoor.

TIDDY (*soothingly*). Hush! dearee, hush!

NELLY. Where am I? (*She goes quickly up stage, and before* TIDDY
can prevent her, lifts curtains of window.) London! (*She gazes
for some moments steadfastly at the distant city, the red light of
the setting sun falling full upon her face.*) The shining city of
my dreams — my dreams! Its spires are bathed in light. (*As
she gazes the light fades from her face, and her voice changes from
one of exultation to one of deep sadness.*) But the darkness is
creeping down, and a shadow rises between me and the

fading light. (*She drops curtains, and turns to* TIDDY.) Where is Job Armroyd?

TIDDY. Nelly, lass! what be coom o'er thee? I dinna loike to see thy eyes so braight an' thy cheek so pale!

NELLY. All is clear to me now. Where is Job Armroyd?

TIDDY. He binna here.

NELLY. He *will* be here! I know it! I *feel* it! (*She grasps* TIDDY's *hands, speaking in a voice of great emotion.*) Tiddy, I must see Job Armroyd before I die!

TIDDY. Die! Dinna talk i' that fashion – we mun hope.

NELLY. I've but one hope on earth – but one – it is to see Job! (TIDDY *is about to speak, but* NELLY *continues with a wild energy.*) I am not mad. I remember all – the delirium! the despair! *All.* (*Her voice sinks into a tone of plaintive sorrow.*) The delirium that has passed, the despair that remains.

TIDDY. It be th' fever that clings to 'ee, darlin'. (*Aside, as she takes* NELLY's *hand.*) It is'na that; her hand be ice-cold. (*Aloud.*) Thee mun return t' bed, Nelly. (*The bells of the distant city strike the hour – eight.*) It be his hour. (*Entreatingly.*) Nelly! Nelly! he munna meet ye – he wunna meet ye.

NELLY. Oh! in mercy!

TIDDY (*speaking rapidly, and with much emotion*). He ha' watched by thy side while the fever wur upon thee, day an' naight! When t' danger had passed, he sought work o' some koind – any koind – so he could be near thee. (NELLY *looks up with a look of wild hope in her face, which dies away as* TIDDY *proceeds.*) For he remembered t' promise gi'en to them as be dead an' gone. He ha' gotten work moor nor ten miles fro' here, but each naight he cooms for news o' thee. (NELLY *covers her face with her hands.*) He sits theer th' long naight thro' (*points to chair*) an' when mornin' dawns, departs to labour – for thee – still for thee.

NELLY. Misery!

TIDDY. But he ha' vowed. (*She pauses in great distress.*) Oh! lass! lass! that I should ha' to say it!

NELLY. Speak! I must know all.

TIDDY. Niver to look upon thy feace ag'in.

NELLY (*with determination*). I will see Job Armroyd! A month ago I would have fled from him, as guilt flies before the avenging angel – but I have that to say which no tongue but mine can speak – no ears but his may hear. (*She stops abruptly, her head bent forward, her whole expression one of eager listening.*) That is his step! (*She makes an involuntary movement towards door, but* TIDDY *intercepts her.*)

TIDDY. For my sake! for his! 'Twould kill him to see thee so sudden loike. (*A heavy step is heard, passing window, then a gentle rapping at door.*)

NELLY (*in agonised entreaty*). Tiddy! dear friend! sister! it is for the last time.

TIDDY. Hush! (*She hastily arranges screen, and motions* NELLY *to conceal herself behind it.*) Thee know'st I would gi'e my loife for thine. (*Aside, as she goes to door at back.*) An' so I know would *he.* (*She opens door, and* JOB ARMROYD *appears on the threshold, but without entering.*) Coom in, lad! coom in! Thee mun be toired wi' thy walk. It be a weary stretch after a day's work. (*She continues to speak rapidly, and bustles about as* JOB *enters.*) Gi'e oi thy hat (*taking hat and stick*) an' sit thee doon. Thee be'st covered wi' dust loike a miller. (JOB, *who has come down stage with his usual slow, heavy step, pauses, and speaking under his voice, motions towards room.*)

JOB. Thee dunna speak o' her. Thee'st no bad news, I hope?

TIDDY. No, no, lad; th' change be for th' better. (*Crossing quickly to chair, which she advances a little nearer fire.*) But it be ill talkin' stan'in. I'll get thee a cup o' tay in a jiffy.

JOB. Thank'ee, lass! thank'ee; but I dunna want for nought. (*He seats himself in chair, as* TIDDY, *after placing an unlighted candle on table, exits.*) I be raight glad she be gettin' hersel' again. (*He looks towards room, shakes his head and sighs.*) Her'sen! no, that can niver be – niver ag'in th' braight happy little wench, whose voice made home doubly home to me, just for all th' world loike th' cricket's chirp on a winter's eve. It were but yesterday, and yet (*he passes hand across forehead*) everything seems in a jumble – a koinder dream. (NELLY *has glided from behind screen and timidly approaches him.*) This be the last naight I shall pass 'neath this roof. It wrings my heart to part wi'out a word, but it munna be – it munna be. (NELLY, *sinking on her knees besides him, pronounces his name.*)

NELLY. Job! (JOB, *with a cry almost of terror, springs to his feet.*)

JOB. Nelly! Woman! what do you here?

NELLY. Job! Job! do not spurn me! (*She makes a movement as to approach nearer, but he checks her by a gesture, at the same time drawing back a pace or two.*) Spurn me, then! but, oh! let me speak! (*She clasps hands.*)

JOB (*speaking, as it were, to himself, his eyes fixed upon the kneeling woman*). Spurn thee! No! no! I couldna hurt a hair o' thy head.

NELLY. You're going away for ever, Job – it is for that I am here. (JOB'S *face is very pale, and he grasps the back of chair convulsively for support. The strong, rough man appears seized with the weakness of a child.*) Have I lost nothing, Job, of that old happy time? Do I suffer nothing in the knowledge of the terrible wrong I've done you? Oh! think of me sometimes as I used to be, long, so long ago. Do not think of me as I am – lost to you – to myself – to everything.

JOB. Nelly! Nelly! I loved thee, and I trusted thee, an' 'twere wi' a sure heart I promised them as be dead an' gone to shield their child fro' harm. I niver thou't to be thankfu' that Isaac Bradley an's wife be sleepin' neath' churchyard grass, but I be, I be.

NELLY. Job!

JOB. Such a love as I'd for thee, Nelly, words canna tell. I were a'most sinfu' proud a-thinkin' thee caredst for me, an' rough an' common as I knew my'sen to be, thee did'st not despise me. A smile fro' thee, a word, a lovin' look, made our bit o' home a sort o' heaven, till I wur most 'shamed to be so joyfu' 'mong my mates, an' know how many hearts wur full o' keer.

NELLY. Job!

JOB. I used to think thee loike them bit flowers we miners coom upon doon in t'mine, a-growin' out o' some wanderin' seed

262

which th' wind ha' blown doon to us; a creatur' o' light springin' up pale an' beautiful in t'midst o' the grimy darkness. Such a flower I had hoped to weer next my heart, an' feel that when my sands were run, t'ud droop a sorrerin' head ower my grave. (*He stops, overcome with emotion – then, with a movement of despair, dashes his clenched hands against his head.*) Thee niver keered for me! Thee couldna ha' keered for me! Fool! fool! that I wur.

NELLY. Job! you must hear me.

JOB (*averting his face*). Dunna speak! I canna bear it! The soun' o' thy voice kills me.

NELLY. I *must* speak! The words are suffocating me! I cannot – I dare not die before I have spoken them! Job! Job! I love you, I love you.

JOB. Me! Love me! (*He gazes at her for a moment with a fixed, haggard look, then utters a short, bitter laugh.*) Love!

NELLY. If I dare approach you; if I dare raise my eyes towards you, thus weeping tears of agony and repentance, let me implore you not to drive me from you.

JOB. It canna be!

NELLY. A little while – but a very little while longer.

JOB. Theer is a shadder between us – a shadder which no light can pierce. (*She endeavours to grasp his hands; he puts her back gently but firmly.*) I am alone! alone! (NELLY *is turning away, her hands tightly pressed to her bosom, when* JOB *again speaks – this time his voice is full of an eager tenderness.*) Thee shanna want for aught the labour o' these two hands can earn – but – we munna – munna meet again.

NELLY. You hate me, Job – you've the right to hate me.

JOB. Hate! (*Sadly.*) We canna change the heart as one moight wish.

NELLY. If a life of repentance – (*She pauses.*) Alas! I have no life to offer. I can but dwell upon the past.

JOB (*his whole manner denoting the struggle within*). Go! go! (*He motions towards door and turns away.*)

NELLY. Job! Job! Say what you will! do what you will! upbraid me! (*She springs forward and clings to him for a moment.*)

Curse me! but do not let us part thus – other punishments I can bear. It is the *kindness* kills. (*She sinks kneeling at his feet, covering her face with her hands.*)

JOB (*with a burst of emotion*). Curse thee! (*He extends his hands.*) I bless thee! bless thee fro' my heart! (*He raises her, then draws back.*) Farewell! for ever! (NELLY *moves a few steps in direction of door, totters, and catches at table for support* – JOB, *with a movement towards her.*) Nelly!

NELLY (*quickly*). It is nothing! nothing! only I've need of rest – a long, long rest. (*She has nearly crossed stage, when her strength again fails, her hands move blindly, as feeling for a support; at the same moment* TIDDY *appears at door, descends steps, and receives the fainting woman in her arms. In obedience to a gesture from* JOB, *she assists* NELLY *up steps. They exeunt.*)

JOB (*his eyes fixed on the retreating figure*). Gone! (*He extends arms as one awakening from a painful dream.*) I canna bear it! I wur mad to think I could bear it! Theer be that in her feace which meks my blood ice, an' my heart stan' still. I ha' killed her! killed *her*, for whose sake I ha' prayed for loife – loife an' strength to work (*he moves towards fireplace, repeating the last words slowly*) – to work. (*He leans for a moment against chimney, his eyes bent on fire.*) I'd best be flittin'! I ha' rested here too long a'ready. (*He takes pen and ink from chimney, placing them on table.*) I mun set doon a few things for Tiddy afore I go. I beant much o' a hond at scribble-scrabble, tho' my feyther used to say 'twernt th' writin' were difficult, but th' readin' o't afterwards. (*Putting down pen, and taking up candle, he stoops to light it by fire. As he does so, he sees the crumpled letter, he picks it up, ignites it by the embers, and is about to apply it to candle when the writing attracts his eye. He crumples out the flame with his fingers, and approaching the paper to the now lighted candle, examines it attentively – tearing open letter.*) His writin'! (*He places candle upon table, holds the charred and blackened paper close to its flame, bending eagerly over it, his trembling hands and quivering face show his emotion.*) I'm goin' blind, I think! (*He brushes hand fiercely across eyes and reads.*) 'I have discovered your prison. I entreat you—'

(JOB *stamps his foot with angry impatience as some of the charred paper crumbles from his fingers.*) It be nigh all burned! I canna mek it out. Stay! What be this? (*Stoops over the paper eagerly, tracing the words with his finger as he reads.*) 'At nine o'clock tonight—must see you—leave door on latch—pass light across window—alone—' (JOB *looking up, his brows fiercely contracted, his face ghastly pale.*) I ha' burned the rest! (*Raises his clenched hands, pressing them tightly on forehead.*) Oh! Nelly! Nelly! Nelly! (*He sinks into chair, but rises instantly as* TIDDY *descends steps and approaches him. She stops abruptly, struck by the expression of his face.*)

TIDDY. Job! What is't, lad?

JOB (*seizing her roughly by the wrist*). Speak, woman! Did *she* know o' this?

TIDDY. Know o' what?

JOB (*placing letter in her hands*). I found it lying on th' hearth. It coom fro' – fro' – (*he again raises hands to his head*) I think oi be a-goin' mad!

TIDDY (*looking at letter*). She knew nothin' o't.

JOB (*fiercely*). Who brought it here?

TIDDY. Honester hands nor them as wrote it, or thee would'na ha' found it theer. (*Pointing to hearth – aside.*) This be what that Blinker were a-pointin' at. He ha' a conscience, that lad! (*She is about to read letter when* JOB *takes it from her hand; at the same time the bells of the city strike the hour.*)

JOB (*who has counted the strokes*). Nine! (*As he turns to* TIDDY, *there is in his face a wild excitement, almost a joy.*) To thy room, lass! to thy room! I would be aloon for awhile. (*He lays his hand on* TIDDY's *arm as she is crossing stage.*) Whativer thee may'st hear, dunna stir till I call ye.

TIDDY (*alarmed*). Job!

JOB. Dost thou doubt my love for *her*?

TIDDY. No, lad.

JOB. I ha' sworn to stan' 'tween her an' harm, an' I wull. (TIDDY *exits.* JOB, *who has followed her to door, stops abruptly as he is re-crossing stage – listening.*) A mon's tread! an' coomin' straight up t' path! It ha' stopped now. (*A short bitter laugh.*)

265

Ah! I had forgot the signal. (*He takes candle from table, passes it several times backwards and forwards before curtain – replacing it on table, he goes up stage to door at back, and raises the swing bar, which* TIDDY *has let fall, then returns to table.*) Now it cooms up th' path ag'in, straight for th' cottage. (*He extinguishes candle – stage in darkness – the latch of door is gently raised, the door opens, and* GILBERT FEATHERSTONE *enters cautiously.*)

GILBERT (*as he advances, stumbles slightly*). No light? (*He comes slowly down stage, as feeling his way in the dark.*) Strange! I saw the light distinctly. Here's a candle at last. (*Takes match from cigar case and strikes a light. Holds up match for a moment glancing about.*) A rough cage this for so pretty a bird. I learnt in the neighbourhood she was alone. (*Leans over table, lighting candle.*) It's lucky; but where's Job, I wonder? (*As he raises his head, his eyes rest upon the motionless figure, and the stern eyes that are now looking direct into his own.*)

JOB. Here!

GILBERT (*recoiling as one who has come upon a crouching tiger*). Job Armroyd here!

JOB. Hegh, lad, wheer *should* he be but under his own roof, when *such* a guest pays 'un a visit?

GILBERT. This is a trap! (*Draws pistol from breast-pocket of his overcoat, but it is wrenched from his grasp by the strong hand of* JOB.)

JOB (*falling back a few paces, and placing pistol on table behind him*). Trap! (*Contemptuously.*) Thee 'rt a man wi' a great estate, on which ivery beast that runs an' bird that flies be claimed by thee. I (*strikes breast*) be a poor mon, yet owner once o' a treasure I would not ha' bartered ag'in thine had ye twenty toimes as much. (*Lays hand upon pistol, but without taking it up.*) A treasure you robbed me of.

GILBERT (*with assumed composure*). Pistol me if you will. If you dare!

JOB. Thee hast robbed me o' that which can niver i' this world be given back agin. It binna in thee to know what she were to me. I be afeared to think o't my'sen and know my loss so great. Young loike her'sen, han'som an' soft-spoken, thee dazed the poor child wi' thy promises an' lies – lured her from her home, an' deceived her loike th' villain that ye are.

GILBERT (*who vainly endeavours to retain his sang-froid under the contempt shown in each look and gesture of the other*). To what does all this lead?

JOB. Thou hast broke her heart. (GILBERT *starts.*) And I tell thee thou'rt a villain! A base, cold-hearted villain!

GILBERT. Job! Job Armroyd! you forget.

JOB. Nothing! I ha' striven hard to get shut on it all, but it be moor powerfu' nor oi. (*Places hand again on pistol* GILBERT *makes movement to hinder him.*)

GILBERT. What would you do? Reflect – the law!

JOB (*with fierce passion*). Law! this house be mine. I foind ye here i' th' naight armed; I know thy arrand. (*Raises pistol.*) What law shall dispute my raight to protect what th' law ha' gi'en me as mine?

GILBERT (*drawing another pistol*). Beware! I, too, am armed.

JOB (*calmly*). I knew it. I felt t'other pistol when I grappled wi' 'ee just now. We Lancashire lads foight fair, an' gi'e even our worst enemies a chance.

GILBERT (*with contemptuous surprise*). A duel! With you?

JOB. Why not? I ha' heerd it be th' fashin' 'mong you fo'ne gentlemen to tek each other's lives for a hard word, a'most for a wry look. (*His manner changes into one of great dignity.*) Had a *king* worked me th' ill thou hast done I'd feel my'sen his equal – ay! – moor nor his equal, fro' th' very greatness o' wrong!

GILBERT (*with involuntary respect*). Job Armroyd! I have deeply – cruelly injured you – I will not add another crime to the catalogue.

JOB. Not foight me! (*Crosses, so as to place himself between* GILBERT *and the door.*) Dunna think to quit this cottage wi'out it! Why th' meanest felon who robs by th' wayside foinds courage, when his toime cooms to stan' th' penalty.

GILBERT (*firmly*). I will not raise my hand against you.

JOB. I say thou shalt. (*Seizes* GILBERT *fiercely by the arm, as the latter endeavours to pass him.*) Thou'st robbed me o' nigh all, but thee shanna cheat me o' my revenge! (*They struggle.*)

GILBERT. Take off your hands, and I will go, never, never to return!

JOB. Will nothing stir thee? Coward! (*He strikes him;* GILBERT *starts back; at the same moment the doors* R. *and* L. *are opened, and* NELLY *and* TIDDY *appear.*)

GILBERT. A blow! (*He raises pistol he still holds in his hand. With a cry* NELLY *rushes forward, and throws herself before* JOB.)

NELLY. Fire *here*, Gilbert Featherstone; that heart (*indicates* JOB *by a gesture*) is struck too deep already! (FEATHERSTONE, *startled and abashed, lowers pistol.*)

JOB. This be no place for thee! To thy room! (*His tone changes into one of alarmed tenderness as he marks the changing expression of* NELLY'S *face.*) Nelly! (*Catches her in his arms as she is about to fall;* TIDDY *also advances in alarmed surprise.* FEATHERSTONE, *horror-struck, his eyes bent upon the sad group, remains without moving.*) Lass! lass! what be this?

NELLY (*raising her head and gazing sorrowfully in* JOB'S *agitated face.*) Death!

JOB. It canna be! it canna be! (*He kneels supporting her;* FEATHERSTONE *covers his face with his hands. A silvery light begins to tinge curtain and back of scene, as from the rising moon.*)

NELLY (*faintly*). Is he gone? (JOB *looks up and half rises as his eyes rest on* FEATHERSTONE, NELLY *laying her hand on his arm.*) Job! Job! look at me! Are you not avenged? (*She sinks back into* TIDDY'S *arms, who, kneeling, supports her.* JOB *has risen, his eyes still fixed on* FEATHERSTONE, *his face showing the fierce struggle of contending emotions.*)

GILBERT (*raising his head, but without advancing*). Job Armroyd, my life is in your hands – take it!

JOB (*pointing to door*). Go!

GILBERT (*abashed by the stern, high look of* JOB, *moves slowly up stage, pausing near door*). If there were atonement possible –

JOB. We canna re-make the past – nor forget it. Begone! (*He points to* NELLY, *who appears to have fainted in* TIDDY'S *arms.*)

Ye carry wi' thee thy own punishment, Gilbert Featherstone.
(*As* GILBERT *exits,* NELLY *raises her head listening.*)

NELLY. Hush! I heard Job Armroyd's voice – where is he?

JOB. Here, lass, here.

NELLY. Job! do you forgive me?

JOB (*with a burst of emotion*). Forgi'e thee! hegh, wench! but I forgave thee long, long ago!

NELLY (*looking earnestly in his face*). Job! think of me sometimes as – as I *was,* and Tiddy! (*taking her hand*) you'll not quite forget me?

TIDDY. Forget! Oh! lass! dunna speak such a word to me.

NELLY (*she moves her hand as feeling for something*). Job! My husband! (*Her heads falls back.*)

JOB. My wife! (*He looks into her face and starts to his feet.*) Air! gi'e her air! (*He rushes up stage to window.*) Sh' ha' swound! on'y swound, I tell 'ee! on'y that! (*He tears aside curtain from window and reveals the distant city, now brought out in strong relief by the rising moon.** *He is about to open window when a cry from* TIDDY *stays him.*)

NELLY (*who has suddenly risen to her feet*). Job! (*She advances towards him, her arms outstretched; he folds her in a convulsive embrace – as he does so her head sinks upon his breast.* TIDDY *is advancing, but he waves her back.*)

TIDDY. She ha' left us! (*Covers her face with hands, sobbing.*)

JOB. But not for ever! not for ever! Though lost in London (*he indicates by a gesture the city now bright with moonbeams*) I shall foind her theer.† (*He points upwards with a bright, hopeful look.* TIDDY *kneeling, raises* NELLY's *hand to her lips.*)

CURTAIN

* The above explains my reason for requiring a great width of window at back. I wish the great city to appear *most distinctly,* as a background to this last act of the drama. The moonlight view will give a beautiful tone to the scene.

† It is required that the silvery light of the moon should fall suddenly upon the figure of Nelly, flooding it as with a glory. W. P.

Under the Gaslight

AN ORIGINAL DRAMA OF AMERICAN
LIFE IN FOUR ACTS

by Augustin Daly

First performed at the New York Theatre, 13 August 1867

CAST

RAY TRAFFORD, a rich young man	*Mr A. H. Davenport*
LAURA COURTLAND, his sweetheart	*Miss Rose Eytinge*
PEARL COURTLAND, her cousin	*Miss Blanche Grey*
EDWARD DEMILT ⎱ fashionable	*Mr Newton*
WINDEL ⎰ members	*Mr Reed*
MRS VAN DAM ⎱ of	*Miss Lizzie Davey*
MISS EARLIE ⎰ society	*Miss Mahon*
SNORKEY, a messenger	*Mr J. K. Mortimer*
MARTIN, a servant	*Mr Fielding*
BYKE, a villain	*Mr J. B. Studley*
JUDAS, his associate	*Mrs Wright*
PEACHBLOSSOM, a servant	*Mrs Skerrett*
BERMUDAS ⎱ street sellers	*Mr C. T. Parsloe*
PEANUTS ⎰	*Master Shea*
JUSTICE BOWLING	*Mr Welsh Edwards*
SPLINTER, an attorney	*Mr James Dunn*
PETER RICH, a vagrant boy	*Master Willie*
POLICEMAN 999	*Mr Sampson*
RAFFERDI, an organ-grinder	*Mr Sullivan*
SAM, a negro	*Mr Williams*
POLICE SERGEANT	*Mr Hurley*
SIGNALMAN	*Mr H. Rayner*

Negro servant, Officers of the police court, Dock boys, Policemen, Ladies and Gentlemen

PAVILION

Licensed by the Lord Chamberlain to THEATRE, WHITECHAPEL ROAD. (Mr. Henry POWELL, 78, Approach Road, Victoria Park.)

COOLEST THEATRE IN LONDON.

RE-OPEN On SATURDAY, July 18th.

Extraordinary Sensation—The Great American Drama of the Day.

UNDER THE GAS LIGHT

With Two of the Greatest and most Marvellous Sensation Scenes ever placed before the Public.

PIERS AND BANKS OF THE RIVER BY STARLIGHT

REAL WATER!

IMMINENT PERIL OF DROWNING & FINAL RESCUE OF THE HEROINE.

THE IRON PILLOW

AND

DOWN EXPRESS TRAIN

Supported by an Entirely New and TALENTED COMPANY.

MASTER PERCY ROSELLE
EVERY EVENING
In one of his most Celebrated Impersonations

On SATURDAY, July 18th, MONDAY, July 20th, and EVERY EVENING until further Notice,

At 8 o'clock precisely, the Comic Drama, entitled—The

IRISH TUTOR!

Under O'Toe's

Master PERCY ROSELLE. Supported by the Company.

After which, at a quarter to Eight, the Extraordinary Sensation Drama, with its Marvellous Scenic Effects, Entitled—

UNDER THE GAS LIGHT

WITH NEW SCENERY & EFFECTS.

Ray Trafford	Mr. C. W. CHAMBERLAINE	Policeman 999 ... Mr. SAMPSON
Snorkey, (a returned Veteran, established as a Soldier Messenger, but upon to anything else) Mr. M. ROBSON		Martin ... Mr. FIELDING
Byke ... (one of the men whom the law is always reaching at but never reaches) Mr. MAYNARD		The Signal Man on the G.N.R. ... Mr. FYSON
Old Judas ... (one of the rising generation) Mr. HIBSON		Dock Boys, &c.
Edward Demilt ... (his friend, 'versed on the street') Mr. THOMPSON		Laura Courtland ... (the Belle of Society) Miss EMILY FORDE
Windel ... (a rival in matter in paper and matches) Master SHAR		Pearl Courtland ... (pretty but no heart) Miss ELLA McCARTHY
Peanuts ... (of doors) Master SHAT		Peachblossom ... (a girl who was never 'brought up') Mrs. HENRY WILLIS
Lillywhite ... (coloured) Mr. WILLIAMS		Mrs. Van Dam ... (one of the waters of Society) Miss MARIE WILLIS
Sam ... (a coloured citizen, ready for suffrage when it is ready for him) Mr. HURLEY		Miss Earlie ... (one of the echoes of the voices) Miss MASON
The Sergeant of the River Patrol		Lizzie Liston ... (another echo) Miss MACY

SCENE—LONDON.

ACT 1.—BETROTHED & DISCARDED
The Home of the Courtland's—The Story of a New Year's Night. The Telltale Letters. The beautiful Waters of Society.

WHERE THE POOR LIVE—A BASEMENT IN RIVINGTON STREET.
A new phase of Paternal Love—Pier of the City and River by Starlight—How the lost tribes spend their evenings.

REAL WATER!

The Heroine hurled Headforemost into the Real Water—her Imminent Peril of Drowning—She Sinks for the Third and Last time—her final rescue by our

Heart of Oak—GRAND TABLEAU OF JOY.

(N.B.—The Effects of this Scene are produced at a cost of over £500 and are duly Registered, and any one infringing or pirating the Registered effects without first obtaining Mr. POWELL's written Permission will be PROCEEDED AGAINST.)

THE IRON PILLOW.—Lesson which the Sad Heart taught the Weak One.

STATION SHED ON THE G.N.R.—PASSING OF THE EXPRESS
Snorkey saved from destruction through the Express Train by the bravery and resolution of Laura—Happiness dawns for the Virtuous and Justice smiles on all

UNDER THE GAS LIGHT.

Concluding, Every Evening, with the Comic Drama of

THE LIMERICK BOY

Miss B—y ... with Song 'True to Luck' ... Mr. M. ROBSON, supported by the whole of the Company.

Private Boxes £1 11s. 6d., £1 1s. 0d., or 2s. each person. Centre Boxes 1s. 6d., Boxes and Stalls 1s. Pit 6d. Gallery 3d. Children in Arms must be Paid for.
Doors Open at Half-past 6; Commencing at 7.   GEO. STEVENS, Theatrical Printer, 81, Langley Place, Commercial Road, E.

Under the Gaslight: Poster for an English adaptation, 1868

ACT I

SCENE I. – *Parlour at the* COURTLANDS, *deep window at back showing snowy exterior – street lamp lighted – time, night – the place elegantly furnished, chandelier, &c.*

RAY TRAFFORD *is discovered lounging on tête-à-tête,* PEARL *is taking leave of* DEMILT, WINDEL, MRS VAN DAM, *and* SUE EARLIE, *who are all dressed and muffled to go out.*

MRS VAN DAM. Goodnight! Of course we'll see you on Tuesday.
PEARL. To be sure you will.
DEMILT. Never spent a jollier hour. Goodnight, Ray.
RAY (*on sofa*). Goodnight.
MRS VAM DAM. You won't forget the sociable on Tuesday, Ray?
RAY. Oh, I won't forget.
ALL (*at door*). Goodnight – goodnight.

Exeunt DEMILT, WINDEL, MRS VAN DAM, *and* MISS EARLIE.

PEARL. Goodnight. Oh, dear, now they're gone and the holiday's gone with them. (*Goes to window.*) There they go. (*Laughter without.*) Ray, do come and look at the Van Dam's new sleigh. How they have come out.
RAY. Yes, it's the gayest thing in the park.
PEARL. I wonder where they got the money! I thought you said Van Dam had failed.
RAY. Well, yes. He failed to pay, but he continues to spend.
PEARL (*as if to those outside*). Goodnight! (*Response from without as sleigh bells jingle 'goodnight'.*) I wish I was in there with you. It's delightful for a sleigh ride, if it wasn't New Year's. Oh! there's Demilt over. (*Laughter outside, cracking of whips,* RAY *saunters up to window, sleigh bells jingle, sleigh music heard to die away,* RAY *and* PEARL *wave their handkerchiefs.*)

PEARL (*closing lace curtains*). Isn't it a frightful thing to be shut up here on such a beautiful night, and New Year's of all others? Pshaw, we've had nothing but mopes all day. Oh, dear, I hate mourning, though it does become me, and I hate everything but fun, larks, and dancing.

RAY. Where in the world is Laura?

PEARL. Oh, do forget her for a second, can't you? She'll be here presently. You're not in the house a minute but it's 'Where's Laura?' 'Why don't Laura come?'

RAY (*taking her hand*). Well, if anybody in the world could make me forget her it would be you. But if you had a lover, wouldn't you like him to be as constant as that?

PEARL. That's quite another thing.

RAY. But this doesn't answer my question. Where is she?

PEARL. I sent for her as soon as I saw you coming. She has hardly been down here a moment all this evening. Oh, dear! Now don't you think I'm a victim, to be cooped up in this way instead of receiving calls as we used to?

RAY. You forget that your mother died only last summer.

PEARL. No, I don't forget. Pshaw, you're just like Laura. She's only my cousin, and yet she keeps always saying 'Poor aunt Mary. Let us not forget how she would have sorrowed for us.'

RAY. Well, don't you know she would, too?

PEARL. I don't know anything about it. I was always at boarding school, and she only saw me once a year. Laura was always at home, and it's very different. But don't let's talk about it. To die – ugh! I don't want to die till I don't want to live – and that'll not be for a million of years. Come, tell me, where have you been today? How many calls did you make?

RAY. About sixty.

PEARL. That's all? You're lazy. Demilt and Windel made a hundred and thirty, and they say that's nothing. Won't you have a cup of coffee?

RAY. No.

PEARL. Ain't you hungry?

RAY. No – you torment.

PEARL. Oh, dear! I suppose it's because you're going to be married shortly to Laura. If there's one time that a man's stupid to his friends, it's when he's going to be married shortly. Tell me whom you saw. (RAY *has sauntered off and is looking over cards on table.*) Where are you? Oh, you needn't be so impatient to see her. Do be agreeable. Sit here and tell me something funny, or I shall drop down and fall asleep.

RAY. You witch! Why didn't I fall in love with you?

PEARL (*laughing*). I don't know – why didn't you?

RAY. You never keep me waiting. (*Listening.*) Ah! that's her step. No.

PEARL. Do sit down.

RAY (*sitting*). This calling's a great bore, but as you and Laura insisted I should go through it I did. First I – (*jumping up*) I knew it was she. (*Goes to door, meets* LAURA, *who enters.*) How you did keep me waiting! (*Kisses both her hands.*)

LAURA. And you, sir, we have been looking for you since eight o'clock.

RAY. Oh, I was fulfilling your orders. I've been engaged in the business of calling from ten o'clock in the morning till now, ten at night.

LAURA. Well, you can make this your last one, for you have leave to spend a nice long hour chatting here before you go. Won't you have some supper?

RAY. I don't care if I do, I'm rather famished.

PEARL. Well, I declare! Did Laura bring your appetite with her? (LAURA *rings.*)

RAY. I don't know how it is, but she brings me a relish for everything in life, I believe. Laura, I think if I were to lose you I'd mope to death and starve to death.

LAURA. Well, that's as much to say I'm a sort of life pill.

Enter MARTIN.

Martin, supper. (*Exit.*)

RAY. You may joke about it, but it's so. You take the lounge. (LAURA *and* PEARL *sit on tête-à-tête.*)

PEARL. You don't want me to go away, do you? (*Putting her head on* LAURA'*s shoulder.*)

LAURA. Certainly not. What an idea!

PEARL. I'm sure you'll have time enough to be alone when you are married. And I do so want to talk and be talked to.

LAURA. Well, Ray shall talk to you.

PEARL. He was just going to tell me about his calls today.

LAURA. That's exactly what we want to hear about. Did you call on everyone we told you to?

RAY. Everyone. There was Miss –

PEARL. Did you go to Henrietta Liston's first?

RAY. Yes, and wasn't she dressed! Speaking of dress, are you going to have your new pink for the sociable Tuesday?

LAURA. Yes, Pearl, and I will do credit to the occasion, as it is our first for a year.

RAY (*taking* LAURA'*s hand*). And *our* last.

PEARL. Our last!

RAY. Laura's and mine. For when we are married, you know, we shall be tabooed – where maids and bachelors only are permitted.

PEARL. Oh, bless me! (*Rising.*) How do you do, Mrs Trafford?

LAURA (*rising, sadly*). I wish you hadn't said that, Pearl. You know the old proverb, 'Call a maid by a married name.'

RAY. Nonsense! (*Putting his arm about* LAURA'*s waist.*) It's only a few days to wait, and we'll live long enough, you know. For nothing but death shall separate us.

MARTIN *appears at door.*

PEARL. Oh, here's supper.

MARTIN. Beg pardon, Miss.

LAURA. What's the matter?

MARTIN. There's a person below, miss, who says he's been sent with a bouquet for you, miss, and must deliver it in person.

LAURA. For me? Whose servant is it?

MARTIN. I don't know, miss, he looks like one of those soldier messengers, red cap and all that.

LAURA. Show him up here. (*Exit* MARTIN.)

PEARL. How romantic. So late at night. It's a rival in disguise, Ray.

Re-enter MARTIN *showing in* SNORKEY *with an air of disdain.* SNORKEY *has a large bouquet in his left hand, and his hat is under the stump of his right arm, which is cut off.*

LAURA. You wished to see me.

SNORKEY. Are you Miss Laura Courtland?

LAURA. Yes.

SNORKEY. Then I was told to give you this.

LAURA. By whom?

SNORKEY. Now, that's what I don't know myself. You see I was down by the steps of the Fifth Avenue Hotel taking a light supper off a small toothpick, when a big chap dressed in black came by, and says he, 'Hallo, come with me if you want to earn a quarter.' That (*confidentially to all*) being my very frame of mind, I went up one street and down another till we came here. 'Just you take this up there,' says he, 'and ask for Miss Laura Courtland, and give it to her and no one else.'

LAURA. It is some folly of our late visitors.

SNORKEY. I'm one of the soldier messengers, miss. A South Carolina gentleman took such a fancy to me at Fredericksburg! Wouldn't have no denial – cut off my arm to remember me by; he was very fond of me. I wasn't any use to Uncle Sam then, so I came home, put a red band round my blue cap, and with my empty sleeve, as a character from my last place, set up for light porter and general messenger. All orders executed with neatness and dispatch.

LAURA. Poor fellow! Martin, be sure and give him a glass of wine before he goes.

SNORKEY. I'm much obliged, miss, but I don't think it would be good for me on an empty stomach after fasting all day.

LAURA. Well, Martin shall find you some supper, too.

SNORKEY. Is this Martin? What a nice young man! Mayn't he have a drop of something, too? He must have caught cold letting me in, he has got such a dreadful stiffness in the back of his neck. (*Exit* MARTIN.)

RAY (*giving pencilled address*). Call on me at this place tomorrow, and you shan't regret it.

SNORKEY. All right, cap'n. I haven't forgot the army regulations about punctuality and promotion. Ladies, if ever either of you should want a light porter think of Joe Snorkey – wages no objection. (*Exit.*)

PEARL (*who has been examining the bouquet*). Oh, Laura, only look, here's a billet-doux.

RAY. Nonsense, crazy-head, who would dare? (*Takes bouquet.*) A letter! (*Takes a paper from bouquet.*)

LAURA. A letter?

PEARL. I am crazy – am I?

RAY. 'For Miss Laura Courtland. Confidential.'

LAURA (*laughs*). Ha, ha! From some goose who has made one call too many today. Read it, Ray.

RAY. 'Dear Laura . . .' (*Refusing the letter and going to* PEARL.)

LAURA (*looks at it a moment, when the whole expression of face changes, then reads slowly and deliberately*). 'I respectfully beg you to grant me the favour of an interview tonight. I have waited until your company retired. I am waiting across the street now.'

PEARL (*runs to window*). A tall man in black is just walking away.

LAURA. 'If you will have the door opened as soon as you get this I will step over; if you don't, I will ring; under all circumstances I will get in. There is no need to sign my name; you will remember me as the strange man whom you once saw talking with your mother in the parlour, and who frightened you so much.' What can be the meaning of this? Pearl – no. (*Goes to bell on table and rings.*)

RAY. Laura, you –

LAURA. Ask me nothing. I will tell you by and by.

Enter MARTIN.

MARTIN. Miss –

LAURA. Admit no one till you bring me the name.

MARTIN. I was about to tell you, miss, that a strange man has forced himself in at the door and asks to see you, but will give no name.

RAY. Kick the rascal out.

PEARL. Oh, don't let him come here.

MARTIN. He's a very strange-looking person, miss.

RAY. I'll find out what this means. (*Is going to door when* BYKE *appears at it smiling and bowing.*)

BYKE. I'll spare you the trouble if you'll hear me a minute.

RAY (*violently*). Who are you, fellow?

BYKE. Don't, I beg you. Don't speak so crossly; I might answer back; then you'd kick me out, and you'd never forgive yourself for it as long as I lived.

RAY. Your business? Come, speak quickly and begone.

BYKE. Business, on this happy day! I came for pleasure – to see Miss Courtland, my little pupil – grown so – only think, sir, I knew her when she was only a little child; I taught her music – she was so musical – and so beautiful – I adored her, and her mother told me I needn't come again. But I did, and her mother was glad to see me, wasn't she, little pupil? (*to* LAURA, *who is pale with terror, leaning on* PEARL) and begged me to stay – but I said no – I'd call occasionally – to see my dear little pupil and to receive any trifling contribution her mother might give me. Won't you shake hands, little pupil? (*Advances suddenly, when* RAY *grasps him by the collar.* BYKE *glares at him a moment, then quickly, as before.*) Don't, please, don't; the stuff is old and I've no other.

RAY. The fellow's drunk. Leave the house.

BYKE. What, after sending that touching bouquet?

LAURA. It was you, then? I knew it.

BYKE. You see she knows me. Ah, memory, how it blooms again where the plough of time has passed.

LAURA. Leave this house at once.

BYKE. Not until I have spoken to you.

RAY (*seizing him*). You miserable rascal.

BYKE. Don't, pray don't. I weigh a hundred and ninety-eight

281

pounds, and if you attempt to throw me about you'll strain yourself.

LAURA. Go; tomorrow in the morning I will see you.

BYKE. Thanks. I thank you, miss, for your forbearance. I am also obliged to you, sir, for not throwing me out at the window. I am indeed. I wish you goodnight and many happy returns of the day. (*Bows and turns to go, then familiarly to servant.*) Many calls today, John? (*Exit.*)

RAY *runs to* LAURA, *who is pale and agitated.*

LAURA (*pointing after* BYKE). See that he goes. (*Exit* RAY, LAURA, *taking both of* PEARL's *hands in her own.*) Pearl, he must know everything.

PEARL. Oh, dear, this is dreadful. I do hate scenes.

LAURA. He must know everything, I tell you; and you must relate all. He will question, he will ponder – leave him nothing to ask.

PEARL. If you wish it, but –

LAURA. I desire it; speak of me as you will, but tell him the truth.

Enter RAY, *hastily.*

Stay with her, don't follow me. (*Exit* LAURA.)

RAY. Pearl, what does this mean?

PEARL. Oh, it's only a little cloud that I want to clear up for you.

RAY. Cloud? How? Where?

PEARL. Don't I tell you I am going to tell you? Sit down here by me.

RAY. He said he knew her. And she gave him an interview for tomorrow. That drunken wretch –

PEARL. Do sit down. I can never speak while you are walking about so. Sit by me, won't you, for I've got something strange to tell you.

RAY. *You* serious? I'd as soon expect to see the lightning tamed. Well, I listen.

PEARL. I have something to say to you, Ray, which you must settle with your own heart. You love Laura, do you not?

RAY. Pearl, I do more; I adore her. I adore the very air that she breathes. I will never be happy without her, I can swear *that*.

PEARL. Laura is twenty now. How do you think she looked when I first saw her?

RAY. Were you at home when she first came into this earthly sphere?

PEARL. Yes.

RAY. Well then, I suppose she looked very small and very pink.

PEARL. She was covered with rags, barefooted, unkempt, crying, and six years old.

RAY (*shocked*). Explain.

PEARL. One night father and mother were going to the opera. When they were crossing Broadway, the usual crowd of children accosted them for alms. As mother felt in her pocket for some change, her fingers touched a cold and trembling hand which had clutched her purse.

RAY. A pickpocket! Well?

PEARL. This hand my mother grasped in her own, and so tightly that a small, feeble voice uttered an exclamation of pain. Mother looked down, and there beside her was a little ragged girl.

RAY. The thief.

PEARL. Yes, but a thief hardly six years old, with a face like an angel's. 'Stop!' said my mother, 'what are you doing?' 'Trying to steal,' said the child. 'Don't you know that it's wicked to do so?' asked my father. 'No,' said the girl, 'but it's dreadful to be hungry.' 'Who told you to steal?' asked my mother. 'She – there!' said the child, pointing to a squalid woman in a doorway opposite, who fled suddenly down the street. 'That is Old Judas,' said the girl.

RAY. Old Judas! What a name. But how does this story interest us?

PEARL. This child was Laura. My father was about to let her go unharmed, but my mother said, 'No, it is not enough. We have a duty to perform, even to her,' and acting on a sudden impulse, took her to our home. On being questioned there, the child seemed to have no recollection save of misery and blows. My mother persuaded father, and the girl was sent to a country clergyman's for instruction, and there she remained for several years.

RAY. Pearl, you are joking with me.

PEARL. In beauty, and accomplishments, and dignity, Laura, as mother named her, exceeded every girl of her age. In gratitude she was all that father could have wished. She was introduced, as you know, into society as my cousin, and no one dreams of her origin.

RAY (*starting up*). Laura an outcast – a thief!

PEARL (*rising*). No, that is what she might have been.

RAY. And this man – tonight?

PEARL. All I know about him is that four years ago this man came with a cruel-looking woman, to see mother. There was a fearful scene between them, for Laura and I sat trembling on the stairs and overheard some awful words. At last they went away, the man putting money into his pocket as he left.

RAY. But who were they?

PEARL. Laura never told me, and mother would not. But, of course, they must have been Laura's father and mother. (RAY *sinks on chair as if overcome.*)

PEARL. Mother made me promise never to tell anybody this, and you would have known nothing had not Laura made me speak. You see, she would not conceal anything from you. Ray, why don't you speak – shall I go after Laura? Shall I tell her to come to you? Why don't you answer? I'll go and tell her you want to see her. I'm going to send her to you, Ray. (*Goes off still looking back at him.*)

RAY (*starting up*). What a frightful story. Laura Courtland a thief. A drunken wretch who knows her history and a squalid beggar woman can claim her at any moment as their own child. And I was about to marry her. Yes, and I love her. But what would my mother think? My friends? Society? No – no – no – I cannot think of it. I will write her – I will tell her – pshaw! she knows, of course, that I cannot wed her now. (*Goes to the table.*) Here is paper. (*Sits.*) What am I about to do? What will be said of me? But I owe a duty to myself – to society – I must perform it. (*Writes.*) 'Laura, I have heard all from your sister.' What have I said? (*crosses out last words*) – 'from Pearl. You know that I love you, but my mother will demand of me a wife who will not blush to own her kindred, and who is not the daughter of obscurity and crime.' It is just – it is I who have been deceived. (*Folds letter and addresses it.*) I will leave it for her. (*Puts on light overcoat which hangs on chair at back.*) I must go before she returns. Her step – too late! (*Crams the letter into pocket of overcoat.*)

LAURA *enters.*

LAURA (*gently*). Ray.

RAY. Miss – Miss Courtland. (LAURA *looks at him a moment, smiles, and then crosses without further noticing him, and sits down on tête-à-tête.*) What have I said? What ought I to have said? (*He takes a step towards her – she rises, without looking at him, goes to window, looks out, then looks over books on table.*) Laura – I –

LAURA. Pshaw, where is my book?

RAY. What book do you want, Laura?

LAURA. Sir!

RAY (*repulsed*). Oh, (*pause*) I've been a fool. How lovely she looks. (*He follows her mechanically to table.*) Can I find it for you?

LAURA (*picking up book and re-seating herself*). Don't trouble yourself, I beg.

RAY (*coming forward and leaning over her seat*). Laura.

LAURA (*without lifting her head*). Well.

RAY (*toying with her hair*). Look at me.

LAURA *turns round and looks full at him.*

RAY. No, no, not that way – as you used to. You act as if I were a stranger.

LAURA. They are only strangers who call me Miss Courtland. (*Resumes reading.*)

RAY. Forgive me, I beg you to forgive me. I was mad – it was so sudden – this miserable story – but I don't care what they say. Oh, do listen to me. I thought you hated reading.

LAURA. I often wish that I were ugly, wretched, and repulsive, like the heroine in this story.

RAY. Why?

LAURA. Because then I could tell who really loved me.

RAY. And don't you know?

LAURA. No, I do not.

RAY. Well, I know.

LAURA. Do tell me then, please.

RAY. He has told you so himself a hundred times.

LAURA. You?

RAY. I!

LAURA (*laughing heartily at him, then seriously*). How happy must those women be who are poor, and friendless, and plain, when some true heart comes and says 'I wish to marry you!'

RAY. Laura, you act very strangely tonight.

LAURA. Will you put this book away?

RAY (*throws it on table*). There, Laura. (*Seats himself beside her.*)

LAURA (*rising*). There's Pearl calling me.

RAY (*rising and taking her hand*). Laura, why don't you let me speak to you?

LAURA. About what?

RAY. About my love.

LAURA. For whom? Not me. This is only marriage and giving in marriage. I hate the very word.

RAY. You did not think so once.

LAURA. I wish I had. I am frightened now; I begin to understand myself better.

RAY. And I am frightened because I understand you less.

LAURA. Do not try to; goodnight. (*Stops by door as she is going out.*) Goodnight Mr Trafford. (*Exit* LAURA, *laughing.*)

RAY. I've been an ass. No, I wrong that noble animal. The ass recognized the angel, and I, like Balaam, was blind. But I see now. After all, what have I to fear? (*Takes letter from pocket.*) No one knows of this. (*Puts it in his pocket again.*) Let things go on; we'll be married, go straight to Europe, and live there ten years. That's the way we'll fix it. (*Exit* RAY – *scene closes in.*)

SCENE II. – (*1st grooves*) – *the gentlemen's coat-room at Delmonico's – opening* C., *for hats and coats. Chairs* L. *Pier-glass on flat.*

Enter WINDEL *and* DEMILT *muffled, and with umbrellas; they proceed to disrobe.*

DEMILT. Phew! wet as the deuce, and cold too. There'll be nobody here.

WINDEL. It's an awful night. The rooms are almost empty.

DEMILT. Sam! Where the dickens is that darkey?

Enter SAM, *fetching in a chair, and boot-black box and brush.*

SAM. Here, sah.

DEMILT (*sitting in chair*). Hurry up with my boots. Who's here?

SAM. Berry few gemman, sah; only lebben overcoats and ten overshoes. Dem overshoes is spilin the polishin' business.

DEMILT. Look out and don't give me any knocks.

WINDEL (*handing in his coat at window and getting check for it*). I wonder if the Courtland girls have come yet.

DEMILT. What did Laura Courtland ever see in Trafford to fall in love with? The Van Dam party is my fancy.

WINDEL (*brushing his hair at glass*). She's ten years older than you, and has a husband.

DEMILT. Yes, a fine old banker, on whom she can draw for everything but attention and affection. She has to get that by her own business tact.

Other parties enter, exchange goodnights, and deposit their coats; some go out at once, some arrange themselves at glass.

DEMILT. That'll do, Sam, take my coat.

Enter RAY TRAFFORD.

WINDEL. Hallo, Trafford, this is a night, ain't it? Have the Courtlands come?

RAY. Not with me. Here, Sam, take my coat. (*His coat is pulled off by* SAM, *and four letters drop out.*) Stupid!

DEMILT. Save the pieces. Mind the love letters.

RAY (*picking them up*). Look out well next time. There's that cursed letter I was going to send to Laura. Confound it, I must destroy it when I go home. (*Puts letter back in overcoat pocket – gets his boots touched up.*)

DEMILT. I say, Trafford, what'll you take and let a fellow read those? Windel, I guess if the girls could get into the cloak-room, it would be better than the dead-letter office. What a time they'd have! Are you ready?

WINDEL. What's the use of hurrying? There is no life in the party till Laura Courtland comes. By Jove, Trafford! you're in luck. She's the prettiest girl in New York.

RAY. And the best. (*March music heard.*)

DEMILT. There's the march music; let's go. (*Gets a final brush as they all go off.*)

RAY. Come along. (*Exeunt.*)

SAM (*picking up a letter dropped from* RAY'S *pocket*). Dere's anoder of dem billy dooses; wonder if it am Mist' Trafford's. Eh, golly! mustn't mix dem gentlemen's letter, – mustn't mix 'em nohow – or nobody or nuffing wouldn't be able to stop fighting in dis city for de nex' month. (*Exit, carrying a chair, &c.*)

SCENE III. – *The blue room at Delmonico's. Waltz music as the scene opens. Waltzers in motion –* PEARL *is dancing with* MRS VAN DAM.

Enter RAY TRAFFORD, DEMILT *and* WINDEL.

PEARL. There's Ray. I've had enough; I want to speak with him. (*Bursts away from* MRS VAN DAM, *runs up to* TRAFFORD. DEMILT *goes up to* MRS VAN DAM.)

PEARL (*to* RAY). You lazy fellow, where have you been?

DEMILT. You're not tired, are you?

MRS VAN DAM. I feel as fresh as a daisy.

DEMILT. Have a waltz with me. (*Waltz music, piano, as they dance,* WINDEL *goes to* MISS EARLIE.)

RAY. Where's Laura?

PEARL. She wasn't ready, and I was dying to come. Been fixed since eight o'clock; so I came with Miss Earlie. So you made it up with Laura?

RAY. Yes. Don't say anything more about the horrid subject. We've made it all up. But what on earth keeps her tonight? It's eleven already. Confound it, I tremble every moment she's out of my sight. I fear that terrible man and his secret.

MRS VAN DAM (*coming up with* DEMILT). Trafford, you look very uneasy; what's the matter?

RAY. Oh, nothing. I think I ought to go for Laura. I will, too. (SERVANT *passes at back.*) Here! go upstairs for my overcoat. (*Gives the man a card, and he goes out.*)

MRS VAN DAM. Nonsense! She'll be here in good time. You shan't leave us. Hold him, Pearl. We want a nine-pin quadrille; we haven't half enough gentlemen. Come, be jolly about it. You lovers are always afraid someone will carry your girls away.

RAY (*uneasy*). I? I'm not afraid.

PEARL. Come, come! I never saw such a restless fellow.

Enter SERVANT *with coat.*

SERVANT. Here's your coat, sir.

MRS VAN DAM. Give it to me. I'm determined you shan't go.

(*Takes coat carelessly.*) I'll make you a promise – if Laura isn't here in fifteen minutes, you shall have your coat, and may go for her.

RAY. Well, I suppose I'll have to wait.

MRS VAN DAM. There, take him off, Pearl. (RAY *goes off with* PEARL – *to* SERVANT.) Here, take this back. (*Flings coat to* SERVANT, *as she does so letters drop from it.*) Well, there! (MISS EARLIE *and another lady run forward and pick up letters.*) Love letters, of course! (*Smelling them.*) Perfumed to suffocation.

MISS EARLIE. Here's one for Laura, it's unsealed and not delivered.

MRS VAN DAM (*tremolo waltz music*). A fair prize, let's see it. (*Music – takes and opens it, puts on eye-glasses and reads.*) 'Laura,' well, come, that's cool for a lover, 'I have heard all from' – something scratched out – ah! 'your sister, Pearl – your obscure origin – terrible family connexions – the secret of the tie which binds you to a drunken wretch – my mother, society – will demand of me a wife who will not blush to own her kindred – or start at the name of outcast and thief. – Signed, RAY TRAFFORD.' (*All stand speechless and look at each other – all this time the rest have been dancing.*)

MISS EARLIE. What can it mean?

MRS VAN DAM. It means that the rumours of ten years ago are proven. It was then suspected that the girl whom Mrs Courtland brought every year from some unnamed place in the country, and introduced to everybody as her niece, was an imposter, which that foolish woman, in a freak of generosity, was thrusting upon society. The rumours died out for want of proof, and before Laura's beauty and dignity, but now they are confirmed; she is some beggar's child.

MISS EARLIE. What do you think we ought to do? (TRAFFORD *surrenders* PEARL *to* DEMILT *and comes down.*)

MRS VAN DAM. Tell it – tell it everywhere, of course. The best blood of New York is insulted by the girl's presence.

RAY. What have you three girls got your heads together for? Some conspiracy, I know.

MRS VAN DAM (*to ladies*). Go, girls, tell it everywhere.

RAY (*as the ladies distribute themselves about the groups*). What is it all about? Your face is like a portrait of mystery.

MRS VAN DAM (*showing letter*). Look at this, and tell me what it means.

RAY (*quickly*). Where did you get this?

MRS VAN DAM. It is you who must answer, and society that will question. So Laura is not a Courtland?

RAY (*overcome*). You know, then –

MRS VAN DAM. Everything! And will you marry this creature? You cannot, society will not permit your sacrifice.

RAY. This is not your business. Give me that letter.

MRS VAN DAM. Certainly, take it. But let me say one word – its contents are known. In an hour every tongue will question you about this secret, every eye will inquire.

RAY. I implore you! Do not breathe a word for her sake. (*She turns scornfully away.*)

MRS VAN DAM. The secret's not mine.

RAY. Who knows it?

MRS VAN DAM. Look! (*points to others who are grouped about whispering and motioning towards* RAY.)

Enter PEARL *and speaks to lady and gentlemen.*

RAY (*wildly*). What will they do?

MRS VAN DAM. Expose her! Expel her from society in which she is an intruder!

RAY. You dare not!

PEARL. Oh Ray, what is the meaning of this?

RAY (*bitterly*). It means that society is a terrible avenger of insult. Have you ever heard of the Siberian wolves? When one of the pack falls through weakness the others devour him. It is not an elegant comparison, but there is something wolfish in society. Laura has mocked it with a pretence, and society, which is made up of pretences, will bitterly resent the mockery.

MRS VAN DAM. Very good! This handsome thief has stolen your breeding as well as your brains, I see.

RAY. If you speak a word against her I will say that what you utter is a lie!

MRS VAN DAM. As you please, we will be silent. But you will find that the world speaks most forcibly when it utters no sound.

PEARL. Oh, go and prevent her coming here.

RAY. That I can do. (*Going up hastily sees* LAURA *entering.*) Too late. (*He retreats.*)

MRS VAN DAM. Come, girls! Let us look after our things. They are no longer safe when an accomplished thief enters. (*Music low, continues while all except* PEARL *and* RAY *pass out, eyeing* LAURA *superciliously.*)

PEARL. Ray, Ray! why do you not come to her?

MRS VAN DAM (*surrounded by others*). Are you not coming with us, Trafford?

PEARL (*to* LAURA). Let us go home.

LAURA. No, stay with *him*! (*Pointing to* RAY, *who has held off.*) He shall not suffer the disgrace long. (*About to faint*; RAY *runs forward, she proudly waves him away.*) It is Heaven's own blow!

ACT II

SCENE I. – *Interior of a basement. Street and railings seen through window at back. Entrance door* L., *stove with long pipe in fire-place*, R. *Table between two windows at back, with flowers, &c. – humble furniture. Table* C., *three chairs. Closet*, L. (*2nd grooves.*)

PEACHBLOSSOM *is discovered polishing stove –* (*a slip-shod girl*).

SONG – PEACHBLOSSOM

A lordly knight and a lovely dame were walking in the
    meadow.
But a jealous rival creeping came, a-watching in the shadow.
They heeded not, but he whet his knife and dogged them in
    the shadow;
The knight was brave, and the dame was true, the rival fared
    but badly;
For the knight he drew and ran him through, and left him
    groaning sadly.
The knight and dame soon wedded were, with bells
    a-chiming gladly.

PEACHBLOSSOM. The stove won't shine. It's the fault of the polish, I know. That boy that comes here just fills the bottles with mud, and calls it stove polish. Only let me catch him. Ah! Ah! (*threatening gesture with brush*) I declare I'd give it up if I didn't want to make everything look smart, before Miss Nina comes in. Miss Nina is the only friend I ever had since I ran away from mother Judas. I wonder where old Judas is now? I know she's drunk, she always was; perhaps that's why she never tried to find out what became of me. If she did she could not take me away. Miss Nina begged me off a policeman. I belong to her. I wonder why she ain't got

293

any other friends? She's awful mysterious. Tells me never to let any strangers see her. She's afraid of somebody, I know. It looks just as if she was hiding. I thought only bad girls, such as I, had to hide. If I was good and pretty like her, I wouldn't hide from the President. (*Still polishing –* JUDAS *appears at window with basket of ornaments, &c.*)

JUDAS. Hum! Is your ma in, my dear?

PEACHBLOSSOM (*starting*). Oh! (*Aside.*) Old Judas! She's found me out at last. No she bain't, or she'd have got me by the hair before she spoke, that's *her* way.

JUDAS (*coming in at door –* PEACHBLOSSOM *keeps her back towards her*). Any old clothes to change for chany, my dear? Where's your ma's old skirts and shawls, my pet? Get 'em quick, before mother comes in, and I'll give you a beautiful chany mug or a tea-pot for them. Come here, my ducky – see the pretty – (*recognises* PEACHBLOSSOM). Eh! why you jail-bird, what are you doing here? Are you sneakin' it? Answer me, or I'll knock your head agin the wall. (*Catches her by the hair.*)

PEACHBLOSSOM. You just leave me be. I'm honest, I am. I'm good!

JUDAS. You're good? Where's my shoe? I'll take the goodness out of you.

PEACHBLOSSOM. Oh, oh! please don't beat me. I ain't good. I'm only trying to be.

JUDAS. You're only trying to be, eh? Trying to be good, and here's me as was a-weeping every night, thinking as you was sent up for six months. Who're you living with – you ain't a-keeping house, are you?

PEACHBLOSSOM. I'm living with Miss Nina.

JUDAS. Nina, what's she, concert saloon girl?

PEACHBLOSSOM. No, she's a lady.

JUDAS. A lady – and have such baggage as you about? Where's my shoe? I'll make you speak the truth.

PEACHBLOSSOM. I don't know what she is. She met me when the police were taking me up for loafin' down Hudson Street, and she begged me off.

JUDAS. Has she any money?

PEACHBLOSSOM. No, she's poor.

JUDAS. Any nice clothes?

PEACHBLOSSOM. Oh, she's got good clothes.

JUDAS. Where are they?

PEACHBLOSSOM. Locked up, and she's got the key.

JUDAS. You're lying; I see it in your eye. You're always shame-faced when you are telling the truth, and now you're as bold as brass. Where's my shoe? (*Making a dash at her.*)

PEACHBLOSSOM (*shouting*). There's Miss Nina. (*As if curtseying to someone behind* JUDAS.) Good morning, miss.

JUDAS (*changing her tone*). Ah, my pretty dear! What a good lady to take you in and give you a home. (*Turns and discovers the deception – in a rage.*) You hussy. (PEACHBLOSSOM *retreats.*) Wait till I get you in my clutches again, and it won't be long. Miss Nina takes care of you, does she? Who will take care of her? Let her look to it. (LAURA *enters, plainly dressed, at back.*) Beg pardon, Miss, I just called to see if you had any old clothes you'd like to exchange.

LAURA. No, I don't want anything, my good woman.

JUDAS (*eyeing her sharply and going to door*). That's her – I'd know here anywhere! (*Malicious glance, and exit.*)

LAURA. You've been very good this morning, Blossom. The room is as nice as I could wish.

PEACHBLOSSOM. Please 'm, I tried because you are so good to me. Shall I sweep out the airy? I guess I'd better – then she'll be alone, as she loves to be. (*Takes broom and exit.*)

LAURA (*opening a package and taking out photographs*). No pay yet for colouring 'till I have practised a week longer. Then I shall have all the work I can do. They say at the photo-grapher's I colour well, and the best pictures will be given me. The best! Already I have had beneath my brush so many faces that I know – friends of the old days. The silent eyes seem to wonder at me for bringing them to this strange and lowly home. (*Picking up letters from table.*) Letters, ah! answers to my advertisement for employment. No, only a circular 'To the lady of this house.' What's that! (*Starting.*)

Only Blossom sweeping. Every time there is a noise I dread the entrance of someone that knows me. But they could never find me in New York. I left them all so secretly and suddenly. None of them can expect I would have descended to this. But it is natural, everything will find its level. I sprang from poverty, and I return to it. Poor Pearl. How she must have wondered the next morning – Laura gone! But three months have passed, and they have forgotten me. Ray will cheer her. (*Wrangling outside;* PEACHBLOSSOM *bursts in, dragging* BERMUDAS, *with his professional tape, pins, blacking, and baskets.*)

PEACHBLOSSOM. Here he is 'm.

BERMUDAS. Leave go, I tell yer, or I'll make yer.

LAURA. What is the matter?

PEACHBLOSSOM. He's the boy that sold me that stove polish what isn't stove polish.

BERMUDAS. What is it then – s-a-a-y?

PEACHBLOSSOM. It's mud! it's mud at tenpence a bottle.

BERMUDAS. Ah, where could I get mud? Ain't the streets clean? Mud's dearer than stove polish now.

PEACHBLOSSOM. And your matches is wet, and your pins won't stick, and your shoe-strings is rotten, there now!

BERMUDAS. Well, how am I to live? it ain't my fault, it's the taxes. Ain't I got to pay my income tax, and how am I to pay it if I gives you your money's worth? Sa-a-y?

LAURA. Do let the boy alone, Blossom. Send him away.

Enter PEANUTS.

PEANUTS. Extra! Hollo, Bermudas! how's your sister? Papers, Miss. Extra! Revolution in Mexico!

LAURA. Dear, dear, this is the way I'm worried from morning till night.

BERMUDAS. Here, just you get out! This is my beat.

PEANUTS. Vell, I ain't blacking or hairpins now, I'm papers. How'm I hurting you?

BERMUDAS. Vell, I'm papers at four o'clock, and this is my beat. Take care of me, I'm training for a fight. I'm a bruiser, I am.

PEANUTS. Hold yer jaw. (*They fight.*)

PEACHBLOSSOM (*beats them with broom*). Get out with you, both of you! (*Grand escapade, and exit of boys.*)

LAURA. Don't let's be troubled in this way again. Have you got the things for dinner?

PEACHBLOSSOM. Lor, no, miss. It's twelve o'clock, and I forgot. (PEACHBLOSSOM *gets shawl, big bonnet from hooks on the wall, basket from closet, while* LAURA *opens her pocket-book for money.*)

LAURA. What did we have for dinner yesterday, Blossom?

PEACHBLOSSOM. Beefsteak 'm. Let's have some leg o' mutton today. We've never had that.

LAURA. But I don't know how to cook it. Do you?

PEACHBLOSSOM. No, but I'd just slap it on, and it's sure to come out right.

LAURA. Slap it on what?

PEACHBLOSSOM. The gridiron!

LAURA (*giving money*). No, we'd better not try a leg of mutton today. Get some lamb chops; we know how to manage them.

PEACHBLOSSOM (*as she is going*). Taters, as usual, 'mum?

LAURA. Yes; and stop, Blossom – while you're buying the chops, just ask the butcher – off hand, you know – how he would cook a leg of mutton, if he were going to eat it himself – as if you wanted to know for yourself.

PEACHBLOSSOM. Yes 'm, but I'm sure it's just as good broiled as fried. (*Exit.*)

LAURA. Now to be cook. (*Laughing.*) The Tuesday Sociable ought to see me now. Artist in the morning, cook at noon, artist in the afternoon.

SNORKEY *raps at the door and enters.*

SNORKEY (*with letter*). Beg pardon, is there anybody here as answers to the name of A. B. C.?

LAURA (*aside*). My advertisement for work – Yes, give it to me.

SNORKEY (*seeing her face*). If I'd been taking something this morning, I'd say that I'd seen that face in a different sort of place from this.

LAURA. Is there anything to pay? Why do you wait?

SNORKEY. Nothing, Miss. It's all right. (*Going – and aside.*) But it ain't all right, Snorkey, old boy. (*Goes out after looking at her, stops at window, and gazes in.*)

LAURA. Yes, an answer to my advertisement. (*Reads.*) To A. B. C. – Your advertisement promises that you are a good linguist, and can teach children of any age. I have two daughters for whom I wish to engage your services while on a tour of Europe. Call at seven o'clock this evening, at No. 207, West 34th Street, Annersley.' Hope at last, a home, and in another land soon. I was sure the clouds would not always be black above me. (*Kisses letter,* SNORKEY *re-entering.*)

SNORKEY. Miss, I say Miss? (LAURA *starts.*) Sh –

LAURA. What do you want?

SNORKEY. Only one word, and perhaps it may be of service to you. I'd do anything to serve you.

LAURA. And why me?

SNORKEY. I'm a blunt fellow, Miss, but I hope my way don't offend. Ain't you the lady that I brought a bouquet to on New Year's night – not here, but in a big house, all bright and rich, and who was so kind to a poor soldier?

LAURA (*faint and leaning against chair*). Whoever you may be, promise to tell no one you saw me here.

SNORKEY. No fear, Miss. I promise.

LAURA. Sacredly?

SNORKEY. No need to do more than promise, Miss – I keeps my word. I promised Uncle Sam I'd stick to the flag – though they tore my arm off, and by darnation I stuck! I don't want to tell on you, Miss, I want to tell on someone else.

LAURA. What do you mean?

SNORKEY. They're looking for you.

LAURA. Who?

SNORKEY. Byke. (LAURA *utters a loud cry, and sinks on chair.*) He's on it day and night. I've got his money in my pocket now, and you've got his letter in your hand this minute. (LAURA *drops the letter in dismay.*)

LAURA. This?

SNORKEY. Yes, it's his writin' – looks like a woman's, don't it?
Lord! the snuff that man's up to would make Barnum sneeze
his head off. He's kept me in hand, 'cause he thinks I know
you, having seen you that once. Every day he reads the
advertisements, and picks out a dozen or so, and says to me –
'Snorkey, that's like my little pet,' and then he sits down and
answers them, and gets the advertisers to make appoint-
ments with him, which he keeps regularly, and regularly
comes back cussing at his ill luck. See here, Miss, I've a
bundle of answers to deliver as usual, to advertisers. I calls
'em Byke's Target Practice, and this time, you see, he's
accidentally hit the mark.

LAURA. For heaven's sake do not betray me to him! I've got
very little money; I earn it hardly, but take it, take it – and
save me. (*Offers money.*)

SNORKEY. No, miss, not a cent of it. Though Byke is a devil,
and would kick me hard if he thought I would betray him.

LAURA. I don't want you to suffer for my sake; take the money.

SNORKEY. No, I stood up to be shot at for thirteen dollars a
month, and I can take my chances of a kickin' for nothing.
But Byke ain't the only one, miss; there's another's looking
for you.

LAURA (*her look of joy changing to fear*). Another! Who?

SNORKEY (*approaching smilingly and confidential*). Mr Trafford.
(LAURA *turns aside despairingly.*) He's been at me every day
for more than six weeks. 'Snorkey,' says he, 'do you remember that beautiful young lady you brought the bouquet to on
New Year's night?' 'Well,' says I, 'Cap'n, the young lady I
slightly disremember, but the cakes and wine I got there
that night I shall never forget.' 'Search for that young lady,'
says he, 'and when you find her' –

LAURA. No, no, no; not even he must know. Do you hear – not
he – not anyone. You have served them well; serve me and
be silent.

SNORKEY. Just as you please, miss, but I hate to serve you by
putting your friends off the track – it don't seem natural –

Byke I don't mind, but the cap'n wouldn't do you any harm. Just let me give him a bit of a hint. (LAURA *makes an entreating gesture.*) Well I'm mum, but as I've only got one hand, it's hard work to hold my tongue. Not the least bit of a hint? (LAURA *appeals to him and then turns away.*) They say when a woman says no she means yes. I wonder if I dare tell her that he's not far off. Perhaps I'd better not. But I can tell him. (*Exit.*)

LAURA. How shall I ever escape that dreadful man? And Ray searching for me too. Our friends, then, remember us, as well as our enemies.

Enter PEACHBLOSSOM, *quickly, shutting the door behind her, with basket, which she places on table.*

PEACHBLOSSOM. Oh, Miss Nina, whatever is into the people? There's a strange man coming down the entry; I heard him asking that red cap fellow about you.

LAURA. Byke! Fasten the door, quick. (PEACHBLOSSOM *runs to door, it is slightly opened, she pushes it against someone on the other side.*)

PEACHBLOSSOM. Oh, dear, he's powerful strong; I can't keep it shut. Go away, you willin: Oh! (*The door is forced and* RAY TRAFFORD *enters.*)

RAY. Laura, it is I!

LAURA. Ray! (*Shrinks from him.*)

RAY. Dear Laura – (*he stops as he becomes conscious that* PEACH-BLOSSOM *with her basket on her arm and her bonnet hanging on her back is staring at him*) I say, my girl, haven't you some particular business somewhere else to attend to?

PEACHBLOSSOM (*seriously*). No, sir, I've swept the sidewalk and gone a-marketing, and now I'm indoors and I mean to stay.

RAY. And wouldn't you oblige me by going for a sheet of paper and an envelope? Here's a dollar – try and see how slow you can be.

PEACHBLOSSOM (*firmly*). You can't sheet of paper me, mister, I'm protecting Miss Nina, and I'm not to be enveloped.

LAURA. Go as the gentleman asks you, Blossom.

300

PEACHBLOSSOM. Oh! (*Takes money, fixes her bonnet.*) First it's 'Keep the man out,' now it's 'Let him stay in alone with me.' But I suppose she's like all of us – it makes a great difference which man it is. (*Exit.*)

RAY (*after watching* PEACHBLOSSOM *out*). Laura, when I approached you you shrank from me. Why did you do so?

LAURA. Look around you and find your answer.

RAY (*shuddering*). Pardon me, I did not come here to insult your misery. When I saw you I forgot everything else.

LAURA. And now it's time for us to remember everything. I told you to look around that you might understand that in such a place I am no longer Laura Courtland, nor anything I used to be. But I did not ask your pity. There is no misery here.

RAY. Alone, without means, exposed to every rudeness, unprotected, is this not misery for you?

LAURA (*laughing*). Oh, it's not so bad as that.

RAY. Laura, don't trifle with me. You cannot have exchanged everything that made you happy for this squalid poverty, and not feel it deeply.

LAURA. I have not time to feel anything deeply. (*Takes basket up, goes to table, busies herself about preparing dinner.*) I work from sunrise till night, and I sleep so soundly that I have not even dreams to recall the past. Just as you came in I was about to cook our dinner. Only think – lamb chops.

RAY. Lamb chops! It makes me shudder to hear you speak.

LAURA. Does it? Then wait till I get the gridiron on the fire and you'll shiver. And if you want to be transfixed with horror stop and take dinner.

RAY. I will not hear you mock yourself thus, Laura. I tell you in this self-banishment you have acted thoughtlessly – you have done wrong.

LAURA. Why?

RAY. Because, let the miserable creatures who slandered you say what they might, you had still a home and friends.

LAURA. A home! Where the very servants would whisper and point, friends who would be ashamed to acknowledge me. You are mistaken. That is neither home nor friendship.

RAY. And you are resolved to surrender the past for ever?

LAURA. The past has forgotten me in spite of myself.

RAY. Look at me.

LAURA. Well, then, there's one who has not forgotten me, but I desire that he may. You speak to me of bitterness. Your presence, your words, cause me the first pang I have felt since the night I fled unnoticed from my chamber, and began my life anew. Therefore I entreat you to leave me, to forget me.

RAY. Laura, by the tie that once bound us!

LAURA. Yes, *once*. It *is* a long time ago.

RAY. What have I said? The tie which still –

LAURA (*sharply turning*). Mr Trafford, must I remind you of that night when all arrayed themselves so pitilessly against me, when a gesture from you might have saved me, and you saw me without stretching a finger to the woman who had felt the beating of your heart. No, you made your choice then – the world without me. I make my choice now – the wide, wide, world without you.

RAY. I have been bitterly punished, for we are never so humiliated as when we despise ourselves. But, by the heaven above us both, I love you, Laura – I have never ceased to love you.

LAURA. I thank you. I know how to construe the love which you deny in the face of society to offer me behind its back.

RAY. Will you drive me mad? I tell you, Laura, your misery, your solitude is as nothing to the anguish I have suffered. The maniac who in his mental darkness stabs to the heart the friend he loved never felt in returning reason the remorse my error has earned me. Everyday it says to me 'You have been false to the heart that loved you, and you shall account for it to your conscience all your life. You shall find that the bitterest drops in the cup of sorrow are the tears of the woman you have forsaken.' And it is true. Oh, forgive me – have pity on me.

LAURA (*moved*). I forgive you. Yes, and I pity you – and so good-bye for ever.

RAY. Of course I am nothing to you now; that is some comfort to

me. I have only to be sorry on my own account, but I come
to you on behalf of others.

LAURA. Whom?

RAY. My mother and Pearl, they ask for you. For them I have
sought you, to urge you to return to them.

LAURA. Dear little Pearl.

RAY. Yes, she has been quite ill.

LAURA. She has been ill?

RAY. Think of those two hearts which you have caused to suffer
and do not drive me from you. It is not only wealth, luxury,
and refinement which you have surrendered – you have also
cast away those greater riches, loving and devoted friends.
But they shall persuade you themselves – yes, I'll go and
bring them to you; you cannot resist their entreaties.

LAURA. No, no, they must not come here, they must never know
where *I* hide my shame, and you must never reveal it.

RAY. I promise it if you will go to them with me. Think, they
will insist on coming unless you do.

LAURA. Poor Pearl. If I go with you, you promise not to detain
me – to permit me to come back and to trouble me and my
poor life no more?

RAY. I promise, but I know you will release me from it when you
see them. I will get a carriage, so that no one will meet you.
Wait for me, I shall not be long. It is agreed?

LAURA (*smiling*). Yes, it is agreed.

Enter PEACHBLOSSOM, *with a sheet of paper foolscap and some
enormous envelopes.*

PEACHBLOSSOM. Here they are.

RAY. That's a good girl, keep them till I come back. In half an
hour, Laura, be ready. (*Exit.*)

PEACHBLOSSOM (*with an air*). What's he going to do in half an
hour?

LAURA. He's going to take me away with him for a little while,
Peachblossom, and while I'm gone I wish you to be a good
girl, and watch the house and take care of it till I return.

PEACHBLOSSOM. I don't believe it, you won't return. (*Crying.*) That's what our Sal said when she went off with her young man, and she never came back at all. You shan't go; I hate him. He shan't take you away.

LAURA (*who is getting ready, putting her hat on, &c.*). Blossom!

PEACHBLOSSOM. I don't care, if you go away I'll go away; I'll bite and scratch him if he comes back. (*Fiercely tearing up the paper and envelopes.*) Let him come back – let him dare come back.

LAURA. Blossom, you're very wicked. Go into the corner this minute and put your apron over your head.

PEACHBLOSSOM (*crying at* LAURA's *feet*). Oh, please, Miss Nina, let me go with you and I'll be so good and not say a word to anyone. Do let me go with you. Let me ask him to let me go with you. (*Figure passes the window.*) Here he is; I see him coming.

LAURA. Run, run, open the door. (PEACHBLOSSOM *runs to door, throws it open, disclosing* BYKE – *exclamation of horror from* LAURA.)

BYKE. Ah, my dear little runaway, found you at last, and just going out. How lucky! I wanted you to take a walk with me.

LAURA. Instantly leave this place!

BYKE. How singular! You are always ordering me out and I am always coming in. We want a change. I will go out, and I request you to come with me.

LAURA. Blossom, go find an officer, tell him this wretch is insulting me.

BYKE. Blossom? Ah – exactly! Here, you Judas.

JUDAS *enters.*

PEACHBLOSSOM. Oh, miss, save me.

BYKE (*throws* PEACHBLOSSOM *over to* JUDAS, *who drags her out*). Take care of that brat, and as for you, daughter, come with me.

LAURA. Daughter!

BYKE. Yes, it is time to declare myself. Paternal feeling has been too long smothered in my breast. Come to my arms, my child – my long-estranged child. (*Takes out dirty handkerchief and presses his eyes with pretended feeling.*)

LAURA. Heavens! is there no help? (*She attempts to escape,* BYKE *seizes her.*)

BYKE. What an unfilial girl; you take advantage of a father's weakness and try to bolt. (*Clutching her by the arm.*) Come, go with me and cheer my old age. Ain't I good to take you back after all these years? (*Drags her out, she calling 'help! help!'*)

SCENE II. – *The Tombs Police Court. Long high desk with three seats across back, from* R. *to* L., *on platform. Railing in front, railing around* L., *with opening* L. C. *In front of railing, a bench* R. *and* L. – *gate in* C. *of railing. Judge* BOWLING *and another* JUSTICE *seated behind high desk* C., *with clerk on his* L. JUSTICE *is reading paper, with his feet upon desk* R. POLICEMEN *at* R. *and* L. POLICEMAN *999 at gate. Hard-looking set of men and women on benches* R. *and* L. – *Lawyer* SPLINTER *is talking to* RAFFERDI, *an organ-man, who is in crowd. As the curtain rises, noisy buzz is heard.*

BOWLING. Smithers, keep those people quiet. (POLICEMAN *handling people roughly.*) Here, easy – officer, treat those poor people decently. Well, whom have you got there?

POLICEMAN (*dragging urchin within railing*). Pickpocket, your honour. Caught in the act.

BOWLING. What's he got to say for himself? Nothing, eh? What's his name?

POLICEMAN (*stooping down to boy as if asking him*). Says his name is Peter Rich.

BOWLING. You stand a poor chance, Rich. Take him away. (BOWLING *consults with another Justice, as the boy is taken off.*)

SPLINTER (*to* RAFFERDI, *who has his monkey and organ*). So you want to get out, eh? How much money have you got?

RAFFERDI. Be jabers! half a dollar in cents is all the money I'm worth in the world.

SPLINTER. Give it to me. I thought you organ fellows were Italians.

RAFFERDI. Divil doubt it! Ain't I got a monkey?

POLICEMAN. Here, you – come up here. (*Takes* RAFFERDI *inside the railing.*)

BOWLING. Now then, what's this, officer?

POLICEMAN (RAFFERDI *takes stand*). Complaint of disturbing the neighbourhood.

BOWLING. What have you got to say for yourself?

SPLINTER. If your honour please, I appear for this man.

BOWLING. Well, what have you got to say for him?

SPLINTER. Here is an unfortunate man, your honour – a native of sunny Italy. He came to our free and happy country, and being a votary of music, he bought an organ and a monkey, and tried to earn his bread. But the myrmidons of the law were upon him, and the Eagle of Liberty drooped his pinions as Rafferdi was hurried to his dungeon.

BOWLING. Rafferdi, you're an Irishman, ain't you? What do you mean by deceiving us?

RAFFERDI. Sure I didn't. It's the lawyer chap there. I paid him fifty cents and he's lying out the worth of it.

BOWLING. You fellows are regular nuisances. I've a great mind to commit you.

SPLINTER. Commit him? If the court please, reflect – commit him to prison? What will become of his monkey?

BOWLING. Well, I'll commit him too.

SPLINTER. You cannot. I defy the Court to find anything in the Statutes authorising the committal of the monkey.

BOWLING. Well, we'll leave out the monkey.

SPLINTER. And if the Court please, what is the monkey to do in the wide world, with his natural protector in prison? I appeal to those kindlier feelings in your honour's breast, which must ever temper justice with mercy. This monkey is perhaps an orphan!

BOWLING (*laughing*). Take them both away, and don't let me

catch you here again, Mr Rafferdi, or you'll go to jail. (SPLINTER *goes down* – RAFFERDI *exits.*)

POLICEMAN (*pulling* SAM, *a nigger, who is drunk, out of a crowd*). Get up here.

SAM (*noisily*). Look yah – don't pull me around.

BOWLING. Silence there! what's all this noise about?

SAM. Whar's de court? I want to see de Judge.

SPLINTER. My coloured friend, can I assist you?

SAM. Am you a Counseller-at-law?

SPLINTER. Yes, retain me. How much money have you got?

SAM. I ain't got no money, but I've got a policy ticket. It's bound to draw a prize.

SPLINTER. Got any pawn tickets?

SAM. Ob course. (*Giving him a handful.*)

BOWLING. Well, what's the charge?

POLICEMAN. Drunk and disorderly.

BOWLING. Well, my man, what have you to say?

SAM. Dis here gemman represents me.

SPLINTER. We admit, if the Court please, that we were slightly intoxicated, but we claim the privilege, as the equal of the white man.

BOWLING (*to clerk*). Very good. Commit him for ten days.

SPLINTER. But this is an outrage, your honour.

BOWLING (*to officer*). Take him off. (*Motioning to* SAM – SPLINTER *sits down discomfited* – SAM *very wroth.*)

SAM. What?

BOWLING. Take him away.

SAM. Look here, judge, hab you read the Civil Right Bill? You can't send dis nigger to prison, while dat bill am de law ob de land.

BOWLING. That'll do, remove him.

SAM. I ain't no gipsy. I'm one of de Bureau nigger, I am. Where am de law? Don't touch me, white man! Dis am corruption – dis am 'ficial delinquency! (POLICEMAN *collars him and carries him off.*)

BOWLING. Any more prisoners? (*Noise.*) What noise is that?

307

(OFFICER *goes out.* BYKE *enters, followed by the* OFFICER, *who escorts* LAURA.)

BYKE. Where is the judge? Oh, where is the good, kind judge?

BOWLING. Well, my dear sir, what is the matter?

BYKE. Oh, sir, forgive my tears. I'm a broken-hearted man!

BOWLING. Be calm, my dear sir. Officer, bring this gentleman a chair. (OFFICER *hands chair.*)

BYKE. Ah, sir, you are very good to a poor distressed father, whose existence has been made a desert on account of his child.

BOWLING. Repress your emotion, and tell me what you want.

BYKE. I want my child.

BOWLING. Where is she?

BYKE. She is here, sir – here – my darling, my beautiful child, and so unfilial – so unnatural.

BOWLING. How is this, young lady?

LAURA (*standing inside railing*). It is all a lie. He is not my father.

BYKE. Not your father? Oh, dear, oh, dear, you will break my heart!

BOWLING. This needs some explanation. If not his child, who are you?

LAURA. I am – I dare not say it. I know not who I am, but I feel that he cannot be my father.

BYKE. Oh, dear – Oh! –

BOWLING (*sharply*). Silence! (*To* LAURA, *sternly.*) You say you don't know who you are. Do you know this man?

LAURA. Yes.

BOWLING. Where and with whom do you live?

LAURA. I have lived alone for four months.

BOWLING. And with whom did you live before that!

LAURA. Oh, forgive me, if I seem disobedient – but I cannot tell.

BOWLING. Then I must look to this gentleman for information.

BYKE. And I will gladly give it. Yes, sir, I will gladly tell. She was taken from me years ago, when she was but a little child, by rich people who wanted to adopt her. I refused – they paid me – I was poor – I was starving – I forebore to claim her –

308

she was happy, but they turned her forth four months ago into the street. I could not see her suffer – my child – the prop of my declining days. I begged her to come – she refused. My enemies had poisoned my daughter's mind against *me*, her father. I am still poor. I taught school, but I have saved a little money, only for her,

BOWLING. How old is she?

BYKE. Nineteen.

BOWLING. Your father is your legal guardian during your minority, and is entitled to your custody, Why are you so undutiful? Try to correct this.

BYKE, Oh, bless you, dear good judge for these words.

LAURA. Oh, have I no friends, must I go with him?

BOWLING. Certainly.

LAURA. Anything then. Exposure! Disgrace, rather than that! (JUDGES *consult.*)

Enter SNORKEY.

BYKE (*aside*). Snorkey! the devil!

SNORKEY. Can I help you, miss? Only tell me what to do, and if it takes my other arm off, I'll save you.

LAURA. Yes, yes, you can help me! (*To* JUDGES.) Will you let me send a message.

BOWLING. You may do that.

LAURA. Run to that house – not my house – but the one in which you saw me first. Do you remember it?

SNORKEY. Don't I, and the wine and cakes.

LAURA. Ask for Miss Pearl. Tell her where I am. Tell her to come instantly. (SNORKEY *going.*) Stay – tell her to bring the ebony box in mother's cabinet. Can you recollect?

SNORKEY. Can I what? Gaze at this giant intellect and don't ask me! The ebony box – all right – I'm off. (*Exit.*)

BOWLING. It would have been as well, young lady, to have answered frankly at first.

BYKE. Oh, sir! Don't be harsh with her! Don't be harsh with my poor child.

BOWLING. Your father has a most Christian disposition.

309

LAURA. Sir, I have told you, and I now solemnly repeat it, that this man is no relation of mine. I desire to remain unknown, for I am most unfortunate; but the injustice you are about to commit forces me to reveal myself, though in doing so I shall increase a sorrow already hard to bear.

BOWLING. We sit here to do right, according to the facts before us. And let me tell you, young lady, that your father's statement is correct. Further, unless the witnesses you have sent for can directly contradict him, we shall not alter our decision.

LAURA. Let it be so. He says he gave me into the care of certain wealthy people when I was a little child.

BYKE. I am willing to swear to it.

LAURA. Then he will be able to describe the clothes in which I was dressed at the time. They were safely kept, I have sent for them.

BYKE. Let them be produced – and I will recognise every little precious garment. (*Aside.*) This is getting ferociously hot for me! Ha!

Re-enter SNORKEY *with* RAY *hastily.*

SNORKEY (*excitedly*). Here's a witness! Here's evidence. (POLICEMAN *admonishes him.*)

LAURA (RAY *takes her hand through the rail*). Ray!

BOWLING. Who is this?

RAY. I am a friend, sir, of this lady.

BYKE. He is a dreadful character – a villain who wants to lead my child astray! Don't – please don't let him contaminate her!

BOWLING. Silence! (*To* RAY.) Can you disprove that this young lady is his daughter?

RAY. His daughter?

LAURA. He knows nothing.

BOWLING. Let him answer. Come – have you any knowledge of this matter?

RAY. I had been told, sir, that – (LAURA *looks at him.*) No – I know nothing.

LAURA. Have you brought the ebony box? It contained the clothes which I wore when –

RAY. I understand; but in my haste, and not knowing your peril I brought nothing. But can you not remember them yourself?

LAURA. Perfectly.

RAY. Write, then! (*Handing her a memorandum book – to* BOWLING.) Sir, this lady will hand you a description of those articles which she wore when she was found thirteen years ago. Then let this scoundrel be questioned – and if he fails to answer, I will accuse him of an attempted abduction.

BOWLING. That's the way.

BYKE (*aside*). It will not be a great effort for me to remember.

BOWLING (*taking the book from* RAY). Now, sir, I will listen to you. (RAY *and* LAURA *are eager and expectant.*)

BYKE (*deliberately*). A soiled gingham frock, patched and torn. (LAURA *gives a shudder and turns aside.*)

BOWLING. What kind of shoes and stockings?

BYKE. Her feet were bare.

BOWLING. And the colour of her hood?

BYKE. Her dear little head was uncovered.

BOWLING (*handing book back*). He has answered correctly.

LAURA. It is useless to struggle more! Heaven alone can help me!

RAY. You can see, sir, that this lady cannot be his daughter. Look at her and at him.

BOWLING. I only see that he has pretty well proven his case. She must go with him, and let her learn to love him as a daughter should.

RAY. She shall not! I shall follow him wherever he goes.

BYKE (*taking* LAURA's *hand*). I appeal to the Court.

BOWLING. Officer, take charge of that person, until this gentleman is gone.

BYKE (*coming forward with* LAURA, *who is dumb and despairing*). My child, try and remember the words of the good judge. 'You must learn to love me as a daughter should.'

SNORKEY (*to* RAY). Stay here, sir, I'll track him. No one suspects me. (*Music – tableau – closed in by next scene.*)

311

SCENE III. – *Exterior of the Tombs, with ballads on strings upon the railings.*

Enter JUDAS, *followed by* PEACHBLOSSOM.

PEACHBLOSSOM. Only tell me where he has taken her, and I'll go with you – indeed I will.

JUDAS. We don't want you, we wouldn't be bothered with you; she's our game.

PEACHBLOSSOM. What are you going to do with her?

JUDAS. Do! why we'll coin her. Turn her into dollars. We've had it on foot for a long time.

PEACHBLOSSOM. What! Is she the rich young lady I heard you and Byke speak of so often before I got away from you?

JUDAS (*savagely*). Heard me speak of! What did you hear?

PEACHBLOSSOM (*dancing off*). Oh, I know! I know more than you suppose. When you used to lock me up in the back cellar for running away, you forgot that doors had key-holes.

JUDAS (*aside*). This girl must be silenced.

PEACHBLOSSOM. What are you muttering about – don't you know how Byke used to throw you down and trample on you for muttering?

JUDAS. I'll have you yet, my beauty.

PEACHBLOSSOM. I think you are a great fool, Judas.

JUDAS. Likely, likely.

PEACHBLOSSOM. Why don't you give up Miss Nina to that handsome young gentleman? He'd pay you well for the secret. He'd give his whole fortune for her, I know, I saw it in his face. And he'd treat you better than Byke does.

JUDAS. Not yet my chicken; besides, what does he care for her now? Isn't he going to marry the other girl – she's the one will pay when the time comes – but we intend to hold the goods 'till the price is high.

PEACHBLOSSOM. Then if you won't, I'll – – I'll tell him all I used to overhear about babies and cradles, and he'll understand it, perhaps, if I don't.

JUDAS (*aside*). Hang her – she'll make mischief. (*Aloud.*) Well, come along with me, my beauty, and I'll talk it over with you.

PEACHBLOSSOM. Don't touch me; I won't trust you with your hands on me. (JUDAS *makes a dart at her.*) I knew that was your game. But I'll be even with you yet. (*Dancing off tantalisingly before* JUDAS – *Both exit.*)

Enter SNORKEY.

SNORKEY (*desponding*). I'm no more use than a gun without a trigger. I tried to follow Byke, but he smoked in a minute. Then I tried to make up with him, but he swore that I went against him in Court, and so he wouldn't have me at no price. Then I ran after the carriage that he got into with the lady, till a darn'd old woman caught me for upsetting her apple stand and bursting up her business. What am I to do now? I'm afraid to go back to the cap'n, *he* won't have me at any price either, I suppose. (*Gazing at ballads, hands in his pockets – going from one to the other.*)

Enter BERMUDAS, *with ballads in his hands, and preparing to take others off the line, as if to shut up shop.*

BERMUDAS (*after gazing at* SNORKEY). What are you a-doing of – sa-a-y? (SNORKEY *takes no notice.*) This here's one of the fellows as steals the bread of the poor man. Reading all the songs for nothin', and got bags of gold at home. Sa-a-y!

SNORKEY. Well, youngster, what are you groaning about? Have you got the cholera?

BERMUDAS. Ah! what are you doing? Taking the bloom off my songs? You've read them 'ere ballads till they're in rags.

SNORKEY. I was looking for the 'Prairie Bird'.

BERMUDAS. Perary Bird, eh? There ain't no perary bird. There's a 'Perary Flower'.

SNORKEY. Now don't go into convulsions. I'll find it. (*Turns to songs.*)

BERMUDAS. Sa-ay – you needn't look no further for that bird! I've found him and no mistake. He's a big Shanghae with a red comb and no feathers.

313

SNORKEY. He's dropped on me.

BERMUDAS. Ain't you a mean cuss, sa-ay? Why don't you come down with your two cents, and support trade?

SNORKEY. But I ain't got two cents. What's a fellow to do if he hasn't got a red?

BERMUDAS (*toning down*). Hain't you? Where's your messages?

SNORKEY. Haven't had one go today.

BERMUDAS. Where do you hang out?

SNORKEY. Nowheres.

BERMUDAS. My eye – no roost?

SNORKEY. No.

BERMUDAS. I tell you what, come along with us – we've got a bully place – no rent – no taxes – no nothin'.

SNORKEY. Where is it?

BERMUDAS. Down under the pier! I discovered it. I was in swimmin' and seed a hole and went in. Lots of room, just the place for a quiet roost. We has jolly times every night, I tell you, on the dock; and when it is time to turn in we goes below, and has it as snug as a hotel; come down with us.

SNORKEY. I will! These young rascals will help me to track that scoundrel yet.

BERMUDAS. Now, help me to take in my shop windows; it's time to shut up shop.

Enter RAY TRAFFORD.

RAY. If what that crazy girl has told me can be true, Laura may yet be restored to her friends, if not to me, for I have dispelled that dream for ever. But that villain must be traced immediately, or he will convey his victim far beyond our reach or rescue. (SNORKEY, *helping to take down songs, sees* TRAFFORD.)

SNORKEY. Hollo! Cap'n!

RAY. The man of all I wanted. You tracked him?

SNORKEY. They was too much for me, sir – two horses was, but I saw them turn into Greenwich-street, near Jay.

RAY. This may give us a clue. I have learned from a girl who knows this fellow that he has some hiding-place over the river, and owns a boat which is always fastened near the pier where the Boston steamers are.

SNORKEY. Well, cap'n, if anything's to be done, you'll find me at Pier – what's the number of our pier, Shorty?

BERMUDAS. Pier 30! Downstairs!

SNORKEY. Pier 30. That's my new home, and if you want me, say the word.

RAY. You will help me?

SNORKEY. You bet, cap'n. I was on Columbia's side for four years, and I'll fight for her daughters for the rest of my life, if you say so. If there's any fightin' count me in, cap'n.

RAY. Thank you, brave fellow. Here take this – no nonsense – take it. Pier 30, is it?

SNORKEY. Pier 30. (*Exit* TRAFFORD.)

BERMUDAS (*eyeing money*). How much, Perary?

SNORKEY. One – two – three – four – four dollars.

BERMUDAS. Four dollars! Sa-ay – don't you want to buy a share in a paying business? I'm looking out for a partner with a cash capital for the ballad business. Or I tell you what to do. Lay your money on me in a mill. I'm going to be a prize-fighter, and get reported in the respectable dailies. 'Rattling Mill, 99th round, Bermudas the victor, having knocked his antagonist into nowheres.'

SNORKEY. Come along, you young imp. I could floor you with my own arm, and then the report would be: '25th round – Snorkey came up first, while his antagonist showed great signs of distress.'

BERMUDAS. Say, Perary, what are you going to do with all that money?

SNORKEY. I won't bet it on you, sure.

BERMUDAS. I'll tell you what to do; let's go and board at the Metropolitan Hotel for an hour.

SNORKEY. What will we do for toothpicks?

BERMUDAS. Oh, go along. You can't get anything to eat for four dollars. (*Exeunt* SNORKEY *and* BERMUDAS *squaring off.*)

SCENE IV. – *Foot of Pier* 30, *North River* – *Transparent set water pieces* – *a pier projecting into the river. A large cavity in front. Bow of a vessel at back, and other steamers, vessels and piers in perspective on either side. The flat gives view of Jersey City and the river shipping by starlight. Music of distant serenade heard.*

Enter BYKE, *sculling a boat, which he fastens to the pier.* JUDAS *is on the pier, smoking pipe, looking down.*

JUDAS. Have you fixed everything across the river?

BYKE. Yes, I have a horse and waggon waiting near the shore to carry her to the farm. Has anyone been around here?

JUDAS. Not a soul. I've been waiting here for an hour. What made you so long?

BYKE. I pulled down the river for a spell to throw any spies off the track. It was necessary after what you told me of that girl's threat to blab about the Boston pier.

JUDAS. Pshaw! she'd never dare.

BYKE. Never mind, it's best to be certain. Is the prize safe?

JUDAS. Yes, she was worn out, and slept when I came away. How her blood tells – she wouldn't shed a tear.

BYKE. Bah! if she'd been more of a woman and set up a screaming, we shouldn't have been able to get her at all. Success to all girls of spirit, say I.

JUDAS. Don't you think it might be worth while to treat with this young spark, Trafford, and hear what he has to offer?

BYKE. Satan take him, no! That'll spoil your game about the other girl, Pearl. He was making up to her all right, and if he gets this one back he'll upset the whole game by marrying her. I tell you he's got the old feeling for her, spite of her running away. Now you can judge for yourself, and do as you please.

JUDAS. Then I do as you do – get her out of the city. When Pearl is married to him we can treat for Laura's ransom by threatening them with the real secret.

BYKE. Then that's settled. (*Taking out flask.*) Here's the precious infant's health. Do you think she'll go easy, or shall we drug her?

JUDAS. Just tell her it's to meet her beau and get her ransom, or give her a reason and she'll be as mild as a lamb.

BYKE. Ha! let me get hold of her, and I'll answer she goes across, reason or no reason. (BERMUDAS *calls outside.*) There's a noise.

JUDAS. It's only the market boys coming down for a swim.

BYKE. Softly then, come along. (*Music – exeunt.*)

Enter BERMUDAS, PEANUTS, *and two other boys.*

BERMUDAS. Say, Peanuts, go down and see if any of the fellows is come yet. (PEANUTS *scrambles down to hole in front on side of dock – comes out again.*)

PEANUTS. There's nobody there.

SNORKEY (*without*). Hollo!

BERMUDAS. Hollo! that's our new chum. Hollo! follow your front teeth, and you'll get here afore you knows it.

Enter SNORKEY, *with more boys.*

SNORKEY. What a very airy location.

BERMUDAS. It's a very convenient hotel. Hot and cold saltwater baths at the very door of your bedrooms, and sometimes when the tide rises we has the bath brought to us in bed, doesn't we, Peanuts?

PEANUTS. That's so.

SNORKEY. Come, what do you do before you go to bed?

BERMUDAS. We'll have a swarry. Say, one of you fellows, go down and bring up the piany forty. (PEANUTS *goes into hole and gets banjo.*) What'll I give you?

SNORKEY. Something lively. (*Music, nigger songs, and various entertainments – trained dogs, street acrobats, &c., ending with dance by boys, given according to capacity and talent. At the end of it a general shout of jubilee.*)

SERGEANT (*aside*). Here, boys! less noise.

BERMUDAS. It's Acton and the police. Let's go to bed. (BERMUDAS *and boys get down into hole.*)

SERGEANT (*entering in patrol boat*). If you boys don't make less noise, I'll have to clear you out.

317

BERMUDAS (*on the pier.*) It's an extra occasion, Mr Acton; we've got a distinguished military guest, and we're entertaining him. (*Boat passes out.*) Come along, Perary, let's go to bed. (SNORKEY *is about to descend.*)

Enter RAY TRAFFORD *on pier.*

RAY. Is that you, Snorkey?

SNORKEY (*quickly whispering*). Here, sir. Anything turned up?

RAY. Byke was overheard to say he intended crossing the river tonight. He will doubtless use that boat which he keeps by the Boston pier. The river patrol are on the watch for him, but I will meet him before he can embark.

SNORKEY. Which Boston pier is it, cap'n? There are three on this river.

RAY. Three?

SNORKEY. Yes, one of them is two slips below. I tell you what, cap'n; you get the officers, go by the shore way, search all the ships; I'll find a boat here, and will drop down the river, and keep an eye around generally.

VOICE (*without*). This way, sir.

RAY. That's the patrol calling me. Your idea is a good one. Keep a sharp eye down the stream. (*Exit.*)

SNORKEY (*alone*). Now for my lay.

BERMUDAS (*popping his head up*). Say, can't I do nothin? I'm the Fifth-Ward Chicken, and if there's any muss, let me have a shy.

SNORKEY. No; get in and keep quiet. (BERMUDAS *disappears.*) I wonder where I can find a boat. There ought to be plenty tied up about here. My eye! (*Discovering* BYKE's.) Here's one for the wishin' – sculls too. I'm in luck. Say, Bermudas, whose boat is this?

BERMUDAS. Yours, if you like. Turn it loose. (SNORKEY *jumps down, enters boat, pushes off.*)

BERMUDAS (*inside*). Keep your toe out of my ear.

Pause – Enter BYKE, LAURA, *and* JUDAS, *on pier.*

LAURA. Is this the place? There is no one here; you have deceived me.

BYKE. Well, we have, but we won't do so any longer.

LAURA. What do you mean?

BYKE (*drawing pistol*). Do you see this? It is my dog Trusty. It has a very loud voice, and a sharp bite; and if you scream out, I'll try if it can't outscream you. Judas, unfasten the boat.

LAURA. What are you about to do? You will not murder me?

BYKE. No, we only mean to take you to the other shore, where your friends won't think of finding you. Quick, Judas!

JUDAS. The boat's gone.

BYKE. Damn you, what do you mean? Where is it? Here, hold her. Where the devil is that boat?

SNORKEY (*re-appearing in boat*). Here!

BYKE. Snorkey! We're betrayed. Come. (*Drags* LAURA *away.*)

SNORKEY. The police are there. Turn, you coward, don't run away from a one-armed man!

BYKE. Judas, take her. (SNORKEY *strikes at him with oar,* BYKE *takes oar from him and strikes him – he falls in boat.*)

SNORKEY. Help! Bermudas! (*The boys hear the noise, and scramble up at back. The patrol boat appears with lights.*)

BERMUDAS. Hi! Ninety-ninth round! First blood for Bermudas! (*Jumps at* BYKE.)

BYKE (*flinging* BERMUDAS *off*). Judas, toss her over. (JUDAS *throws* LAURA *over back of pier.* RAY *enters. Boys all get on pier and surround* BYKE, *fighting him. Officers enter –* RAY *leaps into water after* LAURA *– Curtain – Moonlight on during scene.*)

ACT III

SCENE I. – *Long Branch. Ground floor of an elegant residence – open windows from floor to ceiling at back opening upon a balcony or promenade. Perspective of the shore and sea in distance. Doors* R. *and* L. *Sunset. The curtain rises to lively music.*

Enter PEARL, MRS VAN DAM, MISS EARLIE, *and other ladies in summer costume*, DEMILT *and* WINDEL *with them.*

PEARL. And so the distinguished foreigner is in love with me? I thought he looked excessively solemn last night. Do you know, I can't imagine a more serious spectacle than a Frenchman or an Italian in love. One always imagines them to be unwell. (*To* MRS VAN DAM.) Do fasten my glove – there's a dear.

MRS VAN DAM. Where's Ray?

PEARL. Oh, he's somewhere. I never saw such another. Isn't he cheerful? He never smiles, and seldom talks.

MRS VAN DAM. But the foreigner does. What an ecstasy he was in over your singing; sing us a verse, won't you, while we're waiting for Ray?

ALL. It will be delightful – do.

PEARL. Well!

AIR, *'When the War is Over, Mary'*

> Now the summer days are fading,
>   Autumn sends its dreary blast
> Moaning through the silent forest
>   Where the leaves are falling fast.
> Soon dread winter will enfold us –
>   Chilling in its arms of snow,
> Flowers that the summer cherished,
>   Birds that sing, and streams that flow.

320

Say, shall all things droop and wither,
    That are born this summer day?
Shall the happy love it brought us –
    Like the flowers fade away?
Go; be still thou flutt'ring bosom –
    Seasons change and years glide by,
They may not harm what is immortal –
    Darling – love shall never die!

Now, I've sung that to Ray a dozen times, and he never even said it was nice. He hasn't any soul for music; oh, dear, what a creature!

MRS VAN DAM. Yes, and what a victim you will be, with a husband who has 600,000 dollars per annum income!

PEARL. That's some comfort, isn't it?

Enter RAY TRAFFORD *bowing to others.*

RAY. Going out, Pearl?

PEARL. Yes, we're off to Shrewsbury. Quite a party's going – four carriages – and we mean to stay and ride home by moonlight.

RAY. Couldn't you return a little earlier?

MRS VAN DAM. Earlier! Pshaw! What's in you, Trafford? (*The ladies and gentlemen go up.*)

RAY. You know that Laura will be quite alone, and she is still suffering.

PEARL. Well, she'll read and read, as she always did, and never miss me.

RAY. But at least she ought to have some little attention.

PEARL. Dear, dear, what an unreasonable fellow you are. Isn't she happy now – didn't you save her from drowning, and haven't I been as good to her as I can be – what more do you want?

RAY. I don't like to hear you talk so, Pearl, and remember what she and you were once. And you know that she was something else once – something that you are now to me. And yet how cheerful, how gentle she is. She has lost everything, and does not complain.

PEARL. Well, what a sermon! There, I know you're hurt and I'm a fool. But I can't help it. People say 'she's good-looking, but she's got no heart!' I'd give anything for one, but they ain't to be bought.

RAY. Well, don't moan about it, I didn't mean to reprove you.

PEARL. But you *do* reprove me. I'm sure I haven't been the cause of Laura's troubles. I didn't tell the big ugly man to come and take her away, although I was once glad he did.

RAY. Pearl!

PEARL. Because I thought I had gained you by it. (RAY *turns away*.) But now I've got you, I don't seem to make you happy. But I might as well complain that you don't make me happy – but I don't complain, I'm satisfied, and I want you to be satisfied. There, *are* you satisfied?

MRS VAN DAM (*who, with others, has been promenading up and down the balcony*). Here are the carriages.

PEARL. I'm coming. Can't you get me my shawl, Ray? (RAY *gets it from chair*.)

MRS VAN DAM. And here's your foreign admirer on horseback. (*Exeunt* MISS EARLIE, DEMILT *and* WINDEL.)

PEARL. Bye, bye, Ray. (*Exit* PEARL.)

MRS VAN DAM. Are you not coming, Trafford?

RAY. I? No!

MRS VAN DAM. Do come on horseback, here's a horse ready for you.

PEARL (*without*). Ray! Ray!

MRS VAN DAM. Pearl's calling you. Be quick or Count Carom will be before you, and hand her in the carriage.

RAY (*taking his hat slowly*). Oh, by all means, let the Count have some amusement.

MRS VAN DAM (*taking* RAY's *arm*). You're a perfect icicle. (*They exeunt. Noise of whips and laughter. Plaintive music as* LAURA *enters, and gazes out at them*.)

LAURA. Poor Pearl. It is a sad thing to want for happiness, but it is a terrible thing to see another groping about blindly for

322

it when it is almost within the grasp. And yet she can be very happy with him. Her sunny temper and her joyous face will brighten any home. (*Sits on table, on which are books.*) How happy I feel to be alone with these friends, who are ever ready to talk to me – with no longings for what I may not have – my existence hidden from all save two in the wide world, and making my joy out of the joy of that innocent child who will soon be his wife. (PEACHBLOSSOM *appears at back, looking in cautiously, grotesquely attired.*)

PEACHBLOSSOM. If you please.

LAURA (*aloud*). Who's there?

PEACHBLOSSOM (*running in*). Oh, it's Miss Nina! Oh, I'm so glad; I've had such a hunt for you. Don't ask me nothing yet. I'm so happy. I've been looking for you so long, and I've had such hard luck. Lord what a tramp – miles on miles.

LAURA. Did anyone see you come here? How did you find me?

PEACHBLOSSOM. I asked 'em at the hotel where Mr Trafford was, and they said at Courtlands, and I asked 'em where Courtlands was, and they said down the shore, and I walked down lookin' at every place till I came here.

LAURA. Speak low, Blossom. My existence is a secret, and no one must hear you.

PEACHBLOSSOM. Well, miss, I says to Snorkey – says I –

LAURA. Is he with you?

PEACHBLOSSOM. No, miss, but we are great friends. He wants me to keep house for him some day. I said to him – 'I want to find out where Miss Nina's gone,' and so he went to Mr Trafford's and found he was come to Long Branch, but never a word could we hear of you.

LAURA. And the others – those dreadful people?

PEACHBLOSSOM. Byke and old Judas? Clean gone! They hasn't been seen since they was took up for throwing you into the water, and let off because no one came to Court agin 'em. Bermudas says he's seen 'em in Barnum's wax-work show, but Bermudas is *such* a liar. He brought me up here.

LAURA. Brought you up here?

PEACHBLOSSOM. Yes, he sells papers at Stetson's; he's got the exclusive trade here, and he has a little waggon and a horse, and goes down to the junction every night to catch the extras from the express train what don't come here. He says he'll give me lots of nice rides if I'll stay here.

LAURA. But you must not stay here. You must go back to New York this evening.

PEACHBLOSSOM. Back! No, I won't.

LAURA. Blossom!

PEACHBLOSSOM. I won't, I won't, I won't! I'll never let you away again. I did it once and you was took away and chucked overboard and almost drowned. I won't be any trouble, indeed, I won't. I'll hire out at the hotel, and run over when my work is done at night, when nobody can see me, to look up at your window. Don't send me away. You're the only one as ever was good to me.

LAURA (*aside*). It's too dangerous. She certainly would reveal me sooner or later. I must send her back.

PEACHBLOSSOM. Besides, I've got something to tell you. Dreadful! dreadful! about old Judas and Byke – a secret.

LAURA. A secret! what in the world are you saying?

PEACHBLOSSOM. Is it wicked to listen at doors when people talk?

LAURA. It is very wicked.

PEACHBLOSSOM. Well, I suppose that's why I did it. I used to listen to Byke and Judas when they used to talk about a rich lady whom they called Mrs Courtland.

LAURA. Ah!

PEACHBLOSSOM. Judas used to be a nurse at Mrs Courtland's, and was turned off for stealing. And wasn't she and Byke going to make money off her! and Byke was to pretend to be some beautiful lady's father. Then when they took you, Judas says to me: 'Did you ever hear of children being changed in their cradles?' – and that you wasn't her child, but she was going to make money off the real one at the proper time.

LAURA. What do you tell me?

PEACHBLOSSOM. Oh! I'm not crazy. I know a heap, don't I? And I want you think I'm somebody, and not send me away.

LAURA (*to herself*). She must speak the truth. And yet if I were

324

to repeat her strange words here, I should be suspected of forging the tale. No! better let it rest as it is. She must go – and I must go too.

PEACHBLOSSOM. You ain't mad with me?

LAURA. No, no; but you must go away from here. Go back to the hotel, to your friend – anywhere, and wait for me; I will come to you.

PEACHBLOSSOM. It is a promise?

LAURA (*nervously*). Yes, go.

PEACHBLOSSOM. Then I'll go; for I know you always keep your word – you ain't angry 'cause I came after you? I did it because I loved you – because I wanted to see you put in the right place. Honour bright, you ain't sending me away now? Well, I'll go; goodbye! (*Exit.*)

LAURA (*animated*). I must return to the city, no matter what dangers may lurk there. It is dangerous enough to be concealed here, with a hundred Argus-eyed women about me every day, but with this girl, detection would be certain. I must go – secretly if I can – openly if I must.

RAY (*outside*). No, I shall not ride again. Put him up. (*Entering.*) Laura, I knew I should find you here.

LAURA (*sitting and pretending composure*). I thought you had gone with Pearl.

RAY. I did go part of the way, but I left the party a mile down the road.

LAURA. You and Pearl had no disagreement?

RAY. No – yes; that is, we always have. Our social barometers always stand at 'cloudy' and 'overcast.'

LAURA. And whose fault is that?

RAY (*pettishly*). Not mine. I know I do all I can – I say all I can – but she –

LAURA. But she is to be your wife. Ray, my friend, courtship is the text from which the whole solemn sermon of married life takes its theme. Do not let yours be discontented and unhappy.

RAY. To be my wife; yes. In a moment of foolishness, dazzled by her airs, and teased by her coquettishness, I asked her to be my wife.

LAURA. And you repent already?

RAY (*taking her hand*). I lost you, and I was at the mercy of any flirt that chose to give me an inviting look. It was your fault – you know it was! Why did you leave me?

LAURA (*after conflict with her feelings*). Ray, the greatest happiness I have ever felt has been the thought that all your affections were for ever bestowed upon a virtuous lady, your equal in family, fortune and accomplishments. What a revelation do you make to me now! What is it makes you continually at war with your happiness?

RAY. I don't know what it is. I was wrong to accuse you. Forgive me! I have only my own cowardice to blame for my misery. But Pearl –

LAURA. You must not accuse her.

RAY. When you were gone, she seemed to have no thought – no wish – but for my happiness. She constantly invited me to her house, and when I tried to avoid her, met me at every turn. Was she altogether blameless?

LAURA. Yes, it was her happiness she sought, and she had a right to seek it.

RAY. Oh! men are the veriest fools on earth; a little attention, a little sympathy, and they are caught – caught by a thing without soul or brains, while some noble woman is forsaken and forgotten.

LAURA. Ray, will you hear me?

RAY (*looking at her hopefully*). Yes, speak to me as you used to speak. Be to me as you used to be.

LAURA (*smiling sadly*). I cannot be that to you; but I can speak as the spirit of the Laura who is dead to you for ever.

RAY. Be it as you will.

LAURA. Let the woman you look upon be wise or vain, beautiful or homely, rich or poor, she has but one thing she can really give or refuse – her heart! Her beauty, her wit, her accomplishments, she may sell to you – but her love is the treasure without money and without price.

RAY. How well I have learned that.

LAURA. She only asks in return, that when you look upon her, your eyes shall speak a mute devotion; that when you address her, your voice shall be gentle, loving and kind. That you shall not despise her because she cannot understand, all at once, your vigorous thoughts and ambitious designs; for when misfortune and evil have defeated your greatest purposes – her love remains to console you. You look to the trees for strength and grandeur – do not despise the flowers, because their fragrance is all they have to give. Remember, love is all a woman has to give; but it is the only earthly thing which God permits us to carry beyond the grave.

RAY. You are right. You are always right. I asked Pearl to be my wife, knowing what she was, and I will be just to her. I will do my duty though it break my heart.

LAURA. Spoken like a hero.

RAY. But it is to you I owe the new light that guides me; and I will tell her –

LAURA. Tell her nothing – never speak of me. And when you see her, say to her it is she, and she alone, whom you consult and to whom you listen.

RAY. And you?

LAURA. You will see me no more.

RAY. You will leave me?

LAURA. Something of me will always be with you – my parting words – my prayers for your happiness. (*Distant music heard.*)

RAY (*falling on his knees*). Oh, Laura, you leave me to despair.

LAURA. No; to the happiness which follows duty well performed. Such happiness as I feel in doing mine. (*Picture. During last of this scene the sun has set, and night comes on. Close in. Stage dark.*)

SCENE II. – *Woods near Shrewsbury Station.*

Enter BYKE, *shabbily dressed.*

BYKE. It's getting darker and darker, and I'm like to lose my way. Where the devil is Judas? It must be nine o'clock, and she was to be at the bend with the waggon half an hour ago. (*Rumble of wheels heard.*) Humph – at last.

Enter JUDAS.

JUDAS. Is that you, Byke?

BYKE. Who did you suppose it was? I've been tramping about the wet grass for an hour.

JUDAS. It was a hard job to get the horse and waggon.

BYKE. Give me a match. (*Lights pipe and leans against a tree.*) Did you get the bearings of the crib?

JUDAS. Yes, it is on the shore, well away from the other cottages and hotels.

BYKE. That's good. Nothing like peace and quietness. Who's in the house?

JUDAS. Only the two girls and the servants.

BYKE. How many of them?

JUDAS. Four.

BYKE. It'll be mere child's play to go through that house. Have you spied about the swag?

JUDAS. They have all their diamonds and jewels there. Pearl wears them constantly; they're the talk of the whole place.

BYKE. We'll live in luxury off that girl all our lives. She'll settle a handsome thing on us, won't she? when she knows what we know, and pays us to keep dark – if t'other one don't spoil the game.

JUDAS. Curse her! I could cut her throat.

BYKE. Oh, I'll take care of that!

JUDAS. You always do things for the best, dear old Byke!

BYKE. Of course I do. What time is it?

JUDAS. Not ten yet.

BYKE. An hour to wait.

JUDAS. But, Byke, you won't peach on me before my little pet is married, will you?

BYKE. What's the fool about now?

JUDAS. I can't help trembling; nothing is safe while Laura is there.

BYKE. I've provided for that. I've had the same idea as you – while she's in the way, and Trafford unmarried, our plans are all smoke, and we might as well be sitting on the hob with a keg of powder in the coals.

JUDAS. That we might. But what have you thought to do?

BYKE. Why, I've thought what an unfortunate creature Laura is – robbed of her mother, her home, and her lover; nothing to live for; it would be a mercy to put her out of the way.

JUDAS. That's it; but how – how – how –

BYKE. It's plain she wasn't born to be drowned, or the materials are very handy down here. What made you talk about cutting her throat? It was very wrong! When a thing gets into my head, it sticks there.

JUDAS. You oughtn't to mind me.

BYKE. Make your mind easy on that score.

JUDAS (*alarmed*). Byke, I heard someone in the bushes just there. (*Points off.*)

BYKE (*nervously and quickly*). Who? Where?

JUDAS. Where the hedge is broken. I could swear I saw the shadow of a man.

BYKE. Stop here. I'll see. (*Goes off.*)

JUDAS. I begin to shiver. But it must be done or we starve. Why should I tremble? It's the safest job we ever planned. If they discover us, our secret will save us – we know too much to be sent to jail.

Re-enter BYKE, *slowly.*

BYKE. There are traces, but I can see no one. (*Looking off.*)

JUDAS. Suppose we should have been overheard!

BYKE (*glaring at her*). Overheard? Bah! no one could understand.

JUDAS. Come, let us go to the waggon and be off.

BYKE (*always looking off*). Go you, I will follow. Bring it round by the station, and wait for me in the shadows of the trees. I will follow. (JUDAS *goes off.* BYKE, *after a moment, still looking, buttons up his coat and hides behind wood.*) Heigho! I must be off.

Enter SNORKEY, *slowly.*

SNORKEY. Tracked 'em again! We're the latest fashionable arrivals at Long Branch. 'Mr Byke and Lady, and Brigadier-General Snorkey, of New York'; there's an item for the papers! With a horse and waggon, they'll be at the seaside in two hours; but in the train I think I'll beat 'em. Then to find Cap'n Trafford, and give him the wink, and be ready to receive the distinguished visitors with all the honours. Robbery; burglary; murder; that's Byke's catechism. 'What's to be done when you're hard up? – Steal! What's to be done if you're caught at it? – Kill!' It's short and easy, and he lives up to it like a good many Christians don't live up to their laws. (*Looking off.*) They're out of sight. Phew! it's midsummer, but I'm chilled to the bone; something like a piece of ice has been stuck between my shoulders all day, and something like a black mist is always before me. (BYKE *is behind tree.*) Just like old Nettly told me he felt, the night before Fredericksburg – and next day he was past all feeling – hit with a shell, and knocked into so many pieces, I didn't know which to call my old friend. Well (*slapping his chest*), we've all got to go; and if I can save *them*, I'll have some little capital to start the next world on. The next world! perhaps I shan't be the maimed beggar *there* that I am in this. (*Takes out pistol, examines cap; goes off,* BYKE *gliding after him.*)

SCENE III. – *Railroad Station at Shrewsbury Bend*, R. *Plat-form around it, and door at side, window in front. At* L. *clump of shrubs and trees. The railroad track runs from* L. *to* R. *View of Shrewsbury River in perspective. Night – moonlight. The switch, with a red lantern and a signalman's coat hanging on it* L. C. *The signal lamp and post beside it. As the scene opens, several packages are lying about the stage, among them a bundle of axes. The* SIGNAL-MAN *is wheeling in a small barrel, whistling at his work.*

Enter LAURA, *in walking dress, feebly.*

LAURA. It is impossible for me to go further. A second time I've fled from home and friends, but now they will never find me. The trains must all have passed, and there are no conveyances till tomorrow.

SIGNALMAN. Beg pardon, ma'am, looking for anybody?

LAURA. Thank you, no. Are you the man in charge of this station?

SIGNALMAN. Yes, ma'am.

LAURA. When is there another train for New York?

SIGNALMAN. New York? Not till morning. We've only one more train tonight; that's the down one; it'll be here in about twenty minutes – express train.

LAURA. What place is that?

SIGNALMAN. That? That's the signal station shed. It serves for store-room, depot, baggage-room, and everything.

LAURA. Can I stay there tonight?

SIGNALMAN. There? Well it's an odd place, and I should think you would hardly like it. Why don't you go to the hotel?

LAURA. I have my reasons – urgent ones. It is not because I want money. You shall have this (*producing porte-monnaie*) if you let me remain here.

SIGNALMAN. Well, I've locked up a good many things in there over-night, but I never had a young lady for freight before. Besides, ma'am, I don't know anything about you. You know it's odd that you won't go to a decent hotel, and plenty of money in your pocket.

LAURA. You refuse me – well – I shall only have to sit here all night.

SIGNALMAN. Here, in the open air? Why, it would kill you.

LAURA. So much the better.

SIGNALMAN. Excuse me for questions, miss, but you're a-running away from someone, ain't you?

LAURA. Yes.

SIGNALMAN. Well, I'd like to help you. I'm a plain man you know, and I'd like to help you, but there's one thing would go agin me to assist in. (LAURA *interested.*) I'm on to fifty years of age, and I've many children, some on 'em daughters grown. There's many temptations for young gals, and sometimes the old man has to put on the brakes a bit, for some young men are wicked enough to persuade the gals to steal out of their father's house in the dead of the night, and go to shame and misery. So tell me this – it ain't the old man, and the old man's home you've left, young lady?

LAURA. No, you good, honest fellow – no, I have no father.

SIGNALMAN. Then, by Jerusalem, I'll do for you what I can. Anything but run away from them that have not their interest but yours at heart. Come, you may stay there, but I'll have to lock you in.

LAURA. I desire that you should.

SIGNALMAN. It's for your safety as much as mine. I've got a patent lock on that door that would give a skeleton the rheumatism to fool with it. You don't mind the baggage; I'll have to put it in with you, hoes, shovels, mowing machines, and what is this? axes – yes, a bundle of axes. If the superintendent finds me out I'll ask him if he was afraid you'd run off with these. (*Laughs.*) So, if you please, I'll first tumble 'em in. (*Puts goods in house,* LAURA *sitting on platform looking at him. When all in he comes towards her, taking up cheese-box to put it in station.*) I say, miss, I ain't curious, but, of course, it's a *young man* you're a-going to?

LAURA. So far from that, it's a young man I'm running away from.

SIGNALMAN (*dropping a box*). Running away from a young man;

let me shake hands with you. (*Shakes her hand.*) Lord, it does
my heart good. At your age, too. (*Seriously.*) I wish you'd
come and live down in my neighbourhood awhile; among my
gals (*shaking his head*) you'd do a power of good. (*Putting
box in station.*)

LAURA. I've met an excellent friend – and here at least I can be
concealed until tomorrow – then for New York. My heart
feels lighter already – it's a good omen.

SIGNALMAN. Now, miss, bless your heart, here's your hotel
ready. (*Goes to switch and takes off coat, putting it on.*)

LAURA. Thanks, my good friend, but not a word to anyone till
tomorrow, not even – not even to your girls.

SIGNALMAN. Not a word, I promise you. If I told my girls it
would be over the whole village before morning. (*She goes in,
he locks door.* LAURA *appears at window facing audience.*)

LAURA. Lock me in safely.

SIGNALMAN. Ah, be sure I will. There! (*Tries door.*) Safe as a
jail. (*Pulls out watch and then looking at track with lantern.*)
Ten minutes and down she comes. It's all safe this way, my
noisy beauty, and you may come as soon as you like. Goodnight, miss.

LAURA (*at window*). Goodnight.

SIGNALMAN. Running away from a young man, ha! ha! ha! (*He
goes to track, then looks down it, lights his pipe and is trudging
off.*)

Enter SNORKEY.

SNORKEY. Ten minutes before the train comes, I'll wait here for
it. (*To* SIGNALMAN, *who re-enters.*) Hallo, I say, the train
won't stop here too long, will it?

SIGNALMAN. Too long? it won't stop here at all.

SNORKEY. I must reach the shore tonight, there'll be murder
done unless I can prevent it.

SIGNALMAN. Murder or no murder, the train can't be stopped.

SNORKEY. It's a lie. By waving the red signal for danger the
engineer must stop, I tell you.

SIGNALMAN. Do you think I'm a fool? What, disobey orders and lose my place; then what's to become of my family? (*Exit.*)

SNORKEY. I won't be foiled; I will confiscate some farmer's horse about here and get there before them somehow.

Enter BYKE *at back with loose coil of rope in his hand.*

Then when Byke arrives in his donkey cart he'll be ready to sit for a picture of surprise.

BYKE (*suddenly throwing the coil over* SNORKEY). Will he?

SNORKEY. Byke!

BYKE. Yes, Byke. Where's that pistol of yours? (*Tightening rope round his arm.*)

SNORKEY. In my breast pocket.

BYKE (*taking it*). Just what I wanted.

SNORKEY. You ain't a-going to shoot me?

BYKE. No!

SNORKEY. Well, I'm obliged to you for that.

BYKE (*leading him to platform*). Just sit down a minute, will you.

SNORKEY. What for? (LAURA *appears horror-struck at window.*)

BYKE. You'll see.

SNORKEY. Well, I don't mind if I do take a seat. (*Sits down,* BYKE *coils the rope round his legs.*) Hollo, what's this?

BYKE. You'll see. (*Picks the helpless* SNORKEY *up.*)

SNORKEY. Byke, what are you going to do?

BYKE. Put you to bed. (*Lays him across the railroad track.*)

SNORKEY. Byke, you don't mean to – My God, you are a villain!

BYKE (*fastening him to rails*). I'm going to put you to bed. You won't toss much. In less than ten minutes you'll be sound asleep. There, how do you like it? You'll get down to the Branch before me, will you? You'll dog me and play the eavesdropper, eh! Now do it if you can. When you hear the thunder under your head and see the lights dancing in your eyes, and feel the iron wheels a foot from your neck, remember Byke. (*Exit.*)

LAURA. Oh, Heavens, he will be murdered before my eyes! How can I aid him?

SNORKEY. Who's that?

LAURA. It is I, do you not know my voice?

SNORKEY. That I do, but I almost thought I was dead and it was an angel's. Where are you?

LAURA. In the station.

SNORKEY. I can't see you, but I can hear you. Listen to me, miss, for I've got only a few minutes to live.

LAURA (*shaking door*). And I cannot aid you.

SNORKEY. Never mind me, miss, I might as well die now and here, as at any other time. I'm not afraid. I've seen death in almost every shape, and none of them scare me; but for the sake of those you love, I would live. Do you hear me?

LAURA. Yes! yes!

SNORKEY. They are on the way to your cottage – Byke and Judas – to rob and murder.

LAURA (*in agony*). Oh, I must get out! (*Shakes window bars.*) What shall I do?

SNORKEY. Can't you burst the door?

LAURA. It is locked fast.

SNORKEY. Is there nothing in there? no hammer? no crowbar?

LAURA. Nothing. (*Faint steam whistle heard in the distance.*) Oh, Heavens! The train! (*Paralysed for an instant.*) The axe!!!

SNORKEY. Cut the woodwork! Don't mind the lock, cut round it. How my neck tingles! (*A blow at door is heard.*) Courage! (*Another.*) Courage! (*The steam whistle heard again – nearer, and rumble of train on track – another blow.*) That's a true woman. Courage! (*Noise of locomotive heard, with whistle. A last blow – the door swings open, mutilated, the lock hanging – and* LAURA *appears, axe in hand.*)

SNORKEY. Here – quick! (*She runs and unfastens him. The locomotive lights glare on scene.*) Victory! Saved! Hooray! (LAURA *leans exhausted against switch.*) And these are the women who ain't to have a vote! (*As* LAURA *takes his head from the track, the train of cars rushes past with roar and whistle.*)

Under the Gaslight: Stock poster of the sensational scene

ACT IV

SCENE I. – *An elegant boudoir at Courtland Cottage, Long Branch. Open window and balcony at back – moonlight exterior – tree overhanging balcony. Bed is at* L., *toilette table* R., *arm chair* C., *door* L., *lighted lamp on toilette table – dresses on chair by bed, and by window on* R. *Music.*

PEARL (*discovered, en negligée, brushing her hair out at table before mirror*). I don't feel a bit sleepy. What a splendid drive we had. I like that foreigner. What an elegant fellow he is! Ray is nothing to him. I wonder if I'm in love with him. Pshaw – what an idea! I don't believe I could love anybody much. How sweetly he writes! (*Picks up letter.*) 'You were more lovely than ever tonight – with one thing more, you'd be an angel!' Now that's perfectly splendid – 'with one thing more, you'd be an angel – that one thing is love. They tell me Mr Trafford is your professed admirer. I'm sure he could never be called your lover, for he seems incapable of any passion but melancholy.' It's quite true, Ray does not comprehend me. (*Takes up another letter.*) 'Pearl, forgive me if I have been cross and cold. For the future, I will do my duty, as your affianced husband, better.' Now, did ever anyone hear such talk as that from a lover? Lover! Oh, dear! I begin to feel that he can love – but not me. Well, I'd just as soon break, if he'd be the first to speak. How sweet and fresh the air is. (*She turns down lamp.*) It's much nicer here, than going to bed. (*Settles herself in tête-à-tête for a nap. Pause. Moonbeams fall on* BYKE, *who appears above the balcony. He gets over the rail and enters.*)

BYKE. Safely down. I've made no mistake – no, this is her room. What a figure I am for a lady's chamber. (*Goes to table, picks up delicate lace handkerchief, and wipes his face.*) Phew!

hot! (*Puts handkerchief in his pocket.*) Now for my bearings. (*Taking huge clasp-knife from his pocket.*) There's the bed where she's sleeping like a precious infant, and here – (*Sees* PEARL *in chair, and steals round at back, looking down at her.*) It's so dark – I can't recognise the face. It's a wonder she don't feel me in the air and dream of me. If she does she'll wake sure – but it's easy to settle that. (*Takes phial of chloroform, from his pocket, saturates the handkerchief he picked up, and applies it.*) So – now my charmer, we'll have the earrings. (*Takes them out.*) What's here? (*Going to table.*) Bracelets – diamonds! (*Going to dresses, and feeling in the pockets.*) Money! That's handy. (*He puts all in a bag, and hands them over balcony.*) Now for the drawers; there's where the treasure must be. Locked? (*Tries them with bunch of keys.*) Patent lock of course. It amuses me to see people buying patent locks when there's one key will fit 'em all. (*Produces small crowbar, and just as he is about to force the drawer, a shout is heard, and noise of waggon.*) What's that? (*Jumps, catching at a chair, which falls over.*) Damnation!

PEARL (*starting up*). Who's there? What's that?

BYKE. Silence, or I'll kill you.

PEARL. Help! Help!

BYKE (*running to bureau for knife*). You will have it, my pretty one.

PEARL (*runs to door*). Save me! save me! (BYKE *pursues her, she dodges him round the table, &c. Just as* BYKE *overtakes her, the door bursts open and* RAY *and* LAURA *enter.* BYKE *turns and runs to balcony, and confronts* SNORKEY *and* BERMUDAS, *who have clambered over.*)

LAURA. Just in time.

RAY (*seizing* BYKE). Scoundrel!

SNORKEY. Hold him, governor. Hold him! (*Assists* RAY *to bind* BYKE *in chair.*)

BERMUDAS. Sixty-sixth and last round. The big 'un floored, and Bermudas as fresh as a daisy.

PEARL. Dear, dear Laura, you have saved me.

RAY. Yes, Pearl, from more than you can tell.

LAURA. No, no; her preservers are there. (*Pointing to* BERMUDAS *and* SNORKEY.) Had it not been for the one, I should never have learned your danger, and but for the other, we could never have reached you in time.

SNORKEY. Bermudas and his fourth editions did it. Business enterprise and Bermudas' poney express worked the oracle this time.

BERMUDAS. The way we galloped! Sa-ay, my pony must have thought the extras was full of lively intelligence.

PEARL. Darling Laura, you shall never leave us again.

RAY. No, never!

SNORKEY. Beg pardon, cap'n, what are we to do with this here game we've brought down?

RAY. The magistrates will settle with him.

SNORKEY. Come, old fellow.

BYKE. One word, I beg. My conduct, I know, has been highly reprehensible. I have acted injudiciously, and have been the occasion of more or less inconvenience to everyone here. But I wish to make amends, and therefore I tender you all, in this public manner, my sincere apologies. I trust this will be entirely satisfactory.

RAY. Villain!

BYKE. I have a word to say to you, sir.

SNORKEY. Come, that's enough.

BYKE. My good fellow, don't interrupt gentlemen who are conversing together. (*To* RAY.) I address you, sir – you design to commit me to the care of the officers of the law?

RAY. Most certainly.

BYKE. And you will do your best towards having me incarcerated in the correctional establishments of this country? (RAY *bows.*)

SNORKEY. How very genteel.

BYKE. Then I have to say, if you will, I shall make a public exposure of certain matters connected with a certain young lady.

LAURA. Do not think that will deter us from your punishment. I can bear even more than I have – for the sake of justice.

BYKE. Excuse me, I did not even remotely refer to you.

LAURA. To whom, then?

BYKE (*pointing to* PEARL). To her.

RAY. Miss Courtland?

BYKE. Oh dear – no sir. The daughter of old Judas – the spurious child placed in *your* cradle, Miss Laura Courtland, when you were abducted from it by your nurse.

PEARL. What does he say?

BYKE. That you're a beggar's child – we have the proofs! Deliver me to prison, and I produce them.

RAY. Wretch!

PEARL. Then it's you, dear Laura, have been wronged – while I –

LAURA. You are my sister still – whatever befalls!

PEARL. Oh, I'm so glad it's so! Ray won't want to marry me, now – at least, I hope so; for I know he loves you – he always loved you – and you will be happy together.

RAY. Pearl, what are you saying?

PEARL. Don't interrupt me! I mean every word of it. Laura, I've been very foolish, I know. I ought to have tried to reunite you – but there is time.

RAY. Dear Laura! Is there, indeed, still time? (*She gives her hand.*)

BYKE. Allow me to suggest that a certain proposition I had the honour to submit has not yet been answered.

RAY. Release him. (SNORKEY *undoes his cords.*)

BYKE. Thank you – not so rough! Thank you.

RAY. Now, go – but remember, if you ever return to these parts you shall be tried, not only for this burglary, but for the attempt to kill that poor fellow.

BYKE. Thank you. Good-bye. (*To* SNORKEY.) Good-bye, my dear friend; overlook our little dispute, and write to me. (*Aside.*) They haven't caught Judas, and she shall make them pay handsomely for her silence yet.

Enter PEACHBLOSSOM.

PEACHBLOSSOM. Oh, Miss! Oh, such an accident – old Judas!

LAURA.⎫
BYKE. ⎭ Well?

PEACHBLOSSOM. She was driving along the road away from here just now, when her horse dashed close to the cliff and tumbled her down all of a heap. They've picked her up, and they tell me she is stone dead.

BYKE (*aside*). Dead! And carried her secret with her! All's up. I'll have to emigrate. (*Aloud.*) My friends, pardon my emotion – this melancholy event has made me a widower. I solicit your sympathies in my bereavement. (*Exit* BYKE.)

BERMUDAS. Go to Hoboken and climb a tree! I guess I'll follow him and see he don't pick up anything on his way out. (*Exit* BERMUDAS.)

SNORKEY. Well, there goes a pretty monument of grief. Ain't he a cool 'un? If I ever sets up an ice-cream saloon, I'll have him for head freezer.

PEACHBLOSSOM. Oh, Miss Laura, mayn't I live with you now, and never leave no more?

LAURA. Yes, you shall live with me as long as you please.

SNORKEY. That won't be long if I can help it. (PEACHBLOSSOM *blushes.*) Beg pardon. I suppose we'd better be going! The ladies must be tired, cap'n, at this time of night.

RAY. Yes, it is night! It is night always for me. (*Moving towards door.*)

LAURA (*placing one hand on his shoulder, taking his hand*). But there is a tomorrow. You see, it cannot be dark for ever.

PEARL. Hope for tomorrow, Ray.

LAURA. We shall have cause to bless it, for it will bring the long sought sunlight of our lives.

CURTAIN

The Bells

A DRAMA IN THREE ACTS

by Leopold Lewis

First performed at the Lyceum Theatre, 25 November 1871

CAST

MATHIAS, the burgomaster	*Mr Henry Irving*
CATHERINE, his wife	*Miss G. Pauncefort*
ANNETTE, his daughter	*Miss Fanny Heywood*
WALTER ⎫ friends of Mathias	*Mr Frank Hall*
HANS ⎭	*Mr F. W. Irish*
CHRISTIAN, a gendarme	*Mr H. Crellin*
SOZEL, a servant	*Miss Ellen Mayne*
DR ZIMMER	*Mr Dyas*
NOTARY	*Mr Collett*
TONY ⎫	*Mr Fredericks*
KARL ⎬ guests	*Mr Everard*
FRITZ ⎭	*Mr Fotheringham*
JUDGE OF THE COURT	*Mr Gaston Murray*
CLERK OF THE COURT	*Mr Branscombe*
MESMERIST	*Mr A. Tapping*

Villagers, Officers of the Court, Crowd

ROYAL

LYCEUM THEATRE,

Licensed by the Lord Chamberlain to

Mr. H. L. BATEMAN,

SOLE LESSEE AND MANAGER.

MONDAY, February 12,

AND EVERY EVENING AT 8,

Will be performed

THE NEW DRAMA,

IN THREE ACTS,

BY

LEOPOLD LEWIS,

ENTITLED

THE BELLS

Adapted from "THE POLISH JEW,"

A Dramatic Study by

MM. ERCKMANN-CHATRIAN.

Mathias	Mr. HENRY IRVING.
Walter	Mr. FRANK HALL.
Hans	Mr. F. W. IRISH.
Christian	Mr. HERBERT CRELLIN.
Doctor Zimmer	Mr. DYAS.
Notary	Mr. COLLETT.
Tony	Mr. FREDERICKS.
Fritz	Mr. FOTHERINGHAM.
Karl	Mr. EVERARD.
Catherine	Miss G. PAUNCEFORT.
Annette	Miss FANNY HEYWOOD.
Sosel	Miss ELLEN MAYNE.

With New and appropriate Scenes by HAWES CRAVEN, H. CUTHBERT, and Assistants.

OVERTURE AND ORIGINAL MUSIC

COMPOSED and ARRANGED by M. E. SINGLA.

MUSICAL DIRECTOR. - - - MR. MALLANDAINE.

The Mechanical Effects by Mr. H. JONES. The Properties by Mr. L. ARSOTT & assistants.

Costumes by Mr. SAM. MAY and Mrs. RIDER.

The whole produced under the immediate Direction of

MR. H. L. BATEMAN.

To be had of the Box and Stall Keepers.

Opera Glasses Lent for the Evening.

TO CONCLUDE WITH

PICKWICK,

CHARLES DICKENS.

BY

Adapted and Arranged expressly for the Theatre by

JAMES ALBERY,

Samuel Pickwick, Esq., G.C.M.P.C.		Mr. ADDISON.
Sam Weller		Mr. GEORGE BELMORE.
Alfred Jingle (of No Hall, Nowhere)		Mr. CHARLES WARNER.
Job Trotter		Mr. ODELL.
Mr. Perker (Solicitor)		Mr. F. W. IRISH.
— Nupkins, Esq., (County Magistrate)		Mr. GASTON MURRAY.
Fat Boy		Mr. J. ROYSTON.
Augustus Snodgrass, Esq.		Mr. HERBERT CRELLIN.
Tracy Tupman, Esq.	(M.P.C.'s)	Mr. EDWARD DYAS.
Nathaniel Winkle, Esq.		Mr. W. L. BRANSCOMBE.
Mr. Wardle		Mr. COLLETT.
Mr. Jinks (Clerk to Magistrate)		Mr. FREDERICKS.
Grummer (Village Constable)		Mr. A. TAPPING.
Miss Arabella		Miss LEIGH.
Miss Emily Nupkins	(Wardle's Neices)	Miss MARION HILL.
Miss Witherfield (Mistress of Seminary)		Miss CAROLINE EWELL.
Miss Rachel Wardle (Wardle's Sister)		Miss KATE MANOR.
Miss Smithers		Miss MAUD MORICE.
Mary { Maid at the White Hart, afterwards attendant on Mrs. Winkle}		Miss ANNIE LAFONTAINE.
Ellen { Chambermaid at the "Great White Horse," Ipswich}		Miss MAUDE MIDDLETON.

School Girls, Maid Servants, Gamekeepers, Constables.

N.B.—Emily Wardle in the Book is Emily Nupkins in the Play.

During the Evening the BAND will play the PICKWICK QUADRILLES and the JINGLE GALOP, by FREDERIC REVALLIN, Published by CRAMER, WOOD, & CO., REGENT STREET.

SYNOPSIS OF SCENERY.

SCENE I.

WARDLE'S HOUSE.

SCENE II.

YARD OF WHITE HART INN, BOROUGH.

SCENE III.

SITTING ROOM. No. 8.

SCENE IV.

"THE ANGEL," BURY ST. EDMUNDS.

SCENE V.

Miss WITHERFIELD'S SEMINARY.

SCENE VI.

CORRIDOR IN THE GREAT WHITE HORSE.

SCENE VII.

BEDROOM IN THE GREAT WHITE HORSE.

SCENE VIII.

STREET IN IPSWICH.

SCENE IX.

LIBRARY OF MR. NUPKINS.

The Performance will commence at Seven o'clock with

MY TURN NEXT.

Tarraxicum Twitters (A Village Apothecary)	Mr. GEORGE BELMORE.
	(His original Character.)
Tom Bolus	Mr. JOHN ROYSTON.
Tom Trap	Mr. W. L. BRANSCOMBE.
Farmer Wheatear	Mr. COLLETT.
Lydia	Miss MARION HILL.
Cicely	Miss ELLEN LEIGH.
Peggy	Mrs. F. B. EGAN.

Playbill for the original production of *The Bells*

Mr. IRVING.

ACT I

SCENE I. – *Interior of a Village Inn in Alsace. Table and chairs,
R.; L. an old-fashioned sideboard, with curious china upon it, and
glasses; door, R.; door, L.; large window at back cut in scene, R.;
large door at back cut in scene, L. A candle or lamp burns upon the
table; a stove at back, R., with kettle on it; the pipe of stove going off
through the wing at R. The country covered with snow is seen through
the window; snow is falling; a large clock in L. corner, at back – hands
to work. The Inn is the residence of the Burgomaster. It is Christmas
Eve.*

CATHERINE, *the Burgomaster's wife, discovered seated at a spinning
wheel, L. Music upon rising of curtain.* HANS *passes window; enters
through door at back; he is covered with snow; he carries a gun, and
a large game bag is slung across his shoulders.*

HANS (*taking off his hat and shaking away the snow*). More snow,
Madame Mathias, more snow! (*He places his gun by the stove.*)

CATHERINE. Still in the village, Hans?

HANS. Yes, on Christmas Eve one may be forgiven some small
indulgence.

CATHERINE. You know your sack of flour is ready for you at the
mill?

HANS. Oh, yes; but I am not in a hurry. Father Walter will take
charge of it for me in his cart. Now one glass of wine,
madame, and then I'm off. (*He sits at table, laughing.*)

CATHERINE. Father Walter still here? I thought he had left long
ago.

HANS. No, no. He is still at the Golden Fleece emptying his
bottle. As I came along, I saw his cart standing outside the
grocer's, with the coffee, the cinnamon, and the sugar, all
covered with snow, he, he, he! He is a jolly old fellow. Fond

of good wine, and I don't blame him, you may be sure. We shall leave together.

CATHERINE. And you have no fear of being upset?

HANS. What does it matter? As I said before, on Christmas Eve one may be forgiven some small indulgence.

CATHERINE. I will lend you a lanthorn when you go. Sozel!

SOZEL (*from within*). Madame!

CATHERINE. Some wine for Hans!

SOZEL. Yes, madame.

HANS. That's the sort. Considering the festive character of weather like this, one really must take something.

CATHERINE. Yes, but take care, our white wine is very strong.

HANS. Oh, never fear, madame! But, where is our Burgomaster? How is it he is not to be seen? Is he ill?

CATHERINE. He went to Ribeauville five days ago.

Enter SOZEL, *carrying a decanter of white wine and glass; she places it on table.*

Here is the wine, Master Hans. (*Exit* SOZEL.)

HANS. Good, good! (*He pours out a glass, and drinks with gusto.*) I wager, now, that the Burgomaster has gone to buy the wine for the wedding.

CATHERINE (*laughing*). Not at all improbable.

HANS. Only just now, when I was at the Golden Fleece, it was talked about publicly that the pretty Annette, the daughter of the Burgomaster, and Christian, the Quarter-master of Gendarmes, were going to be married! I could scarcely believe my ears. Christian is certainly a brave man, and an honest man, and a handsome man! I do not wish to maintain anything to the contrary. Our village is rather distinguished in that respect. But he has nothing but his pay to live upon, whilst Annette is the richest match in the village.

CATHERINE. Do you believe then, Hans, that money ought always to be the one consideration?

HANS. No, no, certainly not – on the contrary. Only, I thought that the Burgomaster –

CATHERINE. Well, you have been mistaken; Mathias did not

even ask, 'What have you?' He said at once, 'Let Annette give her free consent and I give mine.'

HANS. And did she give her free consent?

CATHERINE. Yes; she loves Christian, and as we have no other thought but the happiness of our child, we do not look for wealth.

HANS. Oh, if the Burgomaster consents and you consent and Annette consents, why, I suppose I cannot refuse my consent either. Only, I may make this observation: I think Christian a very lucky dog, and I wish I was in his place!

Music. Enter ANNETTE.

ANNETTE. Good evening, Hans! (*Music ceases.*)

HANS. Ah, it is you. Good evening! Good evening! We were just talking about you!

ANNETTE. About me!

HANS. Yes! Oh, oh! How smiling you look, and how prettily dressed; one would almost think that you were going to a wedding.

ANNETTE. Ah, you are always joking.

HANS. No, no, I am not joking! I say what I think, that's all! That pretty cap, and that pretty dress, and those pretty shoes were not put on for the pleasure of a tough middle-aged forest-keeper like myself. It has been all arranged for another – for another I say, and I know who that particular 'another' happens to be – he, he, he!

ANNETTE. (*blushing*). How can you talk such nonsense!

HANS. Oh, yes, it is nonsense to say that you are fascinating, merry, good and pretty, no doubt; and it is nonsense to say that the particular another I refer to – you know the one I mean – the tall one with the handsome moustaches, is a fellow to be envied. Yes, it is nonsense to say it, for I for one do not envy him at all – no, not at all!

FATHER WALTER *has passed the window, now opens door at back and puts his head in.* ANNETTE *turns to look at him.*

FATHER WALTER (*laughing and coming in – he is covered with snow*). Ah, she turned her head! It's not he you expect!

ANNETTE. Who, Father Walter?

WALTER. Ha, ha, ha! That's right. Up to the last minute she will pretend that she knows nothing.

ANNETTE. I do not understand what you mean.

WALTER *and* HANS *both laugh.*

CATHERINE. You are a couple of old fools!

WALTER (*still laughing*). You're not such an old fool as you look, are you, Hans?

HANS. No; and you don't look such an old fool as you are, do you, Walter?

Enter SOZEL *with a lighted lanthorn, which she places upon the sideboard; then exits.*

WALTER. No. What is the meaning of that lanthorn?

HANS. Why, to act as a light for the cart.

ANNETTE. You can go by moonlight!

WALTER. Yes, yes; certainly we will go by the light of the moon! Let us empty a glass in honour of the young couple. (*They fill glasses.*) Here's to the health of Christian and Annette!

They drink – HANS *taking a long time in drinking the contents of his glass, and then heaving a deep sigh, and music commences.*

WALTER. And now listen, Annette; as I entered I saw Christian returning with two gendarmes, and I am sure that in a quarter of an hour –

ANNETTE. Listen! (*Wind off.*)

CATHERINE. The wind is rising. I hope that Mathias is not now on the road!

ANNETTE. No, no, it is Christian! (*Music, forte.*)

CHRISTIAN *passes the window, enters the door at back, covered with snow.*

ALL. Christian! (*Music ceases.*)

CHRISTIAN. Good evening, all. (ANNETTE *runs to him.*) Good evening, Annette.

ANNETTE. Where have you come from, Christian?

CHRISTIAN. From the Hôvald! From the Hôvald! What a snow-storm! I have seen many in Auvergne or the Pyrenees, but never anything like this. (*He sits by the stove, and warms his hands. After hanging up his hat,* ANNETTE *goes out and returns with a jug of wine, which she places upon the stove.*)

WALTER. There, look at that! What care she takes of him! It would not be for us that she would fetch the sugar and the cinnamon and warm the wine.

CHRISTIAN (*laughing*). Do not allow me, Annette, to be crushed by the satire of Father Walter, who knows how to defy the wind and the snow by the side of a good fire. I should like to see the figure he would present if he had been five hours on duty as I have been in the snow on the Hôvald.

CATHERINE. You have been five hours in the snow, Christian! Your duties must be terribly severe.

CHRISTIAN. How can it be helped? At two o'clock we received information that smugglers had passed the river the previous night with tobacco and gunpowder; so we were bound to be off at once. (*Music.*)

ANNETTE. Drink this, Christian; it will warm you.

CHRISTIAN. Thank you, Annette. Ah! that's good!

WALTER. The Quarter-master is not difficult to please. (*Music ceases.*)

CATHERINE. Never mind. Christian, you are fortunate to have arrived this early. (*Wind heard off.*) Listen to the wind! I hope that Mathias will have the prudence to stop for shelter somewhere on the road. (*To* HANS *and* WALTER.) I was right, you see, in advising you to go; you would now have been safely at home.

HANS (*laughing*). Annette was the cause of our stopping. Why did she blow out the lanthorn?

ANNETTE. Oh, you were glad enough to stop!

CHRISTIAN. Your winters are very severe here.

WALTER. Oh, not every year, Quarter-master! For fifteen years we have not had a winter so severe as this.

HANS. No – I do not remember to have seen so much snow since

what is called 'The Polish Jew's Winter'. In that year the
Schnieberg was covered in the first days of November, and
the frost lasted till the end of March.

CHRISTIAN. And for that reason it is called 'The Polish Jew's
Winter'?

WALTER. No – it is for another and terrible reason, which none
of us will ever forget. Madame Mathias remembers it well,
I am sure.

CATHERINE (*solemnly*). You are right, Walter, you are right.

HANS. Had you been here at that time, Quarter-master, you
might have won your cross.

CHRISTIAN. How?

WALTER. I can tell you all about this affair from the beginning
to the end, since I saw it nearly all myself. Curiously enough,
it was this very day, just fifteen years ago, that I was seated
at this very table. There was Mathias, who sat there, and
who had only bought his mill just six months before; there
was old John Roebec, who sat there – they used to call him
'the Little Shoemaker' – and several others, who are now
sleeping under the turf – we shall all go there some day!
Happy are those who have nothing upon their conscience!
We were just beginning a game of cards, when, just as the
old clock struck ten, the sound of horse bells was heard; a
sledge stopped before the door, and almost immediately
afterwards a Polish Jew entered. He was a well-made,
vigorous man, between forty and fifty years of age. I fancy
I can see him even now entering at that door with his green
cloak and his fur cap, his large black beard and his great boots
covered with hare skin. He was a seed merchant. He said as
he came in, 'Peace be with you!' Everybody turned to look
at him, and thought, 'Where has he come from? What does
he want?' Because you must know that the Polish Jews who
come to dispose of seed do not arrive in this province till the
month of February. Mathias said to him, 'What can I do for
you?' But the Jew, without replying, first opened his cloak,
and then unbuckled a girdle which he wore round his waist.
This he threw upon the table, and we all heard the ringing

sound of the gold it contained. Then he said, 'The snow is deep; the road difficult; put my horse in the stable. In one hour I shall continue my journey.' After that he drank his wine without speaking to anyone, and sat like a man depressed, and who is anxious about his affairs. At eleven o'clock the Night Watchman came in. Everyone went his way, and the Jew was left alone!

Chord of Music – loud gust of wind – crash of glass off – hurry.
ALL *start to their feet. Music continued.*

CATHERINE. What has happened? I must go and see.

ANNETTE. Oh! no, you must not go!

CATHERINE. I will return immediately. Don't be alarmed. (*Exit* CATHERINE.)

CHRISTIAN. But I do not yet see how I could have gained the cross in this affair –

WALTER. Stop a minute. The next morning they found the Jew's horse dead under the Bridge of Vechem, and a hundred yards further on, the green cloak and the fur cap, deeply stained with blood. As to what became of the Jew himself has never to this day been discovered. (*Music ceases.*)

HANS. Everything that Walter has stated is strictly true. The gendarmes came here the next morning, notwithstanding the snow; and, in fact, it is since that dreadful time that the brigade has been established here.

CHRISTIAN. But was no inquiry instituted?

HANS. Inquiry! I should think there was. It was the former Quarter-master, Kelz, who undertook the case. How he travelled about! What witnesses he badgered! What clues he discovered! What information and reports were written! and how the coat and the cap were analysed, and examined by magistrates and doctors! – but it all came to nothing!

CHRISTIAN. But, surely, suspicion fell on someone.

HANS. Oh, of course, the gendarmes are never at a loss for suspicions in such cases. But proofs are required. About that time, you see, there were two brothers living in the village who had an old bear, with his ears all torn, two big dogs, and a donkey, that they took about with them to the fairs, and made the dogs bait the bear. This brought them a great deal of money; and they lived a rollicking, dissipated life. When the Jew disappeared, they happened to be at Vechem; suspicions fastened upon them, and the report was that they had caused the Jew to be eaten by the dogs and the bear, and that they only refrained from swallowing the cloak and cap because they had had enough. They were arrested, and it would have gone hard with the poor devils, but Mathias interested himself in their case, and they were discharged, after being in prison fifteen months. That was the specimen of suspicion of the case.

CHRISTIAN. What you have told me greatly astonishes me. I never heard a word of this before.

Re-enter CATHERINE.

CATHERINE. I was sure that Sozel had left the windows in the kitchen open. Now every pane of glass in them is broken. (*To* CHRISTIAN.) Fritz is outside. He wishes to speak with you.

CHRISTIAN. Fritz, the gendarme!

CATHERINE. Yes, I asked him to come in, but he would not. It is upon some matter of duty.

CHRISTIAN. Ah! good, I know what it is!

ANNETTE. You will return, Christian?

CHRISTIAN. In a few minutes. (*Music to take him off. Exit.*)

WALTER. Ah! there goes a brave young fellow – gentle in character, I will admit, but not a man to trifle with rogues.

HANS. Yes, Mathias is fortunate in finding so good a son-in-law; but everything has succeeded with Mathias for the last fifteen years. (*Music commences.*) He was comparatively poor then, and now he is one of the richest men in the village, and the Burgomaster. He was born under a lucky star.

WALTER. Well, and he deserves all the success he has achieved.

CATHERINE. Hark!

ANNETTE. It is, perhaps, Christian returning as he promised.

Hurry. MATHIAS *passes the window, then enters; he wears a long cloak covered with snow, large cap made of otter's skin, gaiters and spurs, and carries a large riding whip in his hand – chord – tableau.*

MATHIAS. It is I – It is I! (*Music ceases.*)

CATHERINE (*rising*). Mathias!

HANS ⎫
WALTER ⎭ (*starting up*). The Burgomaster!

ANNETTE (*running and embracing him*). At last you have come.

MATHIAS. Yes, yes! Heaven be praised! What a snow-storm. I was obliged to leave the carriage at Vechem. It will be brought over tomorrow.

CATHERINE (*embracing him and taking off his coat*). Let me take this off for you. It was very kind of you not to stop away. We were becoming so anxious about you.

MATHIAS. So I thought, Catherine; and that was the reason I determined to reach home tonight. (*Looking round.*) Ha, ha! Father Walter and Hans, you will have nice weather in which to go home. (*He takes off his hat, etc. and gives them to his wife and daughter.*) There! You will have to get all those things dried.

CATHERINE. Sozel, get ready your master's supper at once, and tell Nickel to take the horse to the stable!

SOZEL (*within*). Yes, madame.

ANNETTE. We thought perhaps that your cousin Bôth would have detained you.

MATHIAS (*unbuttoning his gaiters*). Oh, I had finished all my business yesterday morning, and I wished to come away; but Bôth made me stop to see a performance in the town.

ANNETTE. A performance! Is Punchinello at Ribeauville?

MATHIAS. No, it was not Punchinello. It was a Parisian who did extraordinary tricks. He sent people to sleep.

ANNETTE. Sent people to sleep!

MATHIAS. Yes.

CATHERINE. He gave them something to drink, no doubt.

MATHIAS. No; he simply looked at them and made signs, and they went fast asleep. – It certainly was an astonishing performance. If I had not myself seen it I should never have believed it.

HANS. Ah! the Brigadier Stenger was telling me about it the other day. He had seen the same thing at Saverne. This Parisian sends people to sleep, and when they are asleep he makes them tell him everything that weighs upon their consciences.

MATHIAS. Exactly. Annette?

ANNETTE. What, father?

MATHIAS. Look in the big pocket of my cloak.

Enter SOZEL.

Sozel! take these gaiters and spurs; hang them in the stable with the harness.

SOZEL. Yes, Burgomaster. (*Exit*.)

ANNETTE, *who has taken a small box out of the pocket of the cloak, approaches her father. Music.*

ANNETTE. What is it, father?

MATHIAS. Open the box.

She opens the box, and takes out a handsome Alsatian hat, with gold and silver stars upon it – the others approach to look at it.

ANNETTE. Oh, how pretty! Is it for me?

MATHIAS. For whom else could it be? Not for Sozel, I fancy.

ANNETTE *puts on the hat after taking off her ribbon, and looks at herself in glass on sideboard – all express admiration.*

ANNETTE. Oh! What will Christian say?

MATHIAS. He will say you are the prettiest girl in the province.

ANNETTE (*kissing her father*). Thank you, dear father. How good you are!

MATHIAS. It is my wedding present, Annette. The day of your marriage I wish you to wear it, and to preserve it for ever. In fifteen or twenty years hence, will you remember your father gave it you?

ANNETTE (*with emotion*). Yes, dear father!

MATHIAS. All that I wish is to see you happy with Christian. (*Music ceases.*) And now for supper and some wine. (*To* WALTER *and* HANS.) You will stop and take a glass of wine with me?

WALTER. With pleasure, Burgomaster.

HANS. For you, Burgomaster, we will try and make that little effort.

SOZEL *has entered with tray of supper and wine which she has placed upon table.* MATHIAS *now sits at table, helps wine, and then commences to eat with a good appetite.* SOZEL *draws the curtains across window at back, and exits.*

MATHIAS. There is one advantage about the cold. It gives you a good appetite. Here's to your health! (*He drinks.*)

WALTER.⎫ Here's yours, Burgomaster! ⎰(*They touch glasses
HANS. ⎭ ⎱ and drink.*)

MATHIAS. Christian has not been here this evening?

ANNETTE. Yes; they came to fetch him, but he will return presently.

MATHIAS. Ah! Good! good!

CATHERINE. He came late today, in consequence of some duty he had to perform in the Hôvald, in the capture of smugglers.

MATHIAS. Nice weather for such a business. By the side of the river, I found the snow five feet deep.

WALTER. Yes; we were talking about that. We were telling the Quarter-master that since the 'Polish Jew's Winter' we had never seen weather like this.

MATHIAS, *who was raising the glass to his lips, places it on the table again without drinking.*

MATHIAS. Ah! you were talking of that?

Distant sound of Bells heard. To himself – 'Bells! Bells!' *His whole aspect changes, and he leaves off eating, and sits listening. The Bells continue louder.*

HANS. That winter, you remember, Burgomaster, the whole

valley was covered several feet deep with snow, and it was a long time before the horse of the Polish Jew could be dug out.

MATHIAS (*with indifference*). Very possibly; but that tale is too old! It is like an old woman's story now, and is thought about no more. (*Watching them and starting up.*) Do you not hear the sound of Bells upon the road? (*The Bells still go on.*)

HANS
WALTER } (*listening*). Bells? No!

CATHERINE. What is the matter, Mathias? You appear ill. You are cold; some warm wine will restore you. The fire in the stove is low; come, Annette, we will warm your father his wine in the kitchen. (*Exeunt* CATHERINE *and* ANNETTE.)

MATHIAS. Thank you; it is nothing.

WALTER. Come, Hans, let us go and see to the horse. At the same time, it is very stange that it was never discovered who did the deed.

MATHIAS. The rogues have escaped, more's the pity. Here's your health! (*Music.*)

WALTER.
HANS. } Thank you!

HANS. It is just upon the stroke of ten! (*They drink, and go out together.*)

MATHIAS (*alone – comes forward and listens with terror. Music with frequent chords*). Bells! Bells! (*He runs to the window and slightly drawing the curtains, looks out.*) No one on the road. What is this jangling in my ears? What is tonight? Ah, it is the very night – the very hour! (*Clock strikes ten.*) I feel a darkness coming over me. (*Stage darkens.*) A sensation of giddiness seizes me. (*He staggers to chair.*) Shall I call for help? No, no, Mathias. Have courage! The Jew is dead!

Sinks on chair; the Bells come closer; then the back of the Scene rises and sinks, disclosing the Bridge of Vechem, with the snow-covered country and frozen rivulet; lime-kiln burning in the distance. The JEW *is discovered seated in sledge dressed as described in speech in Act I ; the horse carrying Bells; the* JEW'S *face is turned away. The*

*snow is falling fast; the scene is seen through a gauze; limelight.
Vision of a* MAN *dressed in a brown blouse and hood over his head,
carrying an axe; stands in an attitude of following the sledge. When
the picture is fully disclosed the Bells cease.*

MATHIAS (*his back to scene*). Oh, it is nothing. It is the wine and
cold that have overcome me!

*He rises and turns; goes up stage; starts violently upon seeing the
vision before him. At the same time the* JEW *in the sledge suddenly
turns his face, which is ashy pale, and fixes his eyes sternly upon him.*
MATHIAS *utters a prolonged cry of terror, and falls senseless. Hurried Music.*

ACT II

SCENE I. – *Best Room in the Burgomaster's House. Door,* L.;
door, R.; *three large windows at back, looking out upon a street of the
village, the church and the buildings covered with snow. Large stove
in the centre of room, practicable door to stove, tongs in grate; arm-
chair near the stove; at* L. (1st grooves) *an old escritoire; near* L., *a
table and arm-chair; chairs about room. It is morning; the room and
street bright with sunlight.*

As the Curtain rises to Music, MATHIAS *is discovered seated in
armchair at table;* CATHERINE *and* DOCTOR ZIMMER *standing at
back by stove contemplating him. They advance.*

DOCTOR. You feel better, Burgomaster?

MATHIAS. Yes, I am quite well.

DOCTOR. No more pains in the head?

MATHIAS. No.

DOCTOR. No more strange noises in the ears?

MATHIAS. When I tell you that I am quite well – that I never
was better – that is surely enough.

CATHERINE. For a long time he has had bad dreams. He talks
in his sleep, and his thirst at night is constant, and feverish.

MATHIAS. Is there anything extraordinary in being thirsty during
the night?

DOCTOR. Certainly not: but you must take more care of yourself. You drink too much white wine, Burgomaster. Your
attack of the night before last arose from this cause. You had
taken too much wine at your cousin's, and then the severe
cold having seized you, the blood had flown to the head.

MATHIAS. I *was* cold, but that stupid gossip about the Polish Jew
was the cause of all.

DOCTOR. How was that?

360

MATHIAS. Well, you must know, when the Jew disappeared, they brought me the cloak and cap that had belonged to the poor devil, and the sight of them quite upset me, remembering he had, the night before, stopped at our house. Since that time I had thought no more of the matter until the night before last, when some gossip brought the affair again to my mind. It was as if I had seen the ghost of the Jew. We all know that there are no such things, but – (*suddenly to his wife*) Have you sent for the Notary?

CATHERINE. Yes; but you must be calm.

MATHIAS. I am calm. But Annette's marriage must take place at once. When a man in robust health and strength is liable to such an attack as I have had, nothing should be postponed till the morrow. What occurred to me the night before last might again occur tonight. I might not survive the second blow, and then I should not have seen my dear children happy. And now leave me. Whether it was the wine, or the cold, or the gossip about the Polish Jew, it comes to the same thing. It is all past and over now.

DOCTOR. But, perhaps, Burgomaster, it would be better to adjourn the signing of the marriage contract for a few days. It is an affair of so much interest and importance that the agitation might –

MATHIAS (*angrily*). Good heavens, why will not people attend to their own business! I was ill; you bled me – am well again – so much the better. Let the Notary be sent for at once. Let Father Walter and Hans be summoned as witnesses, and let the whole affair be finished without further delay.

DOCTOR (*to* CATHERINE, *aside*). His nerves are still very much shaken. Perhaps it will be better to let him have his own way. (*To* MATHIAS.) Well, well, we'll say no more about it. Only don't forget what I have said – be careful of the white wine.

MATHIAS (*angrily striking the table, turning his back*). Good! Good! Ah!

The DOCTOR *looks with pity towards him, bows to* CATHERINE, *and exits. The church bell commences to ring. Music.*

CATHERINE. Annette! Annette!

ANNETTE (*off*). I am coming.

CATHERINE (*impatiently*). Be quick. Be quick.

ANNETTE. Directly – directly!

MATHIAS. Don't hurry the poor child. You know that she is dressing.

CATHERINE. But I don't take two hours to dress.

MATHIAS. You; oh! that is different. She expects Christian. He was to have been here this morning. Something has detained him.

Enter ANNETTE; *she is in gala dress, and wears the golden heart upon her breast, and the hat given her by* MATHIAS *in Act I.*

CATHERINE. At last, you are ready!

ANNETTE. Yes, I am ready.

MATHIAS (*with affection*). How beautiful you look, Annette.

ANNETTE. You see, dear father, I have put on the hat.

MATHIAS. You did right – you did right.

CATHERINE (*impatiently*). Are you not coming, Annette? The service will have commenced. Come, come.

ANNETTE. Christian has not yet been here.

MATHIAS. No, you may be sure some business detains him.

CATHERINE. Do come, Annette; you will see Christian by and by. (*Exit,* ANNETTE *is following.*)

MATHIAS. Annette, Annette! Have you nothing to say to me?

ANNETTE *runs to him, and kisses him – he embraces her with affection.*

ANNETTE. You know, dear father, how much I love you.

MATHIAS. Yes, yes. There, go now, dear child; your mother is impatient. (*Exit* ANNETTE.)

The villagers, MEN *and* WOMEN *in Sunday clothes, pass the window in couples.* MATHIAS *goes up and looks through the window,* ANNETTE *and* CATHERINE *pass and kiss hands to him – a* WOMAN *in the group says,* 'Good morning, Burgomaster.' *Church bells cease. Music ceases.*

MATHIAS. All goes well! Luckily all is over. But what a lesson,

Mathias – what a lesson! Would anyone believe that the mere talk about the Jew could bring on such a fit? Fortunately the people about here are such idiots they suspect nothing. But it was that Parisian fellow at the fair who was the real cause of all. The rascal had really made me nervous. When he wanted to send me to sleep as well as the others, I said to myself, 'Stop, stop, Mathias – this sending you to sleep may be an invention of the devil, you might relate certain incidents in your past life! You must be cleverer than that, Mathias; you mustn't run your neck into a halter; you must be cleverer than that – ah! you must be cleverer than that.' You will die an old man yet, Mathias, and the most respected in the Province – only this, since you dream and are apt to talk in your dreams, for the future you will sleep alone in the room above, the door locked, and the key safe in your pocket. They say walls have ears – let them hear me as much as they please. (*Music. Takes bunch of keys out of his pocket.*) And now to count the dowry of Annette, to be given to our dear son-in-law, in order that our dear son-in-law may love us. (*He crosses, unlocks the escritoire, takes out a large leather bag, unties it and empties the contents, consisting of gold pieces and rouleaux, upon the table.*) Thirty thousand francs. (*He sits at table and commences to count the money.*) Thirty thousand francs – a fine dowry for Annette. Ah! it is pleasant to hear the sound of gold! A fine dowry for the husband of Annette. He's a clever fellow, is Christian. He's not a Kelz – half deaf and half blind; no, no – he's a clever fellow, is Christian, and quite capable of getting on a right track. (*A pause.*) The first time I saw him I said to myself, 'You shall be my son-in-law, and if anything should be discovered, you will defend me.' (*Continues to count, weighing piece upon his finger – takes up a piece and examines it.*) A piece of old gold! (*Looks at it more closely – starts.*) Ah! that came from the girdle; not for them – no, no, not for them, for me. (*Places the piece of gold in his waistcoat pocket – he goes to the escritoire, opens a drawer, takes out another piece of gold and throws it upon the table in substitution.*) That girdle did us a good turn – without it – without it we were ruined. If Catherine only knew – poor, poor Catherine. (*He sobs – his head sinks on his breast. Music ceases – the Bells heard off; he starts.*) The Bells! the Bells again! They must come from the mill. (*Rushes across to door, calling.*) Sozel! Sozel, I say, Sozel!

Enter SOZEL *holding an open book; she is in her Sunday dress.*

MATHIAS. Is there anyone at the mill?

SOZEL. No, Burgomaster. They have all gone to church and the wheel is stopped.

MATHIAS. Don't you hear the sound of Bells?

SOZEL. No Burgomaster, I hear nothing. (*The Bells cease.*)

MATHIAS (*aside*). Strange – strange. (*Rudely.*) What were you doing?

SOZEL. I was reading, Burgomaster.

MATHIAS. Reading – what? Ghost stories, no doubt.

SOZEL. Oh, no, Burgomaster! I was reading such a curious story, about a band of robbers being discovered after twenty-three years had passed, and all through the blade of an old knife having been found in a blacksmith's shop, hidden under some rusty iron. They captured the whole of them, consisting of the mother, two sons, and the grandfather, and they hanged them all in a row. Look, Burgomaster, there's the picture. (*Shows book – he strikes it violently out of her hand.*)

MATHIAS. Enough, enough! It's pity you have nothing better to do. There, go – go! (*Exit* SOZEL.)

Seats himself at the table and puts remaining money into the bag.

The fools! – not to destroy all evidence against them. To be hanged through the blade of an old knife. Not like that – not like that am *I* to be caught!

Music – sprightly military air. CHRISTIAN *passes at back, stops at centre window and taps upon it.* MATHIAS *looks round with a start, is reassured upon seeing who it is, and says,* 'Ah, it is Christian!' – *he ties up the bag and places it in the escritoire.* CHRISTIAN *enters.* MATHIAS *meets him half way – they shake hands. Music ceases.* CHRISTIAN *is in full dress of a Quarter-master of Gendarmes.*

CHRISTIAN. Good morning, Burgomaster; I hope you are better.

MATHIAS. Oh, yes, I am well, Christian. I have just been counting Annette's dowry, in good sounding gold. It was a pleasure to me to do so, as it recalled to me the days gone by, when by industry and good fortune I had been enabled to gain it; and I thought that in the future my children would enjoy and profit by all that I had so acquired.

CHRISTIAN. You are right, Burgomaster. Money gained by honest labour is the only profitable wealth. It is the good seed which in time is sure to bring a rich harvest.

MATHIAS. Yes, yes; especially when the good seed is sown in good ground. The contract must be signed today.

CHRISTIAN. Today?

MATHIAS. Yes, the sooner the better. I hate postponements. Once decided, why adjourn the business? It shows a great want of character.

CHRISTIAN. Well, Burgomaster, nothing to me could be more agreeable.

MATHIAS. Annette loves you.

CHRISTIAN. Ah, she does.

MATHIAS. And the dowry is ready – then why should not the affair be settled at once? I hope, my boy, you will be satisfied.

CHRISTIAN. You know, Burgomaster, I do not bring much.

MATHIAS. You bring courage and good conduct – I will take care of the rest; and now let us talk of other matters. You are late today. I suppose you were busy. Annette waited for you, and was obliged to go without you.

He goes up and sits by stove in arm-chair, opens stove door, takes up tongs and arranges fire.

CHRISTIAN (*unbuckling his sword and sitting in chair*). Ah, it was a very curious business that detained me. Would you believe it, Burgomaster, I was reading old depositions from five o'clock till ten? The hours flew by, but the more I read the more I wished to read.

MATHIAS. And what was the subject of the depositions?

CHRISTIAN. They were about the case of the Polish Jew who was murdered on the Bridge of Vechem fifteen years ago.

MATHIAS (*dropping the tongs*). Ah!

CHRISTIAN. Father Walter told me the story the night before last. It seems to me very remarkable that nothing was ever discovered.

MATHIAS. No doubt – no doubt.

CHRISTIAN. The man who committed that murder must have been a clever fellow.

MATHIAS. Yes, he was not a fool.

CHRISTIAN. A fool! He would have made one of the cleverest gendarmes in the department.

MATHIAS (*with a smile*). Do you really think so?

CHRISTIAN. I am sure of it. There are so many ways of detecting criminals, and so few escape, that to have committed a crime like this, and yet to remain undiscovered, showed the possession of extraordinary address.

MATHIAS. I quite agree with you, Christian; and what you say shows your good sense. When a man has committed a crime, and by it gained money, he becomes like a gambler, and tries his second and his third throw. I should think it requires a great amount of courage to resist the first success in crime.

CHRISTIAN. You are right, but what is most remarkable to me in the case is this, that no trace of the murdered man was ever found. Now do you know what my idea is?

MATHIAS (*rising*). No, no! What is your idea?

CHRISTIAN. Well, I find at that time there were a great many lime-kilns in the neighbourhood of Vechem. Now it is my idea that the murderer, to destroy all traces of his crime, threw the body of the Jew into one of these kilns. Old Kelz, my predecessor, evidently never thought of that.

MATHIAS. Very likely – very likely. Do you know that idea never occurred to me? You are the first who ever suggested it.

CHRISTIAN. And this idea leads to many others. Now suppose – suppose inquiry had been instituted as to those persons who were burning lime at that time.

MATHIAS. Take care, Christian – take care. Why, I myself had a lime-kiln burning at the time the crime was committed.

CHRISTIAN (*laughing*). Oh, you, Burgomaster!

MATHIAS *laughs heartily.* ANNETTE *and* CATHERINE *pass the window.*

ANNETTE (*as she passes the window before entering*). He is there!

Enter ANNETTE *and* CATHERINE.

MATHIAS. Is the Notary here?

CATHERINE. Yes, he is in the next room with Father Walter and Hans, and the others. He is reading the contract to them now.

MATHIAS. Good – good!

CHRISTIAN. Oh, Annette, how that pretty hat becomes you!

ANNETTE. Yes; it was dear father who gave it to me. (*Music.*)

CHRISTIAN. It is today, Annette.

ANNETTE. Yes, Christian, it is today.

MATHIAS. Well; you know what is customary when father, mother, and all consent.

CHRISTIAN. What, Burgomaster?

MATHIAS (*smiling*). You embrace your intended wife.

CHRISTIAN. Is that so, Annette?

ANNETTE. I don't know, Christian. (*He kisses her forehead, and leads her up to stove, talking.*)

MATHIAS. Look at our children, Catherine; how happy they are! When I think that we were once as happy! It's true; yes, it's true, we were once as happy as they are now! Why are you crying, Catherine? Are you sorry to see our children happy?

CATHERINE. No, no, Mathias; these are tears of joy, and I can't help them. (*Throws herself upon* MATHIAS' *shoulder. Music ceases.*)

MATHIAS. And now to sign the contract! (*Crosses to door and throws it open.*) Walter, Hans, come in! Let everyone present come in! The most important acts in life should always take place in the presence of all. It is an old and honest custom of Alsace. (*Music – 'The Lauterbach,' played forte.*)

Enter HANS *with two* GIRLS *on his arm* – FATHER WALTER *with two* GIRLS – MEN *and* WOMEN *villagers arm-in-arm* – *they wear ribbons in their button-holes* – *the* NOTARY *with papers* – SOZEL. *The* MEN *wear their hats through the whole scene.* MATHIAS *advances and shakes hands with the* NOTARY *and conducts him to table on which is spread out the contract* – *pen and ink on table. The* COMPANY *fill the stage in groups.*

NOTARY. Gentlemen and witnesses – You have just heard read the marriage contract between Christian Bême, Quarter-master of Gendarmes, and Annette Mathias. Has anyone any observations to make?

SEVERAL VOICES. No, no.

NOTARY. Then we can at once proceed to take the signatures.

MATHIAS (*goes to the escritoire and takes out the bag of gold which he places on the table before the* NOTARY). There is the dowry. It is not in promises made on paper, but in gold. Thirty thousand francs in good French gold.

ALL. Thirty thousand francs!

CHRISTIAN. It is too much, Burgomaster.

MATHIAS. Not at all, not at all. When Catherine and myself are gone there will be more. And now, Christian – (*music commences*) – I wish you to make me one promise.

CHRISTIAN. What promise?

MATHIAS. Young men are ambitious. It is natural they should be. You must promise me that you will remain in this village while both of us live. (*Takes* CATHERINE'S *hand.*) You know Annette is our only child; we love her dearly, and to lose her altogether would break our hearts. Do you promise?

CHRISTIAN (*looks to* ANNETTE; *she returns a glance of approval*). I do promise.

MATHIAS. Your word of honour, given before all?

CHRISTIAN. My word of honour, given before all. (*They shake hands. Music ceases.*)

MATHIAS (*aside*). It was necessary. And now to sign the contract. (*He goes to table; the* NOTARY *hands him the pen, and points to the place where he is to sign his name.* MATHIAS *is about to write.*

The Bells heard off. MATHIAS *stops, listens with terror – his face to the audience, and away from the persons upon the stage – aside.*) Bells! Courage, Mathias! (*After an effort he signs rapidly – the Bells cease – he throws the pen down.*) Come, Christian, sign! (CHRISTIAN *approaches the table to sign – as he is about to do so* WALTER *taps him on the shoulder.* MATHIAS *starts at the interruption.*)

WALTER. It is not every day you sign a contract like that.

ALL *laugh.* MATHIAS *heaves a sigh and is reassured.* CHRISTIAN *signs – the* NOTARY *hands the pen to* CATHERINE, *who makes her cross – she then takes* ANNETTE *to table, who signs her name.* CATHERINE *kisses her affectionately and gives her to* CHRISTIAN.

MATHIAS (*aside*). And now should the Jew return to this world, Christian must drive him back again. (*Aloud.*) Come, come, just one waltz and then dinner.

WALTER. Stop! stop! Before we go we must have the song of the betrothal.

ALL. Yes, yes, Annette! Annette! the song of the betrothal.

> *Song,* ANNETTE. *Air – 'The Lauterbach'*
>
> Suitors of wealth and high degree,
>   In style superbly grand,
> Tendered their love on bended knee
>   And sought to win my hand.

Tyrolienne by all, and waltz.

> But a soldier brave came to woo.
>   No maid such love could spurn –
> Proving his heart was fond and true,
>   Won my love in return.

Tyrolienne as before by all, and waltz. MATHIAS *is seated – in the midst of the waltz Bells are heard off.* MATHIAS *starts up and rushes into the midst of the* WALTZERS.

MATHIAS. The Bells! The Bells!

CATHERINE. Are you mad?

MATHIAS *seizes her by the waist and waltzes wildly with her.*

MATHIAS. Ring on! Ring on! Houp! Houp!

Music, forte – while the waltz is at its height the drop falls.

ACT III

SCENE I. – *Bedroom in the Burgomaster's House. The whole back of Scene painted on a gauze; alcove on left; door,* R.; *two windows at back; small table by bed; chair,* L. *Night.*

Music – Enter MATHIAS, FATHER WALTER, HANS, CHRISTIAN, ANNETTE, *and* CATHERINE; SOZEL *carrying a lighted candle, bottle of water and glass, which she places on table. They enter suddenly; the* MEN *appear to be slightly excited by wine.*

HANS (*laughing*). Ha, ha! Everything has gone off admirably. We only wanted something to wind up with, and I may say that we are all as capitally wound up as the great clock at Strasbourg.

WALTER. Yes, and what wine we have consumed! For many a day we shall remember the signing of Annette's marriage contract. I should like to witness such a contract every second day.

HANS. There I object to your argument. Every day, I say!

CHRISTIAN. And so you are determined, Mathias, to sleep here tonight?

MATHIAS. Yes, I am decided. I wish for air. I know what is necessary for my condition. The heat was the cause of my accident. This room is cooler, and will prevent its recurrence. (*Laughter heard outside.*)

HANS. Listen, how they are still revelling! Come, Father Walter, let us rejoin the revels!

WALTER. But Mathias already deserts us, just at the moment when we were beginning to thoroughly enjoy ourselves.

MATHIAS. What more do you wish me to do? From noon till midnight is surely enough!

WALTER. Enough, it may be, but not too much; never too much of such wine.

HANS. There again, I object to your argument – never enough, I say.

CATHERINE. Mathias is right. You remember that Doctor Zimmer told him to be careful of the wine he took, or it would one day play him false. He has already taken too much since this morning.

MATHIAS. One glass of water before I go to rest is all I require. It will calm me – it will calm me.

KARL, FRITZ *and* TONY, *three of the guests of the previous Act, enter suddenly, slightly merry, pushing each other.*

GUESTS. Goodnight, Burgomaster, Goodnight.

TONY. I say, Hans! don't you know that the Night Watchman is below?

HANS. The Night Watchman! What in the name of all that is political does he want?

KARL. He requires us all to leave, and the house to be closed. It is past hours.

MATHIAS. Give him a bumper of wine, and then goodnight all!

WALTER. Past hours! For a Burgomaster no regulations ought to exist.

HANS. ⎫
OTHERS. ⎭ Certainly not.

MATHIAS (*with fierceness*). Regulations made for all must be obeyed by all.

WALTER (*timidly*). Well, then, shall we go?

MATHIAS. Yes, yes, go! Leave me to myself.

CATHERINE. Don't thwart his wish. Follow his directions.

WALTER (*shaking hands with* MATHIAS). Goodnight, Mathias. I wish you calm repose, and no unpleasant dreams.

MATHIAS (*fiercely*). I never dream. (*Mildly.*) Goodnight, all. Go, friends, go.

Music. Exeunt WALTER, HANS, *and the three* GUESTS, *saying,* 'Goodnight, Burgomaster'. CATHERINE, ANNETTE *and* CHRISTIAN *remain.*

MATHIAS. Goodnight, Catherine. (*Embracing her.*) I shall be

better here. The wine, the riot, those songs have quite dazed
my brain. I shall sleep better here; I shall sleep better.

CHRISTIAN. Yes, this room is fresh and cool. Goodnight.

MATHIAS. The same to you, Christian; the same to you. (*They
shake hands.*)

ANNETTE (*running to her father and kissing him*). Goodnight,
dear father; may you sleep well!

MATHIAS (*kissing her with affection*). Goodnight, dear child; do
not fear for me – do not fear.

Music. Exeunt all but MATHIAS. *Music ceases. He goes up cautiously,
locks the door, and puts the key in his pocket.*

At last I am alone! Everything goes well. Christian the
gendarme is caught! Tonight I shall sleep without a fear
haunting me! If any new danger should threaten the father-
in-law of the Quarter-master, it would soon be averted. Ah!
What a power it is to know how to guide your destiny in
life. You must hold good cards in your hands. Good cards! as
I have done, and if you play them well you may defy ill
fortune.

CHORUS OF REVELLERS *outside* (*without accompaniment*)

Now, since we must part, let's drain a last glass;
        Let's drink!
Let us first drink to this gentle young lass:
        Let's drink!
From drinking this toast, we'll none of us shrink;
Others shall follow, when we've time to think.
        Our burden shall be, let us drink!
        The burden to bear is good drink.

Loud laughter heard outside.

MATHIAS (*taking off his coat*). Ha, ha, ha! Those jolly topers
have got all they want. What holes in the snow they will
make before they reach their homes! Drink! Drink! Is it not

strange? To drink and drown every remorse! Yes, everything goes well! (*He drinks a glass of water.*) Mathias, you can at least boast of having well managed your affairs – the contract signed – rich – prosperous – respected – happy! (*Takes off waistcoat.*) No one now will hear you, if you dream. No one! No more folly! – no more Bells! Tonight I triumph; for conscience is at rest!

He enters the alcove. The Chorus of Revellers heard again in the distance. A hand is extended from alcove and extinguishes the candle – stage dark. Curtain at back of gauze rises, disclosing an extensive set of a Court of Justice, arched, brilliantly lighted – at back, three JUDGES *on the bench, dressed in black caps and red robes – at* R. *and* L., *the* PUBLIC, *in Alsatian costumes – in front of the* JUDGES, *but benneath them, a table, on which lies the Jew's cloak and cap – on* R., *the* PUBLIC PROSECUTOR *and* BARRISTERS *– on* L., *the* CLERK *or* REGISTRAR OF THE COURT, *and* BARRISTERS *– a* GENDARME *at each corner of the Court.* MATHIAS *is discovered seated on a stool in* C. *of Court – he is dressed in the brown blouse and hood worn by the* MAN *in the vision in Act I – he has his back to the* AUDIENCE, *face to* JUDGES.

THE CLERK. Therefore, the prisoner, Mathias, is accused of having, on the night of the 24th December, 1818, between midnight and one o'clock, assassinated the Jew Koveski upon the Bridge of Vechem, to rob him of his gold.

PRESIDENT. Prisoner, you have heard the Act of Accusation read; you have already heard the depositions of the witnesses. What have you to say in answer?

MATHIAS (*violently – throws back hood, and starting up*). Witnesses! People who saw nothing; people who live miles from the place where the crime was committed; at night, and in the winter time! You call such people witnesses!

PRESIDENT. Answer with calmness; these gestures – this violence will avail you nothing. You are a man full of cunning.

MATHIAS (*with humility*). No, I am a man of simplicity.

PRESIDENT. You knew well the time to select; you knew well

how to evade all suspicion; you knew well how to destroy all direct evidence. You are a dangerous man!

MATHIAS (*derisively*). Because nothing can be proved against me I am dangerous! Every honest man then is dangerous when nothing can be proved against him! A rare encouragement for honesty!

PRESIDENT. The public voice accuses you. Answer me this; how is it that you hear the noise of Bells?

MATHIAS (*passionately*). I do not hear the noise of Bells!

Music. Bells heard off as before. MATHIAS *trembles.*

PRESIDENT. Prisoner, you speak falsely. At this moment you hear that noise. Tell us why is this?

MATHIAS. It is nothing. It is simply a jangling in my ears.

PRESIDENT. Unless you acknowledge the true cause of this noise you hear, we shall summon the Mesmerist to explain the matter to us.

MATHIAS (*with defiance*). It is true then that I hear this noise. (*Bells cease.*)

PRESIDENT (*to the* CLERK OF THE COURT). It is well; write that down.

MATHIAS. Yes; but I hear it in a dream.

PRESIDENT. Write that he hears it in a dream.

MATHIAS (*furiously*). Is it a crime to dream?

THE CROWD (*murmur very softly among themselves, and move simultaneously, each person performing exactly the same movement of negation*). N-N-N-o!

MATHIAS (*with confidence*). Listen, friends! Don't fear for me! All this is but a dream – I am in a dream. If it were not a dream should I be clothed in these rags? Should I have before me such judges as these? Judges who, simply acting upon their own empty ideas, would hang a fellow creature. Ha, ha, ha! It is a dream – a dream! (*He bursts into a loud derisive laugh.*)

PRESIDENT. Silence, prisoner – silence! (*Turning to his companion* JUDGES.) Gentlemen – this noise of Bells arises in the prisoner's mind from the remembrance of what is past. The prisoner hears this noise because there rankles in his heart the memory of that he would conceal from us. The Jew's horse carried Bells.

MATHIAS. It is false; I have no memories.

PRESIDENT. Be silent!

MATHIAS (*with rage*). A man cannot be condemned upon such suppositions. You must have proofs. I do not hear the noise of Bells.

PRESIDENT. You see, gentlemen, the prisoner contradicts himself. He has already made the avowal – now he retracts it.

MATHIAS. No! I hear nothing. (*The Bells heard.*) It is the blood rushing to my brain – this jangling in my ears. (*The Bells increase in sound.*) I ask for Christian. Why is not Christian here?

PRESIDENT. Prisoner! do you persist in your denial?

MATHIAS (*with force*). Yes. There is nothing proved against me. It is a gross injustice to keep an honest man in prison. I suffer in the cause of jústice. (*The Bells cease.*)

PRESIDENT. You persist. Well! Considering that since this affair took place fifteen years have passed, and that it is impossible to throw light upon the circumstances by ordinary means – first, through the cunning and audacity of the prisoner, and second, through the deaths of witnesses who could have given evidence – for these reasons we decree that the Court hear the Mesmerist. Officer, summon the Mesmerist.

MATHIAS (*in a terrible voice*). I oppose it! I oppose it! Dreams prove nothing.

PRESIDENT. Summon the Mesmerist! (*Exit* GENDARME.)

MATHIAS (*striking the table*). It is abominable! It is in defiance of all justice!

PRESIDENT. If you are innocent, why should you fear the Mesmerist; because he can read the inmost secrets of your heart? Be calm, or, believe me, your own indiscretion will prove that you are guilty.

MATHIAS. I demand an advocate. I wish to instruct the advocate Linder of Saverne. In a case like this, I do not care for cost. I am calm – as calm as any man who has no reproach against

himself. I fear nothing, but dreams are dreams. (*Loudly.*)
Why is Christian not here? My honour is his honour! Let him
be sent for. He is an honest man. (*With exultation.*)
Christian, I have made you rich. Come, and defend me!

Music. The GENDARME *who has gone out returns with the*
MESMERIST.

MESMERIST (*bending to the Court respectfully*). Your honours,
the President and Judges of the Court, it is your decree that
has brought me before your tribunal; without such direction,
terror alone would have kept me far from here.

MATHIAS. Who can believe in the follies of the Mesmerists?
They deceive the public for the purpose of gaining money!
They merely perform the tricks of conjurers! I have seen this
fellow already at my cousin Bôth's, at Ribeauville.

PRESIDENT. Can you send this man to sleep?

MESMERIST (*looking full at* MATHIAS, *who sinks upon chair, unable
to endure the* MESMERIST'S *gaze*). I can!

MATHIAS (*starting up*). I will not be made the subject of this
conjurer's experiments.

PRESIDENT. I command it!

MATHIAS. Christian – where is Christian? He will prove that I
am an honest man.

PRESIDENT. Your resistance betrays you.

MATHIAS (*with defiance*). I have no fear. (*Sits.*)

The MESMERIST *goes up stage to back of* MATHIAS, *makes some
passes. Music.*

MATHIAS (*to himself*). Mathias, if you sleep you are lost. (*His
eyes are fixed as if struck with horror – in a hollow voice*) No –
no – I will not sleep – I will – (*in a hesitating voice*) I will –
not – no – (*Falls asleep. Music ceases.*)

MESMERIST. He sleeps. What shall I ask him?

PRESIDENT. Ask him what he did on the night of the 24th of
December, fifteen years ago.

MESMERIST (*to* MATHIAS, *in a firm voice*). You are at the night
of the 24th December, 1818?

MATHIAS (*in a low voice*). Yes.

MESMERIST. What time is it?

MATHIAS. Half-past eleven.

MESMERIST. Speak on. I command you!

MATHIAS (*still in the same attitude, speaking as if he were describing a vision presented to his sight*). The people are leaving the inn – Catherine and little Annette have gone to rest. Our man Kasper comes in. He tells me the lime-kiln is lighted. I answer him, it is well; go to bed, I will see to the kiln. He leaves me; I am alone with the Jew, who warms himself at the stove. Outside, everything sleeps. Nothing is heard, except from time to time the Jew's horse under the shed, when he shakes his bells.

MESMERIST. Of what are you thinking?

MATHIAS. I am thinking that I must have money – that if I have not three thousand francs by the 31st, the inn will be taken from me. I am thinking that no one is stirring; that it is night; that there are two feet of snow upon the ground, and that the Jew will follow the high road quite alone!

MESMERIST. Have you already decided to attack him?

MATHIAS (*after a short silence*). That man is strong. He has broad shoulders. I am thinking that he would defend himself well, should anyone attack him. (*He makes a movement.*)

MESMERIST. What ails you?

MATHIAS (*in a low voice*). He looks at me. He has grey eyes. (*As if speaking to himself.*) I must strike the blow!

MESMERIST. You are decided?

MATHIAS. Yes – yes; I will strike the blow! I will risk it!

MESMERIST. Go on!

MATHIAS. I must, however, look round. I go out; all is dark! It still snows; no one will trace my footsteps in the snow. (*He raises his hands as if feeling for something.*)

MESMERIST. What are you doing?

MATHIAS. I am feeling in the sledge – should he carry pistols! There is nothing – I will strike the blow! (*He listens.*) All is silent in the village! Little Annette is crying; a goat bleats in the stable; the Jew is walking in his room!

MESMERIST. You re-enter?

MATHIAS. Yes. The Jew has placed six francs upon the table; I return his money; he fixes his eyes steadily upon me!

MESMERIST. He speaks to you.

MATHIAS. He asks me how far it is to Mutzig? Four leagues. I wish him well on his journey! He answers – 'God bless you!' He goes out – he is gone! (MATHIAS, *with body bent, takes several steps forward as if following and watching his victim; he extends his hands.*) The axe! Where is the axe? Ah, here, behind the door! How cold it is! (*He trembles.*) The snow falls – not a star! Courage, Mathias, you shall possess the girdle – courage!

MESMERIST. You follow him?

MATHIAS. Yes, yes. I have crossed the fields! (*Pointing.*) Here is the old bridge, and there below, the frozen rivulet! How the dogs howl at Daniel's farm – how they howl! And old Finck's forge, how brightly it glows upon the hillock. (*Low, as if speaking to himself.*) Kill a man! – kill a man! You will not do that, Mathias – you will not do that! Heaven forbids it. (*Proceeding to walk with measured steps and bent body.*) You are a fool! Listen, you will be rich; your wife and child will no longer want for anything! The Jew came; so much the worse – so much the worse. He ought not to have come! You will pay all you owe; you will no more be in debt. (*Loud, in a broken tone.*) It must be, Mathias, that you kill him! (*He listens.*) No one on the road – no one! (*With an expression of terror.*) What dreaful silence! (*He wipes his forehead with his hand.*) One o'clock strikes, and the moon shines. Ah! The Jew has already passed! Thank God! Thank God! (*He kneels – a pause – he listens – the Bells heard without as before.*) No! The Bells! The Bells! He comes! (*He bends down in a watching attitude, and remains still – a pause – in a low voice.*) You will be rich – you will be rich – you will be rich! (*The noise of the Bells increases – the* CROWD *express alarm simultaneously – all at once* MATHIAS *springs forward, and with a species of savage roar, strikes a terrible blow with his right hand.*) Ah! ah! I have you now, Jew! (*He strikes again – the* CROWD *simultaneously express horror.* MATHIAS *leans forward and gazes anxiously on the ground – he extends his hand as if to touch something, but draws it back in horror.*) He does not move! (*He raises himself, utters a deep sigh of relief and looks round.*) The horse has fled with the sledge! (*The Bells cease – kneeling down*) Quick, quick! The girdle! I have it. Ha! (*He performs the action in saying this of taking if from the* JEW's *body and buckling it round his own.*) It is full of gold, quite full. Be quick, Mathias, be quick! Carry him away. (*He bends low down and appears to lift the body upon his back; then he walks across stage, his body bent, his steps slow, as a man who carries a heavy load.*)

MESMERIST. Where are you going?

MATHIAS (*stopping*). To the lime-kiln. I am there. (*He appears to throw the body upon the kiln.*) How heavy he was! (*He breathes with force; then he again bends down to take up a pole – in a hoarse voice*) Go into the fire, Jew, go into the fire! (*He appears to push the body with the pole, using his whole force; suddenly he utters a cry of horror and staggers away, his face covered with his hands.*) Those eyes, oh, those eyes! How he glares at me. (*He sinks on to stool, and takes the same attitude as when first thrown into sleep.*)

PRESIDENT (*with a sign to the* MESMERIST). It is well. (*To the* CLERK OF THE COURT.) You have written all?

CLERK. All!

PRESIDENT. It is well – awake him now, and let him read himself.

MESMERIST. Awake! I command you!

MATHIAS (*awakes gradually – he appears bewildered*). Where am I? (*He looks round.*) Ah! Yes; what is going on?

CLERK (*handing him paper*). Here is your deposition – read it.

MATHIAS (*takes it and, before reading it, aside*). Wretched, wretched fool! I have told all; I am lost! (*With rage, after reading the paper.*) It is false! (*Tears the paper into pieces.*) You are a set of rogues! Christian – where is Christian? It is a crime against justice! They will not let my only witness speak. Christian! They would kill the father of your wife! Help me – help me!

PRESIDENT. You force me to speak of an event of which I had wished to remain silent. Your son-in-law Christian, upon hearing of the crimes with which you are charged, by his own hand sought his death. He is no more.

MATHIAS. Ah! (*He appears stupefied with dismay.*)

PRESIDENT (*after consulting the other* JUDGES, *rises, speaks in a solemn tone of voice.*) Considering that on the night of the 24th December, 1818, between midnight and one o'clock, Mathias committed the crime of assassination upon the person of one Koveski, and considering that this crime was committed under circumstances which aggravate its enormity – such as premeditation, and for the purpose of highway robbery, the Court condemns the said Mathias to be hanged by the neck until he is dead!

MATHIAS *staggers and falls on his knees. The* CROWD *makes a movement of terror – the death-bell tolls – lights lowered gradually – then curtain at back of gauze descends, disclosing the Scene as at commencement – lights up. Music – a peal of joy bells heard ringing.*

CROWD (*without*). Annette! Annette! The bride!

Hurried steps are heard upon the stairs outside, and then a loud knocking at the door of the room.

CATHERINE (*without*). Mathias! Mathias! get up at once. It is late in the morning, and all our guests are below. (*More knocking.*)

CHRISTIAN (*without*). Mathias! Mathias! (*Silence.*) How soundly he sleeps!

WALTER (*without*). Ho! Mathias, the wedding has commenced – Houp, houp! (*More knocking.*)

THE CROWD (*outside*). Burgomaster! Burgomaster! (*Loud knocking.*)

CATHERINE (*in an anxious voice*). He does not answer. It is strange. Mathias! (*A discussion among many voices is heard without.*)

CHRISTIAN. No – it is useless. Leave it to me!

At the same moment several violent blows are struck upon the door, which falls into the room from its hinges. Enter CHRISTIAN *hurriedly – he runs to the alcove. Music, hurry.*

CHRISTIAN. Mathias! (*Looks into alcove and staggers back into room.*) Ah!

Enter CATHERINE *and* ANNETTE, *followed by* WALTER, HANS, *and the* CROWD, *all dressed for the wedding.*

CATHERINE. What has happened, Christian; what has happened? (*She is rushing to alcove.*)
CHRISTIAN (*stopping her*). Don't come near – don't come near.
CATHERINE (*endeavouring to pass*). I will see what it is. Let me pass; do not fear for me.

MATHIAS *appears from the alcove – he is dressed in the same clothes as when he retired into the alcove at the commencement of the Scene, but his face is haggard, and ghastly pale – he comes out, his eyes fixed, his arms extended – as he rushes forward with uncertain steps, the* CROWD *fall back with horror, and form groups of consternation, with a general exclamation of terror.*

MATHIAS (*in a voice of strangulation*). The rope! the rope! Cut the rope!

He falls suddenly, and is caught in the arms of HANS *and* WALTER, *who carry him to the chair. The Bells heard off. Music, the melody played in the Second Act when promise given. His hands clutch at his throat as if to remove something that strangles him – he looks pitifully round as if trying to recognise those about him, and then his head falls on his breast.* CATHERINE, *kneeling, places her hand on* MATHIAS' *heart.*

CATHERINE. Dead! (*The Bells cease.*)

ANNETTE *bursts into tears. The* WOMEN *in the crowd kneeling;* MEN *remove their hats and bend their heads upon their breasts – tableau.*

CURTAIN

382

Notes on Authors

NOTES ON AUTHORS

ISAAC POCOCK (1782–1835) was born in Bristol, the son of a marine painter. He studied art, and in 1798 became a pupil of Romney. For many years he exhibited at the Royal Academy, and was elected to the Liverpool Academy in 1812. His first play, an operatic farce, *Yes or No?*, was performed at the Little Theatre in the Haymarket in 1808. He was a justice of the peace and magistrate in Berkshire, and died at Maidenhead. Pocock is credited with forty-three plays, and among his most popular melodramas, aside from *The Miller and His Men*, were *For England, Ho* (1813), *The Magpie or the Maid?* (1815), *Robinson Crusoe* (1817), *Rob Roy Macgregor* (1818), and *The Robber's Bride* (1829).

JOHN THOMAS HAINES (1799–1843) regularly provided melodramas for the Surrey and the Victoria, and occasionally acted in his own plays. Little is known of his life; at the time of his death, in Stockwell, Surrey, he was stage manager of the English Opera House. His first play, an adaptation of *Quentin Durward*, was done at the Coburg in 1823. Haines wrote forty-one plays, and specialized in nautical melodramas, of which the most popular was *My Poll and My Partner Joe*. Others include *Jacob Faithful, the Lighter-Boy* (1834), *The Ocean of Life* (1836), *Breakers Ahead* (1837), *The Phantom Ship* (1839), and *Armstrong the Shipwright* (1840).

Of WILLIAM W. PRATT, the actor who adapted *Ten Nights in a Bar-Room* for the stage, I know nothing. TIMOTHY SHAY ARTHUR (1809–85), the author of the novel, was born near Newburgh, New York, the grandson of an officer in the Revolution. He began his lengthy career of writing and editing in the 1830s, being successively editor of two Baltimore periodicals, the *Athenaeum* and the *Saturday Visitor*, and a daily, the *Merchant.*

He founded *Arthur's Home Gazette* in 1850, and a monthly, *The Workingman*, which contained instructively moral stories and articles, in 1870. He died in Philadelphia after writing over a hundred books. Arthur became very influential in the temperance movement, and *Ten Nights in a Bar-Room* (1854) had enormous sales, second only in its time to those of its contemporary, *Uncle Tom's Cabin. Six Nights with the Washingtonians* (1842), *Three Years in a Man-trap* (1872), *Woman to the Rescue* (1874), and *The Strike at Tivoli Mills* (1879) are among his numerous temperance novels.

WATTS PHILLIPS (1825–74) was born in London. His father persuaded him not to go on the stage, and he studied in Paris for several years to advance his chosen career of book illustrator. Turning to writing, he supplied novels for the *Family Herald* and other periodicals. His first play – he wrote twenty-five, almost all strong domestic melodramas – *Joseph Chavigny*, was produced at the Adelphi in 1856. Phillips died in London. Other plays beside *Lost in London* include *Camilla's Husband* (1862), *The Woman in Mauve* (1864), *Maud's Peril* (1867), *Not Guilty* (1869), and *Fettered* (1869).

JOHN AUGUSTIN DALY (1838–99), the dominant American theatrical figure of his age, was born in Plymouth, North Carolina, the son of a ship-owner. He spent ten years as the dramatic critic of the New York *Sunday Courier*, and also wrote for other New York papers. His first play, *Leah the Forsaken*, a melodrama from the German, was performed at the Howard Athenaeum, Boston, in 1862. In 1869 Daly formed his own company at the Fifth Avenue Theatre in New York, moving to the New Fifth Avenue Theatre when the old one burned in 1873. The failure of his melodrama, *The Dark City*, in 1867, forced him to give up the theatre, but he turned the New Broadway Theatre into Daly's in 1879 and opened it with another glittering company, which included John Drew and Ada Rehan. Daly took his company to London in 1884, and to Paris and Berlin in 1886; in all making several tours abroad. He opened a Daly's Theatre in London in

1893, and died in Paris. A meticulous and authoritative director, Daly did much to raise standards of American production, and his fine company excelled in Shakespeare, Sheridan, and Daly's own adaptations from German and French. In all, he wrote and adapted about ninety-six plays, including, in addition to *Under the Gaslight*, *A Flash of Lightning* (1868), *The Red Scarf* (1869), *Frou-Frou* (1870), *Horizon* (1871), *Divorce* (1871) and *Pique* (1875).

LEOPOLD DAVID LEWIS (1828–90), the son of a physician, was born and died in London. He became a solicitor in 1850, and practised in London until 1875. In 1868 he was joint editor of a short-lived, humorous monthly periodical, *The Mask*. A novel, *A Peal of Merry Bells*, was published in 1880. *The Bells* was Lewis' first play, and he wrote only three others: *The Wandering Jew* (1873), *Give a Dog a Bad Name* (1876) and *Foundlings* (1881).

Those nineteenth-century melodramas that were printed are unfortunately entombed in hideous, eye-straining acting editions such as Dicks, Lacy, French, Dewitt, Spencer, etc. A few appeared in regular book form, but most were not published at all; this was especially true in America. Acting editions of melodramas have gone out of print, and it is difficult to buy them second-hand. Diligent readers can find most English melodramas up to 1900 in the Lord Chamberlain's manuscript collection at the British Museum; several American libraries, notably the New York Public Library, have collections of prompt copies and manuscripts. The magnificent Princeton University Press edition in twenty volumes of *America's Lost Plays* (1940–42) contains many previously unprinted melodramas. In England, George Rowell's collection of *Nineteenth Century Plays* (1953) for Oxford includes *Black-Eyed Susan, The Colleen Bawn, Lady Audley's Secret*, and *The Ticket-of-Leave Man*. In separate paperbacks, Montagu Slater has reprinted *Sweeney Todd, Maria Marten*, and *The Drunkard* (Bodley Head, 1943).

The general historical works for the theatre and drama of the nineteenth century are Allardyce Nicoll's indispensable *History of English Drama*, IV and V (1955 and 1959); George Rowell, *Victorian Theatre* (1956); Ernest Reynolds, *Early Victorian Drama* (1936); and E. B. Watson, *Sheridan to Robertson* (1926). Of these, Nicoll and Reynolds have the most thorough studies of melodrama. Also useful is the article on melodrama in the *Oxford Companion to the Theatre* (1957), which is a valuable general work of reference for the theatres of the period. M. W. Disher has written two racy books on melodrama: *Blood and Thunder* (1949) and *Melodrama: Plots that Thrilled* (1954). Other recent helpful books are A. N. Vardac, *Stage to Screen* (1949), a study of the cinema's improvement on nineteenth-century stage techniques; Bertrand Evans, *Gothic Drama from Walpole to*

Shelley (1947), with a chapter on Gothic melodrama, and A. E. Wilson, *East End Entertainment* (1954).

Many theatrical histories and memoirs touch on melodrama. The most useful for accounts of the content of melodrama itself are Percy Fitzgerald, *The World behind the Scenes* (1881), Dutton Cook, *On the Stage* (1883), H. B. Baker, *History of the London Stage* (1904), with a list of the different characteristics of working-class theatres, and H. C. Newton, *Crime and the Drama* (1927). Baker's article, 'The Old Melo-drama', in *Belgravia* (May, 1883) should be read. For French melodrama, Paul Ginisty's *Le Mélodrame* (1910) is a rambling account of the work of Pixérécourt and his followers. Thomas Erle's *Letters from a Theatrical Scene-Painter* (1880) is an invaluable record of melodramatic acting, scenery, and production methods. The novels and articles of Dickens are scattered with references to melodrama and melodramatic acting; James Grant's *Sketches in London* (1838) contains a chapter on the penny gaff (available in a Society for Theatre Research pamphlet). Jerome K. Jerome has amusingly described rehearsals at Astley's where he was a young actor in the 1880s, in *On the Stage and Off* (1891), and presented the character stereotypes of melodrama in *Stage-Land* (1885), superbly illustrated by Bernard Partridge. George Arliss, in *On the Stage* (1928), has left an account of melodrama at the Elephant and Castle in the 1880s; George Bernard Shaw's withering reviews of sensation drama can be found in *Our Theatres in the Nineties* (1931–50). Joe Graham's *An Old Stock Actor's Memories* (1930) shows the problems of touring melodrama in New Zealand in 1875.

For American melodrama, the best studies are H. J. Smith, 'The Melodrama', *Atlantic Monthly* (March, 1907), and G. J. Nathan, *Mr George Jean Nathan Presents* (1917), a vivid and nostalgic recreation of 10–20–30 melodrama. Owen Davis, the leading practitioner of 10–20–30, has written an autobiography, *I'd Like to Do It Again* (1931). Clayton Hamilton defends melodrama in *Studies in Stagecraft* (1914). On the whole, American actors and critics were far less concerned with melodrama than their British counterparts.